EVERY EMPLOYEE'S Guide to the LAW

What You Need to Know About Your Rights in the Workplace— and What to Do If They Are Violated

Revised and Updated to Include New Laws

LEWIN G. JOEL III

Pantheon Books   New York

Library of Congress Cataloging-in-Publication Data
Joel, Lewin G.
Every employee's guide to the law : what you need to know about
your rights in the workplace—and what to do if they are violated /
Lewin G. Joel III
p. cm.
1. Labor laws and legislation—United States—Popular works.
2. Employee rights—United States—Popular works. I. Title.
KF3319.6.J64 2001   344.7301—dc21   2001021501
ISBN 0-375-71445-6

Printed in the United States of America

Revised and Expanded Edition 2001

2 4 6 8 9 7 5 3 1

DEDICATED
TO YOU . . .
WHO WORK HARD FOR A LIVING

Contents

MILITARY LEAVE: Time off to attend reserve meetings; reinstatement following active duty; health insurance

RETIREMENT PLANS: Choice of plans; Who must be allowed to participate? Vesting; "employee welfare plans"

SUMMARY

CIVIL RIGHTS: State and federal civil rights laws; When is it discrimination (age, race, sex, religion, marital status, national origin)? And what can I do about it?

DISCRIMINATION GENERALLY: Types of discrimination (disparate treatment, adverse impact, perpetuating discrimination, statistical imbalance); accommodation

RACE DISCRIMINATION: Title VII of the Civil Rights Act of 1964; Title 42 of the U.S. Code, Section 1981

SEX DISCRIMINATION: Sexual stereotyping; maternity and pregnancy; "fetal protection policies"; What is (and what isn't) sexual harassment? Sexual orientation discrimination

EQUAL PAY ACT: Equal pay for equal work; exceptions; "comparable worth"

HANDICAP DISCRIMINATION: Americans with Disabilities Act (ADA); state laws; Am I a "qualified disabled person"? When and how must an employer accommodate my handicap? AIDS as a disability

AGE DISCRIMINATION: Age Discrimination in Employment Act (ADEA); making an age discrimination case

NATIONAL ORIGIN (ETHNIC) DISCRIMINATION: Harassment; "speak-English-only" rules; height and weight requirements

RELIGIOUS DISCRIMINATION: Reasonable accommodation of religious practices

AFFIRMATIVE ACTION/REVERSE DISCRIMINATION: Government contractors; private employers; affirmative action under fire

SUMMARY

ACCESS TO PERSONNEL FILES: What kinds of records can my employer keep? Confidentiality and employee access to records; Do I have the right to see (and make notes in) my file? Medical records

SEARCH AND SEIZURE: "Legitimate expectation of privacy"; reasonableness of search

SURVEILLANCE AND MONITORING: To what extent can my employer legally eavesdrop on, record, or videotape my activities? Union activities

Tables

EVERY EMPLOYEE'S GUIDE TO THE LAW

Introduction / Overview

BEGINNING *BEFORE* THE BEGINNING

This book is about your rights as an employee. It's about knowing what those rights are and when they've been violated. But it's also about knowing what to do about it. It's easy to say, "This is sexual harassment and that is age discrimination and you shouldn't have to be subjected to either." But, as a practical matter, it's not always so easy to prevent illegal behavior by your employer (or your employer's "agents": managers, supervisors, etc.) or to prove it if it comes to that. (You may still remember the Anita Hill–Clarence Thomas affair.) And, megabucks settlements and court awards notwithstanding, most of us really don't want it to come to that.

All most of us want is a fair chance to compete for a job we think we would like and be good at and, if we get it, fair treatment and a fair wage in exchange for an honest day's work. We don't *want* to be put in the uncomfortable position of having to defend our rights in the workplace. So what is the best way to avoid the situation? *It is for our employers to know that we know exactly what our rights are and what to do about it if they are being violated.*

This book can—and does—define, for example, in precise detail what sexual harassment is. It tells you exactly what penalties the law sets out for a violation. It suggests alternatives for addressing the situation. But it can't guarantee that the behavior will stop or that circumstances will unfold completely in your favor. Unfortunately, when an employer puts you in a difficult spot, there you are, you're in a difficult spot and there may be no easy way out. To continue on in the status quo may be unpalatable. To take action may involve risks. But who said life was going to be easy?

So what *will* this book do?

First, the bulk of the book will take you through the entire employment relationship, from the day you see that job advertisement in the classified section of your Sunday paper or hear about it from a friend or relative until the day you leave it—whether you quit, are fired, or retire—and beyond. It will describe in detail every potential infringement upon your rights along the way, from inappropriate questions on a job application form or in an interview to wage and hour violations; from all possible forms of discrimination to substandard working conditions; from objectionable disciplinary procedures to wrongful discharge. It will even outline your right to workers' compensation and unemployment compensation benefits and your continuing rights to group health insurance benefits and retirement and pension fund contributions after you are no longer employed. In short, in its detailed discussion of more than a hundred employment-related laws, the book will help you decide if you have a potentially valid claim against your employer for violating any one of them.

Second, the book will give you valuable insights into employer strategies, such as issuing disclaimers and getting you to sign various types of authorization forms and waivers of rights. And it will tell you when those disclaimers, authorizations, and waivers are valid and when they aren't worth the paper they're printed on. (Because, of course, as long as you *think* they're valid, they are as valid as they need to be.)

Third, the book will outline your options in case you are the victim of an unfair employment practice. Note the word "options." The book can't tell you what to do. That would be impossible. Yours is a unique case with unique facts and it would be inappropriate for the author to presume to promise that this book will tell you exactly what to do in your unique situation and, in effect, solve your problem. Only you can solve your problem, albeit with the help of either the government agency empowered to administer and enforce the law you feel your employer has broken, or a private attorney (which this book will help you find). What this book *can* and *does* do is outline your *options* in light of your general situation.

Fourth, the book will candidly discuss the potential risks of the decision you make, because whatever decision you make will carry risks. If you decide to do nothing, you risk more of the unwanted or illegal behavior (i.e., sexual harassment, nonpayment of earned overtime, invasion of privacy, etc.), being further unfairly disciplined, or ultimately getting fired (if you haven't already *been* fired). If you do something, whether it's complaining directly to your employer or to a government agency, or adding a private attorney into the mix, you risk retaliatory discipline or discharge by your employer (even if it's illegal in nature) and possibly a long, drawn-out, and costly legal battle that will leave you battered and beaten and broke long before any settlement is ever reached or court decision rendered. In short, this book will give you *practical* options for dealing with your unique situation and will not hesitate to point out the potential (and sometimes inevitable) downside.

Finally, once you have decided on a course of action, this book will chart that course for you. And hopefully, if you have read and understood the laws explained in these pages and apply them reasonably to your situation, that course will lead you to a safe harbor. That safe harbor may lie with one of the many government agencies authorized to administer and enforce employment laws, chief among them the Equal Employment Opportunity Commission and the U.S. (and your state) Department of Labor. If so, the book will lead you step-by-step through the claim-filing process, including hints on what to expect at each turn through the sometimes long and winding corridors of a typical bureaucracy. Or the safest harbor may be an attorney's office, in which case this book will give you the best possible advice on getting . . . the best possible advice. Or maybe the safest harbor will be to cut your losses and start looking for another job. Or perhaps the safest harbor will be for you to wait. (While I do not agree with the adage "The meek shall inherit the earth," I firmly believe that "good things come to those who wait.") But not wait idly. Have a plan. A plan that includes information gathering, building a case.

Because if you learn nothing else, you will learn in the pages that follow that *documentation is the key to any successful unfair employment practice claim.* And you will learn the who, what, where, when, and why of keeping your "personal personnel file." Specifically, with regard to documenting your employment record with your employer, you will learn the importance of:

☞ *Who?*

Everyone: Your employer, supervisor, division manager or other superior, your coworkers, counselors, friends, and even former employees of your company can all be invaluable sources of information for your "personal personnel file," either based on what they may have directly said or done, or as a means to substantiate what you allege one of the others said or did. (Because unless and until you prove it, your claim will remain only an allegation.)

☞ *What?*

Everything: Keep copies of all formal written documents or communications, from the job application form to the company handbook to the "pink slip," performance reviews, informal comments about your work made by superiors either written or oral, notations made in the margins of work you submit, oral statements or assurances (of which you make a written record), witnesses, etc. Buy a cheap manila accordion file folder and keep a job file. In it keep everything even remotely connected with work and your employer. *(You can be sure your employer will keep a file on you!)* Labor lawyers have a saying about employee vs. employer agency proceedings and lawsuits: "The one with the biggest pile of papers wins." It's meant to be funny, but a current of truth runs just below the surface.

☞ *Where?*

Everywhere: Work-related comments, statements, remarks, or actions can be important whether they actually take place in the workplace or during other directly work-related activities, such as business trips or business lunches, or in a less formal atmosphere, such as over dinner, drinks, or even at a chance meeting at a ball game or nightclub. (Although this statement may engender acute paranoia, in the context of this book it is important to note that even ostensibly non-work-related comments made in a non-work environment can be construed as work-related if the object of those comments—you—reasonably interprets them as having a bearing on his or her standing at work.)

☞ *When?*

Immediately. And that means before you even start work. Keep a copy of the job advertisement and the application form; make a written record of your job interview(s), noting any objectionable questions you might have been asked, or objectionable comments or behavior, and by whom. And do it the minute you get out of the interview, while it's still fresh in your mind. Keep a copy of any written tests you were given. If you can't keep a copy, make a note of any questions you feel are discriminatory or otherwise not job-related. Make notes about the physical examination, if any, or drug test, if any. Were you asked to or required to take a lie detector test? If you do not get the job, ask for and note the reasons given. If you do get the job, keep your acceptance letter or make a record of any oral assurances made at the time of hiring. Ask others if they were given the same assurances or subjected to the same objectionable behavior or questionable tactics under similar circumstances. Then keep adding to your file from Day One on the job until your every tie with that employer has been severed.

☞ *Why?*

Because it may be important. Everything may seem all hunky-dory at the outset. But you never know when things might go wrong. Once you are all finished trying to impress each other, you with how industrious you are and your boss with how terrific the company is to work for, the honeymoon will be over and the realities of business will set in. And, at the risk of sounding jaded, what your employer really wants is the best worker he can get for the least money he can get away with paying. That's the nature of business. On the other hand, what you want is the best job (which could mean the easiest, most challenging, most fun, least stressful, or any number of other qualities or combinations thereof, depending on your personality type) for the most pay. That's human nature.

Business nature and human nature. Not always compatible, you'll have to admit. In fact, at its roots, adversarial. Which is where this book comes in.

The goal of this book, then, is to describe in easy-to-understand terms:

☞ Federal and state laws and regulations that protect your employment rights, both statutory law (laws that are actually on the books) and common law (principles that have become part of the law through precedent-setting agency or court action).

☞ How to assess your treatment by your employer (or prospective employer or former employer) and his or her "agents" in relation to those laws and regulations.

☞ The appropriate channels to address your grievance against your employer, be it in-house, through a government agency, or through a private attorney.

☞ The practical aspects of how to actually proceed with a claim, if you decide upon review that your case should be pursued, including how to contact the appropriate government agency and/or hire the right attorney for your case and what to expect from your dealings with that agency and/or attorney.

☞ The trade-offs you might expect, in the form of potential gains (stopping the unwanted behavior, getting that job or receiving that promotion you were denied, or receiving a financial settlement or court award) weighed against potential losses (retaliation by your employer, public embarrassment or humiliation, unsympathetic or even hostile coworkers, loss of wages during a long agency or court battle, or the inability to achieve ultimate satisfaction).

In the final analysis, information is the key to a successful employment relationship. And this book will give you all the information you need to make an educated decision about your situation. And, after all, that's about the best you can hope for in any situation: to make your decision based on the most complete, most accurate, most up-to-date, most intelligible information available.

I hope and trust that, after reading this book, you will be able to make the decision that is the right one for you.

SO, HOW IMPORTANT IS KNOWING YOUR RIGHTS?

How important is it to know your rights in the workplace? Let me give you an example.

The following is a reenactment of a scene that is played out all too often in households across America every single day.

Cast (in order of appearance):

DOMESTIC PARTNER #1: A former employee who until minutes ago worked at any job for any company anywhere in America.

DOMESTIC PARTNER #2: Lives with D.P. #1. D.P. #2 could work full- or part-time and may even have small children to take care of, a task D.P. #1 would, of course, share.

Act I, Scene I:

D.P. #1 *(arriving home early, slamming kitchen door, angrily tossing lunch pail/briefcase on counter and waving pink slip in the air)*: "They can't do this to me! I've got my rights!"

D.P. #2 *(approaching D.P. #1 tentatively, frowning, clearly puzzled)*: "What happened, dear?"

D.P. #1 *(disconsolately, crumpling pink slip and throwing it into trash can in defeat)*: "I got fired."

D.P. #2 *(sympathetically, putting arm around D.P. #1's shoulder)*: "Oh, no. But why? You're such a hard worker."

D.P. #1: "Because I got tired of putting up with all the pinups hanging on the walls and the dirty jokes and lewd remarks. So I complained." (**Note:** Substitute, "Because they hired someone younger for less money." Or, "Because I filed that workers' comp. claim." Or, "Because they don't want minorities/women advancing to management level." Or, "Because they found out I have AIDS." Or, "Because I refused to take a lie detector/drug test." Or any one of dozens of other wrongful reasons for discharging an employee.)

D.P. #2 *(shoulders slumping, a look of concern creasing face)*: "What are you going to do?"

D.P. #1 *(forlornly)*: "What *can* I do? Start looking for another job, I guess."

D.P. #2 *(shaking head absently)*: "Gee, I wish there was something I could do. It's such a difficult time to try to find a new job."

DIRECTOR *(with a look of astonishment)*: "Cut! Cut! Cut!"

D.P. #2: "What's the problem?"

DIRECTOR: "They can't do that to you."

D.P. #1 and D.P. #2 *(simultaneously)*: "They can't?"

DIRECTOR *(addressing D.P. #1)*: "No, they can't. It's against the law."

D.P. #1 *(grinning smugly)*: "But even if it is, what can my character do? Sue them and you'll get blackballed. You'd never get another job."

DIRECTOR: "They can't do that, either. Blackballing is against the law, too."

Blackballing a worker *is* against the law. So is sexual harassment. So is age, race, sex, and AIDS discrimination. So is requiring an employee to take a lie detector test or, in most cases, a drug test. So are hundreds of other common employer practices, from the questions you were asked on your application form or in your interview to the reason you were fired and encompassing just about every other part of the employment relationship in between—and even beyond.

The government of this country and the governments of most of our fifty states have gone out of their way in the past ten or fifteen years to protect the rights of you, its lifeblood, our nation's workers. Our workplaces are now covered by civil rights laws, privacy laws, wage and hour laws, right-to-know laws, laws protecting the disabled, safety and health laws, laws giving employees access to their personnel files, smoking laws, equal opportunity laws, equal pay laws, laws protecting older workers, laws overseeing pension funds, laws protecting military personnel, pregnancy laws, laws requiring continued group health insurance coverage following termination, laws controlling the hiring process, the firing process, the disciplinary process, the treatment of injured workers, the treatment of discharged or laid-off workers, and dozens of other laws and regulations, some of which you've probably never even heard of.

The U.S. Department of Labor's Bureau of Labor Statistics reported recently that union membership continued to decline through the 1980s and into the 1990s to the point where now fewer than one in six of you belongs to a union. That means five out of six of you rely on the laws enacted by your government to get a fair shake at work. *But if you aren't familiar with those laws, what good do they do you?**

You've read the headlines:

Court Awards Workers $57 Million in Unpaid Overtime
(*Owens v. ITT Rayonier,* U.S. District Court of Western Washington, No. C88-533T, March 3, 1991)

Jury Awards $13.5 Million to Whistleblower
(*Green v. Texas Department of Human Services,* Texas District Court, No. 480,701, September 23, 1991)

Employer Liable for Cutting Off Fired Worker's Insurance
(*Kidder v. H&B Marine, Inc.,* U.S. Court of Appeals, 5th Circuit, No. 90-3340, 1991)

---

*See page 15 for information on how to locate cited cases in your library.

Negative Job Reference Makes Former Employee a Millionaire
(*Holton v. Lockheed Corp.,* California Superior Court, No. 642082, January 28, 1991)

Handicap Discrimination Claim Nets Worker $70,000 in Damages
(*EEOC v. Gabbard & Co.,* U.S. District Court of Eastern Michigan, 94 CV 7297, 1995)

Company Settles Age, Sex Bias Case for Half a Million Dollars
(*Jackson v. Casellas,* U.S. District Court of Western New York, No. 88-CV-0654-C, 1995)

Drug Search Violates Worker's Privacy; Gets $550,000 for Emotional Distress
(*Overby v. Chevron USA Inc.,* California Superior Court No. SWC-89552, 1993)

Race Discrimination Settlement Costs U.S. Agency $1.4 Million
(*Lewis v. Brady,* U.S. District Court, District of Columbia, No. 82-0918, November 9, 1990)

$186,000 Awarded in Reverse Discrimination Case
(*Cunico v. Pueblo School District 60,* U.S. Court of Appeals, 10th Circuit, Nos. 88-2727, 87-2779, November 19, 1990)

Sex Discrimination Results in $560,000 Damage Award
(*Helmuth v. Alaska Psychiatric Institute,* Alaska Superior Court, No. 3 AN-93-10461, 1995)

Clause in Handbook Is Contract, Prevents Worker's Firing
(*Badgett v. Visiting Nurses Association,* Iowa Court of Appeals, No. 0-651/90-443, January 29, 1991)

And these are only a few of the stories making news today. More headlines are being made as this book is being written—and as you read it. Tomorrow it could be your case that makes headlines. But what did all of these headline-makers have in common? *They knew their rights!*

Every practicing attorney in the labor and employment field is painfully aware of a simple but startling fact: *Employers do not know the law.* Oh, some of them know some of the basic laws—or think they do; and a handful have staff attorneys or outside law firms who know a great many of the laws—or think they do. But none of them knows all of the laws. That would be virtually impossible. There are just too many of them and they are changing too rapidly. Besides, many of the employers who do know the law will still try to get around it if it suits their purposes. After all, they are the boss, the king (queen) of their castle. Some still feel they have the right to do anything they please in the context of their workplace. *And as long as you don't know your rights—they can get away with it!*

Like the average employer, you probably know a little bit of the law—or think you do. Maybe you know the high-profile stuff, like sexual harassment. (Thank you, Judge Thomas and Professor Hill.) But did you know an employer can be guilty of it without even knowing it's taking place? And do you know what to do if it happens to you? Maybe you know that you forfeit your right to unemployment compensation benefits when you voluntarily quit your job. But did you know that roughly one-third of those who voluntarily quit their jobs and file unemployment claims are awarded benefits anyway? And maybe you know what kinds of on-the-job injuries qualify you for worker's compensation benefits. But do you know how long your employer has to hold your job open for you while you are recovering and under what circumstances he or she can replace you?

The purpose of this book is to fill you in on the *rest* of the story. It will explain the law in simple, straightforward terms with no extraneous material and no "legalese." It will let you know if you are being screwed or have been screwed and what you can do about it without getting screwed worse. It will tell you the appropriate government agency to contact for redress and how to contact them. And it will give you the tools you need to determine whether you need a lawyer (or whether hiring one would be a waste of time and money) and show you how to find the right one if you do.

There have been times in our history when losing your job was not the end of the world, when you didn't have to put up with unfair treatment on the job because all you had to do was quit and get another one. You were in demand in the employment marketplace. But those days are gone—maybe forever. Today your job is more precious than ever and now, more than ever, you need to know how to protect it.

The following pages will show you how.

HOW TO USE THIS BOOK

These are not intended to be scare tactics. In fact, it is neither my position nor my belief that all employers—or even some employers—are intentionally out to get you. But employers are in business for one thing and one thing only: to make money. (Even governmental and nonprofit organizations have to make enough money to stay in business.) What they are best at is making their product or delivering their service . . . not dealing with their employees. After all, they have hired you and their other employees only because you perform tasks they: (a) don't know how to do; (b) don't have time to do; or (c) don't want to do. They may trample on your rights because they perceive you as getting in the way of their objective (making money, remember?): they could hire a younger person for less; a single person would be cheaper to insure. They may trample on your rights because of some antiquated stereotype such as that a younger person would be more productive or a male would be absent from work less frequently or a white would "fit in" better at the workplace. *But most likely they will trample on your rights simply because—just like you—they don't know what those rights are!*

This book will remedy that situation. It will inform you of the rights and protections afforded you by the laws of your state and the United States. However, a note of caution. Remember, your situation is unique. It is *not* the purpose of this book to tell you definitively that you, in your unique situation, have a complaint or cause of action against your employer. This book will merely lay down the ground rules of the game. It will make you aware of the strategies the other side (your employer) will use. It will do its best to prepare you for one of the most important and potentially rewarding (or frustrating) games of your life: the employment game. Then it will hand you the ball. But it is up to you to run with it.

A Word about Conflicting U.S. and State Laws

Before addressing the burning issues, there are one or two procedural nuances you should be aware of. First, there are often two entirely different sets of laws covering a single area of employment: United States law and the law of the state you work in. Often the laws are similar. But at times they conflict. So which law applies to you? Which law must your employer comply with? When considering that question, it is important to understand that there are three possible situations. The issue may be covered:

☞ By state law only;
☞ By federal law only; or
☞ By both state *and* federal law.

The first two situations are fairly clear-cut: If the issue in question is covered by one law only, then you are protected by that law and your employer must comply with it. As for the third situation, sometimes the state and federal laws are virtually the same, so there is no problem. But occasionally the laws conflict—and that can be tricky. (In some areas of the law that is further complicated by the fact that in part the state law is more restrictive and in part the federal law is more restrictive.) But what it all boils down to is this: *In cases where an issue is addressed by conflicting state and federal laws, you, the employee, are covered by the law that affords you the most rights or protections.*

In general, in areas in which there is a conflict, this book simplifies matters by telling you exactly which law or section of the law applies to you and puts the main focus on that law or section.

Note: Judicial interpretation of the various employment laws can vary tremendously from state to state as well as within a single state. What one court calls discrimination another may very well not, and vice versa. What one rules to be wrongful discharge, another may not. And so on down the line. Differences of opinion can occur when there is the slightest distinction between the facts of two cases or even where there is no discernible distinction at all. It is because law is not an exact science. This book, therefore, in its interpretation of tendencies based on court decisions, will adopt the prevailing view, making note of trends as well as frequently occurring dissenting opinions.

Application of Laws by Size of Employer

The second nuance you should be aware of is that laws often apply to employers according to size, as determined by the number of employees in their work force. For example, most federal civil rights laws apply to employers of *fifteen or more employees,* while many individual state civil rights laws apply to smaller employers. The reason some laws are applied to employers by size is because legislators felt that forcing small companies to comply would impose too great a hardship on them; or that statistically it would be impossible to determine whether or not a small employer was in fact complying with the law.

Of course, many employment laws apply to all employers regardless of size. If a law applies only to employers with at least a certain number of employees, that fact will generally be noted at the beginning of the appropriate section.

How to Find Cited Cases

This book outlines employment laws in such a way as to make them as easy as possible to understand without omitting any necessary information. Many case citations and volume references are included, should you wish to read the actual law or case. For your information, individual state statutes, regulations, and case reports are available at most city and town libraries. Federal statutes and regulations, as well as other volumes cited, are available at most university, state, and county law libraries. (State and county law libraries are open to the public. Many university law libraries are, too, especially state universities. But even private universities that limit access to their libraries will generally give you at least a day pass.)

Note: As a practical matter, some of the cited cases may be a bit difficult to find. That is because at the time of this writing some were so recent that they were available only in so-called advance sheets or in looseleaf services. Subsequently many, but not all, will be published in bound form. Therefore, in most cases your librarian should be able to help you find updated citations that will make it easier for you to locate the case. (Be sure to bring the case citation with you.) I hope this is not too burdensome or inconvenient. In any event, the real purpose of providing case citations is to let you know that these things actually did happen. It is expected that only a few *lawyers* will actually want to read the cases in their entirety.

Overlapping Issues

This book makes every attempt to avoid repetition. However, sometimes repetition is unavoidable because legal issues have a tendency to resist clear delineation. For example, the section on wrongful discharge necessarily includes cases of discrimination, which necessitates at least a brief discussion of discrimination issues, even though an entire chapter is reserved for that topic. But to maintain organizational order the discussion of such side issues will be kept to a minimum, with references to the appropriate section for details.

Don't Forget Appendixes

This book has several useful appendixes you should take care not to overlook. There are listings of state and federal agencies, with addresses and telephone numbers; synopses of major employment laws; a glossary of relevant legal terms; and an employment law quiz based on your reading, complete with answers and explanations.

Reading This Book—A Matter of Style

This book is designed to be as comprehensive and easy as possible to use to enable you to refer to it again and again, as needed. How you use it is entirely up to you. Read it from cover to cover, and like the Boy Scouts, "Be prepared." Or take your time. Read it section by section as the need arises. After all, hopefully none of you is trapped in an employment situation that is so tragic you will find every chapter of immediate use. Of immediate interest, yes. Of immediate use, maybe not. But who knows? Today you may need to know how to file an unemployment claim to have the best chance of receiving benefits; another time you may need to know about your civil rights or how to gain access to your personnel files or your right to continue your group health insurance benefits after termination or . . .

But whether this book gives you the ammunition you need to go out and fight for your rights today, this minute; or prepares you for that nearly inevitable day when you will need to know how to defend yourself against an overbearing employer; or simply serves to make you comfortable by reassuring you that you are being treated fairly, it will have served its purpose.

Remember, in the words of the immortal Knute Rockne (or was it Ronald Reagan?): "The best offense is a good defense." *And your best defense against unfair treatment in the workplace is for you and every other employee out there to know your rights. Because if your employer knows you know your rights, he or she will be a little more respectful of them.*

A Word about Gender

The word about gender is "neutral." Of course, it's not quite as simple as that anymore, but it should be. We've gotten very defensive about gender in the past decade.

The problem, I discovered early on in working on this book, is not so much in referring to singular employ*ees*. When referring to a specific case where the gender of the suing employee (actually it is usually by then a *former* employee) is known and matters enough to articulate, I have used the appropriate pronoun. In the abstract I have, insofar as was possible without sounding awkward, used "him or her" and "his or her." At other times I will alternate pronouns so as not to offend anyone by always referring to a "him" or always referring to a "her" as the aggrieved party.

There was more of a problem, as it turned out, in referring to the employ*er*. I considered the impersonal "it," but very soon found it *too* impersonal. After all, it wasn't an "it" who treated you unfairly or fired you. It was a "him" or a "her." However, it wasn't *always* a "him" and it wasn't *always* a "her." But try to write a book referring to "him or her" or "himself or herself" every time a personal pronoun is called for. It very quickly gets cumbersome . . . and tiresome . . . and more than a little bit stilted. So, when in doubt, I called your employer "him." Not because there still are more men than women in managerial positions, though for one reason or another there still are. But simply because I had to choose.

For those of you who may still consider being offended by my choice, consider this: In almost every situation this book discusses, "he" is not a very nice guy.

This book and its author's point of view are strictly gender neutral.

(**Note:** "Employer," as used in this book, refers not only to the actual owner of the business or the chief executive officer or president, as the case may be, but to foremen, supervisors, managers, and others who act as legitimate "agents" of the employer, who is therefore responsible for their actions.)

1

The Hiring Process

The first part of the employment process, of course, is getting out there and getting a job. Which is hard enough without having a strike or two against you—before you've even faced a single pitch. Maybe you're black or female or over forty or pregnant. Maybe you have an arrest record or your credit is not all that great. Maybe you filed a workers' compensation claim on your previous job or maybe you have a permanent disability of some kind. Maybe you're a reformed alcoholic or drug addict. Maybe you're of foreign extraction. In the vast majority of employment situations, none of these things can legally be considered when comparing job applicants. But all too often they are.

Let us now chart your rights throughout the hiring process, from the time you see that first advertisement in the classified section of your local newspaper up until the time you actually walk in the front door of your new workplace.

JOB ADVERTISEMENTS

Let's begin at the beginning. And the beginning is when you decide to start looking for a job. It is important to understand that your employment rights are actually on the job long before you are. They begin to protect you the minute you start to look for employment. The theory, of course, is that everyone with the same qualifications for a job should start out with the same chance to get it; that no one should be disadvantaged by race, sex, age, or anything else unrelated to potential job performance.

Thus, an employer may not advertise a job in such a manner that it would indicate a preference or limitation or otherwise discriminate against anyone based on:

☞ Race;
☞ Color;
☞ Religion;
☞ Age;
☞ Sex;
☞ National origin or ancestry; or
☞ Physical or mental disability.

State Laws: Some states have more extensive antidiscrimination laws that, along with the basics, also prohibit employers from discriminating on the basis of things like marital status and sexual preference.

Notes

Age: Advertisements may specify *minimum* age requirements—as long as the minimum age required is under forty. For example, it would be appropriate to advertise the requirements for a job serving alcohol as "must be at least twenty-one"; or for a hazardous job as "must be at least eighteen." The requirement that any minimum age specified be under forty is because the **Age Discrimination in Employment Act** protects everyone over forty. (Many state laws protect workers under forty from age-based discrimination, too. See Chapter 5: Discrimination and Related Issues.) As a practical matter, specifying any minimum age except in compliance with a law— such as a minimum age requirement to serve alcohol or to work in a hazardous occupation—would be suspect.

"Bona Fide Occupational Qualification or Need" Exception (BFOQ): A rare and narrowly applied exception that allows an employer to specify a job requirement that would otherwise be considered discriminatory is based on a so-called bona fide occupational qualification or need. To fit into this exception, an employer must be able to justify that the requirement is "reasonably necessary to the normal operation of the enterprise." One fairly obvious example of a bona fide occupational qualification or need would be where a private secondary school limits applications for the position of live-in proctor of a girls' residence hall to females. However, it cannot be overemphasized that the BFOQ exception can rarely be applied legitimately and, when it is, must be able to be justified by the employer. In addition, the law specifically states that the exception can be used only "when *religion, sex, or national origin* is a bona fide occupational qualification for employment." (Emphasis added.) 42 United States Code Service Section 2000e-3(b). (I.e., A case generally cannot be made for *race* as a bona fide occupational qualification, except, for example, hiring an actor of a specific race to play a role calling for someone of that race.)

Government Contractors: All government contractors must include the phrase "Equal Opportunity Employer" in all classified ads.

Strikes: Any job advertisement to replace striking union workers must include a statement that a strike is in progress.

Examples: Besides the obvious, some specific and perhaps more subtle examples of job designations that would be discriminatory unless they are within the bona fide occupational qualification or need exception would be:

☞ "Girl" or "Boy," which would indicate both an age and a sex preference;

☞ "Gal Friday," which would indicate a gender and possibly an age preference;

☞ "Young," "Age 25 to 35," "College student," or "Recent college graduate," which would indicate an age preference;

☞ "Able-bodied," which would indicate a prejudice against the handicapped (unless physical strength or endurance are legitimate requirements of the job, such as a job that calls for heavy lifting); and

☞ "Single," which would, pardon the pun, single out unmarried people.

To get just an idea of how little employers know about the fundamental laws of the workplace, all you need do is check the want ads on any given Sunday and count the number of job advertisements that are in direct violation of the law.

Note: For a detailed discussion of civil rights laws see Chapter 5: Discrimination and Related Issues.

WHAT TO DO: Your first and most practical option upon reading a potentially discriminatory job ad would be to notify the federal Equal Employment Opportunity Commission (EEOC). Most states also have an equivalent agency, often a human rights commission. (You can locate agency addresses and telephone numbers in the Blue Pages of your telephone directory under the heading "United States Government" or your individual state.) In most cases, you have 180 days from the date of the employment practice complained of to file charges with the EEOC or your state human rights commission. In practice, the EEOC generally defers action on charges filed directly with it for sixty days to allow the state agency to act on the complaint. (For details of the complaint procedure, see Chapter 11: I'm Getting Screwed; So What Can I Do about It?)

The intent of antidiscrimination laws is not only to force the employer to cease the practice, but, inasmuch as it is possible, to make the victim "whole." Therefore, if a job advertisement is determined to be discriminatory, the company will likely be fined and required to cease placing the offending advertisement. In that effort to make you "whole," the law may also require the employer to pay you lost wages or to hire you and, in some cases, even to contact former victims of the discriminatory practice to notify them that they will be reconsidered for employment if they reapply.

Believe it or not, most courts have ruled that it doesn't matter that you might not have gotten the job anyway, or even that you were not qualified for the job. All that is relevant and that you need to prove to have a claim is that you lost a *chance* to get the job.*

PREEMPLOYMENT INQUIRIES

Whether you send in your resumé, call for an appointment, are referred by a friend or your school's placement department or an employment agency, or simply walk in off the street, eventually you will be asked to fill out a job application form. Then you will likely be further screened in a personal interview.

Which brings us to the types of questions employers are allowed

---

Ruggles v. California Polytechnic State University, San Luis Obispo, 797 Fed. 2d 782, 1986.

to ask you. Such questions are referred to "in the biz" as "preemployment inquiries." Whether you are requested to respond to them in writing on a job application form or orally in a personal interview, preemployment inquiries should be directed at determining your qualifications to perform the job you are applying for. Therefore, *any questions not aimed at the evaluation of your training, education, and experience as they relate to that job are irrelevant—and probably illegal.*

Sample Application / Interview Questions

These days employers must exercise extreme caution even when asking the most routine questions. Otherwise a job applicant may have grounds for a discrimination or invasion of privacy claim. **Table 1** lists some run-of-the-mill preemployment questions along with possible legal objections to them.

Note: Some questions that are objectionable *before* hiring are completely acceptable *after* hiring. For example, an employer who asks a job applicant's age before hiring may be guilty of age discrimination if the applicant is turned down. However, the same employer may legitimately ask an employee's age once he or she is hired if, for example, the information is needed for insurance purposes.

Most-Often-Asked Objectionable Questions: Just because employers are not supposed to ask the questions in Table 1 obviously doesn't mean they never do. In fact, more than three-quarters of workers surveyed in a recent nationwide poll said they had been asked at least one question in an interview that had nothing to do with job performance. In questioning over one thousand people, the National Consumers League of Washington, D.C., found that the objectionable questions most often asked by prospective employers were:

☞ If the applicant lives with a member of the opposite sex;
☞ The applicant's marital status;
☞ The applicant's plans regarding having children;
☞ The applicant's religious affiliation;
☞ Whether or not the applicant smokes off the job;
☞ If the applicant has elderly parents; and
☞ If the applicant has dangerous hobbies.

TABLE **1**

PREEMPLOYMENT INQUIRIES

Question	Before Hiring	Note
Name	*Can* ask your name and if you have worked under another name(s). *Cannot* ask your maiden name or your spouse's maiden name (possible discrimination based on marital status or national origin).	
Address	*Can* ask your present address. *Cannot* ask if you own or rent your residence (is irrelevant and could unfairly tend to single out minorities).	Questions such as how long you have lived at your present address and where you previously resided and how long you lived there are irrelevant and should not be asked.
Age	*Cannot* be asked a question the answer to which would indicate your age, either directly or indirectly. Examples of inappropriate questions: • How old are you? • What year were you born? • What year did you graduate from high school/college? *Can* be asked if you are the minimum age required to perform the job.	*Can* be asked your age for employer-sponsored group insurance purposes *after* you are hired. *Can* be asked to prove that you are of legal age (e.g., to serve alcoholic beverages or to work in a hazardous occupation) *after* you are hired.

TABLE 1 *(Continued)*

Question	*Before Hiring*	*Note*
Marital Status, Family, or Family Plans	*Cannot* be asked a question that would indicate your marital status or family orientation, such as: • Are you married? • Do you have a family? • What is your (or your spouse's) maiden name? • Are you pregnant? • Do you plan to have a family? • What daycare arrangements have you made?	*Can* be asked to provide information about dependents who will be covered by an employer-sponsored insurance plan *after* hiring.
Citizenship	*Can* be asked if you are a citizen, since U.S. law allows preference of a citizen over an equally qualified noncitizen. (Employers must be careful in this gray area, since it is also unlawful to discriminate on the basis of national origin.) *Can* be asked if you are authorized to work in the U.S. *Cannot* be asked if you are a *naturalized* citizen. *Cannot* be asked if you are/were a citizen of a foreign country. *Cannot* be asked if you intend to become a citizen.	*Must* be asked, *after* hiring, to provide proof of eligibility to work in the U.S.

TABLE 1 (*Continued*)

Question	*Before Hiring*	*Note*
National Origin	*Cannot* be asked your nationality, ancestry, native language or that of your family. *Cannot* be asked where you or your parents were born. *Can* be asked if you are eligible to work in the U.S.	*Can* be asked if you are a U.S. citizen. *Can* be asked if you speak a foreign language *if* it is a requirement of the job (i.e., a bona fide occupational qualification). *Must* be asked, *after* hiring, to provide proof of eligibility to work in the U.S.
Group Memberships	*Cannot* be asked any questions regarding social or political group membership (could be considered national origin discrimination).	*Can* be asked about membership in professional, trade, or other organizations that are job-related.
Religion	*Cannot* be asked your religious affiliation or what religious holidays you observe.	*Can* be asked, *after* hiring, about your availability for work and if a religious accommodation will need to be made; *cannot* be refused employment *because* such an accommodation would have to be made.

TABLE 1 *(Continued)*

Question	*Before Hiring*	*Note*
Race	*Cannot* be asked any questions about race or color. *Cannot* be asked to submit a photo. *Cannot* be asked hair, eye, or skin color on an application form.	An interviewer making an observation *cannot* indicate an applicant's race on an application form or report. *Can* be asked by a government contractor if you wish to identify yourself as a minority for purposes of employer's obligation to take affirmative action to hire minorities.* (Such identification must be voluntary.)
Sex	*Cannot* be asked anything about your sex or sexual preference.	*Can* be asked by a government contractor if you wish to identify yourself as a female for purposes of employer's obligation to take affirmative action to hire women. (Such identification must be voluntary.)
Photograph	*Cannot* be asked to submit a photo with your application.	*Can* be asked, *after* hiring, to have photo taken for company ID where needed for legitimate purpose and if all other employees in your job classification are also required to wear a photo ID.

*Questions regarding self-identification should not be on the actual application form but on a separate self-identification form. See Chapter 5: Discrimination and Related Isssues, for more information on "Affirmative Action Under Fire."

TABLE 1 *(Continued)*

Question	*Before Hiring*	*Note*
Handicaps/Disabilities	*Cannot* be asked if you have a disability and, if so, the nature and degree of that disability, *unless* it would limit your ability to perform the job you are applying for.	*Can* be asked about a disability as it relates to your ability to perform the job you are applying for safely and competently. *Can* be asked about a disability as it relates to the type of workplace accommodation necessary for you to perform the job you are applying for. (You *cannot* be disqualified because the employer would have to accommodate your disability.) *Can* be asked by a government contractor if you wish to identify yourself as a handicapped individual for purposes of employer's obligation to take affirmative action to hire the handicapped. (Such identification must be voluntary.)

TABLE 1 *(Continued)*

Question	*Before Hiring*	*Note*
Arrests and Convictions	*Cannot* be asked if you have ever been arrested or charged with a crime (because being arrested or charged with a crime doesn't mean you are/were guilty).	*Can* be asked if you have been convicted of a crime. According to Equal Employment Opportunity Commission *Guidelines,* convictions should be a reason for rejection of an applicant only because of their number, type, or relationship to the job, or because they occurred recently; also, says the EEOC, the employer should consider whether or not you have undergone rehabilitation. The questioner (or application form) should indicate that conviction of a crime cannot, in and of itself, disqualify you from consideration.
Military Service	*Cannot* be asked about military service *unless* such experience is directly related to your ability to perform the job you are applying for. *Cannot* be asked about military reserve duty obligations. *Cannot* be asked about military service for another country. *Cannot* be asked about the type of discharge you received. (Such questions have been found to unfairly disqualify minorities.) *Cannot* be asked about disciplinary record while in the service.	*Can* be asked about experience in military service as it relates to the job you are applying for. *Can* be asked by a government contractor if you wish to identify yourself as a U.S. military veteran for purposes of employer's obligation to take affirmative action to hire veterans. (Such identification must be voluntary.)

TABLE 1 *(Continued)*

Question	*Before Hiring*	*Note*
Height, Weight, and Other Physical Requirements	*Cannot* be required to take a medical or physical exam before hiring. *Cannot* be asked your height or weight *unless* such requirements are a bona fide occupational qualification of the job. (Such requirements tend to eliminate people based on national origin or ancestry and also to eliminate women.)	*Can* be required to take a physical agility test prior to hiring if physical strength or ability is a bona fide requirement for performing the job and if all others in your job classification are also required to submit to the same test.
Job Experience	*Can* be asked virtually unlimited questions relative to job experience, including names and addresses of former employers, job(s) held, wages and hours, dates of employment, and reason for leaving the job(s).	
Education and Training	*Can* be asked questions about education and training, degrees earned, and professional licenses held insofar as they relate to the requirements of the job you are seeking.	*Cannot* be asked questions about education and training that bear no relationship to the requirements of the job applied for (particularly those requiring education or training in excess of reasonable requirements for the job). *Cannot* be asked dates of attendance or graduation. (Such questions would be tantamount to asking for your age.)

TABLE 1 *(Continued)*

Question	*Before Hiring*	*Note*
References	*Can* be asked for job or character references. *Cannot* be asked for references that would indicate religion, sex, race, age, or national origin, or otherwise provide information that could be the basis for discrimination.	References *cannot* be checked without your permission.
Lie Detector Test	*Cannot* be either asked to or required to take a lie detector test.	*Exception:* State and local police departments may request noncivilian personnel to submit to a lie detector test. (Strict guidelines must be adhered to in the administration of such tests.)
Drug Test	*Can* be asked to take an approved urinalysis drug test *if* you are given advance written notice of the employer's intent to conduct the test.	*Observation* is not permitted. *Confidentiality* of results must be scrupulously maintained. You must be given a copy of a positive result.

Note: Employers may sneak in these kinds of questions not for the more obvious discriminatory reasons but because of the effect the answers could have on their group health insurance premiums. Employers may be trying to weed out prospective employees (or their dependents) who could become a burden because of anticipated health problems.

Even so, most of the above questions are unlawful or otherwise objectionable because the answers are personal and/or discriminatory and bear no relationship to job performance.

Employer Strategies

Be prepared to explain gaps in information, such as periods during which you were not employed. Any employer who hasn't been vacationing on another planet for the past ten years will ask you to fill in missing information. **Note:** This is particularly important because employers who are up-to-date on hiring techniques (granted, there aren't many of them, but they're out there) may even ask you to sign an application form that says any misstatement is grounds for discharge at any time. *Courts have almost unanimously held that such misstatements are valid grounds for disqualification or discharge on discovery of the misstatement—as long as the rule is not applied so as to discriminate.* In a precedent-setting case, a black employee who claimed he had passed the bar exam was discharged when the company later found out he hadn't. It just happened the man was a vocal minority rights advocate and he maintained *that* was the real reason he was let go. The court, however, upheld his firing because other employees who had previously done the same thing were either fired or demoted without respect to race.*

Background Investigations

Because of all the laws that protect employees once they are on the job, more and more employers are checking up on job applicants to avoid hiring those "undesirables." It is fairly easy for an employer to check your criminal record and/or your credit history as well as to check on other background information. They can gather some of the desired information themselves with a minimum amount of effort and a little bit of ingenuity. However, many hire investigators to do the work for them. In fact, in recent years companies have sprung up that specialize in checking out prospective employees for employers. Such companies will check out not only such things as criminal records and credit histories but the person's age, race, marital status, and dependents, whether or not he or she has ever filed a workers' compensation claim, and other information an employer is not legally supposed to use in making an employment decision.

Consumer Protection Laws: The **Fair Credit Reporting Act** requires an employer to notify you *in writing* within three days of asking a credit reporting agency to check you out. The notice must tell you:

Williams v. Boorstin, 663 Fed. 2d 109, 1980.

☞ That a credit investigation will be made.

☞ That you have the right to ask the employer to disclose the nature and scope of the investigation. (You must be given any further information about the report within five days of the time you ask for it. But you must ask.)

In fact, according to 1997 amendments fo the FCRA, an employer may not obtain a report for employment purposes unless, in addition to being informed that the report may be made, you specifically authorize the employer to have the report done. Futhermore, before an employer takes any adverse action based on the report (i.e., denies you employment), he has to send you a copy of the background report and a summary of your rights under the FCRA.

Finally, you must be told if a credit report played a part in a decision to deny you a job, and you have the right to be given the name and address of the credit reporting agency so you can get a copy of the report. **Note:** Technically, an employer can use a credit report only to verify the fact that you were employed. The EEOC has ruled that requiring a job applicant to have good credit has a disproportionate impact on minorities and women (based on census figures that indicate many more nonwhites and women are below the poverty level) and is generally against the law unless the employer can justify such a requirement as necessary in a particular business or job. For example, it might be appropriate to require good credit—or rather screen out applicants with poor credit—for jobs whose duties include some fiduciary responsibility, such as handling clients' funds.

Blacklisting Laws: So-called blacklisting laws prohibit employers from belonging to or supporting any agency that provides members with information that would affect a person's ability to secure employment *unless* the information is open to inspection by the person being reported on. (Legitimate credit bureaus are an exception because the information they gather is available to the subjects of their reports.)

WHAT TO DO: You are asked an objectionable question. What do you do about it? An obvious but rarely invoked option: Don't answer it! Leave that section of the application form blank; or politely suggest to the interviewer that you believe he or she is not really supposed to ask your age, religion, marital status, etc. Of course, the problem with this solution is as obvious as the solution itself: First, when we want something (i.e., this job), we realize the best tactic for achieving success is to do what we are told. There will be plenty of time to complain about it later if we don't get the job. And second, in the interview scenario it may be a tad difficult to be diplomatic while telling your prospective employer, "Excuse me, but I believe it's against the law for you to ask me that question."

Of course, even in this day and age of scarce employment, do you really want to work for someone who is so cavalier about your rights? If they behave this way in an interview, think of what actually working for this person would be like.

On the other hand, rather than object to the *question,* you may want to object to the *result.* But remember, if that's the case, your chances of being successful will be significantly fortified with a little of that most basic of legal niceties, evidence. If the offending question is on an application form, keep a copy (or have the employer make you a copy). If the question is asked in an interview, evidence may be a bit more difficult to come by. Were there witnesses? Other job applicants? Other interviewers? Do you know of others who were asked the same objectionable question and also were refused employment? Evidence. It helps.

In any event, if you were asked an unlawful question and feel you were turned down for a job because of your answer, you have a right to complain. (You may even feel you have a *duty*—not only to yourself but to job seekers everywhere—to report it.) As with discriminatory job ads, the easiest and cheapest way to complain is by filing charges with the EEOC or your state human rights commission. Investigating such complaints is their job. If this employer was tactless or ignorant enough to ask you an unlawful question, it is likely that he or she has asked the same kind of discriminatory question to others.

However, as a practical matter, before filing charges you should ask yourself the question: What damages have I suffered? Because your remedies, and thus, the value of the time and effort it will take to establish a claim, depend on the answer. If you can prove you were denied a job even in part because of your answer to a discriminatory question, you may be entitled to that job (if you still want a job with this employer); and/or damages equal to the amount of pay lost between the time you were denied the job and the time you either accept that job or get another; and/or punitive damages—that is, damages assessed to *punish* the employer for breaking the law by denying you your rights. (See Chapter 11: I'm Getting Screwed; So What Can I Do about It?) It is worth a reminder here that you needn't prove you would have gotten the job had you not been discriminated against, only that the employer's discriminatory practice deprived you of a *chance* to get it. **Note:** Besides requiring employers to hire present victims of discriminatory practices, courts have also required employers to contact former victims to notify them that they will be reconsidered for employment if they reapply for the position.

Of course, it may turn out that you are the first person to lodge a complaint against this employer, the very first link in that all-important evidentiary chain, and you may have to be satisfied that the employer will be fined by the EEOC as a result of your complaint, with a greater fine to come if the behavior continues, along with a greater chance that someone else *with more evidence* will achieve even better results in the future. Even if you have a difficult time getting any greater satisfaction than that (like that job you wanted; or money damages), that's okay. The next person who is similarly discriminated against by that employer *will* have evidence—*your* evidence.

Discovering that an employer made an employment decision based on background information about you that he was not legally entitled to gather, such as your age, sex, race, national origin, marital status, previous filing of a workers' compensation claim, and any number of other discriminatory criteria, may be a bit more challenging. What you have to do is be as sneaky and underhanded as you think the employer was. How sneaky and underhanded you can get may depend on your finances, however. True, you are entitled to receive your own credit report from a legitimate credit bureau free of charge simply by calling and requesting it. (Some credit bureaus require the request to be in writing.) But other information may be more costly to come by. You may even have to pay, just as the employer did, to find out what background information is being handed out on you. It may even necessitate hiring an investigator. At this point you (and your attorney?) may be put in a position where you have to decide on a trade-off: the nature and potential value of the information and how sure you are it was used against you illegally versus how likely you are to succeed with a damage suit against the employer and the value of that lawsuit. *Warning:* It is often a difficult call.

Note: For your own protection, you should make a habit of checking with credit bureaus every six to twelve months. You have a right to have your explanation of a poor credit check attached to your credit report, and expunged if you can get a statement from the creditor. (Often old, long-cleared-up debts remain on a credit report because the creditor neglects to notify the credit bureau.)

REFERENCES/RECOMMENDATIONS

What's Allowed

An employer may give a reference on a present or former employee at the request of:

☛ The employee; or
☛ A prospective employer.

An employer can only give truthful, factual *job-related* information about you. The key phrase here is "job-related."

What's Not Allowed

References cannot comment on your personal life or habits. They cannot tell a prospective employer that you filed a discrimination suit or a workers' compensation claim. In short, they cannot provide any information that an employer is not legally entitled to in making an employment decision.

Employer Strategies

To cover himself, the smart employer will ask you to sign a statement authorizing former employers or academic institutions to release information about you. This will allow him to check your references without fear of being called on it later. However, former employers and others providing references still have limits on what they can say about you.

Limits on Giving References

There are a number of factors limiting what an employer (or former employer) can say about you.

Privacy Laws: There are laws that guard the confidentiality of your personnel files and medical records, the results of lie detector and drug tests and arrest and conviction records. (See Chapter 6: Right to Privacy/Access to Records.)

Laws Against Defamation: Defamation laws prohibit libel and slander: giving negative, false information about someone. (Written defamation is libel, oral defamation is slander.) In *Holton v. Lockheed Corp.,* a California jury awarded a fired employee almost $1 million because his former employer provided defamatory job references to prospective employers, which caused the former employee emotional distress, said the jury.*

Civil Rights Laws: An employer cannot give out information regarding your age, sex, race, color, national origin, or disabilities. (See Chapter 5: Discrimination and Related Issues.)

Laws Against Blacklisting: Employers cannot circulate your name with the intent of preventing you from getting a job somewhere else.

Employer Strategies

Some employers try to avoid potential legal problems by limiting their responses to requests for references to "name, rank, and serial number." That is, they will give only your name, dates of employment, positions held, salary, and attendance. (Many employers feel that what references *don't* say is as important as what they *do* say. It's the old "If you can't say anything nice, don't say anything at all" tactic. The implication of course being, if the reference had something good to say about you, they would have said it.) Others will attempt to skirt the reference problem entirely by giving all departing employees a standard, noncommittal reference letter when they leave the job.

WHAT TO DO: One thing you can do, if you suspect a former employer will give you a negative reference, is not give your prospective employer permission to seek a reference from that employer. That could be tricky, however, since a prospective employer might consider an explanation to be appropriate under the circumstances. So you should have one ready.

The best option, however (particularly if you would not expect a glowing reference), is to ask your former employer(s) for a refer-

*California Superior Court, No. 642082, 1991.

ence letter *as you leave your job*. Few employers will risk handing you a negative reference no matter what your reason for leaving the company. Rather, they will either give you a stock "name, rank, and serial number" recommendation or, however reluctantly, a positive reference. You may thus be able to head off the problem of a possible negative reference by attaching the good/neutral reference to your application for the new job.

Note: An employer who fires you but gives you a positive reference (especially if he or she subsequently makes negative comments about you to a prospective employer) is just begging to be hit with a wrongful discharge suit. After all, if you were such a good employee, what was the *real* reason you were fired?

Once again, the importance of evidence cannot be overstated. What can you do about a false negative reference if you have no evidence of it? That underscores the need to get your reference letter from your employer as you leave work. You should also, as a matter of course, request to see and copy your personnel file and demand that either false negative information be deleted or your own statements be added to explain or clarify incorrect or misleading information. You have those rights. (See Chapter 6: Right to Privacy/ Access to Records.)

Note ("negligent hiring"): At least part of the reason employers have become so zealous in recent years about gathering information on prospective employees is the relatively new theory of "negligent hiring." Under the theory, employers can be held liable for their employees' acts even where those acts are determined to have been *outside* the scope of their employment. (Traditionally, employers could be held liable only for conduct of employees acting within the scope of their employment; that is, conduct directly related to the performance of their job). Now, if a "reasonable investigation" would have turned up problems in an employee's past, an employer can be held responsible for his or her acts if there is some link between the job and the act (e.g., the employee's job gains him access to someone's home, where he commits a crime). For example, in an Ohio case, a cable television company was held liable for damages when sued by a customer who was raped by a cable installer after letting him into her house to hook up her cable; and in a Florida case, an employer was even held liable for an attack on a woman by a furniture delivery man who returned to her house to assault her three months after making a delivery.*

Tallahassee Furniture Delivery v. Harrison, 583 So. 2nd 744, 1991.

Note (emerging fields of employer negligence): In recent years several other areas of potential employer negligence have emerged as a result of court decisions.

"Negligent referral": An insurance company that negligently provided a glowing reference for a former employee whom they were actually scared to death of was found liable for negligent referral. (The employee had been fired a few years before for carrying a pistol in his briefcase, the company having concluded that he was "unstable.") That employee, who was hired by another company at least partly as a result of that letter, later shot several coworkers in the cafeteria at his new employer's place of business! According to the court, the insurance company provided the letter "so that the unstable (former employee) would not become angry at Allstate over his termination." This decision has caused employers to rethink whether they will give any employee any kind of reference letter.*

Another case involved a recommendation of a former employee that indicated that he was fit to interact with female employees, even though the employer knew of repeated charges of sexual improprieties against him. The court concluded that an employer who gives a recommendation has a duty not to misrepresent facts that would present a substantial, foreseeable risk of physical injury to a prospective employer or third parties.†

"Negligent supervision": In *Reade v. Cusano,* the court held an employer liable for an employee's physical attack on a fellow worker when the attacker had a history of violent outbursts the employer either knew about or should have known about.‡

"Negligent retention": A Connecticut court recognized a cause of action for "negligent retention" when an employer either knew or should have known that the employee was unfit while nonetheless failing to take any action against the employee prior to the employee causing an injury to someone else.§

Jerner v. Allstate Insurance Co., Fla. Cir. Ct., No. 93-09472, Div. F, 1995.
†*Randi W. v. Muroc Joint Unified School Dist.,* 12 IER Cases 673, Calif. Sup. Ct., No. S051441, 1997.
‡*Reade v. Cusano,* Ct. Sup. Ct. at New Britain, CV97-0481261, 1998.
§*Doe v. Abrahante,* Ct. Sup. Ct. at New Haven, CV97-040311S, 1998.

PREEMPLOYMENT TESTS

These days preemployment tests are all the rage. Employers love them because they think they will be able to use them to weed out . . . there are those "undesirables" again. There are:

☞ *Achievement tests* that are supposed to measure skills and knowledge required to perform the job.

☞ *Physical agility tests* to measure your strength or other attributes required to perform the job (or, what is becoming an even more popular reason for physicals: to have a yardstick by which to measure subsequent on-the-job injuries as they relate to workers' compensation claims).

☞ *Aptitude tests* to measure your general IQ.

☞ *Personality tests* that are intended to measure your motivation, maturity, and/or interests.

☞ *Integrity tests* designed to determine if you will walk off with the store if you are left in charge of it.

Popularity aside, such tests cannot discriminate or be used as an excuse to discriminate against job applicants. Of the five basic types of tests, the easiest for employers to justify giving are achievement tests that measure potential job performance and physical agility tests related to tasks, such as heavy lifting, that will be regularly encountered on the job. However, even these kinds of "justifiable" tests must be proven by employers to be "valid" if use of such tests would have an "adverse impact" on any protected group (i.e., if they limit job opportunities for minorities, women, or the handicapped).

The EEOC has set up *Uniform Guidelines on Employment Selection Procedures* to make sure that selection procedures, including written tests, do not discriminate in violation of **Title VII of the Civil Rights Act of 1964.** The *Guidelines* apply to all employers subject to that law. (Generally, that means employers of fifteen or more employees, though many equivalent state laws apply to smaller employers. See Chapter 5: Discrimination and Related Issues.)

Testing Conditions

In order to be nondiscriminatory, a test that is given to one applicant must be given to all applicants for similar positions. The test must also be given under similar conditions.

The Adverse Impact Question

Congress has long authorized the use of "any professionally developed ability test, *provided that such test, its administration or action upon its results is not designed or intended to discriminate* [emphasis added]." Thus, the main question regarding testing and selection procedures is their effect on equal employment opportunities.

Determining Adverse Impact: Tests that have an adverse impact on the employment opportunities of any race, sex, or ethnic group are presumed to be illegal. ("Adverse impact" means any disadvantage in hiring, firing, discipline, or any other terms and conditions of employment.) The *Guidelines* contain a "rule of thumb" known as the "four-fifths rule" or "80 percent rule" which the EEOC and courts use to determine whether or not a test has an adverse impact. Under the rule, hiring rates for different groups are compared. A selection rate for any sex, race, or ethnic group that is less than four-fifths (or 80 percent) of the rate for the group with the highest selection rate will generally be regarded as having an adverse impact on that group.

Here is an example of how the rule works: Assume that white applicants enjoy the highest selection rate at a particular company. If 10 percent of white applicants are selected, then at least 8 percent (four-fifths of 10 percent) of black applicants must be accepted. To make it simple, let's use round numbers: Say a company tests one hundred white applicants and selects ten of them (10 percent). Let's say the company gave the same test to twenty-five black applicants. To avoid charges of adverse impact, the company must select at least two of them (8 percent of twenty-five). Similar comparisons must be made between males and females, as well as other groups in the applicant pool, except where the number of applicants from a particular group is too small to be statistically significant.

"Bottom Line" Exception: As a practical matter, the EEOC will not investigate an adverse impact claim as long as the employer's "bottom line" shows no adverse impact. That is, if they actually employ a sufficient number of minorities and others from protected groups. The EEOC feels it is more productive to spend their limited resources investigating employers who are actually restricting opportunities for minorities, women, and other protected groups.

Validation of Tests: Even where a test does illegally restrict job opportunities, an employer can justify the test if he can show some business necessity for it. Normally that means it must be *validated* by showing a correlation between test scores and other measures of job performance.

Use of Test Scores

Under the *Guidelines* there are three legitimate ways an employer can use the scores of selection tests:

☞ To screen out those not likely to be able to perform the job successfully;

☞ To group applicants according to the likelihood of their being able to perform the job successfully; and

☞ To rank applicants, selecting those with the highest scores for employment.

Cutoff Scores and Ranking: If an employer uses "cutoff scores" to rank or eliminate applicants, the employer must be able to prove the cutoff points are reasonably consistent with job performance. He can do that by showing how previous test scores are reflected in the performance of workers who are already on the job.

Unscored Tests: If an employer uses unscored tests that result in an adverse impact, either the adverse impact must be eliminated or the procedure must be modified to a more formal one.

Alternative Selection Methods: The *Guidelines* obligate the user of a test shown to have an adverse impact to investigate alternative selection procedures that have substantially the same validity and have less of an adverse impact on protected groups.

Employer Strategies

Some employers try to skirt the adverse impact issue by saying they are testing not only for the actual job opening but for a higher-level job that is the next natural step on the promotional ladder (i.e., so the person must be qualified for that job, too). But the EEOC is wise to that ploy, recognizing the "higher-level job" excuse only if the employer can show that employees are generally promoted to the higher-level job within a reasonable time. But if the progression is not relatively automatic, applicants can be evaluated for only the "entry-level" job.* What is a reasonable time, of course, depends largely on the situation. But federal regulations indicate that a time span is unreasonable when it is so long that "the higher-level job or the employee's potential are likely to change significantly" in the interim.† As a general rule, a time span of more than five years will seldom be considered reasonable.

Affirmative Action Requirements: Using tests that conform to the *Guidelines* does not relieve government contractors of any affirmative action obligations they may have. (See Chapter 5: Discrimination and Related Issues.)

Promotion or Layoff

Tests used to determine promotions or layoffs are subject to the same limitations as for hiring.

WHAT TO DO: If you have been adversely affected by a testing procedure, so probably have many in your "protected class." If you think a test unlawfully put you at a disadvantage (in getting either a job or a promotion) because of your race, sex, or national origin, you can file a complaint with the EEOC. The test can be challenged successfully by proving a pattern of discrimination against a protected group. Once that has been done, the employer must be able to defend the test as job-related or it will be ruled unlawful. Usually if an adverse impact is shown, the employer will be required to alter its testing procedures to conform. It may also be required to take steps to change the makeup of its work force to remedy past imbalances created by the testing procedure.

Once again, it cannot be overemphasized: An EEOC charge has potential merit if you can prove not that you would have actually gotten the job or promotion but that you lost a *chance* to get it because of the alleged discrimination.

Albemarle Paper Co. v. Moody, 422 United States Reports 405, U.S. Court of Appeals, 4th Circuit, 1975.
†Volume 29, Code of Federal Regulations, Section 1607.5I.

EMPLOYMENT VERIFICATION (I-9 FORMS)

The U.S. *Immigration Reform and Control Act (IRCA),* effective November 6, 1986, prohibits employers from recruiting, hiring, or continuing to employ *illegal* aliens. It is administered and enforced by the Immigration and Naturalization Service (INS). The law:

☞ *Requires employees* to prove their identity and eligibility for employment with specific documents and to complete and sign the employee information section of the I-9 "Employment Eligibility Verification" Form after being offered a job;

☞ *Requires employers* to review the documents, complete and sign the employer review section of the I-9 Form, and retain it in their records.

Employees Whose Eligibility Must Be Verified

All employers are required to verify the employment eligibility of *everyone* they hire, part-time and full-time, including U.S. citizens—with two specific exceptions. The first is employees who are "grandfathered" in: that is, employees who were hired before November 6, 1986, and have worked for the employer continuously since. (Employees are considered continuously employed regardless of temporary leaves for things like study, illness, pregnancy, disability, transfer to another location within the company, strikes and layoffs where there was a reasonable expectation of reemployment, promotions and demotions, and vacations and leaves approved by the employer.) The second exception is housekeepers in private homes, where the work is intermittent or periodic.

Important: Employers are supposed to verify the employment eligibility of everyone they hire. They cannot require documentation from only those who they consider "look foreign" or who speak with an accent, and not require it from others.

Document(s) Required

Establishing your eligibility to work in the United States requires proving your identity as well as your eligibility to work. Some documents may be used to establish both identity and employment eligibility. Others can be used to establish only one or the other, as follows:

Single Document for Both Identity and Employment Eligibility: As a newly hired worker, you may use certain documents to establish both your identity *and* your employment eligibility. Showing your new employer the original of any one of these documents will satisfy your requirement of proving your identity and eligibility to work: U.S. passport; certificate of U.S. citizenship (INS Form N-560 or N-561); certificate of naturalization (INS Form N-550 or N-570); unexpired foreign passport having an unexpired I-551 (employment authorization) stamp or a Form I-94 attached to it with the same name as the passport; alien registration receipt card (Form I-151) or resident alien card (Form I-551) with your photograph; unexpired temporary resident card (Form I-688) or unexpired employment authorization card (Form I-688A) with your photograph; an unexpired re-entry permit (Form I-327); an unexpired refugee travel document (Form I-571); or an unexpired employment authorization document issued by the INS, which contains a photograph (Form I-688B).

Two Documents Needed, One for Identity and One for Employment Eligibility:
IDENTITY ONLY: Newly hired workers age *sixteen and over* may establish their identity only with an original of one of the following: state-issued driver's license or ID card with photograph, or which lists name, address, date of birth, sex, height, and eye color; school ID card with a photograph; voter registration card; U.S. military card or draft record; federal, state, or local government agency ID card; military dependent's ID card; Native American tribal document; U.S. Coast Guard merchant mariner card; or Canadian driver's license.

Newly hired workers *under eighteen* who don't have one of the above documents may establish their identity with an original of: school record or report card; hospital or doctor's record; or day care or nursery school record. **Note:** If you are a minor, your parent or guardian may sign the verification form.

EMPLOYMENT ELIGIBILITY ONLY: Newly hired workers may establish their employment eligibility only with an original of one of the following: Social Security card (except one marked "not valid for employment purposes"); certificate of birth in the U.S. (Form FS-545) or birth abroad (Form DS-1350) issued by the State Department; birth certificate with the seal of a state, county, municipality, or U.S. possession (certified copy acceptable); Native American tribal document; U.S. citizen ID card (Form I-197); resident U.S. citizen ID card (Form I-179); or INS-issued unexpired employment authorization document.

Important: Under 1991 amendments to IRCA, it is discriminatory for an employer to ask you for "more or different documents" than those required by IRCA to verify your eligibility for employment, or to refuse to accept documents that "reasonably appear to be genuine." An employer can also be fined for knowingly accepting false documents. An employee, on the other hand, can be fined for presenting false documents or documents that belong to someone else.

Citizenship Preference and National Origin Discrimination—a Rock and a Hard Place for Your Employer

Under IRCA it is *okay* for an employer to favor a citizen over an *equally qualified* noncitizen. However, IRCA also says employers of four or more workers cannot discriminate on the basis of citizenship status or national origin. (**Title VII of the Civil Rights Act of 1964** also prohibits national origin discrimination.) So if you are a noncitizen and an employer favors a citizen over you in hiring or discharges you first because you are not a citizen, you may have a valid discrimination complaint.

Retaliation for Complaining

It is also a discriminatory practice for an employer to intimidate or retaliate against anyone who files an IRCA complaint.

WHAT TO DO: To be successful with an IRCA complaint you have to prove that the employer "knowingly and intentionally" either discriminated against you or engaged in a "pattern or practice" of discrimination. (**Note:** You can also file a charge against an employer for illegally hiring or employing an illegal alien, where that action may have deprived you of a job.)

Here are the steps in the IRCA complaint and enforcement process:

☞ You fill out a complaint of the violation, in writing, identifying the employer, and giving the date, time, and place, as well as details of the act complained of, sign it and file it with the INS.

☞ The INS will then investigate if it feels the complaint may be valid.

☞ If the INS determines the employer violated IRCA, it will issue a citation or a notice of intent to fine the employer, which includes the details of the violation and the penalty. (**Note:** If the INS special counsel notifies you that INS is not going to bring a discrimination complaint, you have ninety days to bring a complaint of your own. INS will provide you with the information necessary to file a complaint; or you may want to hire a lawyer. See Chapter 11: I'm Getting Screwed; So What Can I Do about It?)

☞ The employer may then contest by answering the complaint and requesting a hearing within thirty days of receiving the notice. (If the employer does not contest the complaint, the INS must issue a final order within forty-five days of sending the notice. There is no appeal from a final notice.)

If you feel your IRCA rights have been violated, contact the INS. They are listed in the Appendix and also under Department of Justice in the Blue Pages of your local telephone directory.

Penalties

Fines start at $100 for failing to complete and keep I-9 Forms on file. Employers can be fined from $250 to $10,000 per instance for knowingly hiring a person who is not authorized to work in the United States. Repeated, intentional violations can even result in jail terms. (For more on discrimination complaints and damages see Chapter 5: Discrimination and Related Issues.)

Speak-English-Only Rules: EEOC guidelines point out that rules requiring workers to speak only English while at work are *presumed* to be illegal, as are employment tests that disproportionately exclude applicants of a specific national origin, *unless* they are related to business necessity. Even when a rule requires employees to speak only English at specific times where business necessity can be shown (e.g., when dealing with customers), any adverse employment decision based on the rule will be presumed by the EEOC to be discriminatory *unless* the employer notified employees of the rule, informed them of the circumstances under which English was required, and explained the consequences of breaking the rule.

Note: Generally courts are of the opinion that valid English-only rules do not have a disparate impact on the basis of national origin, especially as applied to bilingual employees. **Title VII** does not protect the ability of workers to express their cultural heritage at the workplace.* However, the rules should apply only to cases of business necessity. In a yet-to-be-reported-on-case decided in early 2000, an employer's requirement that bilingual employees speak only English even to each other in a non-business context was discriminatory.

A WORD ABOUT EMPLOYMENT AGENCIES

Most states have enacted various laws that employment agencies must comply with for your protection. Those laws generally cover various aspects of your relationship with such an agency.

First, there are laws that require employment agencies to be licensed with your state department of labor.

There are also laws that regulate the amount you can be charged for a job referral and that require employment agencies to tell you up front what those fees will be. They also require the partial refund of a fee if you do not remain on the job for a specified minimum length of time.

Such laws also regulate general employment agency practices. For example, employment agencies are subject to discrimination laws the same way employers are. They cannot discriminate in making job referrals on the basis of age, sex, race, color, religion, creed, national origin, ancestry, marital status, or disability.

Should I Use an Employment Agency?

There is no easy answer to this question. However, the first thing you should do—after calling your state labor department to make sure the agency is licensed and authorized to do business under the laws of your state—is find out who pays the fee for referring you for employment. Some agencies charge the fee to the employer, while others charge the fee to you. Obviously, this is an important distinction.

Kania v. Archdiocese of Philadelphia, E. D. Pa., WL 426547, 1998.

Secondly, have you done everything you can—yourself—to secure employment? Getting a job is a full-time job! And you are the most qualified person around to do it. After all, who knows your qualifications better? Who has more at stake in seeing you get the right job? Who will work harder for you? No one.

So, before you start paying someone else, make sure you are doing the job to the best of your ability yourself. Then maybe look into contacting an employment agency as a secondary source of referrals. But don't stop working at it yourself.

SUMMARY

You may have a cause of action if you can prove that you were discriminated against in the job application process. That includes discriminatory limitations or preferences expressed in a job advertisement, objectionable questions on the job application form or in a personal interview, background information collected on you that does not form an appropriate basis for an employment decision, references checked without your permission or references given that include defamatory statements or information that could potentially be used to discriminate against you, preemployment tests that adversely impact a protected group of which you are a member, and IRCA violations such as requiring more or different documentation of employment eligibility from you than from others because of the way you look or the fact that you have an accent.

If you feel you have a legitimate gripe, the first step is to file a complaint with your state human rights commission or the EEOC. If the EEOC can't get you and your employer to settle the matter, the agency will either sue your employer on your behalf, if it thinks you have a good case, or it will notify you that it will not pursue the matter further. You then have every right to hire a private attorney and bring a legal action of your own. (While potentially expensive, hiring an attorney at the outset can reduce the time and aggravation that is always possible when dealing with a bureaucracy. Then again, it is important to get the *right* attorney or you risk not only the added expense but more foot-dragging and aggravation than you ever dreamed of.)

Potential remedies can include an order requiring the employer to cease engaging in the discriminatory hiring practice, to hire you if he used discriminatory hiring practices to deny you a job, and/or to pay you damages for lost wages (with interest), court costs, and attorney's fees.

(For details on how to file charges with your state human rights commission or the EEOC, and how to find the right lawyer, see Chapter 11: I'm Getting Screwed; So What Can I Do about It?)

Phew! You got the job. (Believe it or not, that was the easy part!) So now what happens?

2

The Employment Relationship

S o, you answered that ad in the paper, filled out your application form, went to the interview, no one discriminated against you, and now you've got that job you always wanted. Naturally while you were trying to get the job, you probably didn't give much thought to the day you might lose it. After all, you certainly are qualified for it. And now, after all of your employer's screening and testing you come to find out you're mature, intelligent, honest, and highly motivated, too—not to mention loyal and obedient. You are so good, in fact, that the company chose you over dozens of other qualified candidates. They told you so. You are their man (woman). So you never considered that the road could get rocky ahead. Well, of course it could. So you'd be wise to fasten your seat belt and be prepared—just in case. After all, you may be loyal and obedient but that doesn't give your employer the right to treat you like a dog.

A new job is a new beginning. So, overflowing with optimism, we resolve to work hard to make our new boss glad he hired us, to make ourselves indispensable cogs in the machine. Job security? It's not something most of us think much about in those first halcyon days of welcome and orientation. The company needs us. Otherwise why would they have just hired us?

No, for most of us job security is something that first occurs to us, first *really* occurs to us, when we hit a bump in the road, like when our supervisor starts to criticize our work or when management announces impending layoffs because of a business slump. Up to then job security was going to work, doing our jobs the best we could, and letting the chips fall where they may. But wait a minute. Let's back up to Day One and try a little realistic free association.

I say, "Job security." You say?

"None."

I say, "What are you going to do about it?" You say?

"What *can* I do about it?"

Well, for one thing, you can start thinking about your job security as soon as your new employer offers you that job. Because that is when your employment relationship begins. We've looked at some laws that protect you while you look for a job. Well, there are some laws that protect you from being fired for no reason, too.

Let's take a look at the working relationship between you and your new boss. If you are under contract, which few of us this side of Michael Jordan and Arnold Schwarzenegger are, then your relationship is pretty much spelled out in that contract: You perform your end of the bargain (i.e., score fifty points a game or star in a box office smash) and your employer performs his (i.e., pays you $10 million a year). For the rest of us, however, it's not quite as simple. We are what is called "at-will" employees.

EMPLOYMENT AT WILL

The vast majority of us, those who aren't under written contract with our employer, are termed "at-will" employees in the legal vernacular. (Technically, union members are at-will employees, too. However, most collective bargaining agreements specify that union members can be fired only for "just cause"—i.e., a good reason—giving them a form of contractual protection that nonunion employees do not enjoy.) "At will" means, essentially, that we are employed for an indefinite period *at the will* of our employers . . . and ourselves. Either party is free to terminate the relationship for any reason—good, bad, or indifferent . . . or for no reason at all.

Whose "will" are we talking about? Of course, employers have traditionally been in a much better position to take advantage of the employment-at-will doctrine than we employees. And take advantage of it they did. So much so that the noncontractual employment relationship seemed to be more "at whim" than "at will." So, state and federal legislators, at the urging of their constituents (us employees again), began taking an ever dimmer view of some common employer practices, practices that seemed to be . . . well, a bit unfair.

Unfair then evolved, through legislation, into illegal. Which gave rise to the concept of "wrongful discharge."

"Wrongful Discharge": When At-Will Employment Is Not At-Will Anymore

The concept of "wrongful discharge" evolved from the obvious need to protect workers from unjust acts by their employers, like firing someone in violation of the law or of "public policy," or in breach of an "implied contract," or just firing someone unfairly or in "bad faith." Thus, an employer who discharges an at-will employee under certain circumstances may very well find himself in court defending against that most feared of actions, a wrongful discharge suit. (It has been estimated that it costs the average employer approximately $80,000 to defend a wrongful discharge suit—*even if the employer wins!*)

An employer may quite well be susceptible to a wrongful discharge suit for firing you under any of the following conditions:

☛ In violation of the law.
☛ In violation of "public policy."
☛ Your actions were safeguarded by "whistleblower" protections.
☛ Your employment relationship was covered by an "implied contract." Or,
☛ Your employer had a tacit duty, because of the history of your relationship, to deal with you fairly and in good faith.

Now let's take a closer look at these situations in which at-will employment can be transformed into something else entirely, something whose duration and conditions are no longer subject to the absolute whim and capriciousness of your employer.

Violations of the Law

Even though you are an at-will employee, your employer may not discharge you in violation of the law. For example, **Title VII of the Civil Rights Act of 1964** prohibits discrimination or discharge on the basis of race, sex, religion, handicap, age, marital status, color, ancestry and national origin. (See Chapter 5: Discrimination and Related Issues.) The **National Labor Relations Act** ensures your right to unionize, protecting you and your coworkers against arbitrary discipline and dismissal should you seek to organize. (See Epilogue: Unions and Other Final Thoughts.) The **Fair Labor Standards Act** not only guarantees your right to certain wage and hour considerations but also your right to assert them without fear of retaliation in the form of disciplinary measures or outright discharge. (See Chapter 3: Wages and Hours.) The **Occupational Safety and Health Act** outlines certain requirements of a safe workplace. (See Chapter 7: Health and Safety.) You may not be disciplined or fired for complaining that your employer is not living up to those obligations.

Violations of "Public Policy" and "Whistleblowing"

An employer may not discharge you in violation of a "public policy," something that is in the public's interest. The general rule was articulated in *Shaffer v. Frontrunner, Inc.,** when the court said, simply, that "there is an exception to the at-will employment doctrine . . . for wrongful discharge in violation of public policy."

Specifically, it is in the public's interest that you serve on a jury when called. So you cannot be fired for obeying a court summons to do so. In *Hodges v. S.C. Toof & Co.,*† a company was forced to pay a former employee $575,000 in damages for demoting and subsequently firing him for a thirteen-week absence for jury duty.

It is also in the public's interest that you obey the law, so you cannot be fired for refusing to break the law if your employer asks you to or for refusing to perjure yourself on your employer's behalf. In *Stoeckert v. Primary Plus Inc.,* for example, a nursery school teacher was awarded half a million dollars in damages when she was suspended, transferred and eventually forced to quit because she reported suspected child abuse, which the law required her to do (even though no one was ever officially charged with child abuse in the case).‡

Neither can you be fired in retaliation for reporting safety violations in your workplace or turning in your employer for breaking the law. In *Haynes v. Zoological Society,*§ an animal keeper was enti-

---

*Ohio Court of Appeals, No. 4-88-22, 1990.
†Tenn. Supreme Court, No. 23347-9-TD, 1990.
‡California Superior Court, Santa Clara Cty., No. 724319, 1995.
§Ohio Court of Common Pleas, No. A9005160, 1990.

tled to damages, including damages for emotional distress, when the zoo demoted her in retaliation for reporting unsafe conditions to federal officials investigating a bear attack.

These are called "whistleblower" protections (because you are "blowing the whistle" on your employer). Other whistleblower laws protect you from discipline or discharge for filing a workers' compensation claim or asserting any of your other legally conferred employment rights.

Making a Case: There are three basic steps in presenting a retaliatory discharge case to a court:

☞ You, the employee, must raise a *prima facie* case. (*Prima facie* means, literally, on its face.) That is, you must present evidence that indicates initially that you have the basis of a claim. For example, you filed a workers' compensation claim and some adverse employment action was taken against you shortly thereafter—like, you were fired. Period. That's all the first step requires.

☞ Your employer then gets a chance to rebut your case by showing that his action—firing you—was based on some legitimate business reason other than your workers' compensation claim or your age or whatever unlawful reason you claim it was based on. Legitimate business reasons can include an economic turndown, your incompetence or misconduct, or any number of other things.

☞ Now the hard part: You must be able to prove that the reason given by your employer was a "pretext" to cover up the *real* reason you were fired. For example, you claim you were fired because of your age. You establish your *prima facie* case by showing you are older than forty (under federal law; some states prohibit age discrimination at lower ages) and that you were fired under circumstances that could create the inference that it was because of your age. Your employer counters by saying, "Hey, I fired him because he did lousy work." The burden now falls on you to show that "lousy work" was a pretext for the real reason. You may have evidence that your employer never did anything but compliment your work. You may be able to show that your employer has consistently fired people when they reach age fifty; or that you were replaced by a younger person. All such evidence goes to the question of "pretext" and is a necessary component of making a successful case of retaliatory discharge in violation of the law or of public policy.

Note on whistleblowing: Most states offer some type of protection for whistleblowers, usually in the form of prohibitions against disciplining, discharging, or threatening to discipline or discharge an employee for "blowing the whistle" on specific employer activities. However, whistleblowing can be an iffy proposition. Some states require that you exhaust all of your administrative remedies before pursuing legal action against your employer. That means "going through channels," like to the Occupational Safety and Health Administration about safety violations your employer refuses to correct or to the Immigration and Naturalization Service about illegal aliens employed by your company.

Then, too, whistleblowers are not always the most popular people around. As a whistleblower you risk being branded as somewhat of a traitor in the eyes of your employer and quite possibly even as a "tattletale" by fellow employees. Furthermore, though blackballing is against the law, your name may "coincidentally" become well known in your industry for having "ratted on" your employer, making it difficult if not impossible to obtain another job without moving somewhere where you aren't known. In addition, as with any action following dismissal (particularly in this case, where you may be forced to "go through channels"), it may also be some time before you get any legal satisfaction—if ever. (As we all know, government "channels" can often turn into black holes.) Here are, therefore, ten practical questions you have to ask yourself before blowing the whistle on your employer:

☞ *Am I right?* Make damn sure of the truth of your charges and that you can prove them.

☞ Does my employer have a record of prior violations of the law (especially violations of the same law)? Or a prior record of retaliating against whistleblowers?

☞ Did I give my employer an adequate opportunity to correct the violation on his own? (That is, did you report the violation to the proper authority within the company and wait a reasonable period of time to see if the company corrected it?)

☞ Was there an obvious relationship between my complaint and my firing? (For example, were you summarily fired upon filing your complaint?)

☞ *Can I prove it?* (For example, were any unusual or unconventional disciplinary steps taken against you as a result of your complaint, or did your employer skip any steps in his normal disciplinary procedure in your case?)

☞ Did I receive a prior warning from my employer implying that I would suffer the consequences if I filed a complaint?

☞ Did my employer otherwise retaliate against me because of my complaint? (Did you suffer unwarranted disciplinary action? Were you demoted or given all the company's "dirty work" to do? Were you denied usual company benefits you had been granted in the past?)

☞ Did my employer promise me a promotion or additional benefits if I agreed *not* to file a complaint?

☞ Has my state set a precedent in the area of whistleblowing? That is, have its courts (ordinarily) found in favor of whistleblowers? If so, how long does the judicial process seem to take? And do the size of verdicts warrant taking the chance? (To answer these questions, you'll need the advice of an attorney.)

☞ And finally, is it worth the risk? Of being ostracized? Of being blackballed? Of possibly forfeiting my career? Of suffering financial setbacks for whatever times it takes? Of possibly never getting the kind of satisfaction that may warrant the kind of risk I am about to take?

Whistleblowers do win; and win big. One recent example: Three former Lockheed employees were awarded $45.3 *million* when they were fired after reporting flaws in the company's C5-B aircraft.* But they also lose; and lose big—sometimes even when they "win." So before you take action and turn your employer in for violating the law, *make sure you are right* and then give your employer a chance to correct the situation without government or legal intervention. Then weigh the above factors to estimate your chances of succeeding with a whistleblower complaint. **Note:** It is not a bad idea to run your complaint by an attorney who is a labor specialist before filing your charges. It might be worth paying for an hour or two of someone's time to be sure of your position. (Formally reporting your employer's violation of a law or Occupational Safety and Health Administration regulation can actually add to your job security, if your

Benecke v. Lockheed Corp., California Supreme Court, C621967, 1990.

charge is valid. Any subsequent negative employment decision affecting you is bound to be rigorously scrutinized to determine if it was retaliatory in nature.)

"Implied Contract": Oral or Written Assurances by Your Employer and Employee Handbooks

Any assurances made to you by your employer, either written or oral, can form the foundation of a so-called implied contract and could restrict your employer's right to fire you for anything short of just cause. Specific statements by a superior such as, "You have a job here as long as you keep doing good work," have been found by many courts to limit your employer's ability to fire you. Certain types of conduct between the parties (you and your employer) or even the nature of the employment relationship itself have been construed as forming implied contracts of employment. In fact, "The court can consider the character of the employment, custom, the course of dealing between the parties, company policy, or any other fact which may illuminate . . . circumstances that may alter 'at-will' employment."*

Factors Considered: Whether or not you are a party to an implied contract with your employer depends on a number of circumstances surrounding your employment. Factors considered by most courts include:

☞ The duration of your employment. (Have you worked for your employer for a long time?)
☞ Promotions. (Have you been promoted regularly?)
☞ Lack of criticism. (Has your employer never criticized your work in the past?)
☞ Assurances of continued employment. (Did your employer assure you—or employees generally—by word or deed that you could count on keeping your job?
☞ Acknowledged employment practices. (Did your employer violate some accepted company policy in your firing?) And,
☞ The circumstances surrounding your recruitment. (Specifically, were you hired away from another job?)

*Kelly v. Georgia-Pacific Corp., 46 Ohio St. 3d 134, 1989.

The more of the above factors that exist in your employment situation, the more favorably a court will tend to look on your claim of an implied contract.*

Employee Handbooks: Likewise, clauses in employee handbooks or manuals have been construed by courts to create contractual obligations on the part of employers where the language has been determined to amount to an offer of job security in some way. Such clauses could contain specific statements as to the length of service of certain types of employees or, more often, could be interpreted as *implying* a specific length of "contract" or that termination can only be "for cause." In *Torosyan v. Boehringer Ingelheim,* for example, a Connecticut court ruled that statements in handbooks that employees will only be discharged for "just cause" created an implied contract, so termination could be for cause only.† While another court held that an implied contract for "just cause only" termination could be negated by prominent disclaimers.‡

Not all companies have employee handbooks, but many do. Employee handbooks generally include things like:

☞ A formal welcome to the company;
☞ A company history and profile;
☞ Statements regarding equal opportunity, smoking, sexual harassment, and other applicable laws;
☞ Company rules and policies such as safety regulations, grooming and dress requirements, overtime rules, pay periods, lunch and rest breaks, probationary periods, vacation leave, sick leave, personal days, paid holidays, leaves of absence, promotion and transfer policies, and training and education programs;
☞ Performance appraisals; and
☞ Disciplinary procedures up to termination.

If your company has an employee handbook, dust it off and give it another read *after* you have read this material.

Gardner v. Charles Schwab & Co., California Court of Appeal, 1st District, Division 2, No. A040723, 1990.
†234 Conn. 1, 1995.
‡*Miller v. Crystal Lake Park,* 10 IER Cases, 487, 7th Cir., 1995.

Employer Strategies

Employers publish handbooks for their employees for a number of reasons. Initially a handbook was simply a convenient way to inform workers of company rules and policies, to let them know what was expected of them and what they could expect in return. But gradually it evolved into a tool by which employers could prove, if necessary, that an employee knew (or should have known) about a work rule that he violated—*because it was published in the handbook.* Then courts decided two could play at that game and began enforcing clauses in handbooks as promises that *employers* should be bound to keep.

Nowadays, in the wake of numerous court decisions holding them to their printed statements, employers have begun to scrutinize their handbooks under a brighter light. In fact, many are having *lawyers* scrutinize them under a legal light. Many, but not all. Just so you'll know, any lawyer worth his or her salt will counsel an employer to:

☛ Open the handbook with a general disclaimer, such as: "This handbook is not intended to be construed as a binding employment contract but only as a general source of information. The company reserves the right to make changes at any time." Some courts have found such a statement sufficient to preempt any claim by an employee that the handbook created any contractual rights.*

☛ Avoid making any statement that, either directly or by implication, indicates a specific length of time for which the company intends to retain any individual or group of individuals in its employ, or which gives any job-security assurances to "at-will" employees. And,

☛ Have each employee acknowledge in writing that he or she received a copy of the handbook and is familiar with its provisions.

So, with lawsuits serving as the proverbial bucket of cold water in the face, many employers have moved to tighten those handbook loopholes. But they haven't all closed entirely.

What to Look For: There are still a lot of employee handbooks out there making a lot of promises and assurances, some overtly,

*Miller v. Crystal Lake Park (see p. 59).

some subtly. And courts are holding employers to their promises. Some of the things *you* should be looking for as you scan that handbook:

☞ Does your company's employee handbook have a disclaimer? *Just because a handbook contains a statement that it does not create an employment contract does not necessarily mean it doesn't.* More and more courts have said, in effect, that a promise is a promise—even if the boss says it isn't. In *Badgett v. Visiting Nurses Association,** for example, a former employee was awarded $10,000 for breach of implied contract even though the company's employee manual specifically stated that it was "no guarantee of employment." The court said the employee could have reasonably expected she had a conditional contract of employment and could be fired only for insubordination, misconduct, or unsatisfactory performance as stipulated in the manual.

☞ Are there any statements to the effect that workers will be retained as long as they perform up to a certain standard? Were you fired even though you lived up to that standard? (See *Badgett v. Visiting Nurses Association*, above.)

☞ Does the handbook say you can be fired only "for cause"? If so, then your employer must live up to that promise.†

☞ Does the handbook refer to all employees, or your classification of employees, as "permanent" (as opposed to "full-time")? Even though some employers see them as the same, courts have interpreted the terms much differently. "Permanent" has been ruled to mean indefinite in duration, while "full-time" means working roughly a forty-hour week, as opposed to "part-time" (generally twenty-five hours a week or less).

☞ Does the handbook promise to give you specific training or assistance during an orientation period? If it does, did you receive that training or assistance? If your job performance is rated as poor (possibly causing you to be disciplined or discharged), is it because you didn't get the promised training or help?

☞ If the handbook sets out progressive disciplinary proce-

---

*Iowa Court of Appeals, No. 0-651/90-443, 1991.
†*Vaske v. DuCharme, McMillen & Assoc.,* U.S. District Court, District of Colorado, No. 90-S-274, 1990.

dures, did the company follow them in your case? For example, your company handbook lists verbal warning, written warning, probation, and suspension without pay as the steps on the way to firing. Did they skip any steps with you? If so, was there a good reason? (I.e.: Were there aggravating circumstances—like your behavior—to make your case unusual?) Even an employee who was caught with a can of beer in his hand and was summarily fired had a wrongful discharge claim where the company's employee handbook called for progressive discipline.*

☞ Does the handbook promise a hearing before any dismissal? Did you get one? In *Breshears v. Moore,*† an employee given an oral notice of his discharge had a claim for breach of express contract where the board of directors' written policy required a written statement of the grounds for discharge and provided for a hearing.

☞ Is there a statement to the effect that "all employees will be treated fairly and equally"? Were you, in fact, "treated fairly and equally"? Did the company treat you *the same way* it treats all "departing" employees? Or the same way it treats all employees eligible for promotion (as the case may be)?

☞ Did you follow company procedures as outlined in the handbook and wind up getting fired anyway? A banker fired for refusing to disclose confidential information regarding bank customers, which would have been a violation of company policy, was awarded $6.2 million in damages for wrongful discharge: $600,000 for past and future lost wages, another $600,000 for emotional distress caused by his firing, and $5 million in punitive damages.‡

☞ Does the employee handbook outline a procedure for a certain task, a procedure that is widely disdained in favor of perhaps an easier or increasingly more acceptable way of handling the matter? Were you, in effect, fired for following the accepted procedure, which the company has tacitly condoned in the past?

☞ Does your company's handbook stipulate a probationary period during which you can be terminated for any reason or

Schumaker v. Frito-Lay, Inc., U.S. District Court, District of North Dakota, Northeastern Division, No. A2-89-29, 1991.
†Oklahoma Court of Appeals, No. 70,812, 1990.
‡*Banaitas v. Mitsubishi Bank Ltd.,* Oregon Circuit Court, No. 89-12-07357, 1991.

no reason at all? (The most popular probationary period seems to be six months.) After which time you have earned the right not to be fired except for cause? Such a distinction between being considered a "tryout" and becoming a "regular" has not escaped our court system. If a company handbook makes the distinction, it must live by it . . . by living up to it. If you have worked long enough to become a "regular," you have earned the right to be treated as the handbook promises you will be treated. In *Madani v. Kendall Ford,* * an employee had a cause of action for breach of implied contract based on a manual that assured "productive" employees of a steady job following a probationary period. The handbook listed specific behavior that the company would not "tolerate," and the discharged employee had done nothing on the list to get himself fired.

Remember, read that handbook. Highlight passages that could be interpreted in your favor. If there is a definitive statement that supports your case of unjust dismissal, terrific. But, even if there is something ambiguous, a court (or government agency) may look favorably on your case, since it was your employer who wrote the ambiguous language in the first place . . . and should be held accountable.

Good Faith and Fair Dealing

You may also find that you are protected by that catch-all gray area called "the covenant of good faith and fair dealing." Under it, your employer may have a lawsuit on his hands if he fires you arbitrarily after years of faithful service. (Of course, you may have an age discrimination case as well, depending on your age and the other circumstances surrounding your situation. See Chapter 5: Discrimination and Related Issues.) It depends largely on the nature of the relationship up to that time. One state court awarded $1.7 million in damages to an employee who was fired after seventeen years with the company, saying that after such a long time, there had evolved an obligation on the employer's part to treat the employee fairly and in good faith.†

---

*Oregon Court of Appeals, No. CA A49072, 1990.
†*Lanouette v. Ciba-Geigy Corp.,* California Court of Appeal, 5th Appellate District, No. F008571, 1990.

Note: Courts have specifically held that you cannot be fired for discussing wages and salaries with coworkers. You also cannot be fired for disobeying a company policy or rule that you didn't know about, except if the policy or rule was well published (in your employee handbook) and you *should have* known about it.

The Statute of Frauds

This statute generally requires *written* evidence to prove and enforce a contract of more than a year's duration. (I.e.: An employer's agreement to employ you for more than a year is unenforceable unless it is in writing.) Under the statute, therefore, an oral "contract" claimed to be for an indefinite period, or for "permanent" employment, would technically be considered to be at-will employment, terminable by either party with or without cause. However, recent court decisions have held that an oral employment contract for an indefinite period of time does not fall under the **Statute of Frauds** if it is *possible* for it to be completed within one year (i.e., even when it appears that the contract would be *likely* to extend for more than a year). "Even if the original oral agreement . . . expressly provided the plaintiff permanent employment terminable only on the condition of his subsequent poor performance or other good cause, such agreement, if for no specific term, *could possibly be completed within one year*" (emphasis added).* Note that it didn't matter that the only way the contract could possibly have been completed within one year was if the plaintiff screwed up and got himself fired. All that mattered was that it *could have been completed within one year.*

Promotions and Transfers

For the most part we have been discussing wrongful discharge. However, it is important to recognize that the limitations placed on employers' treatment of those who would otherwise be considered at-will employees apply not only to discharge but to any adverse employment action. That includes denying someone a promotion or transfer or disciplining an employee in any other manner.

Jenkins v. Family Health Program, 262 Cal. Rptr. 798, 1989.

A Word about Employment Contracts

Of course, if you can manage it, you can remove yourself from the "at-will" category by getting your employer to enter into a written employment contract with you. Unfortunately, few of us have the type of clout necessary for such a luxury. However, if you do, here are some things to consider:

☞ Start with the pesky details such as the names, addresses, etc., of the parties.

☞ Make sure it clearly spells out the duties of each party (in a nutshell, your job description and your employer's obligation to pay you a specified wage).

☞ Stipulate the duration of the contract. It is normally in your interest to secure a contract for as long as possible. Reason: You will likely be able to enforce such a provision, while your employer will find it difficult, if not impossible, to enforce from his end. Let's say, for example, you have a contract for three years. Except perhaps for gross misconduct of some kind, your employer will not legally be able to dismiss you during that period. On the other hand, if you quit after a year, a court will not *make* you go back to work for your employer. (Does the word "slavery" ring a bell?) If you provide a unique personal service (e.g., you are a professional ballplayer or an actress whose services obviously cannot be exactly duplicated), you may not be allowed to work for *someone else.* But, short of that, if you are an engineer or a teacher or a pipe fitter and can be replaced with relatively little hardship by another engineer or teacher or pipe fitter (sorry, that's life), you can go merrily on to the next job. (**Note:** If you are in a good enough bargaining position that you can get a contract at all, why not go for a "revolving" one for added security? A revolving contract lets you renew before it expires, so if there is ever any handwriting on the wall, you'll see it in time to start looking for another job. For example, you get a two-year contract renewable for the full term on each year anniversary. That way, if your employer ever refuses to renew, you always have another year to land on your feet.)

☞ Beware of noncompetition and nondisclosure clauses. Courts will enforce a contract term that prohibits you from entering into direct competition with your employer or keeps you from divulging the company's trade secrets after you leave its employ. To be enforceable, the agreement must be "reasonable to protect the employer's legitimate business interest."* The reasonableness of the agreement is measured by its scope, its time period, and its geographical area.† Reasonableness of scope and geographical area are fairly subjective. As for time period, one to three years is commonly considered to be reasonable.

☞ Your employer will no doubt want to include exceptional situations under which you can be fired in spite of the contract (e.g., repeated failure to obey written directions, gross misconduct, theft, etc.). Make sure they are truly exceptional.

☞ *Have your lawyer review it.* You can bet your employer's lawyer will see it.

"PROBATIONARY STATUS"

Okay, now that you know where you stand, and that it isn't necessarily with one foot on a banana peel and the other out the front door, as you may have suspected, let's investigate that initial period when that may be *exactly* where you stand: probation.

Roll the word around on your tongue a bit. "Probation." I don't know about you, but for me it conjures up images of Al Capone and Bugsy Malone, of drug dealers and drunk drivers. "Report to your probation officer every other Thursday, Mr. Employee." Well, actually, the *Random House Dictionary of the English Language*—my *bible*—defines "probation" as "the testing or trial of a person's conduct, character, qualifications or the like." In short, probation is the period of time, usually anywhere from a month to six months, during which your new employer will get to look you over without having to take the big leap, to take a sip of the milk without buying the cow, so to speak. But more and more courts are scrutinizing the probationary relationship as more and more provisionary employees are asking the question: "If my employer has sipped enough of

Rogers v. Runfola & Assoc., Ohio Supreme Court, No. 89-1355, 1991.
†*Perman v. Arcventures, Inc.,* Illinois Appellate Court, 1st District, 3rd Division, No. 1-88-3238, 1990.

the milk, shouldn't he *have* to buy the cow (and make an 'honest' employee out of me)?"

Probation is not a condition universally imposed on new workers. But it is becoming more and more popular with employers not only as a means to assess a new employee's ability to perform the job and fit into the work environment, but also as a kind of tool to make it easier to fire someone who doesn't work out. By classifying you as "probationary," they are saying outright that you have fewer rights to your job than "regular" workers. You are merely "on trial." (But isn't that the same as saying once you are a "regular" worker you have *more* rights? More on this in a minute.)

Many employers don't even provide you with benefits while you are serving your probationary time. That often means no health insurance, sometimes means no paid sick days, and certainly means no vacation time. Usually, however, once you have successfully completed probation, you are accorded benefits on a retroactive basis, at least those that are able to be granted retroactively. (Try getting health insurance to cover that illness you contracted during your probationary period!) For example, you may be given credit toward paid vacation time while working your six-month probationary period, but only if you successfully complete your provisional time and become a regular employee.

Do You Have More Rights Once You Become a "Regular"?

There are a number of things to think about if you had to earn your way onto your employer's regular staff by serving a period of probation. The first is: Because he gave you *less* security (and fewer rights) during your probationary period, does it necessarily follow that you have *more* security (and more rights) now that you have "shown your stuff" and are a properly initiated employee? Depending, as always, on the facts of your case, some courts say "yes." Some questions to ask:

☞ Did your employer assure you (verbally, in the company handbook, through your supervisor or immediate superior, etc.) that once you completed probation you would become a "permanent" employee? "Permanent" may not be interpreted as forever, but it may be interpreted, as it has in some jurisdictions, as conferring more rights than you would have as strictly an "at-will" employee. That could mean your employer now has the right to fire you only upon a showing of "just cause." (**Note:** Some courts have even determined that the fact you had to serve a probationary period *in and of itself* implies that you cannot later be fired for less than just cause. That is to say, no further implication by your employer, by either word or deed, is necessary to elevate your status to something more than at-will.)

☞ Did your employer tell you that once your probation was up you would be a "full-time" employee? If so, your employer may have obligated himself to employ you for a full forty-hour workweek, and subsequently cutting you back to part-time status may amount to a breach of contract.

☞ Did your employer say that once you completed your probation you would be discharged only if your work was unsatisfactory? In just those circumstances courts have found that to mean you can't be terminated *for any other reason* but poor work, not even if it was a downturn in business that made you expendable!*

In summary, separating a newly hired worker from veteran employees can be of great benefit to your employer. Handing out pink slips has, as we all know, become an increasingly sticky proposition. By establishing that ominous "probationary period," your employer is telling you *up front* that you are, in effect, a second-class citizen until you prove yourself. It gives him far more leeway in letting you go during that probationary period. He still can't abridge your rights. He still can't fire you in violation of the law. But he can fire you for almost any other reason. You are on trial and you are on notice of that fact.

But, as we have seen, the sword, as do most, has a sharp side. If, while on probation, you are a second-class citizen with *no* rights, then from that it can be—and often is—inferred that you have acquired *some* rights by successfully completing that probationary period. And the most basic of rights that can be acquired is the right to be fired only for a decent, defendable reason.

WHAT TO DO: If you are an at-will employee who alleges that your employer breached your employment relationship unfairly or ille-

*Foley v. Interactive Data Corp., 3 IER Cases 1729, 1988.

gally, your course of action will depend on *what* you maintain your employer did. If, for example, he fired you because you are black or female, or because of your religious practices or marital status, or because you are handicapped or in violation of some other clause of the **Civil Rights Act of 1964** (or treated you differently because of some discriminatory reason—i.e., fired you, a female, when he merely reprimanded a male for similar conduct), the EEOC is there to hear your charges. If you maintain that you were fired in retaliation for asserting your rights under some other law (e.g., the **Fair Labor Standards Act**), the agency empowered with the administration and enforcement of that law (i.e., the U.S. or your state department of labor) is the proper place to begin the claim process. (See Chapter 11: I'm Getting Screwed; So What Can I Do about It?)

On the other hand, if you believe that your employer breached a contract of employment with you, either express or implied, you are pretty much on your own to seek redress. In which case, you should investigate hiring an attorney who specializes in contract law. (Again, see Chapter 11.)

The potential payoff can be significant. If you can establish that you were wrongfully discharged, you may be entitled to:

☞ Reinstatement to your former job.
☞ Payment of back wages.
☞ Reestablishment of all employee benefits you would have been entitled to had the wrongful discharge not occurred.
☞ Your attorney's fees and court costs. And,
☞ Possibly even punitive damages, if your employer's action is deemed to have been willful.

Proof

It is why you can't wait until you hit those bumps in the road before you take stock of the security—or lack of it—in your position at work. By then it may be too late. You may start out as an at-will employee, but things your employer does or says can change that. It helps to have evidence that proves your employer did or said what you say he did or said. *That is why from the outset you must keep track of every word or action by which your employer indicates that you can expect job security of some kind.* Maintain a file in which you:

☛ Note in detail (word for word if possible) any oral assurances made by your employer before and after hiring, including times, places, dates, circumstances, and witnesses, if any. (Employers often let down their legal guard while making morale-building speeches. Take notes.)

☞ Save any and all written statements, remarks, letters, comments, margin notes, etc., made by your employer that indicate an intention to offer you job security or which compliment your work.

☞ Keep a copy of all employee handbooks, employee manuals, policy statements, etc., issued by your employer, in which you highlight all references, either express or implied, to job security.

Evidence. Having it can make you. Not having it can break you.

It is almost certain that your employer will have a detailed file in which he has noted every time you screwed up, every warning he has ever given you, every possible link in the chain that could establish that he had every right to fire you. If you have nothing to overcome that, to prove you were wrongfully discharged, you are lost before you begin.

Evidence. It will substantially bolster your case. Facts and documents. They are your best defense against arbitrary employment decisions.

SUMMARY

We have seen that there may be more to the employment relationship than meets the eye. Even if you don't enjoy the protections of an express employment contract, you nonetheless still have the protections of the law and, even where there are no specific statutes, the courts. Thus, you may in theory be an at-will employee, able to be terminated for any reason . . . or no reason at all. But in practice there are limits on an employer's "right" to fire you.

Of course, let's not overlook the fact that sometimes employers do have good reasons to fire people: incompetence, poor quality or quantity of work, insubordination, violation of company rules, excessive tardiness or absence, substance abuse on the job, and even "business necessity" (i.e., an economic downturn). **Note:** Courts have begun to recognize that employers have been known to use "business necessity" as a convenient excuse when they lack a legitimate reason for firing an employee. Thus, courts tend to scrutinize carefully "economic reasons" for termination, especially if the discharged employee is a member of a "protected group" (e.g., minority, female, over forty, etc.) and the employer's economic ax has a history of falling particularly heavily on that group.

So if you look at your individual situation realistically and decide that you were, in fact, fired for a justifiable—and well-documented—reason, then perhaps the best option is to cut your losses and just start looking for a new job that suits your talents and interests better than the one you just left.

On the other hand, if you believe—and can substantiate—that your employer's action was capricious or, worse still, a violation of the law, you don't have to stand still for it. *These days, an employer who fires someone without having a good, well-documented reason for it is treading on extremely treacherous terrain—particularly if that someone knows his or her employment rights.*

3

Wages and Hours

N ow for the good part, the reason most of us are out there breaking our backs for someone else: a steady paycheck. Well, just as in every other facet of the employment condition, there are laws out there that protect you. Gone are the days of the turn-of-the-century sweatshops, of endless hours of work for pitiful wages. (Sometimes it just seems they are still around.) There are now laws that cover *when* you have to be paid, *where* you have to be paid, *how* you have to be paid, *how much* you have to be paid, *how much extra* you have to be paid for working especially long hours, and *how long* you can be made to work, among others.

In addition, nowhere in employment law do the states seem to take as much of an interest as in the area of wage and hour controls, where a majority add their own two cents (sorry) to the equation. So, since it's why we leave the house in the morning, let's take a look at some of the major laws regulating our wages and the hours we have to work to earn them.

FAIR LABOR STANDARDS ACT

(**Note:** As you read this chapter, it is important to bear in mind that the general consensus among labor lawyers is that *the* **Fair Labor Standards Act** *is the employment law most violated by employers.*)

Back in the Depression era, when employers were even more demanding and less generous than they are today, the federal government thought it would be a good idea to make them be a bit less demanding and a bit more generous (which is, of course, the only reason they are). Which led to the enactment in 1938 of the **Fair Labor Standards Act** (FLSA). The FLSA, which has undergone numerous amendments over the decades, controls minimum wages, overtime, equal pay, and the employment of minors.

Application of the Law to Individual Employers

There is a complex set of rules that specifies which employers are covered by the provisions of the FLSA and which are not. Those rules have to do basically with whether or not an employer is "engaged in interstate commerce" and whether or not the employer's company does a certain minimum dollar amount of business per year, either as an individual entity or as a total "enterprise" if, for example, the employer operates more than one establishment. There are long, involved definitions of what it means to be "engaged in interstate commerce" or to "produce goods for sale in interstate commerce"; and there are a million ways to figure an employer's dollar amount of business and whether or not any given establishment is to be included in the employer's overall business "enterprise" for purposes of coverage under the act. However, the bottom line, as they say, is that virtually every employer is covered under one or another of the law's coverage tests. In fact, the law is so all-encompassing it *presumes* every employer is covered. Chances are yours is, too.

Application of the Law to Individual Employees

In the case of you and your job, the waters tend to get a little muddier. (You didn't think this was going to be easy, did you? You did? Okay, I'll try to make it as simple as I can.)

Some types of jobs, mostly so-called white-collar jobs, are exempt from both minimum wage and overtime provisions of the FLSA. Other jobs are exempt specifically from either minimum wage or overtime requirements. (The latter will be discussed in the sections on minimum wage and overtime.)

"White-collar" employees who are exempt from both the minimum wage and the overtime provisions of the FLSA include:

☞ Executive, administrative, and professional employees;
☞ Outside salespeople; and
☞ Computer professionals.

Executive, Administrative, and Professional Employees: There are two tests of whether or not you can be considered either an executive, administrative, or professional employee (and, thus, be treated as exempt from minimum wage and overtime laws by your employer). There are so-called long and short tests for each classification. The more involved "long" tests are used to determine if low-paid (between $155 and $250 per week) white-collar employees qualify for exempt status, while the simpler "short" tests are used for higher-paid (at least $250 per week) white-collar employees. (**Note:** Once you qualify as a "white-collar" worker under either the "long" or "short" test, a third test, the "salary basis" test, is used to determine whether you *remain* qualified.)

1. LONG TEST:
   a. Under the "long" test, you are an *executive* if you:
☞ Spend at least 80 percent of your time (60 percent in retail and service industries) managing a department or subdivision and/or directing the work of two or more subordinates;
☞ Have the authority either to hire and fire or to give recommendations regarding hiring, firing, and promotion of employees;
☞ Routinely rely on your own discretion; *and*
☞ Are paid at least $155 a week, not counting any room and board or other facilities, if any, that are provided by your employer.

   b. Under the "long" test, you are an *administrative* employee if you:
☞ Spend at least 80 percent of your time (60 percent in retail and service industries) doing office work; or are on the administration of an educational institution; or perform tasks requiring special training or experience with only general supervision or exercise general supervision over others; or regularly help your employer or an executive or another administrative employee;

☞ Routinely rely on your own discretion; *and*

☞ Are paid at least $155 a week, not counting room and board and other facilities, if any, provided by your employer.

c. Under the "long" test, you are a *professional* employee if you:

☞ Spend at least 80 percent of your time doing work that requires an advanced degree or recognized artistic talent, are a certified teacher in an educational institution, and/or do work that is primarily intellectual;

☞ Routinely rely on your own discretion; *and*

☞ Are paid at least $170 a week.

2. SHORT TEST: Under the short test, executive, administrative, and professional employees are considered "highly paid" employees. You are a highly paid employee (and thus can be exempted by your employer from wage and hour laws) if you are paid *at least $250 a week* and you spend at least 50 percent of your time performing the duties of an executive, administrative, or professional employee described in the "long" tests for each.

Note: You could also be exempt from wage and hour laws if you meet any of the above "long" or "short" test requirements under a combination of the above classifications. For example, you perform both executive and administrative tasks which combined add up to at least 80 percent of your work time and you are paid at least $155 a week.

3. "SALARY BASIS" TEST: If you qualify as a "white-collar" employee under one of the above tests, your employer may treat you as exempt from minimum wage and overtime laws. (Since you are undoubtedly being paid more than minimum wage anyway, the main thing for your employer is that he doesn't have to pay you overtime.) However, as an exempt employee you must be paid a predetermined weekly salary that is not subject to reduction. Under the "salary basis" test, if your employer makes deductions from your weekly salary (other than those required by law), he will lose an otherwise valid exemption, which means he will have to pay you for all that overtime you've been working (*if* you file a complaint with the Labor Department).

Outside Salespeople: In order to qualify as an outside salesperson (and be exempted by your employer from wage and hour laws), you must fit the following profile:

☛ You customarily and regularly work *away from your employer's place of business* while making sales, obtaining orders or contracts for services or for the use of facilities that will be paid for by the client or customer; *and*

☛ You don't spend more than 20 percent of the number of hours worked by your employer's nonexempt employees doing any other kind of work.

A good test to determine if you are exempt from wage and hour laws as an outside salesperson is to ask yourself:

☞ Do I receive significant compensation on a commission basis?

☞ Have I received special sales training?

☞ Do I have little or no (i.e., minimal) direct or constant supervision in doing my daily work?

☞ Do I have a contractual job title that mentions sales?

The more yes answers to the above questions, the more likely you are exempt from wage and hour laws as an outside salesperson.

Computer Professionals: To qualify as a computer professional who is exempt from wage and hour laws, you must be paid at least six and a half times the current minimum wage (or about $57,000 a year, based on the current federal minimum wage) and your primary work responsibility has to be one or more of the following (I admit I have no idea what the following descriptions mean, but presumably if you are one, you do):

☞ Applying systems analysis techniques and procedures, including consulting with users, to determine hardware and software functional specifications;

☞ Designing computer systems based on and related to user specifications;

☞ Creating or modifying computer programs based on and related to system design specifications; or

☞ Creating or modifying computer programs related to machine operating systems.

Nonemployees: Besides "white-collar" workers, others who can be treated as exempt from wage and hour laws are people who are not technically considered "employees" under the law. Basically, this nonemployee category includes apprentices, trainees, and independent contractors.

1. APPRENTICES: You are an apprentice if you are over sixteen and are employed to learn a skilled trade under the terms of a *written* apprenticeship agreement with your "employer." Most states have specific rules limiting the number of hours you may be employed as an apprentice and specifying the percentage of the minimum wage you must be paid for that work. (For example, apprentices are allowed to be paid 85 percent of the minimum wage for up to two thousand hours—after which they must be paid at least minimum wage.) Check the Blue Pages of your telephone book for "Apprentice Training," which will generally be a separate listing under your state's department of labor.

2. TRAINEES: To be considered a trainee, you must be under twenty and your training must be similar to the training you would get at a vocational school. In addition, you cannot displace a regular employee and you cannot be guaranteed a job when your training period is completed. The training must be for your benefit, not the employer's. In addition, you must be aware that your "employer" does not have to pay you according to wage and hour laws during training. Finally, your training period has to be limited to 180 days and you must be paid at least 85 percent of the minimum wage.

3. INDEPENDENT CONTRACTORS: Someone who is sufficiently free from his or her "employer's" control is considered an independent contractor and is exempt from wage and hour laws. According to the Internal Revenue Service definition, an independent contractor is someone who follows a trade, business, or profession independent from that of the person employing him. Thus, if the "employer" has the right to control or direct only "the result of the work and not the means and method of accomplishing it," then the worker is likely an independent contractor. (**Note:** A person is generally considered an employee if the employer controls both *what* must be done and *how* it must be done.) For details, see Chapter 9: Workers' Compensation.

Loss of Exempt Status ("Docking" Employees' Pay): Court cases have determined that legitimate exempt status is lost (i.e., the employer must pay overtime) only if there is an actual practice of making deductions from an employee's salary or a company policy that creates a significant likelihood that such deductions will be made.*

Employer Strategies (Why They'd Want You to Be an Independent Contractor When You're Not)

There are a number of reasons an employer may want to classify you as an independent contractor when you really aren't one. If an employer can classify you as an independent contractor rather than an employee, he can avoid:

☞ Withholding income taxes and Social Security taxes from your paycheck and matching your Social Security contribution;

☞ Paying unemployment insurance taxes to cover you and being responsible for your unemployment benefits when you are discharged;

☞ Having workers' compensation insurance to cover you; and

☞ Providing you with medical insurance and other employment benefits he provides for "employees."

Independent contractors are also not protected by **Title VII of the Civil Rights Act of 1964**, which prohibits discrimination in hiring, firing, compensation, terms, conditions, or privileges of employment on the basis of race, color, religion, sex, or national origin. (See Chapter 5: Discrimination and Related Issues.)

Liability for Misclassification: A company that misclassifies an employee as an independent contractor can be held liable for back wages and overtime. It can also be charged for back taxes with penalties and can risk losing some of the tax benefits of certain qualified profit-sharing pension plans, group term life insurance plans, and other employee benefits plans.

Miscellaneous Exempt Employees: Finally, there are a few other types of people who, although employed, may be exempt from wage and hour laws for various reasons. They include handicapped workers, volunteers, and most agricultural workers.

*Auer v. Robbins, 117 S. Ct. 905, 3 WH Cases 2nd 1249, 1997.

MINIMUM WAGE

Most of us are by now being paid considerably more than the minimum wage. However, if you are a minor or an unskilled laborer, minimum wage may still be an issue. In addition, many restaurant employees are paid the minimum wage and rely on tips for a living wage. Therefore, in the interest of being comprehensive, this book will undertake a brief discussion of minimum wage considerations.

The current federal minimum wage is $6.15 per hour (as of March 9, 2000). However, many states have set a higher minimum wage. In that case, employers who are subject to wage and hour laws must pay the higher of the state and federal minimum wages. (Contact your state department of labor for minimum wage requirements in your state.)

Subminimum Wage

In most states a specified rate that is less than the minimum wage may be paid to apprentices, learners, and handicapped workers with the permission of the state commissioner of labor.

Employees Not Covered

Generally, besides "white-collar" workers, employees who do not have to be paid minimum wage include volunteers in charitable or nonprofit institutions, cleaning people in private homes, people who work on commission, baby-sitters, newspaper delivery people, and members of the employer's immediate family.

Tip Credits

The federal law allows employers to credit up to 50 percent of the tips you receive toward the payment of the minimum wage. (That is, they can credit up to $3.07 an hour toward their minimum wage obligation and actually pay you only $3.08 per hour instead of the full $6.15 an hour.) In order for your employer to legally do that, however:

☞ Yours must be the type of job where you would customarily expect to receive tips (e.g., waiter, waitress, bartender, dock attendant, cabbie, etc.); and
☞ You must be allowed to keep all of your tips.

Note: Some states allow less in tip credits than the federal law does. Contact the wage and hour division of your state department of labor for details.

Facility Credits

The federal law also allows your employer to credit the "reasonable cost" of housing, meals, transportation to work and other facilities he provides toward payment of the minimum wage. To credit the cost of facilities toward payment of the minimum wage, the facilities must be furnished for your benefit (not your employer's) and you must have accepted them voluntarily. "Reasonable cost" refers to the actual cost to your employer, not the retail cost. Some states allow less in facility credits than federal law does. Contact the wage and hour division of your state department of labor for details. **Note:** Items that cannot be credited toward payment of the minimum wage as "facilities" (because they are provided mainly for your employer's benefit) include tools and materials used on the job and uniforms that are required to be worn.

Employer Strategies

Your employer must figure your minimum wage on the basis of the way you are paid. One of the most common ways to pay less than the minimum wage, while appearing to comply with the law, is to average your wages. Things to be aware of if you are paid:

☞ *Hourly:* You have to be paid minimum wage for *all hours worked.* Your employer cannot pay you less for some hours and more for others during the workweek, even though the rate may average out to the minimum wage or more;

☞ *Fixed rate:* The amount of your fixed wage divided by the number of hours you work over the period has to average out to at least the minimum hourly wage;

☞ *Piece rate, incentive rate, or commission:* Your total pay divided by the number of hours you worked in the period has to average out to at least the minimum hourly rate.

"Docking" Pay, Breakage, Shortages, etc.: Your employer cannot "dock" your pay for being late if it would cause your pay for the hours you actually worked to fall below the minimum wage. The same is true of deductions for breakage, cash shortages, or lost items. (In fact, your employer cannot "dock" you at all for time you actually worked. The FLSA expressly states that you must be paid for all time actually worked. So if your employer wants to "dock" you for being late, he must not allow you to work during that time. He cannot have you work and simply not pay you as a form of punishment. For example, you arrive at 8:08 A.M. for an 8:00 shift. Your employer can tell you to go away and come back at 8:30, so you lose half an hour's pay. He cannot put you to work at 8:08 and just not pay you for the time you worked between 8:08 and 8:30.)

Reimbursement (Mileage, Equipment, Uniforms): Employers are not *required* to reimburse you for mileage for business use of your personal car (though most do), unless making you pay your own mileage would bring you below the minimum wage. The same is true of providing your own equipment and uniforms and laundering your own uniforms.

OVERTIME

The FLSA requires employees to be paid time and a half (one and one-half times their regular rate of pay) for every hour they work over forty in a week. (**Note:** Some state laws require employers to pay overtime for more than eight hours worked in a day, which would of course lead to higher pay for employees working overtime. See **Table 2** for the law in your state.)

Exempt Employees

Some employees don't have to be paid overtime under the FLSA. Mostly that depends on whether or not they are "white-collar" workers, as described earlier in this chapter. However, a few other job classifications are specifically exempted from the payment of overtime. They are agricultural workers, car salespeople, cabbies, people who work on commission, merchant mariners, drivers who work for employers who are subject to the Interstate Commerce Commission, anyone whose employer is subject to the Railway Labor Act, and radio and television announcers, editors, and engineers.

TABLE 2

STATE OVERTIME LAWS*

Alabama 8-hour day or 40-hour week for police

Alaska 8-hour day or 40-hour week; 10-hour day or 40-hour week for workers on flex-time by agreement and approval of labor department

Arizona 40-hour week for police, security, and municipal corrections officers

Arkansas 40-hour week

California 8-hour day, 40-hour or 6-day week (generally); 8-hour day, 40-hour week or 4-day, 40-hour week for state employees; many alternate rules for specific employment

Colorado 12-hour day or 40-hour week; 8-hour day or 40-hour week for minors

Connecticut 40-hour week; 48-hour week for hotels, motels, restaurants, and bowling alleys

District of Columbia 40-hour week; 160 hours in 4 weeks for car wash employees

Florida 10-hour day for manual labor, unless written contract otherwise

Hawaii 40-hour week; 48-hour week for 20 weeks a year for most agriculture

Idaho 40-hour week

Illinois 40-hour week

Kansas 46-hour week; 258 hours in 28 days for police, fire, security, and corrections not under FLSA

Kentucky 40-hour week

Maine 40-hour week

Maryland 40-hour week; 48-hour week for hotels, motels, restaurants, bowling alleys, gas stations, and health care facilities (except hospitals); 60-hour week for agriculture not under FLSA

Massachusetts 40-hour week

Michigan 40-hour week; 216 hours in 28 days for fire, police, security, and corrections

Minnesota 48-hour week

Missouri 40-hour week; 52-hour week for recreation areas

Montana 8-hour day or 40-hour week; 48-hour week for students in recreation areas paying room and board

Nevada 8-hour day or 40-hour week; 10-hour day, 40-hour week by agreement

New Hampshire 8-hour day or 40-hour week

New Jersey 40-hour week; 10-hour day, 48-hour week for 10 weeks and 10-hour day, 50-hour week for 10 additional weeks for some agricultural labor

---

*Employers covered by both the federal **Fair Labor Standards Act** and state overtime laws must pay overtime based on the law that would result in the higher wage.

TABLE 2 *(Continued)*

New Mexico 48-hour week; 54-hour week by agreement; 10-hour day, 70-hour or 7-day week for hotels and restaurants

New York 40-hour week; 40-hour or 6-day week for resorts

North Carolina 40-hour week; 45-hours for seasonal recreation

North Dakota 40-hour week; 8-hour day for government employees

Ohio 40-hour week

Oregon 10-hour day or 40-hour week

Pennsylvania 40-hour week

Rhode Island 40-hour week

South Dakota 204 hours in 27 days or 212 hours in 28 days for fire departments

Vermont 40-hour week; 8-hour day or 80 hours in 14 days for hotels, motels, restaurants, and health care facilities with approval of labor commissioner

Washington 40-hour week; 240 hours in 28 days for fire, police, and corrections

West Virginia 40-hour week

Wisconsin 40-hour week; 46-hour week for restaurants

Delaware, Georgia, Indiana, Iowa, Louisiana, Mississippi, Nebraska, Oklahoma, South Carolina, Tennessee, Texas, Utah, Virginia, and Wyoming have no state overtime rules. Employers covered by the FLSA must pay overtime for work in excess of 40 hours in a week.

~~~~~~

Regular Rate of Pay

Note that overtime has to be based on your regular rate of pay. Generally, your "regular rate" includes all payments you get for working except:

☞ Gifts (including for Christmas, your birthday, or other special occasions) that aren't related to hours, productivity, or efficiency;

☞ Vacation pay, holiday pay, pay for sick days, or any other pay you get for nonwork time;

☞ Reimbursement of travel expenses;

☞ Discretionary bonuses (i.e., bonuses that your employer didn't *have* to give you under the terms of a contract);

☞ Payments your employer makes on your behalf to a bona fide profit-sharing or savings plan;

☞ Contributions your employer makes to your retirement plan or life, accident, or health insurance plan; and,

☞ Premium pay you receive for working extra hours during a

day or week, for working on weekends or holidays, or for working outside hours set by an employment contract or collective bargaining agreement. (**Note:** Premium pay can actually be credited toward any overtime you work during the same week you earn the premium pay.)

"Hours Worked"

In order to figure your rate of pay for overtime purposes, you have to know what, legally, is working time an employer must pay you for, and what is not. Generally, working time includes all time you are required to be at the workplace and all the time you are either *required to or allowed to work* or be on duty.

Meal Breaks. Meal breaks of thirty minutes or more, where you are relieved of duty, do not have to be counted as hours worked (i.e., you don't have to be paid for the time). However, you do have to be paid for the time during which you eat if your employer either makes you or lets you keep working or remaining on duty during that time. (**Note:** There is no federal law that requires employers to give their employees meal and/or rest breaks during the workday, though of course most employers do. However, a number of state laws require your employer to give you a specified meal or rest break at a certain point during the day. See **Table 3.**)

"Coffee Breaks." You have to be paid for break periods that are less than 20 minutes.

Waiting Time. Your employer has to pay you for any time you have to be on the premises even though he doesn't provide you with any work.

On-call Time. Your employer has to pay you for all time you are required to be on call *at a place designated by your employer,* even though you are not actually working. (For example, your employer tells you to stay at home and wait for his call to report in.) On the other hand, if you are required only to keep your employer informed of where you are, you have to be paid for only the time between when he calls you to give you your assignment and when you finish the assignment. (For example, you have to call in to tell your supervisor where you will be; or you are given a beeper and have to respond when your employer calls.)

TABLE 3

STATE MEAL AND REST BREAK REQUIREMENTS*

California 30-minute mealtime within 5 hours if over 6-hour day; 10-minute rest per 4 hours; special rules for preparers of farm products, certain motion picture employees, and wood manufacturing

Colorado 30-minute mealtime within 5 hours if over 6-hour day; 10-minute rest per 4 hours

Connecticut 30-minute mealtime in 7½-hour day, between hour 2 and hour 5½, unless employer gives 30-minute paid mealtime

Delaware 30-minute mealtime in 7½-hour day between the first 2 hours and the last 2 hours

Hawaii 45-minute mealtime for government employees

Illinois 20-minute mealtime within first 5 hours of 7½-hour or longer day

Kentucky reasonable mealtime 3 to 5 hours into shift; 10-minute rest per 4 hours (except employers subject to federal Railway Labor Act)

Maine 30-minute rest time within 6 hours (except where under 3 employees on duty and workers get frequent breaks)

Massachusetts 30-minute mealtime within 6 hours

Minnesota 30-minute mealtime within 8 hours; reasonable time each 4 hours to use the restroom

Nebraska 30-minute mealtime and able to leave workplace between noon and 1 P.M. for assembly and mechanical plants and workshops (except if operate 24 hours a day)

Nevada 30-minute mealtime within 8 hours; 10-minute rest per 4 hours

New Hampshire 30-minute mealtime within 5 hours, unless allowed to eat on the job (and is counted as paid time)

New Mexico 30-minute meal or rest during workday

New York 45-minute noontime (11 A.M.–2 P.M.) meal for mercantile and similar employers and 60-minute mealtime for factories; additional 20 minutes for evening shifts and 45 (mercantile) to 60 (factories) minutes for morning shift

North Dakota 30-minute mealtime 3 to 5 hours into shift

Oregon 30-minute mealtime within 5 hours for shift of at least 6 hours; 10-minute paid rest per 4 hours; by agreement for employees working 24 or more consecutive hours

Pennsylvania 30-minute mealtime within 5 hours for seasonal farm workers

Rhode Island 20-minute mealtime within 6 hours, except 6½-hour shift ending by 1 P.M. and 7½-hour shift ending by 2 P.M. and worker can eat on the job

---

*Generally, alternate meal and rest periods can be agreed upon through collective bargaining agreements, agreements between employers and employees, and by permission of the state labor department, and can be expected during emergencies.

TABLE 3 *(Continued)*

Tennessee 30-minute mealtime, between hour 2 and hour 6

Washington 30-minute mealtime 2 to 5 hours into shift; additional 30-minute mealtime during overtime of 3 or more hours after regular workday; 10-minute rest per 4 hours

West Virginia 20-minute mealtime in shift of 6 or more hours; must be counted as hours worked; reasonable sleep and mealtime by agreement for employees on duty 24 hours or more in a row (considered work time without agreement)

Wisconsin 30-minute mealtime within 6 hours recommended (required for minors under 18)

Alabama, Alaska, Arizona, Arkansas, District of Columbia, Florida, Georgia, Idaho, Indiana, Iowa, Kansas, Louisiana, Maryland, Michigan, Mississippi, Missouri, Montana, New Jersey, North Carolina, Ohio, Oklahoma, South Carolina, South Dakota, Texas, Utah, Vermont, Virginia, and Wyoming do not have laws that require employers to give employees meal or rest breaks.

~~~~~~

Travel Time. Your employer has to pay you your regular rate for any required travel. For example, if you are told to drive or take a train or fly to a conference in another city or state, the time it takes you to get there is considered work time and you have to be paid for those hours (i.e., not just the time you are at the place and actually on the job). Of course, your employer doesn't have to pay you for the time it takes you for your regular commute to work. However, if you have to report to someplace other than your usual work site on a given day, he has to pay you your regular rate for the extra time, if any, the commute takes you.

Special Overtime Rules for Hospitals

Hospitals and other health care institutions are allowed to use a fourteen-day work period to figure overtime. (I.e., they don't have to pay overtime unless an employee works more than eighty hours during the fourteen-day period.)

Special Overtime Rules for Fire Fighters and Police

Fire fighters and police can be put on a "tour of duty" of up to twenty-eight days during which they don't have to be paid overtime until they work more than 212 hours.

Compensatory ("Comp.") Time

Private employers generally are not allowed to give compensatory time off, so-called comp. time, instead of paying overtime. State and local government employers, however, can give comp. time within certain limits: Comp. time must be given at one and a half times the overtime hours worked. For example, if you, a state employee, work 10 hours overtime, you have to be given 15 hours of comp. time. However, after 160 hours of overtime (240 hours of comp. time), you must be paid any additional overtime in cash. For emergency and safety personnel the limit is 320 hours of overtime (480 hours of comp. time).

Employer Strategies

An employer may try to get you to waive overtime or accept comp. time instead of money. Neither is legal (except you can be given comp. time instead of overtime if you are a public employee, as noted above). Unless you are exempt from overtime, you must be paid time and a half for overtime hours. You cannot agree to waive payment of overtime, and any agreement to do so is invalid. **Note:** *You can sue your employer for back overtime payments even if you signed an agreement to waive it.*

Records and Notices

Employers are required to keep accurate records of all hours worked and wages paid. Therefore, courts don't place the burden on you to prove the number of hours you worked, but on your employer to disprove your contention by producing the required records.

Your employer is also required to display prominently a U.S. Department of Labor poster that outlines your rights under the FLSA and tells you how to recover any wages you feel are owed to you but haven't been paid.

LIMITS ON HOURS OF WORK

Many states set limits on the number of consecutive hours and/or days you can be required to or allowed to work in certain occupations. The occupations are many and varied, but in general they are hazardous or safety-related. For example, most states set some restrictions on the number of hours in a row truck and bus drivers, miners and railroad workers may work before having a certain number of hours in a row off to rest. For limits on hours in other occupations in your state, if any, check with the wage and hour division of your state department of labor.

JURY DUTY, WITNESS DUTY, AND VOTING TIME

Jury Duty

Under the federal **Jury System Improvement Act of 1978,** an employer can't fire you for serving on a federal jury. State laws also prohibit employers from disciplining, discharging, or threatening action against you for responding to a summons to serve on a jury in state court. Under most circumstances an employee can't be forced to use vacation days for jury time, either. As far as getting paid for the time you are on jury duty, federal law bars employers from making any deductions from the salary of an exempt employee for being absent for less than a week, which would include time served on a jury. So, if you are a salaried employee, your employer would have to pay you for the first week you serve on jury duty. (Employers can offset any fee you get paid for jury duty against your wages, though.) Several state laws do require employers to pay you at your regular rate while you are on jury duty. See **Table 4.**

Witness Duty

Similarly, you can't be disciplined or discharged for being summoned to court as a witness. However, you do not have to be paid for the time (except if you are an exempt salaried employee, in which case you would have to be paid for the first week, as with jury duty).

TABLE **4**

STATE JURY DUTY LAWS*

Alabama Regular wages, offset by the amount the juror is paid for duty over and above actual expenses, while serving on a jury

Colorado Regular wages up to $50 per day for first 3 days of service (includes part-time and temporary workers), except in cases of demonstrated hardship, by application to court

Connecticut Regular wages for first 5 days of service (only employees, including temporary workers, who work at least 30 hours a week)

Massachusetts Regular wages for first 3 days of service, except in cases of demonstrated hardship, by application to court (state will then pay up to $50 a day for first 3 days)

Nebraska Regular wages, offset by the amount the juror is paid for duty over and above actual expenses, while serving on a jury

New Jersey Regular wages, offset by the amount the juror is paid for duty, while serving on a jury (state, municipal, and mass transit workers only)

New York $15 a day for first 3 days (employers of more than 10 employees)

Tennessee Regular wages, offset by the amount the juror is paid for duty, while serving on a jury

*Wages required to be paid to nonexempt (i.e.: hourly, piece work, etc.) employees while serving on jury duty. (Under the FLSA, exempt employees must be paid for up to a week of jury duty.) **Note (excuse from service):** Federal law specifies that loss of earnings is not a valid excuse for not serving on a jury. However, a court will usually entertain a single request by the person summoned, made to the clerk of the applicable court, for a postponement of the date of service. Certain limited job classifications, such as schoolteachers, can often be dismissed from jury duty on application of the employer. Finally, some courts will postpone jury duty if an employer applies to the court and is able to demonstrate a serious hardship on business operations will result if the employee is required to serve on the appointed date.

〜〜〜〜〜〜〜〜〜〜〜〜〜〜〜〜〜〜〜〜〜〜

Voting Time

There is no federal law that says your employer has to give you time off to vote. But several states do make employers give you time off to vote if you don't have enough time outside working hours to make it to the polls. See **Table 5.**

CHILD LABOR LAWS

In order to protect minors, the federal FLSA—as well as most state laws—limits the type of jobs and the number of hours minors may work.

TABLE 5

STATE LAWS ON TIME OFF TO VOTE*

Alaska 2 hours unless employee has 2 consecutive nonwork hours to vote; no deduction from wages

Arizona 3 hours unless employee has 3 consecutive nonwork hours to vote; no deduction from wages

Arkansas No time off required but employees' schedules must allow time for voting

California No time off required unless employee does not have time before or after work to vote; no deduction from wages up to 2 hours

Colorado 2 hours unless employee has 3 consecutive nonwork hours to vote; no deduction from wages

Georgia 2 hours unless employee has 2 consecutive nonwork hours to vote; pay not required

Hawaii 2 hours unless employee has 2 consecutive nonwork hours to vote; no deduction from wages

Illinois 2 hours; pay not required

Iowa 3 hours in general elections; no deduction from wages

Kansas 2 hours; no deduction from wages

Kentucky 4 hours; pay not required

Maryland 2 hours unless employee has 2 consecutive nonwork hours to vote; no deduction from wages

Massachusetts First 2 hours polls are open for manufacturing, mercantile, and mechanical employees; pay not required

Minnesota Unspecified length of time in the morning; no deduction from wages

Missouri 3 hours unless employee has 3 consecutive nonwork hours to vote; no deduction from wages

Nebraska 2 hours; no deduction from wages

Nevada 3 hours unless employee has enough time during nonwork hours to vote; no deduction from wages

New Mexico 2 hours unless employee has 2 hours before or 3 after work to vote; no deduction from wages

New York 2 hours unless employee has 4 nonwork hours to vote; no deduction from wages up to 2 hours

Ohio Reasonable time to vote; no deduction from wages for exempt employees

Oklahoma 2 hours; no deduction from wages

*Most state laws apply to general and primary elections. Employees normally must apply in advance for time off to vote and the employer may designate which hours the employee can take off to vote. (A number of states do not allow employers to designate mealtimes as the hours employees must take off to vote.)

TABLE 5   *(Continued)*

South Dakota 2 hours unless employee has 2 consecutive nonwork hours to vote; no deduction

Tennessee 3 hours unless employee has 3 consecutive nonwork hours to vote; no deduction from wages

Texas Unspecified length of time unless employee has 2 consecutive nonwork hours to vote; no deduction from wages

Utah 2 hours; no deduction from wages for exempt employees

Washington 2 hours unless employee has 2 consecutive nonwork hours to vote; no deduction from wages

West Virginia 3 hours; no deduction from wages unless employee has 3 consecutive nonwork hours to vote

Wisconsin 3 hours; pay not required

Wyoming 1 hour; no deduction from wages

Types of Jobs

Under federal law, *minors under eighteen* may not work in any job that is considered hazardous by the Secretary of Labor. **Note (hazardous occupations):** According to the Secretary of Labor, hazardous occupations specifically include coal mining, logging, slaughtering or meat packing, wrecking and demolition, and roofing and excavation. Specific hazardous jobs include operating or helping on a motor vehicle, working in explosives plants, any job that involves exposure to radioactive substances, and working on power-driven machinery, bakery machines, paper products machines, circular band saws, or guillotine shears.

Minors under sixteen specifically cannot work in mining, manufacturing and processing, occupations involving the operation or tending of hoisting apparatus or power-driven machinery other than office machinery, the operation of motor vehicles or service as a helper on motor vehicles, or in public messenger service or hazardous occupations. *Exceptions:* Minors under sixteen may work delivering newspapers and in agriculture. They may also be employed as actors or performers with movies, theater, television, or radio; and they may be employed by their parents in jobs other than manufacturing, mining, and such hazardous occupations.

Minors under twelve cannot be employed except on a family farm and minors twelve to fourteen can be employed only on the same farm as their parents and with parental consent.

Hours of Work

Federal law does not restrict the number of hours minors between the ages of sixteen and eighteen may work.

Minors between fourteen and sixteen may *not* work:

☞ During school hours.

☞ More than eight hours a day and forty hours a week when school is not in session (i.e., during school vacations).

☞ More than three hours a day and eighteen hours a week when school is in session. And,

☞ Between 7 P.M. and 7 A.M. (From June 1 through Labor Day they may work until 9 P.M.)

State Law

Many states place more restrictions on the types of jobs and the hours minors may work than does the federal government. For instance, in many states minors under twenty-one may not serve alcoholic beverages. Of course, as with all employment laws, where there is a conflict between the federal law and the law of your state, employers have to comply with the law that gives employees the most rights or protections. So, if your state places additional restrictions on the employment of minors, your employer must comply with those restrictions. For details on your state's specific requirements, look under the state listings in the Blue Pages of your telephone directory. Most states list a separate number for "Employment of Minors" under the department of labor.

PAYMENT OF WAGES

Almost every state has laws or regulations covering when, where, how, and how often employees must be paid. Most require wages to be paid by cash or negotiable check, draft or order payable upon presentation at local banks or other financial institutions. (Most also allow direct deposit to a bank specified by the employee, too.) In the absence of an agreement otherwise, payment normally must be made at a convenient place designated by the employer (usually the work site), or by mail if the employee is on vacation or leave of absence, has quit or been discharged, or will be absent from work for any length of time for some other reason. However, state laws and regulations vary greatly with regard to how often employees have to be paid and how soon after termination employees have to be paid, depending on whether they quit, are fired, are laid off, or go out on strike.

Table 6 outlines basic state requirements on how regularly wages must be paid, and **Table 7** on how soon after termination wages must be paid. For more detailed information contact the wage and hour division of your state's department of labor.

WITHHOLDINGS AND DEDUCTIONS FROM WAGES
Authorized Deductions

All state laws and regulations require employers to withhold the following from your wages:

☞ Federal (and state) income taxes;
☞ Social Security taxes; and
☞ Court-ordered attachments against your wages to pay debts or spousal or child support. (For details, see Court-Ordered Judgments Against Your Wages, on p. 100.)

In addition, most states allow employers to deduct amounts you authorize in writing to be deducted for health and life insurance premiums, hospital and surgical insurance, union dues, credit union contributions, stock purchases, retirement and other benefit plans, and other payments that are for *your* benefit (not your employer's). Many also authorize deductions for repayment of loans made to you by your employer *if* there is written evidence of the loan.

Amounts That Cannot Be Deducted

Except for amounts required or authorized to be deducted from your paycheck as described above, most states severely limit what employers can deduct from your wages. In fact, many specifically prohibit deductions for such things as:

☞ Amounts to cover losses, breakage, shortages, or thefts caused or committed by customers;

(Continued on p. 96)

TABLE 6

STATE FREQUENCY OF WAGE PAYMENT LAWS*

Alaska monthly; twice monthly if employee chooses (except employees exempt from FLSA)

Arizona twice monthly (except school employees)

Arkansas twice monthly (except coal mining); monthly for some exempt employees

California twice monthly, 1st half due by 26th of month and 2nd half by 10th of next month (22nd and 7th for farm workers), except counties and schools; monthly, by 26th of month for executive, administrative, and professional; monthly for farm and domestic workers receiving room and board

Colorado monthly, within 10 days of end of pay period, except municipal government and schools; monthly within 10 days of end of pay period for farm and domestic workers receiving room and board

Connecticut weekly, within 8 days of end of pay period

Delaware monthly within 7 days of end of pay period; weekly for public works; every 2 weeks, within 14 days of end of pay period for railroads

District of Columbia twice monthly within 10 days of end of pay period; except government, railroad, and executive, administrative, and professional

Georgia twice monthly, except farm; monthly for executives

Hawaii twice monthly within 7 days of end of pay period, except government

Idaho monthly within 10 days of end of pay period

Illinois twice monthly within 13 days of end of pay period, except state and federal government; monthly for executive, administrative, and professional

Indiana twice monthly (every 2 weeks if requested), within 10 days of end of pay period, except farm; every 2 weeks, by request

Iowa monthly within 12 days of end of pay period, except employees on commission

Kansas monthly within 15 days of end of pay period, except government

Kentucky twice monthly within 18 days of end of pay period; 15th and 30th of month for mining with at least 10 employees

Louisiana twice monthly within 10 days of end of pay period for manufacturing, mining, and drilling with at least 10 employees

Maine weekly within 8 days of close of pay period

Maryland twice monthly, except executive, administrative, and professional

---

*List represents the *minimum* frequency of paychecks. Most states accept different payment schedules by collective bargaining agreement and by permission of the department of labor. For other limitations and exceptions, contact the wage and hour division of your state's department of labor. See Appendix. (**Note:** Most states provide that, where a regularly scheduled payday falls on a nonwork day, wages must be paid on the *preceding* day.)

TABLE 6   *(Continued)*

Massachusetts weekly within 6 days of end of pay period; twice monthly for salaried; monthly for farm and domestic

Michigan twice monthly, 1st half due by 1st and 2nd half by 15th of next month; monthly if paid by 1st of following month

Minnesota every 30 days; every 2 weeks for migrant workers

Mississippi twice monthly within 10 days of end of pay period for manufacturers with 50 or more employees and state government

Missouri every 15 days, within 5 days of end of pay period for manufacturers (immediately on close of pay period for mines, except coal mines within 5 days); twice monthly, within 16 days for railroads and companies with laborers, mechanics, and similar workers; monthly for executive, administrative, professional, and sales

Montana within 10 days of end of pay period, except federal government; monthly for salaried

Nebraska by agreement, except state government; twice monthly, 1st half due by 1st of next month, 2nd half by 15th for railroads

Nevada twice monthly, 1st half due by last day of month and 2nd half by 15th of next month

New Hampshire weekly, within 8 days of end of pay period or every two weeks if paid by next day; less often only if paid in advance

New Jersey twice monthly, within 10 days of end of pay period; monthly for executive, administrative, and professional

New Mexico every 16 days, 1st half due by 25th and 2nd half by 10th of next month (end of month and 15th of next month for payroll from out-of-state); monthly for executive, administrative, professional, and sales; monthly, by 10th of next month for piece rate, task, and commissioned employees by agreement

New York twice monthly; weekly, within 7 days of close of pay period for manual laborers (by following Thursday for Tuesday close for railroads); monthly for executive, administrative, professional, and sales

North Carolina monthly; annually for wages calculated by commission; twice monthly for railroads and repair shops with over 10 employees

North Dakota twice monthly

Ohio twice monthly, 1st half due by 1st day of next month and 2nd half by 15th of next month; or monthly, by next day

Oklahoma twice monthly, within 11 days of end of pay period; monthly for government and executive, administrative, and professional

Oregon every 35 days

Pennsylvania within 15 days of end of pay period; weekly, within 7 days of end of pay period for seasonal farm labor; weekly, within 2 weeks of end of pay period for railroad

Rhode Island weekly, within 9 days of end of pay period except salaried and government employees

TABLE 6 *(Continued)*

South Carolina weekly for textiles

South Dakota monthly or on regular paydays designated in advance

Tennessee twice monthly, 1st half due by 5th of next month and 2nd half by 20th of next month for private employers of 5 or more

Texas twice monthly, 1st and 15th if not designated by employer, except government; monthly for employees exempt from overtime under FLSA; weekly if hired by day or week and monthly if by month for farm, factory, and stores

Utah twice monthly, within 10 days of end of pay period, except government, domestic, dairy, and agriculture

Vermont weekly, within 6 days of end of pay period; twice monthly with written notice

Virginia twice monthly for hourly, monthly for salaried

Washington monthly

West Virginia every 2 weeks

Wisconsin monthly, within 31 days of close of pay period, except schools; quarterly for agriculture and logging

Wyoming twice monthly, 1st half due by 1st of next month and 2nd half by 15th of next month, for railroads, mines, factories, mills, and production of oil and gas; monthly for state employers, by last day of month

Alabama and Florida do not have laws that specify frequency of wage payment for all employers generally.

~~~~~~

(Continued from p. 93)

☞ Inducements to get or keep your job;

☞ Medical examinations required by your employer; and

☞ Medical expenses for work-related injuries.

WHAT TO DO: If you believe you were or are now being underpaid in violation of the FLSA or state wage and hour laws, you should contact your state department of labor. The agency will investigate, and if they feel your complaint has merit, they will conduct an audit of your employer's wage payment policies. (In the usual situation, if your employer is underpaying you, he is probably underpaying a lot of other employees; and numbers tend to stimulate an agency's interest.) Your complaint can be kept confidential so you do not risk retaliation by your employer. (Of course, retaliation is illegal, but that doesn't always stop employers from harassing employees who report a violation of the law.) If your employer is found to have violated wage and

(Continued on p. 99)

TABLE 7

STATE LAWS CONCERNING PAYMENT OF WAGES ON TERMINATION*

Alaska *All terminations:*† within 3 workdays

Arizona Fires: sooner of 3 workdays or end of pay period (schools: within 10 days); Quits: next payday

Arkansas *Fires:* immediate (within 7 days if employee requests wages by mail)

California *Fires:* immediate (except some seasonal 3 days and some oil and motion picture within 1 workday); *Quits:* within 3 days of notice or quit

Colorado *Fires:* immediate; *Quits, strikes:* next payday

Connecticut *Fires:* next business day; *Quits, layoffs, strikes:* next payday

Delaware *All terminations:* next payday

District of Columbia *Fires:* next workday (4 workdays for employee handling money); *Quits:* sooner of next payday or 1 week; *Strikes:* next payday

Hawaii *Fires:* immediate, if possible, or next workday; *Quits:* next payday (immediate if employee gives 2 weeks' notice); *Strikes, layoffs:* next payday

Idaho *Fires, quits, layoffs:* sooner of 10 workdays or next payday (except 2 days on written request)

Illinois *Fires, quits:* immediate, if possible, or by next payday; *Strikes, layoffs:* next payday

Indiana *Fires, quits, strikes:* next payday

Iowa *Fires:* next payday

Kansas *Fires, quits:* next payday

Kentucky *Fires, quits:* later of next pay period or 14 days

Louisiana *Fires,* within 3 days; *Quits:* sooner of next payday or 15 days

Maine *Fires, quits:* sooner of next payday or 2 weeks of demand

Maryland *Fires, quits:* next payday

Massachusetts *Fires:* immediate (except Boston employers when accounts certified); *Quits:* next payday

Michigan *Fires:* within 4 workdays (some agricultural labor: 1 workday); *Quits:* next payday (some agricultural labor: 3 days)

Minnesota *Fires:* immediately (except state), within 3 workdays for sales (except immediate for independent contractor), 1 day for migrant workers, 10 workdays for employee handling money; *Quits:* within 5 days (1 day for employee giving 5 days' notice), 6 days for sales (3 days with notice, immediate if independent contractor), 1 day for migrant workers, 10 days for employee handling money; *Strikes:* next payday

---

*Most states allow payment by mail on or before required day, at employee's request. Collective bargaining agreements generally supersede these requirements.

†"All terminations" refers to loss of employment for any reason, including "quits," "fires," "layoffs," and "strikes."

TABLE 7 *(Continued)*

Missouri *Fires:* immediate (within 7 days if employee requests wages by mail); except commissioned employees

Montana *All terminations:* within 3 days (6 days if out-of-state payroll); State: sooner of next payday or 15 days; *Fires for cause:* immediate

Nebraska *Fires:* sooner of next payday or 2 weeks (except state)

Nevada *Fires:* immediate; *Quits:* sooner of next payday or 1 week

New Hampshire *Fires:* 3 days; *Quits, layoffs:* next payday (3 days if employee gives pay period's notice); *Strikes:* next payday

New Jersey *All terminations:* next payday

New Mexico *Fires:* within 5 days (10 days for task, piece, commission, or similar-rate employees); *Quits, strikes:* next payday

New York *Fires, quits:* next payday

North Carolina *All terminations:* next payday

North Dakota *Fires:* 1 day (except by certified mail, sooner of 15 days or next payday); *Quits, strikes:* next payday

Oklahoma *Fires, quits:* next payday

Oregon *Fires:* immediate; *Quits:* 5 workdays if no notice, immediate if employee gives 2 workdays' notice; *Strikes:* sooner of next payday or 30 days; *Seasonal layoffs:* next payday

Pennsylvania *Fires, quits, strikes:* next payday; *seasonal agriculture:* next workday

Rhode Island *Fires, quits:* next payday

South Carolina *Fires:* later of 2 days or next payday; *Strikes:* next payday

South Dakota *Fires:* sooner of 5 days or when employee returns employer's property; *Quits, strikes:* next payday or when employee returns employer's property

Texas *Fires:* within 6 days (except railroad within 15 days); *Quits:* next payday

Utah *Fires:* 1 day (except commissioned salesperson in charge of financial accounts); *Quits:* 3 days (immediate if employee gives 1 day notice); *Strikes:* next payday

Vermont *Fires:* 3 days; *Quits:* next payday (next Friday if no regular payday)

Virginia *Fires, quits:* next payday

Washington *Fires, quits:* next payday

West Virginia *Fires:* 3 days; *Quits:* next payday (immediate if employee gives pay period notice)

Wisconsin *Fires:* within 3 days (1 day if caused by shutdown); *Quits:* within 15 days (except commissioned sales)

Wyoming *Fires, quits:* within 5 workdays; *Strikes, layoffs:* next payday

Alabama, Florida, Georgia, Mississippi, Ohio, and Tennessee do not have laws that specify wage payment on termination.

(Continued from p. 96)

hour laws, you—and everyone else who is underpaid as a result of the employer's illegal wage payment practice—are entitled to:

☞ Back pay.
☞ Liquidated damages equal to the amount of unpaid back wages. "Liquidated" means the damages are preset or calculated exactly, rather than estimated. For example, if you weren't paid for a certain number of hours of overtime, that amount can be figured precisely, and damages awarded in an equal amount would be referred to as "liquidated." (**Note:** The award of liquidated damages in an action to recover wages in a FLSA violation is automatic. So if you win your case, you will automatically be awarded *twice* what your employer owes you.)
☞ Your attorney's fees and court costs.

If the department of labor notifies you that they will not pursue the matter, you may bring a private legal action against your employer. You must bring your wage and hour action within two years of discovering the violation. Practically speaking, though the statute of limitations is two years, you should bring your action as soon as possible to be sure to preserve your rights. (**Note:** The statute of limitations is extended to three years if your employer's violation was intentional.)

Note: If you can get the department of labor to do your "dirty work" for you, so much the better as far as keeping your out-of-pocket expenses down. However, as with most bureaucracies, because most departments are overworked and understaffed, they tend to proceed at a rather "casual" pace. But you can exert a modest amount of control over how aggressively they pursue the matter. Don't be afraid to "bug" them early and often. And call and write to your legislator if they don't respond (with copies to your contact at the agency). As my mother always says—yours probably does, too: "The squeaky wheel gets the grease."

Given the frequency with which employers violate the **Fair Labor Standards Act** *and the fact that they rarely violate it for one employee, but rather for entire classifications of employees, and because of the enormous amounts of money often involved, a wage and hour audit by the department of labor is one of the agency actions most feared by employers!*

COURT-ORDERED JUDGMENTS AGAINST YOUR WAGES

Your employer is required by law to withhold any amounts ordered to be withheld from your wages by a court. He doesn't have a choice in the matter and, in fact, can be held responsible for the payments himself if he doesn't make the deductions and pay the amount withheld to a sheriff or other court officer who is authorized to collect the withheld funds.

In most jurisdictions the procedure for someone to gain an attachment of your wages (sometimes called a "garnishment") is as follows:

☞ A creditor wins a lawsuit against you in court. The creditor can be anyone you owe money to, including the federal, state, or local government for back taxes, a vendor to whom you owe money for the purchase price of goods, a bank or anyone else who loaned you money which you have not repaid, or your spouse and/or dependent children for alimony or support. (Of course, you must have been notified at the time of the lawsuit by a sheriff, who serves you with a summons to appear, and have been given an opportunity to defend the suit.)

☞ You refuse or neglect to pay the judgment against you as ordered, either in a lump sum or in periodic payments.

☞ The creditor returns to court to get an attachment of your wages for the amount of the debt.

☞ A sheriff serves the attachment order on your employer.

☞ Your employer notifies you of the attachment. (In most jurisdictions you have the right at this point to appeal to the court not to attach your wages.)

Limit on Amount Withheld

The federal **Consumer Credit Protection Act** places a limit on the amount that can be deducted from your paycheck to pay a judgment. Many states also place limits on attachments. Your employer is required to deduct according to the formula (federal or state) that deducts less from your paycheck (i.e., leaves you with more money).

Federal Limit on Attachments for Debts Other Than Support:
Federal law limits the amount of money that can be taken from your

wages to pay debts other than support, such as debts for consumer credit transactions. Under federal law you are able to keep at least 75 percent of your weekly disposable earnings or thirty times the federal minimum wage, whichever is more. ("Disposable earnings" is what is left after deductions for taxes, Social Security, normal retirement contributions, group health and life insurance premiums, and union dues.) The court can order any amount in excess of that to be attached and withheld from your paycheck each pay period until the entire amount of the debt is paid off. The court order usually specifies how much your employer is to deduct.

Federal Limit on Support Orders: Federal law also limits the amount that can be withheld from your wages to pay for the support of a spouse or minor children. However, more of your pay can be attached to pay support than to pay other debts. In support attachments you are allowed to keep at least 40 percent of your weekly disposable earnings. However, you get to keep at least 50 percent if you are already supporting another spouse or child. (These drop to 35 percent and 45 percent, respectively, if the support order is more than twelve weeks old.) In any event, a support order can't leave you with less than $100. Anything over these amounts can be attached and withheld from your regular paycheck until the total amount is paid off.

Orders of a Bankruptcy Court, and State and Federal Taxes: The above limits on wage attachments do not apply to orders made by a bankruptcy court judge in a case in which you are a debtor. Nor do the limits apply to the amounts you owe for state or federal taxes. (It is usually a good idea to contact the Internal Revenue Service or your state taxing authority to try to work out some reasonable payment schedule for delinquent taxes, rather than wait for them to lower the boom on you with a big-time wage attachment.)

Priority of Attachments: Generally, support orders have priority over orders to pay other debts, no matter which was served first. In other words, if your employer is already deducting from your wages for a debt you owe on a car, and another sheriff comes along with an order to attach your wages for support, the support order takes precedence. So your employer must pay the support order to that sheriff first. Then if there is anything left of your wages over the amount the law says you get to keep, your employer will deduct the rest to pay the other order. (**Note:** Orders for child support ordinarily take precedence over spousal support orders.)

In the case of two attachments of the same kind, the normal rule is first come, first served (or rather, first served, first paid.)

Discharges Because of Attachments: Federal law prohibits your employer from discharging you because your wages have been attached for any one indebtedness. This means you can't be fired over a court-ordered attachment for a single debt regardless of how many times your employer has to withhold money from your paycheck to satisfy it. (Federal law would allow your discharge if your wages are attached for more than one indebtedness. Some state laws, however, do not. See below.)

State Laws

As noted above, many states have formulas different from the federal law's for calculating the limits on amounts that can be withheld from your paycheck to satisfy a court-ordered judgment. In that case, the formula that has to be used is the one that allows you to keep the most money from your paycheck. Most states also prohibit discharge or discipline of an employee because his or her wages have been attached for a number of debts. Contact your state department of labor for the withholding limit in your state, as well as restrictions on discipline for more than one attachment. See Appendix.

WHAT TO DO: A court-ordered attachment against an employee's wages can be a tricky thing for an employer. On the one hand, he has an obligation to the creditor to comply with the attachment and withhold the required amount or face potential liability for the portion of the debt he was supposed to withhold and didn't. On the other hand, he has an obligation to the employee, too. First, he must notify you of the attachment so you have a chance to dispute the claim and get it reversed or reduced, if possible. Then he must be careful not to deduct more than the limit imposed by law for the type of attachment involved because you can hold your employer liable for amounts he withholds and pays over to a sheriff that are in excess of what is legally allowed to be withheld. (**Note:** A lawsuit against your employer for not properly complying with a wage attachment order is a private cause of action. Unlike usual wage and hour actions, such as minimum wage and overtime violations, the department of labor has no interest and will not pursue the matter for you.)

Finally, as noted, federal law prohibits your employer from discharging you because your wages have been attached for a single debt. It also prohibits an employer from refusing to hire you, or disciplining or discharging you because of an attachment for child support. In addition, many state laws also protect you from discharge or discipline even if your wages have been attached numerous times. If your employer disciplines or discharges you because your wages were attached once (under federal law), you can enlist the aid of the EEOC because in essence the **Consumer Credit Protection Act** is a law against discrimination. (Negative employment decisions based on wage attachments have been found to have a greater impact on minorities.) And, of course, if your employer disciplines or discharges you because your wages were attached more than once (in many states), you can go to your state human rights commission to file charges. Or you may have a right to bring a lawsuit on your own.

If your employer is found to have disciplined or discharged you in violation of the law, you are entitled to be "made whole"—that is, put in the position you would have been in had your employer not discriminated against you. For example, if you were demoted, you can be returned to your previous job (and awarded the differential pay you would have received had you not been demoted). If you were denied a promotion and a raise, you can be awarded the promotion and raise—the raise retroactively. If you were fired, you can be reinstated with back pay and interest, along with damages in an amount equal to your back pay. You can also recover attorney's fees and court costs.

Note: In either case, whether you are represented by the EEOC or your own lawyer, you have to weigh the *real* potential for gain against the real potential for loss. In the situation where you are fired because of a wage attachment, the loss (i.e., your job, your wages, etc.) and potential gain (i.e., your job, your wages, damages, etc.) may be quite clearly defined. However, if you were disciplined, the potential for gain and loss may not be so clearly defined. For example, if you were merely "given a talking-to," stirring up the waters by bringing in the EEOC may be overkill and lead to more problems than it solves. That's because there is no way to legislate away negative feelings created between you and your employer, which could lead to more subtle negative action against you in the future. Do you want to risk that for such a minor form of discrimination? Maybe. But that's up to you.

How about if you were given a written warning? Many states allow you to put explanatory notes in your personnel file, and this may be enough to satisfy your sense of principle. (See Chapter 6: Right to Privacy/Access to Records.) In any event, as the disciplinary measures escalate and begin to cost you money and/or job security or promotional potential, you will have to decide when it is appropriate to take steps of your own. That is, when you feel that your potential for gain outweighs what you have already lost *and your potential for future loss*. Just knowing you are right isn't always enough. Be sure you take a good hard look at the down side before standing on principle.

SUMMARY

It is not illegal for our employers to pay us less than we think we are worth. If that were true, every single one of us would be calling our lawyer first thing tomorrow morning. However, underpaying us in violation of the FLSA or state wage and hour laws *is* illegal.

A great many employers habitually violate wage and hour laws, some to save money, but most out of negligence or just plain ignorance. High on the list of violations is misclassifying hourly workers as "white-collar" exempt employees (i.e., executive, administrative, or professional employees), and paying them a "salary" to avoid paying overtime.

If you feel that you—and likely, therefore, everyone in your job or pay category—are not being paid what you should be being paid, either as a result of minimum wage or overtime violations or any other violation of the FLSA or state wage and hour laws, file a complaint with the U.S. or your state department of labor. You can request confidentiality, which is obviously a good idea. A word to the wise, however: Depending on the circumstances, your employer may be able to figure out it was you who complained anyway. Have you complained to him before going to the department of labor? Are you the only one in your pay category?

To back up just a bit, you *could* bring up your gripe with your employer before going to the department of labor to see if the company will voluntarily change its wage and hour practices. But if the company refuses to change its stance and *then* you go to the department of labor, your hope of confidentiality is pretty much blown. Your employer may be greedy, but he isn't stupid!

Another tactic would be to write an anonymous letter suggesting your employer review its wage and hour practices. Obviously, it will be truly anonymous only if you are one of many affected employees.

So the department of labor may be your last resort. But certainly not the least effective. If your employer has been underpaying you, he has probably been underpaying a lot of people for a lot of pay periods. Back pay, interest, fines—the total payout could be staggering. It's no wonder the words "department of labor wage audit" strike only slightly less fear into the heart of an employer than the words "your in-laws are in town."

4

Fringe Benefits

The employment relationship is a two-way street. Maybe it doesn't always seem that way, but it is. Employers are trying to get the best employees they can, and one way to do that is to offer a few "extras." Of course, some of these extras have become so commonplace over the years that employees have come to expect them: things like group health insurance, paid vacation days, paid sick days, paid holidays, retirement plans, and leaves of absence. (**Note:** In 1993, the federal government passed the **Family and Medical Leave Law,** which requires employers to allow qualified employees to take unpaid leaves of absence for certain family or medical emergencies. A number of states have similar laws. Details appear later in this chapter.)

Most of these employer policies share two things:

☞ They are established voluntarily by your employer. That is, there is no law requiring them to offer these benefits. (Except in the case of certain family and medical leaves in some states as noted above.)

☞ Once these policies are established and promised to employees, employers are obligated to follow through on them. (However, an employer may be able to reserve the right to alter the terms of a policy after giving employees adequate notice of the proposed change.) Also, employers cannot discriminate in providing benefits. (i.e., If an employer provides benefits to a certain class of employees, it must provide that benefit to everyone in that class regardless of sex, race, etc.)

Now let's take a look at some common employee benefits and potential problem areas.

GROUP HEALTH INSURANCE

Group health insurance is one of those benefits employees have grown so accustomed to that some think it is required. But all you have to do is check the statistics to realize that this isn't the case. The statistics? Some *thirty-five million* Americans have no health insurance! And a conservative estimate of the number who are underinsured would top twice that figure. Of course, some of them are unemployed. But most of them (or their spouses or parents) work for small employers who can't afford to provide health insurance for their employees. In good economic times, when jobs are plentiful and companies are making money, providing group health insurance becomes almost a must for employers who want to compete for the best workers. But in bad times, expensive health insurance plans are often the first benefit to be cut back on or even to be left by the wayside entirely.

So, no, employers don't have to provide health insurance for their employees. But if they do, there are certain rules they have to follow.

Types of Coverage

Providing health insurance is an expensive undertaking for your employer (and for you if, as with most group insurance, you have to contribute to the cost). Therefore, the kind of health insurance plan the employer has should be critical in your choice of jobs—if, given the current state of the economy, you are lucky enough to have a choice.

Employers have a wide variety of benefit plans to choose from for their employees. Increasingly these benefit plans require contributions from covered employees, including deductibles and co-pay provisions. Insurance coverage and how much you will have to contribute toward it yourself is something you should factor into the wage you are being offered. Having no insurance or being under-covered or overcharged can end up being extremely costly. It is something you should investigate *before* accepting that job.

Many state laws require employers who do offer health insurance to employees to provide certain minimum (mandated) coverage, such as medical and surgical benefits, treatment of alcoholism and drug abuse, mammograms, treatment of mental illness, and the like. (In other words, employers don't have to provide health insurance, but if they do, they must provide specific minimum coverage.)

WHAT TO DO: The laws requiring minimum coverage for employers who provide health insurance are complex and vary greatly from state to state. Check with your state's health commissioner if you question whether your employer's health insurance plan provides the minimum mandated coverage. (They will be able to tell you what illnesses and conditions must be covered by all group insurance plans.) Then check the list against the benefits covered by your employer's insurance carrier. An employer who does not offer required coverage can be held liable for medical expenses you incur as a result. You can pursue your complaint either through your state's department of health and welfare or through private legal action. It might be best to begin with the department of health and welfare, since if you are being shortchanged, so too are your fellow employees. Generally, the more people who are affected, the more interest agencies tend to have in a case.

Note (older employees and female employees): There are specific rules regarding providing health care benefits to older workers and women:

Older Workers: As of May 1, 1986, employers have to offer workers over age sixty-five the same health insurance coverage they offer to younger workers and their spouses. In addition, if participation in the plan is mandatory, the employer can't make older workers pay any more than younger workers to belong. If participation is voluntary, premiums charged to older workers can't be any higher than actuarial tables show costs for older workers to be in relation to costs for younger workers.

Women: The **Pregnancy Discrimination Act** requires that "women affected by pregnancy and related conditions must be treated the same as other applicants and employees on the basis of their ability or inability to work." In the area of health insurance benefits, that means employers who provide health insurance have to provide the same coverage to women who can't work because of childbirth or other "disabilities" related to pregnancy as they provide to all employees for other disabilities. (See below.)

Mastectomies: Effective for plan years after October 21, 1998, federal law requires group health plans, health insurance issuers, and HMOs to provide coverage for reconstructive surgery associated with mastectomies.

Continuation of Coverage (COBRA)

Once you have health insurance, the next most important question is how to keep from losing it through no fault of your own. The question comes to the forefront when you are fired or, if you have your health insurance through your spouse's job, when your spouse is fired, or when you and your spouse are divorced or separated, or your spouse dies, or you are dropped from the insured group for any other reason (including voluntarily quitting your job). Other coverage questions arise from layoffs or reductions in hours that make you ineligible to continue in the group for health insurance purposes. A federal law with the formidable name **Consolidated Omnibus Budget Reconciliation Act of 1986** (COBRA, for short) requires your employer to offer you the opportunity to continue your health insurance (and that of your spouse and dependents) if you are terminated *for any reason (except gross misconduct)*. COBRA applies to employers of twenty or more employees. (**Note:** Many states have their own versions of COBRA covering smaller employers. Some even cover all employers who offer group insurance to their employees. Most of the state laws don't offer as much overall protection as the federal law does. However, some offer longer periods of continuation in specific situations. In any case, as with all areas of labor and employment law where you are covered by separate state and federal laws, you—or your spouse or ex-spouse or dependent—can choose the law you wish to be covered under. That, of course, would be the one that gives you the longer period of protection.)*

COBRA has specific requirements concerning when you must

*There is some question as to whether state COBRA laws are preempted by the federal **Employee Retirement Income Security Act** (ERISA) as "employee benefit plans," which by law are subject only to federal regulation. If they are, employers would only have to comply with the federal COBRA law. (Most lawyers in states having their own COBRA laws have advised their employer/clients to follow both laws until the issue is settled.)

be notified of your rights to continued coverage, when you (or your spouse or dependents) must notify your employer of your intention to exercise those rights, the maximum premium you can be charged, the minimum period of extended coverage (which depends to some extent on the reason you are no longer eligible for group coverage), and the reasons continued coverage can be terminated prematurely.

Conversion Rights: In addition to your continuation rights, you (and your covered dependents) must also be given the right to convert to an individual policy at the end of your continuation period. (You can—and will—be charged individual rates, though).

Table 8 outlines COBRA's continuation requirements.

Table 9 is an example of the type of notice your employer should give you regarding your COBRA rights. It is based on the U.S. Department of Labor's model notice. Though the form may vary, to be in strict compliance with the law, the contents of your employer's notice should be substantially equivalent to those in the sample.

WHAT TO DO: Both your employer and the insurance company that provides coverage can be held liable for any additional expenses you incur as a result of not being offered continuation of group health insurance coverage. For example, where the employer informed a terminated employee only of his right to convert to an individual policy and not of his right to continue under the group plan and the man was subsequently injured, the employer and the insurer had to share the additional medical bills the man had to pay because the individual policy was less comprehensive than the group plan.*

PAID DAYS OFF

After health insurance, probably the next most critical benefit question is "How many paid days off do I get?" This question encompasses the areas of paid holidays, vacation days, sick days, and "personal" days.

Kidder v. H&B Marine, Inc., U.S. Court of Appeals, 5th Circuit, No. 90-3340, 1991.

TABLE 8

CONSOLIDATED OMNIBUS BUDGET RECONCILIATION ACT (COBRA) REQUIREMENTS: CONTINUATION OF HEALTH INSURANCE

Situation Covered	*COBRA Requirement*
Employers Covered	Employers of 20 or more employees, except churches and the federal government. (A number of states have COBRA-type laws that cover smaller employers. Check with your state's insurance commissioner for possible additional coverage in your state.*)
Notice of Rights	*Employees joining the plan:* Employers must notify each employee and his or her spouse of their COBRA rights as soon as they join the insurance plan. *Insurance company:* Employers have 30 days to notify the plan administrator (i.e., their insurance company) that an employee (or spouse or dependent) is no longer eligible to continue in the group. *Employees no longer eligible:* The insurance company (or the employer, if the plan is self-administered) has 14 days from the date notice is received that the employee is no longer eligible for the group to inform the employee (or spouse or dependent) of his or her right to continue his or her insurance.
Notice of Election	Anyone qualified to continue insurance under COBRA (including divorced or separated spouses and dependents who lose coverage through marriage or age) has 60 days to elect to do so. Individuals (i.e., the employee, spouse, and dependent) may make the election separately.

*See footnote, p. 109.

TABLE 8 *(Continued)*

Situation Covered	*COBRA Requirement*
Due Date of Initial Premium	Anyone electing continuation of coverage must pay the first premium within 45 days of making the election. (i.e., since you have 60 days to elect coverage—an initial 30 days plus a 30-day grace period—and another 45 days to pay the first premium, that gives you up to 105 days to pay the first premium. However, the employer can bill you retroactively for the premiums due.)
Due Date of Subsequent Premiums	After the first premium payment, you must pay additional premiums within 30 days of when they are due (or longer, if so required by the insurer).
Duration of Continued Coverage	
Termination of employment for any reason except death ("Any reason" includes being fired, quitting, having hours reduced so you no longer qualify for coverage, and being laid off):	18 months for former employee, spouse, and dependents. (**Note:** Spouse and dependents can get up to a maximum total of 36 months if employee dies or divorces spouse during 18-month continuation period.)
Death of the employee, or divorce or legal separation from the employee, or employee becoming entitled to Medicare:	36 months for surviving or former spouse and dependents.
Dependent losing coverage through marriage or becoming too old to qualify as a dependent:	36 months for dependent.
Employee disabled at the time of ineligibility for group insurance:	29 months for disabled employee, spouse, or dependents. (Anyone who becomes disabled during the initial 18 months of continuation coverage has 60 days to inform the plan administrator in order to get the added 11 months of coverage.)

TABLE 8 *(Continued)*

Situation Covered	*COBRA Requirement*
Duration of Continued Coverage	
Gross misconduct:	No right of continuation. (**Note:** "Gross misconduct" is not clearly defined by the law. At least one court defined it as: • Deliberate or negligent disregard of the employer's interests; • Deliberate violations of reasonable standards of conduct set by the employer; • Behavior so careless or negligent as to amount to wrongful intent. The court noted that inefficiency, poor conduct or performance, ordinary negligence, and errors in judgment are not enough for gross misconduct (*Paris v. Korbel & Brothers, Inc.,* U.S. District Court, Northern California, No. C-89-1278 TEH, March 14, 1990).
Employer files for bankruptcy:	Retirees (or their surviving spouses) who lose coverage within a year before or after the employer sponsoring their health plan goes bankrupt can continue coverage until their death. When retiree or his or her surviving spouse dies, their dependents may continue coverage for 36 months.
Active military duty:	Employees called to active military duty may continue coverage while on active duty. (**Note:** Military personnel who are called to duty and who discontinue their health insurance coverage must be reinstated immediately upon return to work with no waiting period.)
Maximum Amount of Premiums Charged	Coverage is continued at the individual's expense. Employer may charge up to 102% of the applicable group premium. In the case of a disabled person the employer can charge up to 150% for the 19th through 29th months of continued coverage. (**Note:** Employers who self-insure can set premiums based either on actuarial estimates or the prior year's premium plus an adjustment for inflation.)

TABLE 8 (*Continued*)

Situation Covered	*COBRA Requirement*
Termination of Continued Coverage before End of Maximum Period	Right to continuation of coverage ends if: • The covered person doesn't pay the premiums; • The employer terminates the group health plan for all its employees; • The covered person becomes eligible for Medicare; or • The covered person becomes eligible under another group health plan. (**Note:** Employers can end coverage only if the other plan doesn't exclude or limit coverage for preexisting conditions.)
Conversion to Individual Policy	Covered individuals must be given the right to convert to an individual policy (at individual rates) at the end of the continuation period.

"Legal Holidays"

Despite the fact that certain days are traditionally referred to as "legal holidays," there is actually no legal requirement that your employer give you any paid holidays off. Of course, most employers do give paid holidays off. In fact, surveys indicate the average employer gives full-time employees nine paid holidays off per year. Also, many part-time employees are given holiday pay according to the number of hours they normally work in a day. (For example, a part-timer who works four hours a day would be paid for four hours on Christmas. Note, however, that there is no requirement that an employer pay part-timers anything, even if full-timers are given holidays off with pay.) In addition, employers are free to set their own standards regarding eligibility for paid holidays. Some require employees to work a certain probationary period before they are eligible for paid holidays. (**Note:** There is no requirement that your employer pay you overtime for working on a holiday unless it puts you over forty hours for the week.)

TABLE 9

SAMPLE COBRA NOTICE

Dear (Employee and Spouse):

Under the Consolidated Omnibus Budget Reconciliation Act (COBRA), enacted April 7, 1986, most employers who sponsor group health insurance plans are required to offer covered employees and their dependents the chance to extend their health coverage for a specified period of time at group rates under certain circumstances when insurance coverage would otherwise end. This notice is to inform you of your rights and obligations under the COBRA law.

As an employee of (Company Name), covered by (Group Insurance Plan), you are entitled to elect to continue your insurance coverage if you lose your job other than for gross misconduct.

As the spouse of an employee of (Company Name), covered by (Group Insurance Plan), you are entitled to elect to continue your insurance coverage if you would otherwise lose coverage for any of the following reasons:

- Your spouse loses his or her job or has his or her hours reduced;
- You are divorced or legally separated from your spouse;
- Your spouse applies for and becomes entitled to Medicare; or
- Your spouse dies.

The dependent child (or children) of an employee of (Company Name), covered by (Group Insurance Plan), is entitled to continue their insurance coverage if they would otherwise lose coverage for any of the following reasons:

- Your parent loses his or her job or has his or her hours reduced;
- Your parents are divorced or legally separated;
- Your parent applies for and becomes entitled to Medicare;
- Your parent dies; or
- You no longer qualify as a dependent under the plan.

Spouses of retirees also have the right to continuation of insurance upon the death of, or their divorce from, the retiree. In addition, retirees, retirees' spouses, and surviving spouses also have the right to continuation of insurance in the event (Company Name) files for bankruptcy.

To be eligible to elect COBRA continuation coverage, the covered employee or family member must notify (Group Health Plan Administrator) within 60 days of a divorce or legal separation, or when a child no longer qualifies as a dependent under the plan, or by the date coverage would be lost as a result of any of these events. (Company Name) must notify (Group Health Plan Administrator) of the covered employee's termination of employment, reduction in hours, or death.

When (Group Health Plan Administrator) is notified of the occurrence of one of the above "qualifying events," (Group Health Plan Administrator) will notify you that you have the right to elect continuation of coverage. You then have 60 days from the date you would otherwise lose coverage to inform (Group Health Plan Administrator) you want to continue coverage.

If you do not elect continuation coverage, your insurance coverage under (Group Insurance Plan) will terminate as scheduled.

TABLE 9 *(Continued)*

If you elect coverage, (Company Name) must give you the same coverage provided to similarly situated employees or family members. You must be allowed to continue your insurance coverage for up to 18 months if your coverage would be lost due to termination of employment or a reduction in hours; or 36 months if your coverage would be lost for any other reason. **Note:** The 18-month period may be extended to 36 months if you are divorced or legally separated from a covered spouse, or the covered spouse becomes eligible for Medicare or dies within the 18-month period. The 18-month period may be extended to 29 months if you are disabled under Social Security disability rules and so notify (Group Health Plan Administrator) within 60 days.

You should be aware that, under COBRA, your continuation coverage can be ended before the full 18-, 29- or 36-month period, as the case may be, in the event of any of the following:

- You do not pay your insurance premiums within the required grace period;
- You become covered under another group insurance plan (except one that limits or does not cover a preexisting medical condition which you have);
- You become eligible for Medicare;
- It is determined that you are no longer disabled (and you had qualified for an 11-month extension of coverage based on your disability: insurance can be canceled at the beginning of the month following such determination); or
- (Company Name) ceases to provide group health insurance for any of its employees.

You do not have to demonstrate insurability in order to elect COBRA continuation coverage. However, you may have to pay part or all of the premium for such coverage. You must be allowed at least 45 days to pay your initial premium, which (Company Name) can charge retroactively. You must be given at least 30 days to pay subsequent premiums.

You also have the right to convert your (Group Insurance Plan) policy to an individual policy at the end of your COBRA continuation coverage period.

If you have any questions, please contact (Group Health Plan Administrator, Address, Phone). Also, please provide timely information to (Group Health Plan Administrator) regarding any changes of status (i.e., divorce, separation, etc.) that would affect your insurance coverage

---

Vacation Pay, Sick Pay, "Personal" Days, Severance Pay, Etc.

Vacation pay, sick pay, "personal" days, and severance pay are not, as some employees believe, an inalienable right. As an employee, you have no right to these benefits unless they are given to you by your employer. However, it has come to be recognized that employees need paid time to regenerate their juices; to attend funerals of close friends or to mourn the passing of family members; or to recover from brief illnesses (or to get back on their feet after a layoff or discharge that was not their fault). Most employees expect these benefits and most employers have long had policies concerning them, maybe not so much out of the goodness of their hearts as out of a business necessity—to be competitive in the labor market. Employers have virtually unlimited latitude in setting policies regarding paid days off. However, they cannot discriminate in giving those benefits. If they give certain paid days off to some employees, they have to give them to all employees in that category (for example, all full-time employees). But in any case, once your employer set a policy conferring these benefits, it creates rights that you can enforce.

Accruing Paid Time Off: Employers vary according to size and type of business as to whether or not they allow employees to accrue paid time off (i.e., vacation days, sick days, etc., not used). Many of those who do allow accrual of paid days off set a limit on the number of days that can be accrued. If employers have a policy of paying terminated employees for accrued time, they must comply with that policy. If they do not, you can sue for double the unpaid amount under federal (and some state) wage and hour laws, plus your attorney's fees and court costs.

Part-time Employees: Employers often give paid days off to part-time employees on a prorated basis according to the number of hours a day they generally work. For example, if full-time employees get a week's vacation after six months, an employee who usually works four hours a day would get two and a half days paid vacation after six months. Again, however, employers are not required to give paid days off to part-timers any more than they are to full-timers. (But if they do give some part-timers prorated paid time off, they must give it to all in the same category—i.e., who work the same number of hours.)

MATERNITY AND PREGNANCY LEAVE

The federal **Pregnancy Discrimination Act**, which is an amendment to **Title VII of the Civil Rights Act of 1964**, prohibits employers from discriminating against employees based on pregnancy. The law, which applies to employers of fifteen or more employees, requires that "women affected by pregnancy, childbirth or related medical conditions . . . be treated the same for all employment-related purposes . . . as other personnel" who are not pregnant but are "similar in their ability or inability to work." That means:

☞ Employers can't *require* maternity leave of a certain length that bears no relation to the woman's ability or inability to work.

☞ Employers must offer those returning from maternity leave reinstatement to the same or an equivalent job, benefits, and seniority.

☞ Employers have to offer leaves of absence for pregnancy- and childbirth-related "disabilities" under the same terms as they offer it for other "disabilities."

Maternity Leave Policies That May Discriminate Against Men: According to the EEOC, employers who grant liberal maternity leave to female employees *without tying it directly to pregnancy-related disabilities* may be opening themselves up to sex discrimination charges from male employees. Male employees may have valid sex discrimination claims if their employers don't offer *separate:*

☞ Parental leave for *all employees,* male and female, for the birth or adoption of a child; and

☞ Disability leave, including leave for pregnancy-related disabilities.

FAMILY AND MEDICAL LEAVE

The federal **Family and Medical Leave Law** was passed in late 1993 to allow qualified employees to take unpaid leave for family or medical emergencies without risking loss of their jobs. The law requires all employers (both public and private) of fifty or more employees to provide eligible employees up to twelve weeks of unpaid family and medical leave in any twelve-month period.

A number of states have passed their own family and medical leave laws as well. They range from laws as rudimentary as those in Colorado and New York, requiring employers to give employees who are adopting a child the same paternity and maternity leave they give to employees for a natural childbirth, to Connecticut's, requiring up to sixteen weeks of leave during any two-year period for most family emergencies. For a synopsis of state family and medical leave requirements, see **Table 10.** (Remember that, as with other overlapping federal and state requirements, employers who are subject to both state and federal family and medical leave laws must comply with both laws. That means if there is any inconsistency between the state and federal statutes, your employer must follow the law that is most generous to you.)

What follows is a summary of the federal law. Refer to **Table 10** for any provisions of your state law that may be more beneficial to you.

Effective Date: The Act took effect for most employees on August 5, 1993. If you were subject to a collective bargaining agreement that was in effect on that date, however, the Act did not take effect for you until either the agreement expired or on February 5, 1994, whichever came earlier.

Is my employer covered? Any employer who employed fifty or more workers in the current or preceding calendar year is covered by the Act. (The fifty or more workers can work either at a single worksite or within a 75-mile radius.)

Am I eligible to take leave? You are eligible for leave if you have worked for your present employer for at least a year and have worked at least 1,250 hours in the year leading up to the date you are taking the leave.

What reasons qualify me to take leave? You can request leave for the birth and care of a child, the adoption of a child (or placement of a foster child in your care), the care of your spouse, child, or parent who has a serious health condition, or for your own serious health condition if it makes you unable to perform your job. (The law defines a serious health condition as an illness, injury, impairment, or physical or mental condition that involves inpatient care or continuing treatment by a health care provider.)

How long a leave can I take? You are entitled to take up to twelve work weeks of leave during any twelve-month period. Note, however, that your employer does not have to let you take your leave intermittently, or on a reduced schedule basis unless it's medically necessary. If your employer does agree to let you take intermittent leave or work a reduced schedule (or it is proven to be medically necessary), he may require you to transfer temporarily to an available alternate position for which you are qualified and which has equivalent pay and benefits and better accommodates these recurring periods of leave.

Note (FMLA vs. ADA): If you are eligible for leave under both the **Family and Medical Leave Law** and the **Americans with Disabilities Act** (as a reasonable accommodation of your disability), your employer must let you take an indefinite leave in accordance with the ADA. (See Chapter 5: Discrimination and Related Issues.)

How long before taking leave do I have to notify my employer?
Where the need to take the leave is foreseeable based on the birth, adoption, or foster care placement of a child, or the medical treatment of you or your spouse, child, or parent, you are required to give your employer thirty days' notice of your intent to take leave. If for some reason the date of birth, placement, or medical treatment would require your leave to begin in less than thirty days, you have to give as much notice as you can. If the leave is for foreseeable medical treatment—whether for you, or your spouse, child, or parent—you have to make a reasonable effort to schedule the treatment so as not to disrupt your employer's business unduly.

Once you have notified your employer of your need for leave, your employer has to inform you in writing, within two business days, of your obligations under the law and what will happen if you don't meet them.

Can my employer make me take vacation days or sick days instead of family and medical leave? In a word, "Yes." Your employer may require you to substitute (or you may choose to substitute) any accrued vacation, personal, or sick leave you may have coming for any part of the twelve-week period you request for family and medical leave. If your employer is going to require you to make the substitution, he has to notify you in writing by your next payday.

Do I have to provide proof of my need to take leave? If you request leave for a medical reason, your employer may require certification by a health care provider of the date on which the serious health condition began, the probable duration of the condition, and appropriate medical facts regarding the condition. If the leave is requested for the care of your spouse, child, or parent, the certification must contain a statement that you are needed to care for the individual and an estimate of the length of time you will be needed for that care. If the leave is for your own serious health condition, it must contain a statement that the condition makes you unable to perform your job. (If you are requesting intermittent leave or a reduced work schedule, the health care provider's statement must specify the medical necessity of such a schedule.) **Note:** If your employer doesn't believe you, or questions the validity of the certification you provide, he may require you, at company expense, to get a second opinion from a health care provider designated or approved by the company (but not regularly employed by the company) to verify any information in the original certification.

What happens if my spouse and I work for the same employer?
The answer to this question depends on the reason the leave is needed. If the leave is for your own illness, or your spouse or child's illness, each of you is allowed to take the full twelve-week leave. However, if the leave is for the birth, foster care placement, or adoption of a child, or for the illness of a parent, your employer can limit the amount of leave to a total of twelve weeks between the two of you.

What happens to my medical insurance while I'm on leave?
Nothing. Your employer has to continue to cover you under his group health plan while you are on family and medical leave the same as if you had continued working as usual. Note, however, that if you don't return to work after your leave expires, your employer has the right to come after you for the premiums the company paid while you were on leave. That is, unless the reason you didn't return to work was because of your own serious health condition, or that of your spouse, child, or parent, or other circumstances beyond your control.

Warning: If you are eligible for leave under both the **Family and Medical Leave Law** and the **Americans with Disabilities Act,** all things being equal, you may be better off taking family and medical leave, since under the **Family and Medical Leave Law** your employer has to continue providing your health insurance while you are on leave and under the ADA he does not (unless other employees' insurance is continued under similar circumstances). (See Chapter 5: Discrimination and Related Issues.)

Can my employer make me report in while I'm on leave? Your employer may require you to update him periodically during your leave on your medical status and your intention to return to work.

What happens when I return to work? When you return to work after family and medical leave, you must be returned to the same job you held when your leave began, or to an equivalent position with equivalent benefits, pay, and other terms and conditions of employment. This means you are entitled to all accumulated seniority, retirement, fringe benefits, and other service credits you had when your leave started. However, you are not entitled to accrue seniority or other benefits while you are on leave.

If you took leave because of your own serious health condition, your employer can require you to provide certification from a health care provider that you are able to resume work, but only if the employer has a policy which requires all employees returning from medical leave to do the same.

Warning: Under the **Americans with Disabilities Act,** you must be returned to the same (not just an equivalent) job. So, if this is a concern and you are eligible for leave under both the **Family and Medical Leave Law** and the ADA, you would be better off taking leave under the ADA. (See Chapter 5: Discrimination and Related Issues.)

Note (highly paid employees): If you are among the highest paid 10% of your company's employees within a seventy-five-mile radius of the site where you work, your employer may refuse to return you to the same or equivalent job if to do so would cause the company "substantial and grievous economic injury." In that case, your employer would have to notify you of his intent not to return you to your regular job as soon as he determined that such an economic injury would occur; and he would have to give you the opportunity to return to your regular job when you are so notified.

Does my employer have to tell me about the law? Employers are required to post a notice summarizing the main provisions of the law. The poster must be put up in a conspicuous place, such as on a bulletin board where notices to employees and applicants are normally posted.

How does state law fit into all this? If your state has its own family and medical leave law (see **Table 10**), your employer is required to comply with both the state and federal laws. As in all such situations, where there are inconsistencies between provisions of the state and federal laws, your employer has to follow the law that is most generous to you. For example, the Connecticut **Family and Medical Leave Law** allows eligible employees to take up to sixteen weeks of leave in any two-year period. Thus, though it is yet to be tested in court, it appears that Connecticut employers subject to both laws may, under some circumstances, have to allow eligible employees up to twenty-eight weeks of leave in a two-year period. That is, an employee could take sixteen weeks of leave under the state law in year one, and in year two be entitled to twelve additional weeks of leave under the federal law.

Trendsetter? In 1998 Massachusetts enacted a law called the Small Necessities Leave Act, which provides 24 hours of leave per year (in addition to the leave available under federal law) to participate in a child's school activities, such as attending parent-teacher conferences and interviewing for a new school, or to take a child or elderly relative for routine medical or dental appointments.

How about confidentiality? Your employer must keep your family and medical records strictly confidential.

MILITARY LEAVE

The federal law has for some time protected the employment rights of members of the military reserve and national guard. But it was 1990–91's Persian Gulf War that put reservists' employment rights squarely on the front page. It was also the huge call-up of reserves during that conflict that pointed out some flaws in the previous laws that covered non-career military personnel. The **Vietnam Era Veterans' Readjustment Act** and the **Veterans Reemployment Act,** the two laws that provided most of the protection for employee/reservists, have since been superseded by the **Uniformed Services Employment and Reemployment Rights Act** (USERRA), which took effect in late 1994.

USERRA, as did the prior laws, covers virtually all employee/reservists, whether their service is voluntary or required, and

(Continued on p. 127)

TABLE 10

STATE FAMILY AND MEDICAL LEAVE LAWS*

California *Coverage:* Employers of 50 or more workers. *Eligibility:* Employees who have worked for employer for at least a year. Requires reasonable notice, where possible; proof, where requested by employer; use of vacation or other leave, where possible. *Requirements:* Up to 4 months of unpaid leave in a 2-year period for care of a seriously ill family member; 5 months for maternity leave. *Other:* All employers must give up to 5 months of maternity leave and time off to attend teacher conference for suspended child. Employers of 25 or more workers must give up to 4 hours per child for school visits, grades K-12.

Colorado *Coverage:* All employers. *Requirements:* Leave for adoption (except for the adoption of the child of the employee's spouse) must be granted on the same basis as for birth of a child, including extended leave for adoption of a seriously ill or handicapped child.

Connecticut *Coverage:* Employers of 75 or more. *Eligibility:* Must have worked for employer for at least 1 year, including at least 1,000 hours during the year preceding leave. *Requirements:* Up to 12 weeks of unpaid leave during first year the law applies to the employer, up to 16 weeks in any subsequent 2-year period for birth or adoption of a child, or serious illness of the employee, or employee's child, spouse, or parent. May be offset against other leave entitlement. Must be fully reinstated with full benefits.

District of Columbia *Coverage:* Employers of 20 or more workers. *Eligibility:* Must have worked for employer for at least 1 year, including at least 1,000 hours during the year preceding leave. Highest-paid 5 employees (employers of fewer than 50) or highest-paid 10% of employees (employers of 50 or more) do not have to be eligible for leave. *Requirements:* Up to 16 weeks of unpaid leave during any 2-year period for birth or adoption of a child, for the employee's serious illness, or for the serious illness of employee's child, spouse (including domestic partners), or parent. Must be kept on employer's health insurance plan and fully reinstated upon return to work.

Hawaii *Coverage:* Employers of 100 or more. *Eligibility:* Must have worked for employer for at least 6 months. *Requirements:* Up to 4 weeks of unpaid leave per year for birth, adoption, or to care for seriously ill child, spouse, or parent.

---

*In general, employees are entitled to be returned to the same or equivalent job, status, pay, and benefits upon return from leave. Most employers must continue to provide benefits while the employee is on leave, though often the employee must pay for them. Penalties for violation include full reinstatement, lost wages, reimbursement for any financial loss suffered as a result and, in some cases, suit for damages. For details, contact your state department of labor.

†The above table outlines the requirements for private employers. A number of states also have family and medical leave requirements for state employees.

TABLE 10 *(Continued)*

Illinois *Coverage:* Employers of 50 or more workers. *Requirements:* Up to 8 hours leave per year (no more than 4 hours at a time) for school conferences that cannot be scheduled during non-work hours.

Kentucky *Coverage:* All employers. *Eligibility:* Employees must request leave in writing. *Requirements:* Up to 6 weeks of unpaid leave for adoption of a child under age 7.

Maine *Coverage:* Employers of 25 or more. *Eligibility:* Must have worked for employer for at least 1 year. Must give 30 days' notice, except in cases of medical emergency. Medical certificate, at employer's request. *Requirements:* Up to 10 weeks of unpaid leave during 2-year period for birth or adoption of a child, or serious illness of the employee, or employee's child, spouse, or parent.

Massachusetts *Coverage:* Employers of 6 or more workers. *Eligibility:* Women who have worked for employer full-time for at least 3 months. *Requirements:* Up to 8 weeks of unpaid leave for birth or adoption.

Minnesota *Coverage:* All employers (Up to 16 hours a year for school conferences that cannot be scheduled outside work hours); employers of 21 or more (birth, adoption, or illness of a child). *Eligibility:* Must have worked for employer for at least 1 year, averaging at least 20 hours per week. Notice of leave may be required, where leave can be anticipated. At least 2 weeks' notice required before returning from a leave of more than 1 month. *Requirements:* Up to 6 weeks of unpaid leave for birth, adoption, or serious illness of a child (including adopted child). Up to 16 hours of unpaid leave per year for children's school conferences that cannot be scheduled around work time.

Nevada *Coverage:* All employers. *Requirements:* Must be allowed to leave work for school conferences that cannot be scheduled outside work hours, and for family emergencies involving the employee's child that occur during work hours.

New Jersey *Coverage:* Employers of 50 or more workers. *Eligibility:* Must have worked at least 1 year for employer. Highest-paid 5 percent of salaried workers or 7 highest-paid salaried workers (whichever is greater) do not have to be eligible for leave. Leave not required if it would cause undue economic hardship on employer. Notice required. Medical certificate, at employer's request. Leave must be scheduled, if possible, so as not to unduly disrupt employer's business. *Requirements:* Up to 12 weeks of unpaid leave during any 2-year period for birth or adoption of a child, or for serious illness of child, spouse, or parent.

New York *Coverage:* All employers. *Requirements:* Leave for adoption must be granted on the same basis as for birth of a child, except for the adoption of a child of at least school age. Exception does not include handicapped children under 18.

TABLE 10 *(Continued)*

Oregon *Coverage:* Employers of 25 or more workers (birth or adoption), 50 or more workers (serious illness). *Eligibility:* Must have worked for employer for at least 90 days (birth or adoption); at least 180 days of at least 25 hours a week (serious illness). Seasonal and temporary workers hired for less than 6 months ineligible. Thirty days' notice required or employer may reduce or delay leave by 3 weeks. *Requirements:* Up to 12 weeks of unpaid leave in a 2-year period for birth or adoption of a child under 6, or the illness of a child, spouse, or parent.

Rhode Island *Coverage:* Employers of 50 or more (private); and city, town, and municipal agencies that employ 30 or more. *Eligibility:* Must have worked for employer for at least 1 year, averaging at least 30 hours a week. Thirty days' notice required, except in cases of medical emergency. *Requirements:* Up to 13 weeks of unpaid leave within 2-year period for birth or adoption of a child, or for serious illness of employee, or employee's child, spouse, parent, or in-law.

Tennessee *Coverage:* Employers of 100 or more. *Eligibility:* Women who have worked for employer for at least 1 year. Thirty days' notice required, with statement of intent to return, except in cases of medical emergency. *Requirements:* Up to 4 months of unpaid leave for pregnancy or childbirth; up to 30 days for adoption.

Vermont *Coverage:* Employers of 10 or more workers (birth or adoption); 15 or more (family leave). *Eligibility:* Must have worked for employer for at least 1 year, including an average of at least 30 hours a week. *Requirements:* Up to 12 weeks of unpaid leave in 1 year.

Washington *Coverage:* Employers of 100 or more (family leave); all employers (medical leave and equal leave for adoption and childbirth). *Eligibility:* Must have worked for employer for at least 1 year, averaging at least 35 hours a week. Employers may require employees to use other accrued leave toward family and medical leave. Employer may refuse leave for up to 10 percent of work force classified as key personnel. Thirty days' notice required (birth or adoption); 14 days' notice (care of terminally ill child), except in cases of medical emergency; or employer may reduce or delay leave by 3 weeks. Medical certificate, at employer's request. *Requirements:* Up to 12 weeks of unpaid leave (in addition to disability-related pregnancy leave) during any 2-year period for birth or adoption of a child under 6, or to care for terminally ill child under 18. Employee may take sick leave for a child's illness on same basis as for him- or herself. Leave for adoption of a child under 6 must be granted on the same basis as for birth of a child, including extended leave for adoption of a seriously ill or handicapped child.

Wisconsin *Coverage:* Employers of 50 or more. *Eligibility:* Must have worked for employer for at least 1 year (at least 1,000 hours during the year). *Requirements:* Up to 6 weeks of unpaid leave during any 1-year period for birth or adoption of a child, or for serious illness of child, spouse, or parent. Up to 2 weeks of unpaid leave per year for employee's own illness.

(Continued from p. 123)

whether they work full- or part-time, are employed in the public or private sector, and no matter what type of business the employer runs or how many workers he employs. And the law protects reservists whether they are required to attend periodic reserve meetings or drills during work time or are actually called to active duty for an extended period.

Meetings, Training, and Drills

Employers have to allow employees leave of absence during work hours to attend required military reserve or national guard meetings, training sessions, and drills.

Call to Active Duty

Employers have to keep reservists' jobs open when they are called to active duty and reinstate them when they complete their service. The law specifically addresses the following questions:

- ☞ **Request for leave of absence:** Employees who are called to active duty must give their employer advance notice, either oral or written, of the need to take a leave of absence, except where notice would be impossible, or unreasonable, or is precluded by military necessity. Not giving advance notice could jeopardize a reservist's reemployment rights. (**Note:** A congressional report indicates that last-minute notice, when notice could reasonably have been given earlier, should be viewed unfavorably.)
- ☞ **Pay:** Employers do not have to pay employee/reservists during the time they are on active duty.

   Note: Though employers are not required to pay employee/reservists while on active duty, many larger companies do offer at least to make up the difference between the employees' military pay and regular wages. As with all benefits, however, they cannot discriminate. If they pay any active-duty reservists, they must pay them all on the same basis.
- ☞ **Insurance:** Employers do not have to maintain employee/reservists' medical insurance while they are on active duty. (The military covers reservists'—and their dependents'—medical insurance while they are on active duty.)

Note: Employers that don't cover reservists called to active duty have to offer them the chance to continue their insurance coverage at their own expense, but at group rates. (See COBRA, above.) If a reservist's employer-sponsored insurance is cut off while he or she is on active duty, the employer must reinstate it immediately upon their return to work, with no waiting period.

☛ **Pension plans:** Military service cannot be considered as an interruption of continuous employment for the purposes of vesting requirements of pension benefits. (See Retirement Plans below.)

☛ **Vacation time:** An employer cannot require an employee/reservist to use earned vacation time while on active duty.

Return from Active Duty

Notice of return to work: In order not to jeopardize their reemployment rights, a returning reservist must under most circumstances (i.e.: unless it would be impossible or unreasonable) give his or her employer the following amount of notice of the intention to return to work:

- *Military service of less than 31 days:* No later than the start of the first full regularly scheduled work period that starts at least 8 hours after discharge;
- *Military service of 31 to 180 days:* Within 14 days of discharge;
- *Military service of more than 180 days:* Within 90 days of discharge.

   Not giving the required notice does not mean the reservist loses all rights to reemployment. However, the reservist does lose the protection of USERRA. That means that he or she must be treated the same way the employer treats any employee who is absent from scheduled work, whether by company policy or general practice.

Reinstatement: An employer must reinstate an employee who returns from active military duty as soon as reasonably possible. Reinstatement must be to the same or an equivalent job at the same level of seniority, status, and pay. Reservists returning from active duty have up to ninety days after the date of their discharge to apply for reemployment (or less for short periods of service. See "Notice of return to work," above). They *must* be reinstated if:

☞ Their civilian job was other than temporary. (According to court decisions, a "temporary" job is one that isn't expected to continue indefinitely. Thus, part-timers and seasonal workers employed continuously or regularly can expect to be reinstated just as full-timers can.)

☞ The total length of their active service, adding the most recent and previous absences, was five years or less. (There are a number of exceptions to this requirement, including where the individual's initial period of required service was over five years.)

☞ They were honorably discharged.

RETIREMENT PLANS

There are a series of extremely complex laws that govern your right to participate in your employer's retirement plan, if he has one, and when you acquire an unqualified right to the contributions made to that plan, either by you or by your employer. (I'll try to simplify the discussion of them as much as possible.) Basic among these laws is the **Employee Retirement Income Security Act** (ERISA). ERISA also requires your employer to file certain government disclosure forms and tax reports to make sure the retirement plan stays on the up-and-up and that your employer isn't using your retirement money to fund his Cancun hideaway. But the government's tight reins (particularly those held by the Internal Revenue Service) are your employer's problem. Your biggest concerns are your right to participate in the plan and your right to actually get the money you and your employer have put into it over the years should you leave your job for any reason. (The potential—indeed, the temptation—to abuse retirement plans would be obvious if, for example, you forfeited your right to contributions made to the plan on your behalf when you left your job for any reason. If that was permitted, your employer could just fire you on the eve of your retirement and keep the money!)

Once again, as with most fringe benefits, company sponsorship of a retirement plan is purely at the discretion of your employer. Your company doesn't have to participate in a retirement plan. But there are obvious advantages to participation for both employers and employees. Companies do it to attract good workers and to provide an incentive for those good workers to stay with the company for the long haul. They also get certain tax advantages, since their contributions to the plan are tax-deductible and the plan's earnings are tax-exempt. Employees, on the other hand, have a means to save for those fabled "golden" years. Their contributions and the earnings of the retirement plan's investments are deferred until they actually start receiving the benefits after retirement—at which time they will likely be in a lower tax bracket. And they also get a boost in their ultimate benefits if their employer contributes to the fund on their behalf, which most employers do to varying degrees.

Choice of Plans

Employers have various plans to select from. Rarely do you, the employee, have a choice in the matter. Employers generally select a plan on the basis of obvious considerations: how much it is likely to cost them in both the short term and the long term, and how much risk they are undertaking in the profitability of the investments the funds are put into.

Even though your active role in the plan is usually limited to forking over your money, brief descriptions of some of the more popularly used plans follow because you should know what's happening to your money . . . and surveys show that, in the area of retirement plans, you don't.

The two basic types of plans are the more traditional "defined benefit" plans, which commit employers to pay a certain benefit amount when you retire, and the increasingly popular "defined contribution" plans, which commit your employer to contributing a certain amount each year. Defined *benefit* plans have fallen out of favor because they require employers to pay out a certain amount when you retire regardless of how the investments did during your working life. If the investments falter, your employer has to make up the difference. Defined *contribution* plans, on the other hand, guarantee a specific contribution from your employer, which can be tied to profits. If profits drop, so does your employer's obligation to pay into your retirement fund. It adds up to less risk for your employer.

Specific defined contribution retirement plans include:

Profit-Sharing Plans, in which a designated percentage of the company profits are added to employee contributions, which go into a trust fund that will finance retirement benefits. The portion of your employer's contribution to the plan that goes into your individual account is usually pegged to your wages.

Stock-Option Plans, which either give employees stock in the company or give them the opportunity to buy shares. Again, how many shares you are either given or allowed to purchase usually depends on your income level.

401(k) Plans (named after Section 401(k) of the Internal Revenue Code, under which they are allowed), which give employees the choice of deferring payment of part of their wages until retirement. The deferred amount, which some employers match at least in part, is then invested for retirement. These 401(k)s have become especially favored by smaller companies because the investment risk is shifted to the employees, since they usually are given a voice in selecting how their funds will be invested. In a sense, everyone wins: You and your employer both get tax advantages, you for deferring part of your income, and your employer for matching your contributions. In addition, you have a voice in how your own money will be invested, and your employer has less to worry about if the investments go bad. (At least 70 percent of the company's employees have to participate in the plan for the employer's contributions to be tax deductible, which gives employers an added incentive to contribute. The more the company puts in, the more attractive the plan will be to potential participants.)

Individual Retirement Accounts (IRAs), which let you contribute a maximum amount ($2,000 for individuals; $2,250 if you have a spouse who doesn't work) to a tax-deferred account. Though we usually think of IRAs as personal retirement plans, they can also be sponsored by your employer.

Participation in the Plan

Once an employer sets up a pension or retirement plan, he cannot pick and choose who will be allowed to participate in it. Under most circumstances, you must be allowed to participate in your employer's plan if you:

☞ Are over twenty-one years old. And,

☞ Have worked for the company for a year. (To get credit for a year of service with the company, you must have worked at least one thousand hours in the previous twelve months.)

Exceptions: There are a couple of exceptions to the basic requirements for participation. The first applies to all employers: An employer can require employees to be with the company for two years to be eligible for participation in the plan if, when they join the plan, their rights to their benefits becomes 100 percent vested immediately. (See the discussion of vesting below.) The second exception applies only to tax-exempt educational institutions, which can require employees to be twenty-six years old to participate.

Note (older workers): Generally, older newly hired workers cannot be excluded from participation in pension or retirement plans. (The single exception is with defined *benefit* plans, which can exclude newly hired workers who are within five years of normal retirement age.)

Vesting (Absolute Right to Accrued Benefits)

Once you become an official participant in your employer's pension or retirement plan, the first important question is, What happens to the contributions to my individual retirement fund if I leave the company's employ before I retire?

The answer involves something called "vesting."

"Vesting" refers to the point when your right to the contributions made to your fund become yours absolutely. If you leave the company, they leave with you—in one form or another. That is, you may or may not be able to take the cash, but you retain a nonforfeitable right to those benefits when you retire—whatever company you ultimately retire from.

Now, in most retirement plans both you and your employer are making contributions. Let's consider your vesting rights in both. First, your own contributions. You are 100 percent vested in your own contributions immediately. That is, you own those funds and any earnings made by those funds absolutely, from the first time you make a contribution. Period.

The real question is when your rights to your employer's contributions to your individual fund become vested. That's a bit more complicated, especially since the rules changed for plan years beginning in 1989. Here's the scoop:

Vesting for Plan Years Beginning in 1989 or After:

☞ If your employer's plan requires you to work for the company for more than one year before you can participate in the plan (remember, it can't require you to work for him for more than two years to be eligible to participate), you own 100 percent of all contributions and accruals immediately.

☞ If you are eligible to participate at age twenty-one or after working for your company for a year, the plan has two vesting options:

- You become 100 percent vested after five years with the company; or
- You become 20 percent vested after three years, and 20 percent more after each additional year with the company. So, vesting is more gradual until you are fully vested after seven years.

Vesting for Plan Years That Began in 1988 or Before: Some of you may belong to plans you were eligible for prior to 1989. For your information, much more gradual vesting was allowed then. The basic requirement was that employees be at least 50 percent vested after ten years and 100 percent vested after fifteen years. However, these more gradual vesting schedules are no longer available to employers. The result is that employees have a legal right to the funds sooner than they used to.

Note (leaving before retirement): If you leave your job before retirement with a vested interest (Oh, that's what that means!) in your retirement account, you may be entitled to receive the accrued amount in a lump-sum payment, which, of course, would be taxable. However, many plans make you wait until you actually retire before paying you the benefits. So, though the money may be yours, you may have to wait until you retire to get it.

"Breaks in Service"

What happens if you leave your job before you are eligible to participate in your employer's retirement plan, or before you are fully vested, and you subsequently return? Do you have to start all over again? Not as long as you return to work within five years. If you do, you retain credit for all time you previously put in toward participation in the plan or acquiring vesting rights.

Note (maternity and paternity leave): When you take time off your job for maternity or paternity leave, not only do you retain credit already built up toward participation and vesting, you must actually be given credit for the time you are on leave just the same as if you were working during that time. (The limit on earning credit while you are on maternity or paternity leave is 501 hours. Why 501 hours, who knows, but after that you no longer have to be given credit toward participation and vesting for the time you take off.)

Other Fringe Benefits

Of course, there are many other types of fringe benefits besides health insurance and retirement plans offered by employers who can afford them. There are life and disability insurance policies, tuition grants, employee assistance programs to help with such things as drug and alcohol problems and mental disorders, child care programs, prepaid legal plans, and severance pay plans, to name some of the more widely used. These are all so-called employee welfare plans that are subject to ERISA and its many reporting, claims, termination of benefits, and enforcement requirements.

Employers normally make fringe benefit programs available to all employees, since making benefits available only to highly compensated employees, for example, would negate any tax advantages the employer (and the employee) would otherwise gain from contributing to the program.

WHAT TO DO: If you suspect you are being unfairly deprived of fringe benefits in any way—for example, you are not covered by your company's group health insurance plan, or you weren't offered the opportunity to continue that insurance coverage after termination from your job; or you have worked long enough to be eligible for participation in your company's retirement plan but have yet to be offered that right; or you leave the company and are not apprised of the amount of your accumulated vested funds and how and when they are payable; or you are denied equal rights to participate in any other benefits offered by your employer:

☞ Approach your employer (or the person at your company who is in charge of administering benefits) for an explanation of your situation. In the case of insurance or retirement matters, he may refer you to the insurance carrier or retirement plan administrator. (He should be able to give you a specific name and telephone number.) But, in any case, someone should be able to give you a satisfactory answer to your question. If he or she can't—or won't . . .

☞ In the case of insurance matters, contact your state insurance commissioner.

☞ If your question concerns your company's retirement plan, contact the U.S. Labor Department or the U.S. Treasury Department, which have joint responsibility for administering ERISA. (**Warning:** Dealing with one bureaucracy is difficult and frustrating enough; two of them can make you suicidal. Large doses of persistence are likely to be required. DO NOT TAKE NO FOR AN ANSWER! If you are shuttled back and forth without getting an answer to your question, call your state senator's or representative's office for help cutting the bureaucratic red tape. Someone at their office will usually be glad to give you the information you request. After all, you elected them. They are listed in the Blue Pages of your phone book under "United States," normally under the subheading "United States Congress Representatives," by name and district. In any event, both the U.S. Secretary of Labor— and you, as a plan participant—have the right to take your employer to court to enforce the provisions of ERISA as they relate to your retirement, pension, or other "employee welfare plan."

For answers to questions about other benefits, call or write your state department of labor.

SUMMARY

Though it is true that it is entirely up to your employer whether or not he will provide most fringe benefits, he certainly doesn't decide to do it out of the goodness of his heart. He does it to attract you and other good workers away from the competition. And once he promises that he will provide benefits, he can't just pull the rug out from under you. He is then, at least to an extent, required to provide them. Because he promised them, those fringe benefits, in effect, become part of your compensation package and must be "paid" to you when due, just like your wages.

For example, in most cases, though your employer may cancel his group insurance coverage for all employees, he must give you adequate notice of cancellation. If he has a practice of paying employees for accrued and unused sick leave days, he must pay you for them according to company practice. If he has a retirement or pension plan, you must be given an unforfeitable right to the accrued funds he has contributed to the plan according to the plan's vesting schedule. In short, you acquire an inalienable right to promised fringe benefits and your employer has a legal obligation to "pay" them.

5

Discrimination and Related Issues

Okay, let's be honest: Some of you skipped the first four chapters and started out right here, didn't you? Well, as I said at the outset, this book is designed so you don't *have* to read it cover to cover. And, unless you are an average-looking white agnostic heterosexual male of no discernible national origin who is under forty and has no handicap or even something that could be perceived as a handicap, this section deals with your situation. Because unless you are a nonhandicapped, agnostic, born-in-America white male under forty, you are in a so-called protected group. You are female. You are African American, Hispanic, Oriental, Native American, or a member of another minority group. You are over forty. You or your family are natives of Italy, Germany, Japan, England, Ireland, or anywhere else. You are Jewish, Hindu, Buddhist, Muslim, Christian Scientist, Jehovah's Witness, or maybe even Catholic or Protestant. You are in a wheelchair, wear a prosthesis, have a bad back or a communicable disease—even AIDS. Or you may be "More Than One of the Above."

The "bottom line," as they say, is that today fully 70 percent of us are members of at least one protected group. (And that's not even considering the issue of *reverse* discrimination, which means we also can't be discriminated against because we are *not* members of a protected group.) All of which presents an obvious problem for employers, who are prohibited by various civil rights laws from discriminating against any employee because he or she is (or is not) a member of a protected group.

What with the passage of the **Civil Rights Act of 1991**, along with the Clarence Thomas–Anita Hill "affair," President Bill Clinton's "indiscretions," and other more recent headline-making events, it's no wonder you skipped to this chapter—even if the *other* 30 percent of you just want to be sure *not* to discriminate against or harass the rest of us.

There are a veritable gaggle of laws out there that protect us from various forms of on-the-job discrimination and harassment. Among them are **Title VII of the Civil Rights Act of 1964**, the **Civil Rights Act of 1991, Title 42 of the United States Code, Section 1981**, the **Americans with Disabilities Act of 1990**, the **Age Discrimination in Employment Act**, the **Equal Pay Act of 1963**, and the **First Amendment to the U.S. Constitution**. There are, of course, others, but these are the ones that protect us in most employment situations. And, obviously, some of us are protected by more than one of them.

Let's have a look. Then, after we've determined whether you may have a discrimination claim, we'll briefly check out the procedure for filing a complaint with the Equal Employment Opportunity Commission (EEOC) and what happens to that claim once you've filed it. (For details, see Chapter 11: I'm Getting Screwed; So What Can I Do about It?) And we'll also investigate other action you can take when you are being discriminated against.

So here we go, wading into the ever-more-treacherous waters of employment discrimination.

CIVIL RIGHTS

According to **Title VII of the Civil Rights Act of 1964**, as well as most state human rights laws, an employer may not refuse to hire you when you are applying for a job, and may not discriminate against you once you have one, because of your race, color, religion, sex, or national origin. Though the law applies only to employers who have at least fifteen employees, your state's human rights law has pretty much the same restrictions and many of them apply to smaller employers than does the federal law. See **Table 11**.

If you read the newspaper, you know that civil rights laws have undergone some major growing pains in recent years. The problems started in 1989, when the U.S. Supreme Court made a number of rulings that limited the ability of workers to sue successfully for

TABLE 11

STATE CIVIL RIGHTS LAW COVERAGE
(PRIVATE EMPLOYERS)*

State	Number of Employees	State	Number of Employees
Alabama	no state requirement	Montana	1 or more
Alaska	1 or more	Nebraska	15 or more
Arizona	15 or more	Nevada	15 or more
Arkansas	9 or more	New Hampshire	6 or more
California	5 or more†	New Jersey	1 or more
Colorado	1 or more	New Mexico	4 or more
Connecticut	3 or more	New York	4 or more
Delaware	4 or more	North Carolina	15 or more
Dist. of Columbia	1 or more	North Dakota	10 or more
Florida	15 or more	Ohio	4 or more
Georgia	no state requirement	Oklahoma	15 or more
Hawaii	1 or more	Oregon	1 or more
Idaho	5 or more	Pennsylvania	4 or more
Illinois	15 or more‡	Rhode Island	4 or more
Indiana	6 or more	South Carolina	15 or more
Iowa	1 or more	South Dakota	1 or more
Kansas	4 or more	Tennessee	8 or more
Kentucky	8 or more	Texas	15 or more
Louisiana	15 or more	Utah	15 or more
Maine	1 or more	Vermont	1 or more
Maryland	15 or more	Virginia	no state requirement§
Massachusetts	6 or more	Washington	8 or more
Michigan	1 or more	West Virginia	12 or more
Minnesota	1 or more	Wisconsin	1 or more
Mississippi	no state requirement	Wyoming	2 or more
Missouri	6 or more		

*The above table reflects coverage of state civil rights laws for private employers. Government employers are covered in most states. *Number of Employees* refers to the minimum size of work force required before the state civil rights law applies to an employer.
†15 or more in the case of a mental disability
‡1 or more in the case of a disability, or sexual harassment
§Though no minimum number of employees is specified, state laws give employees who work for employers with more than 5 but fewer than 15 employees the right to sue in state court for discriminatory dicharge.

employment discrimination. *Patterson v. McLean Credit Union,**perhaps the most dramatic of those decisions, narrowed the scope of the civil rights statute most often used to bring race discrimination complaints: **Title 42 of the United States Code, Section 1981.** In the *Patterson* decision the High Court ruled that the statute barred discrimination only in the formation of the employment contract (i.e., at the time you are hired, and in the kinds of promotion decisions where you are effectively being hired for a completely new job). That meant it did not protect you against harassment or against other discriminatory conduct by your employer (or your employer's agents or your coworkers) once you were on the job, or even against discriminatory firing.

Well, it didn't take Congress long to see that the effect of the Supreme Court decisions was to subvert their general intention in passing the civil rights law, which was to protect their constituents against all forms of racial discrimination in employment. Enter the **Civil Rights Act of 1991**, which was finally passed after much wrangling over whether it or previously proposed—and vetoed— bills would force employers into hiring quotas. Anyway, the long and short of it is that the new act simply restores the punch of the old act—with two key additional advantages to workers in several protected groups: the right to seek damages and the right to request a jury trial.

Damages

Under previous civil rights laws, only a worker claiming intentional discrimination based on race or ethnic background could make a claim for monetary damages. Damages awarded could be either compensatory, designed to compensate the worker for things like emotional pain and suffering and mental anguish; or punitive, which served to punish the employer for his wrongdoing. Of course, in an appropriate situation a worker could be awarded both compensatory and punitive damages. However, that was true only of a worker who was subjected to intentional racial or ethnic discrimination and sued under **Title 42 U.S. Code, Section 1981** or **1983.** If you happened to have been discriminated against because you were a woman, or because you were handicapped or because you were a member of a religious minority, you were limited to seeking

*109 Supreme Court 2363, 1989.

reinstatement to your old job (if you still wanted it) and whatever back pay you had lost.

Now, under the new civil rights law, anyone claiming to have been the victim of intentional employment discrimination can sue for damages. The only fly in the ointment is that the law limits the amount of damages that can be awarded to those suing for intentional sex, religious, and handicap discrimination according to the size of their employer's work force, based on the following formula:

☞ 15 to 100 employees: $50,000;
☞ 101 to 200 employees: $100,000;
☞ 201 to 500 employees: $200,000; and
☞ 501 or more employees: $300,000.

(**Note:** Victims of race and national origin discrimination can sue for damages with no limits. And victims of handicap discrimination may not be entitled to any damages at all if the employer attempted a reasonable accommodation of the person's handicap. Read on for more on handicap discrimination.)

In recent years a number of congressional committees have debated various bills that would eliminate the damage award limits in some cases in all lawsuits and in other cases in all lawsuits except those against smaller employers. The reasoning is that damage awards that would force small employers out of business would do more harm than good by displacing the very employees the law is designed to protect. (**Note:** Compensatory damages are available in all discrimination lawsuits, subject to the limits outlined above. However, punitive damages can be awarded only in cases where an employer "engaged in a discriminatory practice . . . with malice or with reckless indifference" to the complaining person's rights. In practice, that means he either purposefully violated your rights or showed such blatant disregard for your rights that it appears he didn't care.)

Jury Trials

The second bit of good news flowing from passage of the new act is that it allows anyone seeking damages for employment discrimination to opt for a jury trial. As with damage awards themselves, the law previously allowed only those suing for race or ethnic discrimination to ask for a jury trial. Women, the handicapped, and members of religious minorities were left standing before a judge whether they liked it or not.

It is these two developments—the ability to seek damages, along with the right to have your case heard by a jury—that have eliminated a lot of the guesswork for potential plaintiffs (that's you, my friends). They have already led to a significant increase in the number of lawsuits for employment discrimination. (And no doubt will lead to a significant increase in damage awards when these cases are finally settled or litigated.) That's because some of you who might not have sued when your lawyer said you couldn't recover damages may change your minds now that you can. And so may your lawyer, who will now have greater incentive to represent you with more money potentially in the offing. And the addition of a jury option can serve only to sweeten the pot, since juries have more of a tendency to make decisions based on emotion than judges do; and more often than not, their emotions will be sympathetic toward you rather than your big, bad, oppressive employer. (After all, when they're not heeding the call to jury duty, aren't most of them *employees,* too?)

On the other side of the coin, just knowing that damage awards and juries are available to plaintiffs, defense attorneys representing employers may be quicker to advise their clients to settle before trial to avoid just such a situation: a sympathetic jury and a potential damage award. Just think of the possibilities if Congress eliminates the cap on damages!

DISCRIMINATION GENERALLY

These days most employers are enlightened enough (they have either a social conscience or an attorney) that they won't purposefully discriminate against you in violation of the law. However, there are more subtle ways to discriminate. You don't have to say, "We don't hire blacks," or "We don't hire women to do that particular job because _____" (fill in the blank with any antiquated stereotype), or "You're too old to work here anymore."

Your employer may treat you differently as an individual than he treats other employees (so-called disparate treatment). He can have a business policy or practice that affects the entire protected group of which you are a member differently than it affects members of other groups ("adverse impact"). He may continue a policy or practice which looked at by itself may seem innocent enough, but which taken in the context of his workplace has the actual result of continuing past discrimination ("perpetuating discrimination"). He may use a hiring or promotion practice that results in the hiring or promotion of fewer members of your protected group than other groups (in their relation to the number of qualified members of each group in the local labor pool), which is referred to as a statistical imbalance. Or he may fail to take reasonable steps to adapt his workplace, business practices, or policies to members of your protected group when he is legally required to do so ("accommodation"). The latter normally occurs in the case of religious practices or observances, or physical or mental handicaps, whereas the others normally involve race or sex discrimination.

Disparate Treatment

There are three key questions you have to ask yourself before you start thinking about accusing your employer of discrimination, and bringing a lawsuit against him or filing a complaint with the EEOC. That goes for all forms of discrimination: race, sex, national origin, religious, handicap, and age. Those three all-important questions are:

☞ Am I a member of a protected group because of my race, sex, religious affiliation, national origin, physical or mental handicap, age, or sexual orientation?
☞ Am I being treated differently from other "similarly situated" employees? ("Similarly situated" means that they do the same or similar work as you do.)
☞ Is it *because* I'm black, female, over forty, handicapped, or a member of any other protected group?

For example, you are a woman who is paid less than a male contemporary who performs essentially the same job. (Also, see **Equal Pay Act** on p. 156.) If it is solely because you are a woman, that is discrimination. But if the man is paid more because he is more qualified or better educated, it may not be. (Unless that is simply a "pretext" used by your employer to get away with paying the man more than he pays you. See below.) Or maybe you are black and were disciplined more severely for an infraction of work rules than a white fellow worker was. Again, if it is because you are black and he is white, that is discrimination. But if it is because of some other valid reason, like this is your second offense or you have been warned for many other previous rule infractions of other types, it may not be.

So, are you in a protected group? Are you being treated differently than similarly situated employees? And is it because you are a member of that group? If the answer to all of these questions is yes, then you may have a valid basis for a discrimination complaint. For example, the only woman teacher in a college art department (and one of the oldest faculty members, to boot) made a case for disparate treatment by showing it was because of those reasons she was assigned to courses she didn't want, wasn't given adequate supplies, and was the only teacher whose class enrollment was monitored.*

Adverse Impact

There are, of course, other more subtle ways your employer can discriminate against you. One such form of discrimination occurs when the effect of a company policy or work rule, even when the rule appears on its face to be impartial, falls more heavily on a protected group of workers than on other workers. And these are the types of cases we see more and more of in the courts. They involve situations where an employer either acted out of ignorance of the effect of a policy on a protected group, or simply continued a perhaps long-time practice, which resulted in limiting employment opportunities for minorities.

Take something as seemingly benign as a restaurant's policy against employees wearing beards, a policy presumably invoked for sanitary reasons. Well, a Domino's Pizza franchise had exactly such a policy. And a federal court of appeals found that the policy discriminated against blacks because of a common skin disorder suffered by black males. Statistics show that the disease, with the formidable name pseudofolliculitis barbae, affects approximately 50 percent of all black males, half of them so severely that they can't shave. Thus, according to the court decision, the policy had an adverse impact on blacks, since it "effectively excludes almost 25 percent of the potential black male work force from employment," and it did not similarly exclude white males.†

---

*Sischo-Nownejad v. Merced College District, U.S. Court of Appeals, 9th Circuit, 1991.
†Bradley v. Pizzaco of Nebraska, Inc., dba Domino's Pizza, U.S. Court of Appeals, 8th Circuit, No. 89-2271NE, 1991.

Other policies which may have an adverse impact on a protected group might be rules that require employees in a certain job to have a college education, when the requirement isn't really necessary to perform the job in question. Such a policy would tend to affect minorities to a greater extent than whites. Or to screen out anyone with an arrest record, no matter what their other qualifications might be, again because such a policy would impact minorities—negatively—to a greater degree than whites. Even a residency requirement for local police officers, apparently neutral on its surface, can be discriminatory where it bears no relation to job performance if it tends to screen out a large minority population in a neighboring city.*

Having minimum height requirements has been found to adversely affect women and members of certain ethnic groups; and some preemployment tests used to measure physical strength have been ruled to discriminate against women when the tests are an invalid measure of the physical requirements of the job.

Making an Adverse Impact Case: There is a specific legal tango that must be danced by the participants (you and your employer) in order to make a case for adverse impact. It involves the question of whether or not a company policy or rule affects your protected group—adversely—to a greater degree than it does other groups; and if so, whether there is a valid reason for your employer to have such a rule or policy. (For example, the physical exam just mentioned may indeed turn out to be an accurate measure of what is required for the job.)

The procedure you must follow involves what is called the "burden of proof." The burden of proof starts with you. You must make a *prima facie* case of discrimination. That is, you have to show that what happened looks for all the world like discrimination. Again, using the physical exam example, let's say you prove that 95 percent of the men taking the exam pass and only 5 percent of the women taking the same exam pass. A court might say, "Okay, that taken alone looks like discrimination."

Then the burden of proof shifts to your employer to prove that there is a business necessity for having the physical exam. He may be able to show that there are, in fact, certain physical requirements for the job that the test accurately measures.

*Newark Branch, NAACP v. Town of Harrison, U.S. Court of Appeals, 3rd Circuit, No. 90-5897, 1991.

That done, the burden shifts back to you to show that the examination requirement is a pretext for discrimination. That, for example, the test was instituted for the purpose of screening out *you,* the only woman employee potentially eligible for the promotion, when you have shown yourself capable of performing all the necessary physical aspects of the job in question.

Perpetuating Discrimination

Your employer may no longer be actively guilty of a particular form of discrimination but may still have a policy or practice that has a tendency to continue, or perpetuate, discriminations of the past. You may have a discrimination claim even if that effect is inadvertent. For example, a policy of posting managerial openings only in departments occupied exclusively by white employees (or male employees) may amount to employment discrimination if there are no other avenues for women and minorities to hear about the job openings. Though the policy, taken alone, would not be discriminatory, taken in the context of the specific workplace, it is discriminatory because it effectively perpetuates a previous discrimination through a more subtle form of exclusion. The result of the policy is to continue to hold women (or minorities) back.

Statistical Imbalance

Your employer may also be guilty of discrimination if a specific practice the company uses has created a statistical imbalance in his work force to the disadvantage of the group of which you are a member. That is, if you are Hispanic and, based on the statistical makeup of the qualified local labor pool, you can show that a certain preemployment examination or interview process or other selection method used by your employer or prospective employer has a "disparate impact" on Hispanics (that is, puts Hispanics at a decided disadvantage in getting a job or being promoted), you may have a discrimination case against the company. And, in fact, another side effect of the **Civil Rights Act of 1991** is that it has made it easier for you to do exactly that. Another of the controversial 1989 U.S. Supreme Court decisions mentioned earlier in this chapter ruled that your employer had to show only a business *justification* for the practice that led to the imbalance in its work force.* However, the

*Ward's Cove Packing Co. v. Atonio, 49 FEP Cases 1519, 1989.

new civil rights law requires your employer to show a business *necessity* for the practice, a much higher standard.

Accommodation

Finally, an employer may be guilty of discriminating if he fails to accommodate a particular need you may have because of your membership in a specific protected group (which usually means you are handicapped, you practice a certain religion or, in some cases, you are pregnant). For details, see **Sex Discrimination, Handicap Discrimination,** and **Religious Discrimination,** below.

Now, let's take a look at specific types of discrimination in the context of the employer-employee relationship.

RACE DISCRIMINATION

U.S. equal rights laws provide specifically that "all persons within the jurisdiction of the United States shall have the same right in every State and Territory to . . . the full and equal benefit of all laws for the security of persons and property as is enjoyed by white citizens." (It is important to note that courts have specifically given whites standing to sue under the law where they allege racial discrimination.) In addition, both federal law (**Title VII of the Civil Rights Act of 1964**) and the human rights laws that exist in most states prohibit race discrimination. As previously mentioned, the federal antidiscrimination law applies to employers whose work forces have at least fifteen employees, while many state laws apply to smaller employers. See **Table 11.** In any event, for cases of racial discrimination, there is also **Title 42 of the United States Code, Section 1981,** which prohibits racial discrimination as well as discrimination against any ethnic minority; and it applies to all employers.

Of course, we all hope that no employer intentionally discriminates against members of any racial or ethnic group. But did you know that an employer can be guilty of racial bias even if he doesn't actively participate in the discriminatory practice? Or condone it? That's right. All that's necessary is that your employer knew or should have known (i.e., the only way he couldn't have known was to have his head in the sand) that your supervisor or even your coworkers were engaged in racist behavior and he did nothing to try to stop it. For example, he either actually heard other employees make racial comments or even heard *about* such comments being made, and yet did nothing to stop the behavior.

An employer's selection processes may not be racially biased, either. Any tests you have to pass to qualify for a job must be given to all prospective employees applying for the same job or job classification. The conditions they are given under must also be the same for everyone. And they must be free of all racial bias. In fact, to be safe, any employer who gives a preemployment test has to be sure it is designed to measure the examinee's qualifications for the job and nothing else.

Upon the complaint of someone who claims to have been adversely affected by a preemployment test because he or she is a minority, the EEOC will require the employer to "validate" the test, if it feels the test operates to weed out a disproportionate number of minorities. To validate a test, the employer must prove a relationship to actual job performance and also show that there isn't an alternate test that would accomplish the same result without having an adverse impact on minorities.

So it is important to restate that, though blatant race discrimination is obviously illegal (and may be subject to punitive damage awards against employers), so too is any company policy, practice, or rule that limits opportunities for minorities, or has a greater negative impact or effect on minorities, even though that effect may be unintended. If your company has such a policy and it has a negative effect either on you individually or the entire minority group of which you are a member, you may have a claim—either as an individual or in a class action. (A class action suit is one that is pursued by one or more plaintiffs on behalf of an entire class or group of similarly disadvantaged people who join to sue the defendant—in this case, the employer.)

Vicarious Liability: Note that at least one district court has applied the relatively new "vicarious employer liability" standard used in sexual harassment cases to racial harassment.* See **"Vicarious" Employer Liability** in the sexual harassment section, below.

Booker v. Budget Rent-A-Car Systems, 67 USLW, No. 4, 1056, M.D. Tenn., 1998).

SEX DISCRIMINATION

Sex discrimination (like race and other types of discrimination) occurs when you are treated *differently* because of your sex (race, etc.).

Sexual harassment is, of course, the form of sex discrimination we are all reading about these days. But as we all know, it takes many forms. As with race discrimination, many of the more blatant forms have, thankfully, passed the way of the dinosaur. But some have not; or at least not entirely.

Again, it is federal, and state, civil rights laws that protect you from being discriminated against because of your sex. Although most cases of sex discrimination are brought by women, men, too, have sued successfully for sex discrimination where they have shown that they were refused a job, fired, or discriminated against in any other terms or conditions of employment based on their sex. According to the EEOC, that means your employer (or prospective employer) can't do things like:

☞ Classify a job as "male" or "female," or advertise a job using a "male" or "female" preference, *except* in the case of a bona fide occupational qualification.

☞ Maintain a separate line of progression for males and females within occupations, or discriminate in promotions in any way based on sex.

☞ Maintain separate seniority lists for males and females.

☞ Pay males and females different wages for the same work done under the same or similar working conditions. (See **Equal Pay Act**.)

☞ Refuse to hire married women.

☞ Deny health insurance or offer health insurance on different terms for males and females.

☞ Treat pregnancy differently than any other "disability."

☞ Deny participation in pension or retirement plans or offer them on different terms based on sex.

☞ Offer vacations, severance pay, holidays, or any other benefit or advantage of employment on a different basis to males and females.

Sex discrimination also includes any discrimination based on pregnancy, child-bearing capacity, sterilization, fertility, or related medical conditions. In other words, an employer can't discriminate against you because of the following:

☞ You are married (and thus may have a family and increase the company's health insurance premiums or, that nasty old stereotype, move around the country willy-nilly following hubby's job transfers);

☞ You are pregnant (and will require time off to deliver and care for your baby and will potentially incur higher health insurance and medical costs than a male);

☞ You have or plan to have a family (once again, those nasty health insurance premiums and child care problems); or

☞ You are or are not sterile.

Note: A recent U.S. Supreme Court decision banned so-called fetal protection policies, whereby employers didn't allow women of child-bearing age to work in certain hazardous—and usually higher-paying—jobs. The Court concluded that, although employers with such policies contended they were designed to protect women and their fetuses, the policies were an excuse for "denying women equal employment opportunity" and that "decisions about the welfare of future children must be left to the parents who conceive, bear, support and raise them."*

Bona Fide Occupational Qualification

There is one area, however, where an employer can legally specify a preference for a member of one sex over another for a particular job or class of jobs. That is where the employer can show that being a female (or male) is a bona fide occupational qualification. For example, limiting applicants for the role of Cleopatra to females, or hiring only males as security guards in an all-male prison. EEOC guidelines, however, specify that the concept is to be construed narrowly. That means an employer still can't:

☞ Refuse to hire women based on comparative employment characteristics of women, such as turnover rates;

☞ Refuse to hire women based on stereotypes, such as "lack of aggressiveness," or

☞ Refuse to hire women because of preferences of coworkers, clients, or customers.

*United Auto Workers v. Johnson Control, Inc., U.S. Supreme Court, No. 89-1215, 1991.

Sexual Harassment

Now for the sticky issue.

Regardless of whom you believed or where you stood on the question of Senate confirmation hearings as The Inquisition revisited, there is no doubt that since the Clarence Thomas–Anita Hill "affair" in the early 1990s, a great deal of attention has been focused on the issue of sexual harassment. And the subsequent "problems" of former President Clinton only added fuel to the fire.

There are degrees of sexual harassment. First, the obvious ones. There are unwelcome sexual advances, requests for sexual favors, or *any* conduct of a sexual nature where submission to the conduct is the basis of employment decisions affecting the employee. For example, your supervisor threatens to fire you or give you all the department's dirty work to do if you don't sleep with him, or promises you a promotion or other favorable treatment if you do.

And then there is the more insidious type of sexual harassment, where you are subjected to an overall "hostile working environment" that unreasonably interferes with your job performance. In this situation, there doesn't need to be any economic inducement (promotion, demotion, etc.) for there to be sexual harassment. All that's necessary is that there be a "hostile working environment." Examples would be: unwelcome sexual comments, joking, or unwanted physical contact, like constantly brushing up against you. This form of sexual harassment is obviously more difficult to prove. Generally, there must be a pattern of the type of offensive conduct involved. Take, for example, a male supervisor who tells his female subordinate, "The only way you'll get more money is to be a prostitute or do sexual favors." Is that sexual harassment? Not when the offensive comment or behavior is an isolated incident, or accidental, or part of sporadic behavior, according to a Connecticut federal court.* Rather, to amount to sexual harassment, the comments must be part of a general pattern or practice. And according to the U.S. Court of Appeals in Chicago, you can't make a claim for sexual harassment if you previously participated in the sexual joking you are now complaining of, like the female jailer at a sheriff's department did, even though she claimed it was because she felt it was the only way she could be accepted in the male-dominated profession.†

*Olmstead v. North East Council on Compensation Insurance, Civ. No. H-90-646, 1991.
†Reed v. Shepard, U.S. Court of Appeals, 7th Circuit, 1991.

It is also important to note that sexual harassment, though generally a woman-as-victim scenario, *can* be a two-way street. For example, two men who were forced to engage in sexual activity with their supervisor's secretary as a condition of keeping their jobs were victims of sexual harassment.*

Likewise, heterosexuals are not the only potential victims of sexual harassment. Homosexuals can be victims, too.

"Vicarious" Employer Liability: Perhaps the least-known aspect of sexual harassment—and that goes for both employers and employees—is the fact that your employer can be held liable for sexual harassment by his agents (supervisors, managers, etc.), even if he is unaware of it and even if the company has a policy against it. A couple of recent U.S. Supreme Court decisions have broken the issue of vicarious employer liability into two distinct situations:

1. Where a supervisor's harassment results in "a significant change in employment status" (including decisions on hiring and firing, promotion or failure to promote, demotion, undesirable reassignment and a change in wages or benefits); and

2. Where the harassment involves simple teasing, offhand comments, or isolated incidents that are not "extremely serious." (These types of behaviors, however, would rise to the level of "extremely serious" if they alter the conditions of the victim's employment enough to create a "hostile working environment.")

The Court determined that an employer is *always* liable for the first type of harassment, involving a significant change in employment status.† However, in the case of incidents determined not to have been of an extremely serious nature, an employer can limit liability, or even avoid liability entirely, by showing that:

*He (your employer) exercised reasonable care to prevent and correct any harassment. And

*You (the employee) unreasonably failed to take advantage of any preventative or corrective opportunities provided by the employer or that you failed to do anything else reasonable to avoid whatever harm you may have suffered.

Sexual Harassment Policies: For an employer to take advantage of any potential defense available to him actually requires that he

---

Showalter v. Allison Reed Group, Inc., Rhode Island District Court, No. 90-0168L, 1991.
†*Burlington Industries Inc. v. Ellerth,* 118 S. Ct. 2257, 1998.

have an anti-harassment policy in effect.* To provide an effective defense, such a policy requires:

☞ a clear explanation of the prohibited conduct;
☞ an assurance that a complaining employee will be protected from retaliation;
☞ a clear complaint procedure;
☞ confidentiality insofar as that is possible;
☞ a prompt, thorough and impartial investigation; and
☞ immediate and appropriate corrective action if a determination is made that harassment took place.

Finally, the policy must be "published." That means, simply, that workers must be aware of its existence and its requirements.

Does your company have a sexual harassment policy? Have you seen it?

Coworkers and Outsiders: Your employer may even be held liable for harassment by your coworkers. But in the case of coworkers, you have to be able to prove that your employer knew (you reported it or he—including "vicariously" through a supervisor—witnessed it) or at least should have known about the harassment and took no remedial action.†

Finally, your employer can even be held responsible for sexual harassment by outsiders (visitors, customers, etc.) if he or his agents knew or should have known about the conduct and didn't take immediate steps to stop it. Liability in this situation depends on the extent of your employer's control or legal responsibility over the nonemployee. Was the visitor a relative of his? A business associate? Someone he invited onto the premises?

Note: Sexual harassment is not necessarily limited to the workplace, either. If your employer invites you to a "business" dinner and his hormones take over halfway through dessert, you may have a valid complaint. Did he either explicitly or tacitly make your job or that promotion or other work terms conditional on acceptance of his advances? Did you run into your supervisor at a nightclub, where he suggested that if you didn't take him home and model your pink slip, he'd give you a pink slip? (Sorry.)

Sexual harassment can be a difficult call. On the one hand, well-

*Faragher v. City of Boca Raton, 118 S. St. 2275, 1998.
†Prunty v. Arkansas Freightways Inc., 5th Cir., 1993.

intentioned compliments can amount to sexual harassment if a reasonable person of the same sex as the employee would consider them sufficiently offensive as to create a "hostile working environment." But on the other hand, the law doesn't require a completely "desexualized" workplace.* The court didn't elaborate, but it could be presumed they meant that at least the normal types of male-female interaction, such as mild flirtations, can't be completely legislated out of the work environment.

Sexual Harassment on the Information Highway: Just when you thought it was safe to turn on your computer . . . Speaking to the ingenuity of man, a recent court case considered perhaps the newest way to sexually harass a subordinate: via e-mail. In its decision, the court concluded that sexually explicit e-mail messages were admissible evidence of sexual harassment.† For more on e-mail (particularly employer monitoring of employees' e-mail messages) see Chapter 6: Right to Privacy/Access to Records.

Summary: Know what sexual harassment is—and what to do about it if it happens to you. Knowing what it is is important from both sides of the fence, since one way your employer can protect himself from liability is to discipline an employee for doing it; and that may include anything from a reprimand to a transfer to firing, depending on the severity of the offense.

All the recent articles about sexual harassment make "what it is" seem like a morass of conflicting opinions. And, true enough, what is sexual harassment to one person may be a compliment for another. Like it or not, men and women are different: Conduct a man might consider flattering coming from a woman, a woman might find offensive coming from a man. Perhaps that is why at least one court has adopted what is called the "reasonable woman" standard of evaluating what sexual harassment is. Saying that the usual reasonable *person* standard tends to be male-biased and tends to systematically ignore the experiences of women, the court essentially said sexual harassment should be evaluated from the perspective of the victim.‡ And that's what you should do, too. Use your common sense. The workplace is not the local tavern. People do not

---

Ellison v. Brady, U.S. Court of Appeals, 9th Circuit, No. 89-15248, 1991.
†*Strauss v. Microsoft Corp.,* SD NY, 1995 U.S. Dist. LEXIS 7433, 1995.
‡*Ellison v. Brady,* p. 139

come to work to get "picked up." They come to do their jobs. Period.

If you are the victim of sexual harassment, what you do about it will likely depend on the severity and persistence of the objectionable conduct. For objectionable but relatively mild behavior, a simple "I'm not interested" or "Please, I find that kind of talk offensive" may be enough. A second incident might require a more stern reprimand and a third a report to your supervisor (or if he is the culprit, his superior), or the specific person listed in your employer's sexual harassment policy as the one to whom such complaints are to be made. Of course, more objectionable behavior may not call for a second warning before reporting the incident; and really objectionable behavior may not warrant even a single warning. And it is what is objectionable to *you* that counts, not what might be objectionable to a man—or maybe to Madonna.

What you do from there depends on how offensive and persistent the behavior was and what your employer now does in response to your complaint. For details of the EEOC complaint process, see Chapter 11: I'm Getting Screwed; So What Can I Do about It?

Remember: Be sure to document the details of the offensive behavior, including the time and place, the person(s) involved, the exact nature of the conduct or words spoken, and any witnesses.

Sexual Harassment and Job Security: Employers are on the run. And perhaps with good reason. In a case called *Wheeler v. Southland Corp.,* the court ruled that a manager who was afraid she might have to keep working under the man who had sexually harassed her had a wrongful discharge claim even though she actually quit her job. The court said she was "constructively discharged" even though her employer was sympathetic and had urged her to "hang in there."*

Cases like *Wheeler* might start you thinking that a sexual harassment complaint would be a good way to solidify your position at work; that your employer would be too afraid of a retaliatory discharge suit if he ever fired you. While there may be something to that, it's not foolproof—as one woman found out. Six months after making a sexual harassment complaint, which led to the harasser's suspension and ultimate termination, the woman was fired for what the company called poor performance. She claimed the real reason

*Wheeler v. Southland Corp., 875 Fed. 2d 1246, 1989.

was her sexual harassment complaint. Finding that the firing was justified, the court said, "Although reprehensible, sexual harassment does not entitle the victim to lifetime tenure at her place of employment."*

Depending on the circumstances of the harassment and the state you live in, you may have other claims against your employer and the harasser, such as assault, battery, or infliction of emotional distress. If the harassment causes significant stress or trauma or you become temporarily disabled, you may even have a claim for large compensatory and punitive damages. It may be helpful if you can prove that you were so traumatized you had to see a physician or a psychiatrist. However, proving you sought medical attention is not absolutely necessary to establish a claim of emotional distress.†

On the other hand, if you are the victim of a false accusation of sexual harassment, you have rights, too, as well as a reputation to maintain. You, too, could have a valid legal claim, including for defamation, against both your accuser and your employer, if he didn't investigate the incident fairly.

Sexual Orientation

A number of federal court decisions have held that **Title VII of the Civil Rights Act of 1964** also protects job applicants and employees from discrimination based on their sexual orientation. In general, "sexual orientation" refers to a present or past preference for heterosexuality, homosexuality, or bisexuality, or identification with such preferences. The latter phrase is intended to include individuals who, for example, may not be homosexual or bisexual, but who for one reason or another may be labeled as such. A few states also have laws specifically prohibiting discrimination based on sexual orientation.

EQUAL PAY ACT

Another law that specifically addresses the issue of equality of the sexes in the workplace is the **Equal Pay Act of 1963,** which requires equal pay for substantially equal work (work that requires

---

Juarez v. Ameritech Mobile Communications, U.S. District Court, Northern Illinois, No. 89 C 00017, 1990.
†*Harris v. Forklift Systems Inc.,* USDC Midd. Tenn., No. 3:89-0557, 1994.

roughly the same skill, effort, and responsibility) done under similar circumstances. Fringe benefits are considered "pay" under the act, and employers must therefore provide equal benefits to men and women even if there happens to be a difference in the cost of providing them.

Whether work is substantially equal depends in large part on a case-by-case comparison of duties and the conditions under which they are performed, but courts will consider the following factors in determining whether one job merits higher pay than another:

☛ Is any additional education, experience, training, or ability actually necessary to perform the job?
☛ How much additional effort and/or time is really required to perform the job?
☛ Is any extra work that is performed really important to job performance, or is it merely a perfunctory task?

The main question, of course, is whether or not any minor difference in duties or conditions justifies a difference in pay. One crutch employers sometimes lean on is an employee's unwillingness or inability to work overtime. According to the EEOC, the question, again, is whether not working overtime is "substantial" enough to make the work unequal.

Part-timers and "Temps"

Workers employed for twenty or fewer hours a week and workers hired for temporary assignments can be paid at lower rates than full-timers. However, employers may be found guilty of attempting to subvert the purpose of the **Equal Pay Act** if an inordinate percentage of part-time or temporary workers are women and they are paid less than full-time male employees doing substantially equal work.

Exceptions: Employers do not violate the law where pay differentials are based on a valid seniority system or merit system, a system based on quantity or quality of production, or any other bona fide system that is not sex-based.

Lowering Pay of Male Employees: The act specifies that an employer cannot lower the pay of any employees (i.e., men) in order to comply with the law. They must raise the pay of the lower-paid employees (i.e., women).

Comparable Worth: There is a relatively new theory on the equal pay front. It's called "comparable worth." Where the **Equal Pay Act** requires that people performing essentially the same job be given the same pay regardless of sex, the theory of comparable worth argues that people performing *different jobs* having roughly the *same value to the employer* should be paid the same rates regardless of sex. The justification is that such a requirement would narrow the gap in wages between men and women, since historically women have been overrepresented (and underpaid) in some job classifications. Under the theory, employees could make a case for wage discrimination if they were paid less than members of the opposite sex who perform jobs of substantially the same *value* to their employer (as opposed to substantially equal work under the **Equal Pay Act**).

Obviously, the difficulty comes with trying to evaluate the relative worth of different jobs to an employer. That's probably why many of the court decisions to date on the "comparable worth" issue have dealt with government employment, where job classifications are easier to compare. In any case, the comparable worth theory is probably stronger in cases where intentional discrimination is being alleged, particularly where entire job classifications that are predominantly occupied by women are underpaid.

Courts are still wrestling with the question of how to apply the comparable worth theory. If you are a woman working in a job that is filled predominantly by women and the job is paid less than jobs that are filled predominantly by men, your employer should be prepared to justify the pay differentials on the basis of the training, education, and experience required to perform the jobs. If he can't, you may just have a case under the comparable worth theory.

HANDICAP DISCRIMINATION

On July 26, 1992, the **Americans with Disabilities Act** (ADA) took over from the **Vocational Rehabilitation Act of 1973** (the Rehab Act) as the main federal law protecting handicapped and disabled workers. It applies to all employers of 15 or more workers. The Rehab Act applied only to government contractors and private employers who received government assistance. (The majority of those employers were—and are—also required to take affirmative action to hire the handicapped.)

For purposes of both the Rehab Act and ADA, a handicapped individual is a person who has a physical or mental impairment that limits one or more major life activities, has a record of such an impairment (i.e., has recovered from a previous condition), or is *perceived* as having such an impairment. (A person is perceived as having a handicap when he isn't actually handicapped but people think he is; for example, he is suspected of having AIDS.) Handicaps under both acts include contagious diseases, as long as the person isn't in danger of infecting coworkers, and even drug or alcohol addiction if the person can still perform the job safely and competently.

State Laws

Though the relatively Johnny-come-lately ADA has grabbed most of the limelight, many state civil rights laws have been doing a creditable job protecting the rights of handicapped workers for years. Of course, it depends on what state you live in whether your employer is large enough to come under the law's umbrella (see **Table 11**) and, if so, whether your condition qualifies in the eyes of your state court as a "handicap." Obviously, some conditions, such as a certain degree of blindness or paralysis, would qualify as handicaps in all jurisdictions. However, some are not so cut and dried. For example, a New York court has ruled that being overweight can be a handicap and a Michigan court has ruled that being a narcoleptic can constitute a handicap, too. Others have found that being color-blind or left-handed is not a handicap, nor is transvestism. (In the "we'll try just about anything" category, a highly publicized 1994 California decision held that *body odor* was not a handicap that required accommodation under the ADA.) For many courts, the question boils down to the time-honored standard: Does the "disability" limit one or more major life activities—such as breathing, walking, seeing, hearing, etc.? And are you still able to perform the job despite the disability? The latter question can really be answered only on a case-by-case basis, depending on the type of disability you have and the type of job involved.

Americans with Disabilities Act (ADA)

Now the one that some employers are still griping about: the **Americans with Disabilities Act.** (President Bush actually signed the act into law in 1990 and, knowing employers would resent it, gave them until 1992 to get ready for it.) In the employers' defense, what most are griping about isn't the idea of employing the handicapped but the cost of accommodating their handicaps. However, as we will see, those fears are generally unfounded, since many accommodations can be accomplished at little or no cost; and if they would present an "undue hardship," the employer doesn't have to make them at all.

The basic provision of ADA prohibits discrimination against qualified disabled people (specifically including people with AIDS) by requiring employers to make reasonable accommodation for those who can perform the essential functions of the job, unless that accommodation would cause the employer an undue hardship. Let's break down some of those terms.

What does it mean to be a "qualified disabled person"? What are a particular job's "essential functions"? What constitutes a "reasonable accommodation"? And what makes such an accommodation an "undue hardship" on the employer?

Are You a "Qualified Disabled Person"? The first thing you (and your employer or prospective employer) must determine under ADA is whether you are a qualified disabled person whose disability must be accommodated. That requires you to ask yourself two basic questions:

First, do you have a "disability" that qualifies you for the protection of the ADA? You do if your impairment substantially limits your ability to work. That is, it significantly restricts your ability to perform either an entire category of jobs or a wide range of jobs in a number of categories as compared with the average person with comparable qualifications.

Second, are you otherwise "qualified" for the job? To be qualified, you must be able to perform the "essential functions," or primary duties, of the job regardless of whether or not an accommodation would be necessary to enable you to do so. In other words, the *fact* that you have a handicap that would need to be accommodated can't eliminate you from consideration. Now, what the "essential functions" of a job are is a bit more objective. That depends to some extent on the employer's judgment, but mostly on the amount of time spent on each task, and how much of a problem would be created by not requiring you to perform the task. In deciding if your employer is justified in calling a duty an essential function of the job, the

EEOC will look at both written job descriptions and the work experience and job duties of past and present people in the job.

Reasonable Accommodation: Okay, you're a "qualified disabled person who is able to perform the essential functions of the job," so your employer (or prospective employer) has to provide a "reasonable accommodation" for your handicap. What does that mean? It means that, if necessary, he has to:

☞ Modify the job application process so you can be considered for the job you are applying for in the first place. (Such things as altering application forms, preemployment tests, and other aspects of the screening process.)

☞ Adjust the work environment or the way the job is usually performed so you'll be able to perform the essential functions of the job. (This may include major things like altering the structure of his existing facility to make it readily accessible, or acquiring new equipment; or relatively minor things like modifying work schedules, training materials, or company policies, or putting a desk on blocks so your wheelchair can slide under it, or otherwise modifying the equipment he already has.)

Note: An accommodation does not have to be the best one possible, as long as it meets the job-related needs of the person being accommodated. For example, your employer wouldn't have to buy a whole new computer station if simply raising the height of the existing terminal would allow you to perform the essential duties of the job. And an accommodation does not have to be made at all if it would impose an "undue hardship" on the employer.

Undue Hardship: Whether or not requiring an accommodation would impose an undue hardship on an employer depends on the type and cost of the accommodation needed, the size and type of the employer's business, and how much money the employer has. (A large, rich company would have to go to greater lengths than a small company clinging to solvency by its teeth.)

An accommodation can be considered an undue hardship if it would unduly disrupt other employees or customers, *but not* if the disruption is simply caused by fear or prejudice. (Remember, the ADA's protections specifically extend to people with AIDS.) In any event, an employer can be required to provide an alternate accommodation that would not be an undue hardship.

Special Situations: The EEOC has some guidelines that cover several special situations, such as:

☞ *Threat to health or safety:* An employer can refuse to hire you if you would be a direct threat to the health or safety of other workers or customers. But such a determination must be based on current medical knowledge. (Your employer had better not make that kind of determination without the advice of a qualified professional, or he's just asking for trouble.)

☞ *Drug and alcohol abuse:* ADA does not protect current users of illegal drugs and lets employers hold alcoholics to the same employment standards as other workers. (**Note:** ADA *does* protect people who are participating in or have successfully completed rehabilitation and no longer use alcohol or illegal drugs.)

☞ *Food service:* The Secretary of Health and Human Services has compiled a list of communicable diseases that can be transmitted through the handling of food. Employers can refuse to hire a person with any of these diseases for a food handling job. However, the EEOC "suggests" that employers try to accommodate current employees by reassigning them to an available position that does not involve handling food.

☞ *Insurance:* You must have equal access to whatever insurance is available to other employees regardless of your disability. (However, insurance policies can still have pre-existing condition clauses. That is, they can exempt an existing condition from coverage.)

☞ *Medical exams and questions: Before* offering you a job, an employer can ask only if you can perform job functions. He can't require you to take a medical exam or to answer questions about your medical history until *after* he has offered you a job. A job offer can be conditioned on the results of a post-offer medical exam or answers to questions about your medical history, but only if all entering employees in the same job class have to take the same exam or answer the same questions *and they are job-related.* If you are excluded based on the exam, the employer must show that there was no reasonable accommodation available that would have enabled you to perform the essential functions of the job.

AGE DISCRIMINATION

Let's start with the good news: You're not getting older, you're getting better. At least that was the result of a study commissioned by the Commonwealth Fund of New York. According to that study, if you are over fifty, you are cheaper to hire and train, have lower absenteeism and turnover rates, cost less in terms of damage and theft, are more amenable to flexible schedules, and are more efficient and productive than your younger coworkers. So why are so many employers out there discriminating against you because of your age? Well, you are also more likely to be at the higher end of the company's wage scale and cost more to provide health insurance for. Thus, the **Age Discrimination in Employment Act,** which is no doubt more a result of the increased power of an aging population (and aging politicians) than any sudden social conscience.

The Age Discrimination in Employment Act (ADEA)

The ADEA protects you from being discriminated against because of your age, but only if you are over forty and work for an employer who employs at least twenty people. (Some state human rights laws protect you even if you are under forty. And some kick in for employers with fewer than twenty workers. See **Table 11.**) That means employers can't indicate any age preference or limitation in job ads except minimum age requirements, for example, to serve alcoholic beverages or to work in hazardous jobs; and they can't refuse to hire you, or pay you less or discriminate against you in any way because of your age. In fact, they can't even make wisecracks about your age. In *Sischo-Nownejad v. Merced College District,* which I've mentioned before, a female teacher claimed she was given the worst classes and subjected to closer scrutiny than other faculty members because of her sex and her age. On the latter count, the court agreed when it heard that her colleagues referred to her as "the old war-horse" and made other denigrating remarks about her age. And in a recent case,* a Hartford, Connecticut, television station was found guilty of age discrimination after they systematically demoted and then eventually fired an anchorwoman in her mid-forties (a decidedly youth-oriented profession).

Exceptions: As with any rule, the ADEA has exceptions:

☞ If you have been in a bona fide executive or in a high policy-making position for at least the past two years and are entitled to an immediate, nonforfeitable pension of at least $44,000 a year, you can be let go at age 65.

☞ If age is a bona fide occupational qualification (BFOQ) of your job, you can be terminated when your age becomes a relevant factor. The BFOQ exception is limited to jobs where an employer can legitimize a cutoff age for reasons that are "reasonably necessary to the normal operation of the enterprise." Age as a BFOQ has been upheld for public safety personnel, for example (police and fire fighters).

☞ If you are let go as a result of the operation of a bona fide seniority system, retirement plan, or apprentice system.

Making an Age Discrimination Case: Courts recognize four elements necessary to make a *prima facie* case for age discrimination. The four elements are:

☞ That you are in the protected age group—over forty under ADEA; younger under some state laws, as listed below.

☞ That you were let go, or demoted, or were the object of some other adverse job decision.

☞ That you were qualified for your job. (This one shouldn't be difficult if you have been with the company for a while and have consistently been given good performance reviews, raises, etc. It may be a bit tougher if you were hired fairly recently.)

☞ That your dismissal came under circumstances that give rise to an inference of age discrimination. (Relevant circumstances vary, but the big one here is that you were replaced or passed over for a promotion by a younger employee.)

*Peckinpaugh v. Tribune Broadcasting Co., USDC, 2nd Cir., 1998.

Good Cause; Elimination of Your Position; Cost Reduction:
Once you have established the elements required to make that *prima facie* case, the ball is in your employer's court. In order to return it, he must provide a nondiscriminatory reason for his decision. One way he can do that is by showing that the person he hired was, in fact, better qualified for the job. He might have a problem, though, if he says you are "overqualified" for the job. A federal appeals court in New York ruled that, while it may be reasonable to think that an overqualified younger worker would keep looking for a job that was a better "fit," that alternative isn't always a reality for an older worker. "Overqualified" is not the same as "unqualified," the court noted, saying that, in this case, the word was being used as a euphemism for "too old."*

But being older isn't a free ticket. Your employer can win out by showing that there was another valid reason for firing you that was unrelated to your age. For example, poor performance, or "just cause," or economic reasons. (In other words, your job is not safe if you don't do it. Or if you are insubordinate. Or if the company can no longer afford to pay you.)

It is also more difficult to make a case if you are fired but not replaced. In a Connecticut case, a company was able to show that an employee was transferred because of poor performance and later discharged as part of a reduction in force that eventually led to the closing of the company's Connecticut plant. The woman was not replaced. Instead, her work was spread among remaining workers, some of whom, the company pointed out, were the same age as the woman who was let go. The company won.†

Legitimate reductions in force like the one in the *Blanchard* case are troublesome areas for workers, even workers in protected groups. One court indicated that to establish a case of age discrimination during a reduction in force, you would have to show that you were treated worse than younger employees, either individually or as a group.‡

Finally, at least one court *(Bay v. Times Mirror Magazines, Inc.)* has ruled that an employer can even discharge you because he thinks your salary is too high for current market conditions, as long as the decision is purely financial and doesn't impose a general rule

---

Taggart v. Time, Inc., U.S. Court of Appeals, 2nd Circuit, No. 90-7318, 1991.
†*Blanchard v. Stone Safety Corp.,* Conn. Superior Court, Civ. No. 89-55, 1991.
‡*Branson v. Price River Coal Co.,* 853 Fed. 2d 768, 1988.

that has a discriminatory impact on older workers.* The *Bay* case involved a fairly unique set of circumstances in which a fifty-four-year-old worker's company was bought out by another company. He ended up working for a boss who was not only younger than he was but whose salary was less than his—which is decidedly poor form. Anyway, as in *Bay,* your employer would probably have to show that an economic hardship made it difficult, if not impossible, to pay your salary. A thriving business could not expect to be safe from legal action if it just went around cutting its higher-paid older staff and replacing them with lower-paid younger workers.

Group Health Insurance: ADEA requires your employer's group health insurance plan to offer any employee (or spouse) who is sixty-five or over the right to group coverage under the same conditions as any covered employee (or spouse) who is under sixty-five. That means that your premiums and benefits have to be the same as those of younger workers.

Medical Exams: ADEA doesn't prevent your employer from requiring you to take a medical exam to determine if you are still qualified for your job. But only if your job requires certain physical capabilities that would make a medical exam appropriate.

Employee Benefit Plans: In 1989 the U.S. Supreme Court ruled that the ADEA did not apply to employee benefit plans, as long as employers weren't using them as a way around ADEA.† However, a law called the **Older Workers Benefit Protection Act,** which applies to any benefit plan established or modified after October 16, 1990 (the date the act was signed into law), reversed that decision, so ADEA now *does apply* to benefit plans. The law says that if an employer has an employee benefit plan, he must either provide equal benefits to older and younger workers or incur equal costs in providing them. In other words, benefits for older workers can be less than for younger workers if the employer spends the same amount to provide them. (As noted above, this does not apply to health insurance coverage, for which premiums and benefits must be equal.)

Bay v. Times Mirror Magazines, Inc., U.S. Court of Appeals, 2nd Circuit, No. 91-7089, 1991.
†*Public Employees' Retirement System of Ohio v. Betts,* 50 FEP Cases 104, 1989.

Waiver of ADEA Rights: Oh, those sneaky employers. Is there no end to what they'll try to get away with? Apparently not. You get yourself some rights, and they slide a piece of paper in front of you and try to entice you into signing them away for nothing. Well, the government is wise to that ploy, too. That's why they included a clause in the **Older Workers Benefit Protection Act** that specifically states that a waiver of rights or claims under the ADEA is valid only if it is made "knowingly and voluntarily." A waiver—usually an agreement to retire early (you know, the old "golden handshake")—is not considered "knowing and voluntary" under the law unless, at a minimum:

☛ The agreement is in writing and easy to understand;
☛ The waiver specifically refers to your ADEA rights or claims;
☛ You cannot waive any rights or claims that may arise *after* the date of the waiver;
☛ You receive something of value in exchange (i.e., *in addition to* what you were already entitled to by law and by any applicable company policy);
☛ You are advised in writing to consult an attorney before executing the waiver;
☛ You are given at least twenty-one days to consider the agreement (forty-five days in the case of retirement incentive programs offered to a group or class of employees, in which case you must be given additional written information about eligibility for the group program, its time limits, the ages and job titles of those selected to participate, and the ages of those not selected); and
☛ The agreement is revocable for up to seven days after execution.

Remember, the ADEA applies to employers of twenty or more employees, but your state human rights law probably prohibits age discrimination, too, and may well apply to your employer if he's not already covered by ADEA.

State Age Discrimination Laws

The following states have age discrimination laws similar to ADEA's, but which protect employees in the following age ranges:

☞ *18 and over:* Iowa, Kansas, Minnesota, Oregon, Vermont, and New York.

☞ *18 to 65:* District of Columbia.

☞ *40 and over:* Arizona, Arkansas (state employees only), California, Idaho, Illinois, Kentucky, Massachusetts, North Dakota, Ohio, Oklahoma, Pennsylvania, South Carolina, South Dakota (state employees only), Tennessee, Texas, Utah, Washington, West Virginia, and Wisconsin.

☞ *40 to 70:* Colorado, Delaware, Georgia, Indiana, Louisiana, Missouri, Nebraska, North Carolina, Rhode Island, and Wyoming.

☞ *No specified limit:* Alabama, Alaska, Connecticut, Florida, Hawaii, Maine, Maryland, Michigan, Mississippi (state employees only), Montana, New Hampshire, New Jersey, New Mexico, Nevada, and Virginia (state employees only).

Note: Several states also have laws that limit the number of hours older workers may be employed in certain jobs, though generally they can consent to waive those limits. Those laws are administered and enforced by state departments of labor.

NATIONAL ORIGIN (ETHNIC) DISCRIMINATION

The only question a prospective employer can legally ask you regarding your national origin is if you are authorized to work in the United States. Then, after you are hired, he *must* have you submit documentation to verify that fact. See Chapter 1: The Hiring Process.

Under federal (and most state) law, you can't be discriminated against in employment because of your place of origin or because you have physical, cultural, or linguistic characteristics of a certain nationality (because you "look foreign" or have a "foreign accent"). In fact, you can't even be discriminated against because of *someone else's* national origin: An employer was found guilty of discrimination for giving a bad performance review to a Caucasian employee because her husband was Hispanic.*

The only time an employer could legitimately favor someone

Chacon v. California Department of Corrections, U.S. District Court Central Calif., 1991.

based on national origin would be in the case of a bona fide occupational qualification, which would be rare. (For example, hiring someone Chinese to wait on tables in a Chinese restaurant.) An employer may also legally favor an American citizen over an equally qualified noncitizen. See Chapter 1: The Hiring Process.

Harassment

The prohibitions of **Title VII of the Civil Rights Act of 1964** against harassment on the basis of national origin are essentially the same as for sexual harassment. In a nutshell, ethnic slurs or conduct denigrating someone's national origins (or ethnic background) is harassment when the effect is to create a hostile working environment, or to interfere with the person's performance, or to otherwise affect the person's employment opportunities. As with sexual harassment, your employer is directly responsible for harassment by your supervisor, even if he didn't know about it, and in fact, even if he forbids it. He may also be liable for harassment by your coworkers if he knew or had reason to know about it and did nothing to stop it.

"Speak-English-Only" Rules

Can your employer require you to speak English on the job all the time? Some of the time? The EEOC presumes that any requirement that employees speak English *all the time* (including on their own time, like during lunch or coffee breaks) is discriminatory. However, your employer may require you to speak English when there is a business necessity for it, such as when dealing with customers who speak English. But in order for your employer to enforce such a rule without being guilty of discrimination, he must have told you about the rule and the consequences of breaking it.

Note: At least one federal appeals court has rejected the EEOC's position that English-only rules are presumed to violate Title VII. The U.S. Court of Appeals in San Francisco has held that such a work rule "does not inexorably lead to an abusive environment" for workers whose first language is not English. Rather, each case said the court, must be evaluated in its own "factual context"* What that means, at least in that jursidiction, is that the plaintiff still has to prove that the rule had a discriminatory effect *first,* before the burden of defending

Garcia v. Spun Steak Co., 62 FEP Cases 525, 1993.

it with a valid business reason shifts to employer (rather than the other way around), just as in other disparate impact cases.

Height and Weight Requirements

Height and weight requirements, unless they bear a demonstrable relationship to job requirements, have consistently been ruled to be discriminatory. (Few but the Boston Celtics or Chicago Bears would escape EEOC scrutiny.) In a landmark case, the City of San Francisco's requirement that police officers be at least five feet six inches tall was judged to discriminate against Hispanics, Asians, and women.*

RELIGIOUS DISCRIMINATION

So who's going to know or care if you're Catholic or Protestant or Jewish or Hindu or Muslim or Worshippers of the Great Pumpkin? As for employers, first of all, they shouldn't know because they're not supposed to ask. And second of all, why pick on religion? Well, why pick on sex or race or national origin? Some just do it because it's there. And others, well, others do it because a religion may be associated with people of a certain race or national or ethnic background and that's the real basis of their discrimination.

In any event, it's not usually your religion per se that's at issue. More likely than not it's your religious *practices,* and the degree to which your employer is required to accommodate them. As with a person's handicap, an employer has a responsibility to reasonably accommodate your religious practices, but only if it doesn't impose an undue burden on his business.

What is reasonable depends on the type of job and the size of the company, but it can include altering work schedules, reassigning or transferring you, or relaxing dress codes. On the one hand, an employer would probably be justified in not hiring you for a one-of-a-kind job where your religious practices conflict with the job requirements. (For example, you are a sports trainer and you apply for a job with a football team. Your religion prohibits you from working on Saturdays, but the team plays its games on Saturdays.) On the other hand, if it is a large company, a court might have greater

---

Officers for Justice v. Civil Service Commission, City and County of San Francisco, 473 Fed. Supp. 801, 1979.

expectations that your employer would be able to offer you a similar job in another department where your religious practices wouldn't conflict with scheduling requirements.

As for what is an undue hardship, the U.S. Supreme Court has ruled that, in accommodating your religious practices, your employer isn't required to incur more than minimal cost, doesn't have to violate the terms of a bona fide seniority system, and does not have to pick the accommodation that you prefer. (For example, your employer doesn't have to let *you* choose the day of the week that will be your Sabbath if by doing so he would have to adapt his business operations to your religious practices.) Likewise, you may give up your right to a reasonable accommodation of your religious practices if you don't tell your employer in advance of your potential need for an accommodation, or if you aren't reasonable about accepting the accommodation offered. (And, of course, that would depend on your specific situation.) Remember, your employer doesn't have to offer you the *best* possible solution, only one that is reasonable in light of his business circumstances.

AFFIRMATIVE ACTION/REVERSE DISCRIMINATION*

One of the basic ideas behind civil rights and equal opportunity laws, of course, was to level the playing field for minorities, women, and the handicapped. Because of that, various federal (and some state) laws encourage employers to modify employment practices voluntarily when they act as barriers to equal employment opportunities. They even encourage affirmative action, in effect, to right previous wrongs (and in the case of affirmative action for military veterans, because "it's the right thing to do"). A distinction is made, however, between affirmative action for government contractors and for other employers.

Government contractors—and for the most part that includes both state and federal government contractors—are generally *required* to take affirmative action to hire minorities, women, the handicapped, and veterans.

However, employers, especially private employers, who embark on an affirmative action course must beware of the fact that equal

*See "Affirmative Action Under Fire," later in this chapter, for a discussion of the future of affirmative action.

opportunity laws can, and have, been used by whites to sue for *reverse* discrimination.

Federal Government Contractors

If that job you are applying for is with a government contractor or subcontractor, he probably has a legal obligation to publish job openings with a pronouncement that he is an "affirmative action/equal employment opportunity employer," along with a legal obligation to fulfill that promise. Generally, employers with government contracts of $2,500 or more must take affirmative action to hire the disabled and handicapped (under **Section 503 of the Rehabilitation Act of 1973**), while contracts of $10,000 or more require affirmative action to hire women and minorities (**Executive Order 11246**) and Vietnam veterans and disabled veterans of all wars (**Vietnam Era Veterans' Readjustment Assistance Act of 1974**).

The above laws have complex requirements for employers, including how they must advertise job openings and the type of notice they must give to unions and employment services. There are also written affirmative action plan requirements. And what would a federal law be without paperwork—scads of paperwork? But the end result for you is that if you are a minority, a woman, or a Vietnam or disabled vet, virtually all government contractors must take affirmative action to hire you.

Affirmative action laws are administered by the Office of Federal Contract Compliance Programs (OFCCP), a division of the EEOC. Part of the OFCCP's requirements are for employers to encourage people to identify themselves as members of groups who are given hiring (and promotion) preference under the law. The OFCCP does, however, caution employers to make it clear to job applicants as well as to current employees that any such identification is voluntary, will be kept confidential, and will be used for affirmative action purposes only.

State Government Contractors

State laws requiring affirmative action in public contracts are generally administered by your state's Commission on Human Rights and Opportunities or equivalent agency. (**Note:** Some larger cities have their own similar laws and agencies.)

Reverse Discrimination

White males are just about the only employees left who aren't in a "protected group" (those not over forty or handicapped, that is). But what if you are rejected for employment in favor of a less qualified minority or woman? Do you have any rights? You may.

As it turns out, private employers are free (or at least fairly free) to take affirmative action to modify employment practices that present barriers to equal employment opportunities. Of course, they must also take care that they don't overstep themselves. Court decisions in reverse discrimination cases have fairly universally ruled that it is appropriate for an employer to take affirmative action:

☞ When he can show that an adverse impact results or is likely to result from a certain employment practice. Or,

☞ To correct an imbalance in his work force determined by comparing it with an appropriate segment of the available labor pool.

The EEOC stresses that any resulting affirmative action plan has to be "reasonable" in relation to the problems uncovered and the goals and timetables set for correcting them; and it must avoid unnecessary restrictions on opportunities for the rest of the employer's work force. It can really do that only if the employer has proof that women and/or minorities are (or were before he took affirmative action) significantly underrepresented in his work force.

So can you prove that the less qualified minority or woman who was hired or promoted over you is not qualified to perform the job? Or that your employer's affirmative action plan is not reasonable in light of the statistical makeup of his work force? Or that you were laid off before a less senior minority or woman? Now you're talking lawsuit.

WHAT TO DO: When you are the object of any kind of discrimination at work, your options are many and varied. You can start by filing a complaint with the EEOC (or the EEOC's OFCCP in the case of a government contractor or subcontractor). Alternatively (or in addition), you may bring legal action through your own private attorney. Details of the EEOC complaint procedure, as well as weighing the merits of a potential lawsuit and selecting an attorney, are discussed in Chapter 11.

Affirmative Action Under Fire

There has always been a certain amount of controversy over affirmative action programs, and a 1995 U.S. Supreme Court ruling once again brought the debate to the forefront. In the case of *Adarand Constructors v. Pena,** the Court ruled 5-4 that the federal government should be held to stricter standards to justify affirmative action. Specifically what those stricter standards are will not be totally clear until people start to sue under them, but what is clear is that the decision will make it more difficult for the federal government to justify affirmative action programs.

The Court refused to rule against all affirmative action programs as forms of reverse discrimination, but it did say that such programs should be strictly scrutinized and "are constitutional only if they are narrowly tailored measures that further compelling governmental interests." According to the decision, affirmative action plans can be justified only when they are necessary to further a compelling government interest (which can include evidence of prior discrimination), and when they are narrowly tailored to meet that goal (which means, among other things, that no non-race-based alternatives are available). The new strict standard is applicable to all federal government affirmative action plans based on race or ethnic background. (The case did not directly address the issue of affirmative action plans that benefit women.)

Private employers: The ruling did not affect voluntary affirmative action plans formulated by private employers. Those plans will still pass muster if there is a "manifest imbalance" between the percentage of available qualified minorities in the labor pool and the number working for the employer. (Private plans have always had to pass the additional, narrow tailoring test.)

State laws: At the same time the Supreme Court was tightening the rules for justifying affirmative action programs, the Governor of California issued an Executive Order that seriously cut state affirmative action programs. The order discontinued some affirmative action programs entirely, while requiring all state agencies to hire and promote, as well as employ contractors on the basis of merit only, without regard to sex or race.† Meanwhile, a number of other states have proposed laws opposing racial preferences.

Note: In any event, *equal employment opportunity* is still the law.

---

*1995 US LEXIS 4037, 1995.
†California Executive Order W-124-95, 1995.

SUMMARY

"All men—and women—are created equal." And all employers have to treat them that way. They aren't always required to treat you *well,* but if they treat you lousy, they'd better be treating everybody else just as lousy. As we have seen, this equality of treatment is particularly important from your employer's standpoint when he is dealing with members of a protected group (minority, female, over forty, handicapped). And, since upwards of 70 percent of us are now in one—or more—protected groups, he has to be particularly on guard.

If you are in a protected group and an employer takes adverse employment action against you—he doesn't hire you, passes you over for a promotion, pays you less than your counterparts who do essentially the same work, subjects you to higher standards of production or behavior, disciplines you a bit more harshly or hastily than your coworkers, lays you off or fires you—the situation may merit a closer look. You already have the ingredients of that *prima facie* case we've been harping on: membership in a protected group and getting dumped on by your employer.

To parry your initial thrust, your employer would then have to prove that the nonprotected group member he hired or promoted over you was, in fact, more qualified; or that the job he pays you less to do isn't as demanding as the jobs he pays the other guy more for; or that, though his productivity goals are ambitious and his discipline tough, he measures everyone against the same published policy; or that you were laid off first not because of your age or sex or handicap or race but because you were the junior member of the staff or the worst at your job.

Finally, to make a case that can stick, you must counter that your employer's action or policy is simply a pretext, a sham, and that the *real* reason for the action taken against you (or in favor of someone else) is that you are black, Hispanic, female, handicapped, sixty-three years old, Muslim . . . If you can do that, or if you can prove that clearly discriminatory remarks were made, there is a jury award out there with your name on it.

6

Right to Privacy/Access to Records

hat privacy rights do I keep and what do I give up
when I arrive for work? Can my employer look
through my locker or desk or other place where I
keep my personal things? Can he watch me on closed-circuit television or tape my conversations? How about the legality of computer
monitoring or electronic mail interception? Do I have to submit to a
drug test and, if so, under what circumstances? How about an AIDS
or other medical test? Or a lie detector test? And, finally, do I have
the right to see what's in my personnel file or medical records? After
all, my employer may be making decisions about my job or promotion based on them. And, if I do have the right to check them out, do
I then have the right to demand that incorrect or outdated information be removed? And what about the right to slip in a statement explaining my side of the story?

Well, as we'll see, the answers to these and many other workplace
privacy questions often depend on where you live.

ACCESS TO PERSONNEL FILES

There are reams of records your employer is required by law to
keep concerning you and every other worker in his employ, including how they must be kept and how long they must be kept on file—
things like payroll records, time sheets, tax information, records of
occupational injury or illness and other safety records, workers'
compensation records, records of participation in group health in-

surance plans and retirement plans, and more. There are even requirements regarding how and how long he keeps employment records he isn't even required to keep, like application forms, pre-employment test scores, and records concerning hiring, promotion, demotion, transfer, or termination.

Of course, it's generally not the required records that cause the problems, but those optional things such as performance appraisals, credit checks, disciplinary records and the like. We *know* how much money we make (not enough) and the hours we work to make it (too many). What we *really* want to know is why we were denied that promotion, or why we were the first one laid off, or why we were fired or demoted. Or maybe we're just curious to see what's in there. (Maybe they've got something in there they shouldn't have.) After all, it *is* the sum total of our work life, at least from our employer's perspective.

In these days of lawsuits and counter-lawsuits, you can bet your employer is going to keep a detailed account of every step you make during the period spent in his employ. What he wants is a "paper trail" that will prove to any court in the country that the reason he didn't hire you, or the reason he didn't promote you or, in fact, demoted you or fired you or whatever other negative employment action he took against you was completely justified and there's not the proverbial "snowball's chance" that a case of illegal discrimination or retaliation can be made against him. Of course, in their zeal for self-preservation, employers often overstep the bounds of law regarding *what* records they can keep and/or how they can use them.

So, we know what kind of information your employer is *required* to collect and keep in your file. The big questions are:

☞ What other kinds of information besides that required by the various governmental agencies is your employer legally allowed to collect about you?
☞ Do you have the right to examine your own personnel file and, if so, how broad is that right and what limitations are placed on it?
☞ Who else has a right to see your personnel file?
☞ What about your medical records: the results of any company medical examination, records of your medical history, medical conditions, disabilities, etc.?
☞ Do you have the right to insist that your employer correct false information or delete obsolete information? Do you

have the right to insert explanatory comments if your employer refuses? And do you have the right to copy your file?

The answer to the first question is fairly universal. Any information your employer collects about you should be strictly job-related and based on business necessity. That is, it should have a bearing on how you will be able to perform your job or do, in fact, perform your job, including your respect for reasonable company rules and policies and anything else that has an effect on the employer's ability to run his business. Anything else is likely to be suspect. In addition, some laws allow employers to collect certain information, but restrict how they can use it. For example, a prospective employer can seek information about you from a credit bureau, but the **Fair Credit Reporting Act** limits the employer's use of the information to verification of previous employment. That is, he's not supposed to use it to see if your credit is good. (Sort of like telling the jury to disregard the question that was already asked.) You must also be told that the credit check will be made, and that you have the right to find out the scope of the check and get a copy. If you were denied a job or promotion, you must be told what part the credit check played in that decision.

If your employer has an affirmative action plan, he can ask you if you want to identify yourself as female, a minority, or a veteran for purposes of his affirmative action goals or obligations. (**Note:** Questions regarding self-identification should not be on the actual application form but on a separate self-identification form. See Chapter 5: Discrimination and Related Issues, for a discussion of "Affirmative Action Under Fire.") However, he cannot use that information for any other purpose, and he is not supposed to include the fact that you are black, for example, in your personnel file. (Obviously, you may have a proof problem regarding *how* your employer used information in a way he shouldn't have unless other signs point the same way. For example, if he has a statement in your file that indicates that you are black, or says "poor credit," or the like.)

Now, the answer to the second question, access to your personnel file and what limits can be placed on that right, depends a great deal on where you live, since state laws generally cover the availability of personnel files. Many states allow you to inspect your own personnel records at reasonable intervals (e.g., once or twice a year). Usually the inspections have to be done on your own time (coffee breaks or a lunch hour, if you are still employed at the company) and in the presence of a company official, so your employer retains some control over the integrity of the records. In some states your employer can require that any request to see your file be made in writing. Most states include virtually every piece of information your employer collects about you and uses to evaluate you for hiring, promotion, disciplinary action, a raise in pay or termination, as part of your personnel file and, thus, open to your inspection. That includes application forms, preemployment tests, performance evaluations, comments by supervisors, etc.

There are exceptions under most laws: information employers can legally screen from your records before you see them. Those exceptions generally include information being gathered as part of a criminal investigation, reference letters, at least insofar as the author is capable of being identified, and any other information which, if shown to you, would violate the privacy of another person. Some laws also except results of preemployment examinations to the extent that disclosing the results would invalidate the test.

As for who has the right to see your file, most (smart) employers will restrict access to employees' (and former employees') personnel files strictly to those with a "need to know." To ensure confidentiality, your employer should keep personnel files under lock and key so they are not available for public consumption. Otherwise, they are asking for an invasion of privacy—or even defamation—suit. In fact, one court went so far as to hold that an employee was defamed by a negative performance review in her personnel file, even though the only people to see it were a couple of high-ranking company officials who were evaluating her for a promotion and, presumably, had a "need to know." And even though defamation requires "publication" of the offending material. That is, the material either has to be told to someone (slander), or shown to someone (libel).* And if an employer can't show a performance review to management personnel whose job it is to make employment decisions . . . Needless to say, this is a decision that has some employers wondering if they should ever risk letting a supervisor write a bad performance review again (and if they do, if they should include it in the employee's personnel file).

To make a long story short, at the very least your fellow employees should not know what is in your personnel file unless you tell them.

Medical records are treated differently than other personnel

*Cary v. AT&T Technologies, Inc., New Jersey Superior Court, No. W-027817-87, 1991.

records by some state laws. A few specifically include the results of medical examinations conducted by your employer and medical histories he compiles as part of your personnel file. As such, they too are open to inspection. However, some specifically exclude them, at least to the extent they are available to you through other means, such as from a doctor or health care facility. Others restrict access to medical records insofar as necessary to protect your health (whatever that means—and sometimes you can determine what that means only by taking your employer to court).

Note: No matter whether your employer considers your medical records as part and parcel of your entire personnel record, federal law now requires that personnel records and medical records be kept separately. That is, they must be maintained in separate files.

The confidentiality of your medical records is expressly covered by the **Americans with Disabilities Act** (ADA). Under the ADA, results of any medical examination or information concerning your medical condition or history must be kept on separate forms and in a file separate from your personnel records and must be kept confidential. The only people who may be given access to your medical records are:

☞ A supervisor or manager who may need to be informed if you have a condition that would require your duties to be restricted, or if you have a disability that must be accommodated;

☞ First aid or medical personnel, if you have a condition or disability that may require emergency treatment; and

☞ Government officials investigating your employer's compliance (or lack of compliance) with the ADA.

If your employer has fewer than twenty-five employees (and thus is not covered by the ADA), he may still be taking a big risk by letting anyone other than the above people see your medical records. For example, letting leak the fact that you have AIDS (even if it turns out that you don't) could cost your employer big bucks.

Finally, a number of state laws expressly allow you to request that your employer remove erroneous or dated information from your file and insert an explanation of any document you disagree with. That explanatory comment must then remain a part of the file so that anyone who sees it will also see your explanation. Many state laws allow you to get a copy of your file, too, though most require you to pay your employer for the reasonable cost of making copies.

TABLE 12

STATE LAWS ON ACCESS TO PERSONNEL FILES*

State	Personnel Files	Medical Records	Remove/Explain
Alaska	√	—	—
Arizona	public employees	—	—
Arkansas	√	√	—
California	√	—	—
Connecticut	√	√	√
Delaware	√	√	√
District of Columbia	District employees	†	√
Illinois	√	—	√
Indiana	public employees	—	—
Iowa	√	—	—
Kentucky	public employees	public employees	—
Louisiana	—	√	—
Maine	public employees	—	—
Massachusetts	√	—	√
Michigan	√	—	√
Minnesota	√	—	√
Nebraska	public employees	—	—
Nevada	√	—	employer's option
New Hampshire	√	—	√
New Mexico	—	‡	—
North Carolina	public employees	public employees†	public employees
North Dakota	public employees	public employees	public employees
Ohio	—	√	—
Oklahoma	public employees	√	—
Oregon	√	—	—
Pennsylvania	√	—	√
Rhode Island	√	—	—
South Dakota	public employees	—	—
Tennessee	public employees	—	—
Texas	public safety personnel	—	—
Utah	public employees	—	—
Washington	√	—	√
Wisconsin	√	—	√

Personnel Files: √ indicates that, in general, both public and private employees are covered by the law requiring access to personnel files. "Public employees" means only public employees must be given access to their files and that private employers are not expressly covered.
Medical Records: √ indicates that medical records are expressly included among the records to which employees must be given access. (A √ under *Medical Records* only indicates that the law refers to medical records specifically and not to personnel records in general.)
Remove/Explain: √ indicates that employees are allowed to request that their employer remove erroneous or dated material or material with which the employee does not agree; or in the alternative, the employee has a right to insert an explanation, which must remain a permanent part of the file.
†except if a prudent doctor would not release them
‡records may be released to the employee by a health care provider
Note: States not listed do not have specific laws regarding access to personnel files.

Table 12 contains a synopsis of state records-inspection laws. But even if your state isn't among those that require your employer to provide you with access to your records, don't despair. In the event of a lawsuit, state (and federal) courts will generally compel your employer to produce all records that are relevant to your case.

SEARCH AND SEIZURE

The key factor most courts will consider in deciding whether or not you are safe from employer intrusions into areas normally subject to your exclusive control, such as your locker or desk drawer (the two most frequent situations where the issue arises), is the extent to which you have a "legitimate expectation of privacy" in those areas.

Of course, your employer's main interest in gaining access to those and other areas subject to your control is ostensibly to prevent pilferage of his inventory or other company property, to prevent the use of alcohol on the job or the use of and potential traffic in illegal drugs on his premises. Legitimate reasons all, but not so legitimate if they contravene your right to privacy, your right to maintain that one small space of your own in which to keep personal, private items (such as that file folder full of work-related documents you've been compiling since you applied for this job).

Legitimate Expectation of Privacy

So, what is a "legitimate expectation of privacy," anyway? In short, it is the reasonableness of your belief that your "stuff" was safe from the prying eyes of your employer. That reasonableness, in turn, is measured by the degree to which you thought you controlled the space in question. For example:

☛ Was your locker, desk, etc., locked and did you have the only key? If so, you certainly would have a "more legitimate" expectation of privacy than if it was not locked or if coworkers or your secretary or especially your employer had a key, too.

☛ Does your employer have a policy that such areas are *not* your exclusive province, but are the property of the company and, as such, subject to search at his discretion? And were you given notice of that policy? If so, your expectancy of privacy is significantly diminished.

The *reasonableness* of your employer's search, in terms of its scope and intrusiveness, may also have an impact on its legitimacy in the eyes of a judge. In one case, an employee sued his employer for searching his knapsack on his way out of the building. The employer had an inspection policy to prevent theft of his property, but the employee didn't actually know about it, which the court said made the employee's expectation of privacy legitimate. However, the court ruled in favor of the employer anyway, citing the fact that employees were encouraged to check their personal packages before entering the workplace, and searches, when conducted, were neither forcible nor unduly intrusive.* In another case, a worker who was fired for refusing to turn over his wallet during a random drug search was awarded $550,000 for lost wages and emotional distress. The company's actions were called a violation of California's right to privacy laws. The court said a person's wallet or purse is an intensely private possession that should be subject to search only when there is a specific reason to suspect the employee is concealing drugs or stolen property.†

How legitimate your expectation of privacy is can also depend on your job. For example, an employer's search of your car while it is in his parking lot may be acceptable at a correctional facility for security reasons and unacceptable under less compelling circumstances. Likewise, the degree to which you have a presumed expectation of personal privacy may depend on the type of employment situation, although courts concede much more of an expectancy of privacy in your body than in other areas "under your control." In order for a body search, even a pat-down, not to amount to an invasion of privacy, you would generally have to be in some kind of a security position. Even then, your employer would have to have some overriding reason to search you: for example, reasonable cause to believe you were guilty of theft or some other type of wrongdoing warranting such an intrusion.

Just a note: Based on court decisions, you generally have less of an expectation of privacy in desks, lockers, and other areas under your exclusive control if you work for the government than if you work for a private employer, although even there, cases have gone both ways.

So, whether or not you have a legitimate expectation of privacy will depend on several factors, including your employer's published

*Chenkin v. Bellevue Hospital Center, 479 Fed. Supp. 207, DC SNY, 1979.
†Overby v. Chevron USA Inc., Calif. Sup. Ct., No. SWC-89552,1993.

policy regarding searches, the exclusivity of your control over what is searched (your body vs. your desk), the reason for the search, and the intrusiveness of the search relative to that reason. Search and seizure laws work on a basic principle: The more intrusive the search, the more likely it will be found to be an invasion of your privacy.

Detention: You aren't in high school anymore. Your employer can't detain or confine you against your will—such as requiring you to wait in his office while he calls the police because he may think you have stolen something. (An employer who does detain or confine an employee against his or her will could be found guilty of a charge of false imprisonment.) However, he may, of course, discipline you appropriately if you leave your work station during working hours.

SURVEILLANCE AND MONITORING

How much covert surveillance goes on in the workplace? And is it legal?

The answer to the first question is merely a guess, but you don't have to be a rocket scientist to realize that the more technological advances our society makes, the more potential there is for surveillance. Conclusion: Since our employers aren't telling, you can bet it's being done more than you realize. Computer monitoring and monitoring of telephone conversations seem to be the favorites, with closed-circuit television close behind.

There is, as usual, a method to employers' madness, though whether it is more method or madness is open to conjecture. They do it, they say, to stimulate productivity, or to improve customer service, or to decrease theft of company property, or to see to it that employees don't spend their time on company computers or telephones for their own personal use. Employee advocacy groups, however, counter that it is an invasion of privacy, and besides, what employers gain in productivity or customer relations is more than offset by losses due to an increase in employees' stress levels and the inevitable dropoff in morale.

Unfortunately, a lot of this new-age watchdog stuff is legal when conducted in actual work areas. However, like other information your employer tries to gather about you, it should have a legitimate business purpose (spurring productivity, stemming theft, improving customer relations, etc.). Also, like other information gathering, the results should yield information your employer is legally entitled to have. Finally, like other information in your personnel file, it should be accessible only on a need-to-know basis. It may be okay for your employer to get information about you through electronic surveillance, but if he blabs the results all over the place, he's open to an invasion of privacy suit.

Prior Written Notice. A growing body of law suggests that employees must be given prior written notification, via the posting of a notice, of any and all monitoring that will take place in the workplace, including the types of monitoring that may occur.*

And there are other restrictions on how snoopy an employer can be.

Federal Law

A federal law called the **Omnibus Crime Control and Safe Streets Act of 1968** prohibits intercepting "wire, oral or electronic communications." One big exception, however, is that employers are expressly allowed to use extension phones to monitor employees' calls "in the ordinary course of business." But the law also says they are required to hang up as soon as they determine that the call is personal.

State Law

Though in theory most workplace monitoring done "in the ordinary course of business" is acceptable (maybe not to you, but to the law), many state laws restrict *where* employers can go with their surveillance. For example, employers take a big risk when they undertake electronic monitoring of activities in areas designated for employees' personal comfort or for safeguarding their possessions. For example, it would be pretty difficult to prove a business justification for having a closed-circuit television set in an employee rest room; also, although perhaps to a lesser extent, in a locker room, lounge, or other employee area.

On the "more technology, more snooping" front, an increasing number of cases have been popping up regarding privacy rights in electronic mail (mostly invasion of privacy suits filed by employees who were disciplined or fired as a result of messages sent through

*Conn. Pub. Act No. 98-142, 1998.

their company's e-mail). In one case an employer tapped into an employee's personal computer messages and then used the information to can him for allegedly stealing company secrets. In another, two women objected when their boss tapped into their (they thought private) e-mail messages—in which they made some rather unflattering references to him. Though the **Omnibus Crime Control and Safe Streets Act of 1968** prohibits a third party from intercepting electronic communications, it does not address the matter of employers monitoring computer message networks. Nor, specifically, does the **Electronic Communications and Privacy Act.** However, most courts—including the ones in these two cases—have ruled that employers are within their rights to tap into employees' e-mail. Apparently, the theory is that if you are using e-mail, you should know that it is not necessarily a completely private form of communication. In fact, employers can assume they are on fairly firm ground if the monitoring, no matter what the form, has a legitimate business purpose, if they let employees know they are being monitored, and if, once it has been established that a communication is personal, the monitoring ceases.

Note (e-mail about workplace issues): In a 1997 case *(Timekeeping Systems, Inc. v. Lawrence Leinweber),* the National Labor Relations Board (NLRB) determined that an employee who was fired after sending e-mail to coworkers complaining about the employer's vacation policy was engaged in a "protected activity" under the National Labor Relations Act (NLRA) and should be reinstated with back pay. While the NLRA is concerned primarily with employees' organizational and collective bargaining rights, according to the NRLB it also addresses other "concerted activity" for mutual aid and protection in the workplace. According to the NLRB, this includes the actions of two or more employees "seeking to initiate or induce or to prepare for group action." Examples include complaints about safety violations, discussions about wages and benefits, and walk-outs because of inadequate or non-functioning heating or cooling systems. In short, all employees of employers engaged in interstate commerce are protected by the NLRA whether or not they are unionized. So workers enjoy great latitude in using e-mail to communicate with coworkers about workplace issues.

With the advent of voice mail and video mail, among other technological advances on the horizon, the potential for snooping seems to be growing exponentially. Even so, a number of bills addressing workplace monitoring have stalled in Congress in recent years. Specifically, a bill introduced by Sen. Paul Simon (D-Ill.), though it would not have prohibited electronic monitoring per se, would have required employers to use some means to let employees know when they were being monitored (i.e.: a flashing light or a beeping tone when surveillance was under way). It would also have limited the type of information that could be gathered and how it could be used.

Alas, without a current champion of the cause of techno-privacy in the workplace, the best advice is "cyber-worker beware."

Union Activities

The National Labor Relations Board expressly prohibits employers from using *any* technique to intentionally observe, overhear, or record (i.e., spy on) employer-employee contract negotiations, union meetings, or any other union activities. To do so is categorized as an unfair labor practice.

Is it superfluous to say that electronic surveillance of employees is likely to be a bigger and bigger issue in the future, as more and more businesses make significant technological advances? Indeed, if you spend most of your work time on the telephone or at a computer terminal, Big Brother may already be watching.

LIE DETECTOR (POLYGRAPH) TESTING

We've all watched enough TV movies to know they still can't use lie detectors in most courtroom situations. But can they use them at work? The answer is no. But, again, it is a qualified no.

Federal Law

The federal **Employee Polygraph Protection Act of 1988** prohibits most private employers not only from *requiring* job applicants or employees to submit to a lie detector test but even from *requesting* that they take one. Then, if your employer (or prospective employer) does ask you to take a lie detector test in spite of the law against it, he is prohibited from disciplining, discharging, or otherwise discriminating against you for refusing to take it.

Under the federal law, a polygraph, or lie detector, includes any type of mechanical or electrical device or procedure either used or claimed to be used to examine, test, or question a person to determine if he or she is telling the truth.

So exactly what does that mean? It means that most private employers may not:

☞ Request, require, suggest, or cause an employee or prospective employee to take a lie detector test as a condition of getting a job or keeping his or her job.

☞ Discharge, in any way discipline, or make an adverse employment decision based on an employee's refusal to take a lie detector test.

☞ Use or ask about the results of a lie detector test given to an employee or job applicant. Or,

☞ Retaliate against an applicant or employee for filing a complaint or otherwise asserting his or her rights under the act.

Exception (Workplace Theft)

The law *does* allow your employer to ask you to take a lie detector test when workplace theft or other misconduct is causing him to lose money, but only under the following conditions:

☞ Your employer has to be investigating a *specific* incident or activity (as opposed to a loss of property that has taken place over a period of time). Examples of appropriate incidents or activities include theft, embezzlement, sabotage, and misappropriation.

☞ You must have had access to the missing property.

☞ Your employer must have a reasonable suspicion that you were involved in the incident or activity. Generally, this means that an objective, disinterested person would have reached the same conclusion from the same set of facts or evidence.

☞ You must be given a written notice of the incident being investigated and the reason you are suspected at least forty-eight hours before the test. (Your employer has to keep a copy of the notice on file for at least three years.)

Note: Even if you take a lie detector test in response to your employer's legitimate request that you take one, the results cannot be the sole reason for discharging or disciplining you.

Exceptions (Employers Not Covered)

The federal polygraph protection law does not cover federal, state, or local government employees, or employees of the Department of Defense or FBI contractors.

In addition, employers in the following businesses are permitted to require job applicants to take a polygraph test:

☞ *Security companies:* This exception applies only to applicants for certain security positions: those primarily engaged in handling, trading, transferring, or storing "currency, negotiable instruments or proprietary information." It does not include security alarm or guard services provided to other types of businesses or to private homes. Neither does it include non-security personnel within qualified companies (such as janitors or secretaries), or to companies who hire employees for their *own* company's security.

☞ *Drug and pharmaceutical companies:* This exception applies only to applicants for jobs that will actually put them in contact with controlled drugs.

The Rules of the Game

Even in the limited context where polygraph tests are allowed, actual testing is subject to numerous restrictions—before, during, and after the test is given. If your employer has a legitimate right to ask you to submit to a lie detector test, he must:

☞ Give you reasonable advance *written* notice of the test, including the date, time, and conditions of the test and the instruments that will be used to conduct the test.
☞ *Read* to you and ask you to sign:
  • a list of prohibited questions (which includes all the usual suspects, like anything concerning your religious beliefs, racial opinions, sexual preferences, political affiliation, union membership or leanings, etc.);
  • a statement regarding your right to refuse to take the test;
  • a statement indicating that you cannot be required to take the test as a condition of employment;
  • a statement regarding how the results of the test can be used: that is, that your answers, along with other evidence,

could affect your job (i.e., be used as a reason not to hire you, or to discipline or fire you); and

- your legal rights if the test isn't administered properly.

Testers

As if all that wasn't enough, the person who actually conducts the test must be licensed and bonded and must comply with certain procedural, record-keeping, and notice requirements. And he has to be honest about certain details of the testing process. Specifically, the tester:

☛ Has to inform you that you can refuse to take the test or quit taking it at any time.

☛ Can't ask you questions about race, religion, sex, etc., or questions that would otherwise invade your privacy. And,

☛ Can't disclose test results to anyone other than you and your employer. (**Note:** The tester *can* disclose the results to a government agency that jumps through the right legal hoops to get them, but *not unless* you have admitted to committing a crime.)

Finally, the act requires employers to post a notice outlining the law's requirements and restrictions where employees and job applicants can readily see it.

Summary: So unless you are a government employee, work around something really valuable (like drugs or money), or are reasonably suspected of swiping something of your employer's that you had access to, you can't even be asked to take a lie detector test, and can refuse without penalty if you are. And if you do happen to qualify to be tested, remember: After your employer complies with all the pretesting requirements, you can refuse to take the test without penalty, you can stop taking it any time you wish, and even if you agree to take it and flunk, you can't be refused employment, disciplined, demoted, or fired based on the test results alone.

State Laws

But there's more. More than half the states have polygraph protection laws of their own, which, like other state laws, apply to the extent that they outdo the federal law in protecting you from intrusions into your privacy. Many of these states prohibit employers from requiring job applicants to take polygraph tests as a condition of employment. Period. Take Rhode Island, for example. A police department violated the state's polygraph protection law by asking a civilian employee to take a lie detector test to help "clear up" an investigation into wrongdoing—even though the employee was not disciplined for refusing to take it.*

A few states go so far as to prohibit *any* employer from requesting *any* employee or job applicant to take a lie detector test under *any* circumstances. However, most states except government agencies, law enforcement agencies, and drug and pharmaceutical companies.

Lie detector tests may also be further restricted by local laws and union contracts.

WHAT TO DO: The situations under which a private employer can legally ask you to take a lie detector test are so narrow that if yours (or one with whom you are applying for a job) does, consult a lawyer. See Chapter 11: I'm Getting Screwed; So What Can I Do about It? for details on finding the right lawyer.

DRUG AND ALCOHOL TESTING

The first thing to know about drug testing (including that most ubiquitous of drugs, alcohol) is that it can be quite an expensive undertaking for an employer. That's because, like getting pregnant, it's kind of hard to do without going all the way. Particularly if an employer has decided he is going to test job applicants (which we will see is easier than testing people he already employs), it's difficult to justify testing just some of them. How do you choose whom to test without discriminating? By the way they dress? The way they talk? What they look like? The color of their skin? Their sex? See what I mean?

So drug testing is a big can of worms. But more and more employers are willing to open the can, and there are several reasons why. First, the job they are screening for may have a legitimate need for a sober occupant (operating heavy machinery, driving a delivery truck, etc.). Second is the pay-me-now-or-pay-me-later syndrome: It's worth it to go to the trouble and expense of screening job applicants for drug use now rather than face the down-the-road expenses

Carr v. Mulhearn, Rhode Island Supreme Court, No. 91-89-M.P., 1992.

due to lateness, absence from work, decreased productivity, and turnover that drug users inevitably involve. And third, they are trapped in a fright cycle (perhaps with good reason) that tells them we are living in a drug culture, and if more and more employers screen for drug use and they continue not to, word will get out and they will end up with all the druggies.

Government Contractors

A number of laws and government regulations passed in the late 1980s require most federal contractors, employers who receive federal funding, and both public and private transportation companies to have drug awareness programs. A brief synopsis of each follows:

Drug Free Workplace Act of 1988: Under the Act, most government contractors have to:

☞ Have a policy prohibiting drug use that would affect the workplace and require employees to abide by it;
☞ Establish a drug-free awareness program for employees;
☞ Require employees to notify them within five days of being convicted of a drug offense;
☞ Notify the proper agency of an employee's drug conviction within ten days of being informed by the employee; and
☞ Take appropriate disciplinary action against the drug offender, up to and including termination.

The act doesn't require drug testing.

Department of Defense Rules: The DOD rules also require contractors to train and educate employees concerning drug abuse. However, the DOD rules specifically require drug testing of employees in sensitive jobs. Basically, those jobs involve national security or public health and safety. In addition, drug testing is allowed for all job applicants, for employees whom the employer reasonably suspects of drug use, for employees who are involved in an accident, and as part of a voluntary testing program.

A recent Supreme Court case tested the right of the Department of Justice (a division of the DOD) to require job applicants to take a drug test. The case involved an attorney who refused to take the test. The Supreme Court ruled in favor of the agency, saying that because of the extensive background checks known to be done by the DOJ prior to hiring, job applicants had a reduced expectation of privacy. They added that the government's interest in "maintaining public confidence and trust" outweighed applicants' privacy rights.*

Department of Transportation Regulations: The DOT regulations require random drug testing of employees in safety-sensitive jobs in industries regulated by the agency. That includes virtually every employee having to do with bus, rail, sea, or air travel, from maintenance to actual operation. Under the regulations, with regard to most of these safety-sensitive positions, you can be tested as a condition of employment, be given periodic or random tests, and be tested where there is a reasonable suspicion of drug use or after being involved in an accident.

Of course, each administration subject to the DOT (Aviation, Highway, Railroad, Coast Guard, etc.), as well as city mass transit commissions, has very strict rules regarding how frequently employees may be tested and the privacy of those being tested, as well as for collection, chain-of-custody (who has possession of a blood or urine sample between its donor and its analysis), and confirmation and confidentiality of results.

Nuclear Regulatory Commission Regulations: The NRC regs cover employees with access to protected areas of nuclear plants and those involved with plant emergency response operations. Besides education and training programs, the regs require testing of employees within two months before they are given unescorted access to a protected area, plus random tests, and tests for cause, including after an accident, exposure, radiation leaks, and other safety breaches.

Drug-Free Schools and Communities Act of 1989: Department of Education rules require all schools receiving federal funds to take steps to implement programs to prevent the unlawful possession, use, or distribution of drugs by students and teachers. The rules do not call for drug testing.

Willner v. Barr, U.S. Supreme Court, No. 88-67, 1991.

Drug and Alcohol Abuse as a Protected "Handicap"

There are two laws that offer limited protection to drug and alcohol abusers as "handicapped individuals": The **Rehabilitation Act of 1973,** which applies to federal contractors and recipients of federal funds, and the parallel **Americans with Disabilities Act of 1990,** which covers all employers of fifteen or more workers. For details of handicap discrimination in general, see Chapter 5: Discrimination and Related Issues.

Both acts generally protect "qualified handicapped individuals" from job discrimination and require employers to offer reasonable accommodation of their handicap in order to enable them to perform the essential duties of the job, as long as it doesn't cause an undue hardship for the employer.

The question: To what extent is drug or alcohol abuse a "qualified handicap" protected by ADA (or the Rehab Act)?

The answer: To the extent that the employee (or job applicant) is a *former* user who has undergone rehabilitation or is presently undergoing rehabilitation and is now "clean." Current alcohol use or use of illegal drugs is not protected. (As one court put it, "Reasonable accommodation in the context of alcoholism must be limited in scope, since continued accommodation would enable an alcoholic to keep drinking."* So, if you are a current user of alcohol or illegal drugs, an employer can refuse to hire you, or can discipline or fire you, and you have no recourse to the protection of "handicap" laws.

What all this means, then, is that your employer is free to:

☞ Prohibit drug or alcohol use or possession at work.
☞ Hold current drug and alcohol users to the same performance standards as nonusers.
☞ Require employees' behavior to conform to the **Drug Free Workplace Act.**
☞ Require employees in "sensitive" jobs (as defined by the DOD, DOT, and NRC regulations) to comply with those regulations. And,
☞ Discipline or fire an employee for poor performance or breach of work rules even if it is caused by drug or alcohol impairment.

Fuller v. Frank, U.S. Court of Appeals, 9th Circuit, No. 89-15559, 1990.

Drug Testing under the ADA: While ADA suggests that reasonable employer policies can include drug testing, it doesn't imply that employers should or should not test for drug or alcohol use. It does, however, prohibit preemployment drug tests unless a job offer has already been made and unless the test is given to everyone applying for that job classification.

The Rules of the Game

Neither the Rehab Act nor the ADA prevents employers from trying their best to keep drugs out of their workplaces. However, once an employer does decide he will test job applicants and/or current employees for drug use, there are certain rules he has to follow, some of which are prescribed by statute (the Rehab Act, ADA, or individual state drug-testing or handicap discrimination laws) and others that have evolved over the past ten or fifteen years from court decisions in various jurisdictions. The rules vary somewhat from state to state, and also depending on your job, but break down pretty much as follows:

Job Applicants: The law generally recognizes an employer's right to hire workers whose performance or behavior will not be impaired by drug or alcohol use. Thus, preemployment medical exams that include urinalysis drug tests are acceptable in most situations. However, to protect your privacy rights, an employer should include a drug test only when:

☞ He gives applicants prior notice that employment is conditioned on passing a drug test.
☞ He has already made a job offer. (The job offer can be conditioned on passing the drug test, though.)
☞ All applicants for the same type or classification of job are tested.

Of course, the way in which the test is conducted (by a certified laboratory) must also comply with privacy and confidentiality requirements. For example:

☞ Where a urine sample is collected (urinalysis drug tests using gas chromatography and mass spectrometry are a common testing method), it must be done without observation of the donor;

☞ The chain of custody of samples (i.e., who has possession of them between the donor and the test) must be guarded so as to ensure the integrity of the sample;

☞ A positive test result must be confirmed by an independent test; and

☞ Results of the test must be kept confidential.

Current Employees: If an employer wants to test current employees for drug use, the standards are much stricter. To protect your privacy, an employer can require a drug test *safely* only when:

☛ The employer has a written drug-testing policy known to employees.

☛ The employer has an appropriate grievance procedure for employees who refuse to be tested.

☛ An employee's insobriety could present a danger to himself or herself or others (e.g., drivers, operators of heavy machinery, etc.).

☛ The employer has a reasonable suspicion that drug use is affecting the employee's job performance. (This is the tough one for most employers. They are not drug counselors. Nor are they trained in detection of drug or alcohol use. They may think an employee "acts" drunk or drugged, and they may hear rumors of substance use at work, but when are they safe in accusing a worker? "Reasonableness" implies that a reasonable person could tell that the worker was under the influence. But unless the employer is pretty damn sure—and that means he has proof other than just the observation of an untrained supervisor—he is taking a calculated risk that the employee isn't just sick or tired or stressed out and will turn around and sue him for invasion of privacy, defamation, wrongful discharge, and a slew of other offenses.)

☛ All the rules of sample collection, custody, and analysis are followed, as outlined above.

☛ The confidentiality of test results is scrupulously maintained.

☛ An employee who has an independently confirmed positive test result is given an opportunity for rehabilitation.

Refusing to Take a Drug Test: Can you be fired for refusing to take a drug test? Of course you can be fired. But do you have recourse? That's not an easy question to answer with a quick yes or no. The answer really depends on the answers to a few more questions:

☞ Are you able to perform the essential functions of your job?
☞ Are you a threat to the safety or property of others?
☞ What is your past work record?
☞ How has your employer dealt with similar problems in the past?
☞ Does he have sufficient evidence that you were under the influence of drugs or alcohol on the job?
☞ Was there a grievance process that allowed you to air your objections to being tested?
☞ Were you given an opportunity for rehabilitation?

Now, your employer doesn't have to ask himself all of these questions before he shows you the door, but if he doesn't, he may be leaving that door open for your return ... with your lawyer.

By the way, in case you were wondering, if an employer forces you to take a drug test or extracts a blood sample without your consent, he faces additional charges of assault and battery.

AIDS TESTING

Let's take it from the top: You aren't going to get AIDS at work. Not unless you have a pretty weird job. And you can't be discriminated against because you have AIDS (or if you are suspected of having AIDS). The fact is that AIDS is transmittable only by the kind of intimate contact most of us just don't have on the job.

A 1987 U.S. Supreme Court decision listed the three factors that could be used to determine whether an employee can be refused a job or terminated because of *any contagious disease* (including AIDS). Those factors are:

☞ The nature, duration, and severity of the risk.
☞ The potential harm to others.
☞ The probability of transmission.

In the case of AIDS, while the first two factors may be significant, the third is virtually nil. This is to say that, though the effects of the disease are horrible, and the harm to anyone who contracts it is supreme, the chance of getting it at work is just about zero. (The risk is so insignificant, in fact, that the State of Connecticut refused to mandate AIDS tests for health care professionals because, according to the state health commissioner, even the risk of *infected health care professionals* passing the virus on to patients "is so small, so remote, that it can't even be measured.") That's why the **Americans with Disabilities Act** specifically includes victims of AIDS as "qualified disabled individuals" entitled to the law's protections against employment discrimination. And while some states also specify that AIDS is a protected disability, even in those states that don't, AIDS victims would probably be protected by state civil rights or fair employment laws as handicapped individuals.

So, what about AIDS testing?

Americans with Disabilities Act

Under the ADA, job applicants can neither be asked if they have AIDS nor be given an AIDS test unless having AIDS could be considered "job-related and consistent with business necessity." (And, of course, a test can't be given, or a question asked, unless a job offer has already been made.) As we have seen, the chances of that are virtually zero.

Jobs Handling Food: The ADA does treat jobs that require food handling (meat packer, cook, waiter, waitress, etc.) differently. An employer can refuse to hire someone with a communicable disease for a job handling food *if* the disease can be transmitted through the handling of food. (**Note:** An employer can't decide what jobs those are. The Secretary of Health and Human Services has compiled a list—which is updated annually to reflect current medical knowledge.) However, current employees should be offered the accommodation of reassignment to an alternate position that doesn't involve food handling. What that means, essentially, is that if your employer has an alternate position available that you are qualified to do, he should give you the chance to take that job.

State Law

In most states AIDS is treated as a handicap either by statute or court precedent. Most prohibit involuntary AIDS testing or the use of test results to affect employment decisions.

Chain of Logic

Here's a geometry-type proof for you:

Statement	*Reason*
☞ AIDS is virtually impossible to catch through contact at work.	☞ The Centers for Disease Control say so.
☞ Having AIDS would not render an employee incapable of performing the essential duties of the job.	☞ AIDS is virtually impossible to catch at work.
☞ An AIDS victim cannot be fired (or disciplined) if he or she can otherwise perform the essential duties of the job.	☞ **Americans with Disabilities Act,** state AIDS testing and handicap laws and court decisions.
☞ Whether or not an employee has AIDS is irrelevant as long as he or she can still perform the essential duties of the job.	☞ Having AIDS does not render an employee incapable of performing the essential duties of the job.
☞ Testing an employee for AIDS is pointless and stupid.	☞ AIDS victims cannot be fired or disciplined as long as they can still perform the essential duties of the job.
☞ Your employer shouldn't ask you to take an AIDS test, and if he does you probably have every right to sue him down to his last penny.	☞ Testing an employee for AIDS is stupid and pointless.

Q.E.D. (*Quod Erat Demonstrandum:* that which was to be proven)

SUMMARY

You *do* give up some degree of personal freedom when you enter the workplace. Actually, it would be more accurate to say that you may have to sacrifice some personal freedom in order to keep your job. And part of the freedom you must sacrifice on the altar of *The God of a Roof and Three Squares* is in the area of privacy. But, as we have seen, you don't have to make the supreme sacrifice. You don't give up *all* of your privacy when you punch that clock.

Though more and more employers are invading what we consider to be our personal space, like our computer files and telephone conversations, there are laws that protect us if those invasions are unjustified or too intrusive. For example, once your employer determines that the telephone conversation he is eavesdropping on is personal, he is legally required to hang up.

We have also seen that, in the private sector, at least, few employers have the right to ask you to take a lie detector test without some pretty hard evidence that you are involved in a theft of company property. And almost *no* employer is justified in giving you an AIDS test.

Of course, once your employer has gathered all this information on you, the law restricts how he can use it and to whom he can divulge it. Most employees have the right to see whatever is in their own personnel files; and many have the right to have their employer add an explanation of anything they disagree with. But beyond that your employer is taking a risk when he divulges any information about you to anyone other than on a "need-to-know" basis.

Finally, in search and seizure cases, courts will consider:

☞ How legitimate your expectation of privacy was.
☞ Whether your employer had an express policy regarding the area that was searched.
☞ The reason for the search.
☞ The validity of your employer's cause to search *you*. And,
☞ The intrusiveness of the search in relation to the reason for it.

In short, whether the privacy issue involves a drug test, an AIDS test, a lie detector test, a search of your desk or personal property or person, disclosure of the reason you were fired or other information in your personnel or medical file, or tapping into your computer or telephone, a court will weigh the degree of the intrusion on your privacy against your employer's legitimate business interest.

7

Health and Safety

O nce upon a time, for a lot of people a good day at work meant getting home in one piece. Actually, for some workers that may still be true today. In fact, a study by the Bureau of Labor Statistics reported that about 6.7 million workers were injured or became ill at work in 1993. Though the rate of workplace injury and illness actually decreased from 8.9 per 100 workers in 1992 to 8.5 per 100 workers in 1993, the 1992 rate had been the highest in over ten years. Compare that to highway department statistics and it's easy to see that for many American workers, driving home is safer than being at work. And prior to the enactment of the **Occupational Safety and Health Act of 1970,** it was worse. Before that states enacted their own health and safety laws, which in general were enforced piecemeal if at all. The federal act has established some basic workplace safety standards and instituted some overall enforcement measures that offer workers more protection than they have ever had. But still, given the law's limited enforcement capabilities, much of the responsibility for overseeing compliance rests with employers to do the right thing—and with you to report them if they don't. Read on for warnings.

OCCUPATIONAL SAFETY AND HEALTH ACT

The federal **Occupational Safety and Health Act** applies to all private employers engaged in business affecting interstate commerce (which is virtually all employers). The act is administered and enforced by the Occupational Safety and Health Administration, a division of the U.S. Department of Labor. Though most employers are covered by the act, OSHA tends to concentrate its enforcement efforts on the more hazardous industries, such as construction.

OSHA encourages the states to develop their own safety and health laws but approves them only if they are at least as effective in assuring workplace safety and health as the federal standard. States whose occupational safety and health laws have been approved by OSHA include: Alaska, Arizona, California, Connecticut,* Hawaii, Indiana, Iowa, Kentucky, Maryland, Michigan, Minnesota, Nevada, New Mexico, New York,* North Carolina, Oregon, South Carolina, Tennessee, Utah, Vermont, Virginia, Washington, and Wyoming.

SAFETY AND HEALTH STANDARDS

The **Occupational Safety and Health Act** requires employers to comply with two separate safety standards, a general standard, which applies to all workplaces, and a specific standard, which applies to conditions in particular work environments.

General Standard

Under the act, your employer has *a general duty to provide a workplace that is free from "recognized hazards" that are likely to cause death or severe physical harm.* "Recognized hazards" include conditions or situations that are obviously dangerous, or that your employer knows about, or that are generally considered hazardous in his particular industry.

So, in order to prove that your employer violated the general duty clause, OSHA would have to show that (1) your employer "failed to render [his] workplace free of a hazard [which was] (2) recognized and [which was] (3) causing or likely to cause death or serious physical harm."†

---

*Connecticut and New York occupational safety and health laws apply only to state and local governments, not private employers.
†*National Realty & Construction Co. v. Occupational Safety and Health Review Commission,* 489 F. 2d 1257, U.S. Court of Appeals, D.C. Circuit, 1973.

Specific Standards

In addition to the general standard, OSHA has established safety and health standards covering virtually all conceivable aspects of the workplace environment. Though they are too numerous to list in their entirety, let alone to detail, some of the specific standards cover:

☞ Control of ventilation, temperature, and noise levels;
☞ "Hazard communication," or "right-to-know" laws (see below);
☞ Keeping the workplace clean and orderly, and keeping entrances, exits, and stairways clear;
☞ Having emergency exits, fire protection and alarm systems, sprinklers, and evacuation plans;
☞ Medical and first-aid treatment;
☞ Handling and storage of compressed gas, radiation, flammable materials, explosives, hazardous waste, and other toxic or hazardous materials;
☞ Personal protective equipment for eyes, face, head, feet, and respiratory systems;
☞ Maintenance of work areas;
☞ Training on and operation of machinery and hand-held equipment;
☞ Electrical standards; and
☞ General working conditions (waste disposal, toilets, showers, changing rooms, and food handling). See below.

WORKING CONDITIONS

OSHA and most states have detailed requirements concerning general environmental controls in the workplace. (Many more apply to workplaces using, producing, or distributing toxic or carcinogenic substances or other potentially harmful agents. See Right-to-Know Laws below.)

Basic Requirements

Some of the basic environmental considerations in the workplace include:

Housekeeping: Workplaces must be kept in clean and orderly condition to the degree allowed by the nature of the work. Rest rooms and water fountains should be cleaned regularly. Floors should be swept and kept free of unnecessary obstructions.

Waste Disposal: Receptacles used for rotting waste must not leak and must be kept sanitary.

Water: The workplace must have water that is suitable for drinking and washing.

Toilets: Separate toilets must be maintained for males and females (except if they can be locked from the inside and used by one person at a time), as follows:

Number of Employees	Number of Toilets
1–15	1
16–35	2
36–55	3
56–80	4
81–110	5
111–150	6
Over 150	1 more toilet for each additional 40 employees

Hot and cold water must be available in rest rooms.

Showers and Changing Rooms: Generally, if your employer provides you with work clothes that get wet or are washed between shifts, the clothes have to be dry before reuse. If you are required to wear certain clothing as protection against contamination from toxic materials, your employer has to provide a changing room with storage facilities for street clothes and separate storage facilities for protective clothes. When showers are required, there must be at least one for every ten employees (or fraction thereof) of each sex.

Food Handling: All employee food service facilities must be hygienic. Food must be wholesome and unspoiled, and prepared and stored so it is not contaminated.

Eating: Eating may not be allowed in rest rooms or where food would be exposed to hazardous chemicals.

Temperature: Temperatures should be maintained at a comfortable level. OSHA has no specific temperature requirements. However, the "general standard" would prohibit allowing temperatures to get so cold or so hot that workers' health or safety would be affected.

Noise: Employees generally may not be exposed to constant noise above a certain level. And when noise levels exceed eighty-five decibels over eight hours, employees must be provided with protective gear and be tested periodically.

Lighting: Lighting should be adequate to prevent eyestrain and angled to reduce glare.

Elevators: Smoking cannot be permitted in elevators.

Medical and First Aid

At the very least your employer is supposed to have first aid equipment on hand to deal with minor injuries. Depending on the type of industry, more may be required. Specifically, OSHA regulations require the following medical and first aid considerations:

☞ There must be medical care available within a reasonable distance of the workplace.
☞ If there is no emergency clinic or hospital relatively near the workplace, there should be someone on hand who is trained to give first aid. (First aid supplies must be approved by a consulting physician.) If there is no one available who is trained to give first aid, the employer may have to have a specific doctor on call when needed. And,
☞ If workers are exposed to potentially dangerous corrosive materials, the workplace is supposed to have suitable facilities for immediate flushing of the eyes and body.

Fire Extinguishers

Unless a workplace has an OSHA emergency fire prevention plan, which includes an alarm system, evacuation plan, and trained people to assist in the evacuation, it must have fire extinguishers available within a certain distance, depending on the type of potential fire:

Class A Fire (fire involving ordinary combustible materials, such as paper, wood, cloth, and some types of rubber and plastic): There must be an extinguisher within seventy-five feet of employees.

Class B Fire (fire involving combustible liquids, flammable gases, and similar materials): There must be an extinguisher within fifty feet of employees.

Class C Fire (fire involving combustible metals): There must be an extinguisher within seventy-five feet of combustible work area.

Note: OSHA also has specific requirements regarding the type of extinguishers that must be used.

Fire Alarms

A building has to have fire alarms if the building is big enough so that the outbreak of the fire itself would give adequate warning to employees that there is a fire.

OSHA INSPECTIONS

OSHA inspectors have the authority to enter and inspect workplaces to determine compliance with the law. Inspections may be made without advance notice, either on a routine basis or in response to a complaint. Inspections generally must be made during working hours.

Inspections usually include a check of company records, a review of compliance with the federal hazard communication standard ("right-to-know" laws), an examination of workers' personal protective gear and fire protection measures, and a review of the company's general health and safety plan. Random investigations are done more often, of course, in the more hazardous industries such as construction and public utilities. However, because of the relatively small number of OSHA inspectors, investigations are most commonly conducted as a result of complaints and, unfortunately, in the wake of accidents resulting in serious injury or death.

ACCIDENT REPORTS

Most state occupational safety and health laws (as well as workers' compensation laws) require employers to report all workplace accidents that result in serious physical injury to an employee. "Serious physical injury" is generally considered to be an injury that causes an absence from work of at least a week, or that results in death. In any case, your employer should report all workplace accidents resulting in serious physical injury to the state department of labor, occupational safety and health division, as soon as possible. Reports should include the injured worker's name; the time and place of the accident; the nature of the worker's injury; and the type of machine, if any, the employee was using.

Workers' Compensation Laws

In addition to the occupational safety and health law requirement that your employer report all "serious physical injuries," most state workers' compensation laws require him to:

☞ Keep a record of all on-the-job injuries resulting in an absence from work of one day or more; and

☞ File a weekly report of on-the-job injuries with the commissioner of labor, including the time of the injury and any notices of claims for compensation that he has received.

For details see Chapter 9: Workers' Compensation.

OSHA REPORTING REQUIREMENTS

OSHA has a slew of reporting requirements. They're really your employer's problem, but they are required to be kept mostly for your benefit. So here is a synopsis of the main ones:

Log and Summary of Injuries and Illnesses (OSHA Form No. 200)

OSHA requires *employers of more than ten workers* to keep a log of occupational injuries and illnesses and post a summary of them in the workplace.

Log of Injuries and Illnesses: The employer's log of injuries and illnesses has to include those that result in:

☞ A fatality.
☞ Lost days of work. Or,
☞ Transfer to another job, termination of employment, medical treatment (not including first aid), unconsciousness, or restriction of work or motion.

Employers are supposed to record these injuries as soon as possible, but at the latest within six days of when they happen. As an employee or former employee, you (or your attorney) must be given access to the log upon request. It must also be made available to OSHA representatives during inspections.

Posting Annual Summary: By February 1 of each year, employers have to post an annual summary of occupational injuries and illnesses in the workplace (part of OSHA Form No. 200). The summary must remain posted at least until March 1, and must include:

☞ The year's total recordable occupational injuries and illnesses (from OSHA Form 200).
☞ The calendar year covered.
☞ The company's name and address.
☞ The signature and title of the person signing the form. And,
☞ The date.

Record of Occupational Injury or Illness (OSHA Form No. 101)

Employers of more than ten workers also have to keep records of all injuries and illnesses. The records have to include:

☞ The employer's name and address.
☞ The injured or sick employee's name, Social Security number, address, sex, age, occupation, and department.
☞ Details of the accident, including the place, whether or not it happened on the employer's premises, what the employee was doing at the time, and how the accident happened.
☞ A description of the injury or illness, including the part of the body affected, the object or substance that caused the injury, the date it occurred, and the diagnosis. And,

☛ The name and address of the doctor and hospital, if the employee was hospitalized, the date of the report, and the name and title of the person who prepared the report.

OSHA Forms 200 and 101 must be retained by employers for at least five years.

Note: Employers of ten or fewer employees and employers in some "low-hazard" industries are exempted from OSHA record-keeping and posting requirements. Industries considered "low hazard" include most retailers, finance companies, real estate companies, insurance companies, and companies in the service industry.

Reporting Fatality or Hospitalization of Five or More Workers

All employers (including those with ten or fewer workers) are required to report to the area director of OSHA, within forty-eight hours, any accident resulting in a fatality or serious injury to five or more workers, including:

☞ The circumstances of the accident.
☞ The number of fatalities. And,
☞ The extent of nonfatal injuries to other employees.

KEEPING MEDICAL RECORDS

OSHA requires employers to keep employees' medical records (except first aid records) for at least *thirty years* after termination of their employment. "First aid" is considered any one-time treatment and follow-up visit for things like minor scratches, burns, cuts, and splinters which do not ordinarily require medical care.

POSTING REQUIREMENTS

Employers are also required to post OSHA notices informing their employees of the act, including:

☞ OSHA "Job Safety & Health" poster;
☞ Annual Summary of Occupational Injuries and Illnesses (OSHA Form No. 200); and
☞ Copies of any OSHA citations for violations.

RIGHT-TO-KNOW LAWS IN GENERAL

Under OSHA's hazard communication rule—the so-called right-to-know law—your employer is required to inform you of the presence of any and all hazardous chemicals or toxic substances he uses or produces in the manufacture of any item, product, or material; or which he uses for research, experimentation, or treatment. He is also required to label hazardous chemicals, train employees in how to handle hazardous chemicals safely, develop a written hazardous communication program, and provide a material safety data sheet (called an MSDS) for each hazardous chemical. See the following section for details.

Originally, the right-to-know law was intended to apply only to chemical manufacturers. But in 1988 it was extended to nonmanufacturers, and in 1989 it was further extended to the construction industry.

In addition to the federal standard, most states (and some local governments) also have right-to-know laws. Most of the state laws are similar to the federal law. However, some have even tighter restrictions, including extending coverage to all employers, requiring the posting of right-to-know notices and prohibiting discipline or discharge of employees who assert their rights under the law. The question of whether an employer has to follow the federal or state standard is still unsettled, but it is OSHA's position that the federal standard preempts state and local standards *unless* the state standard was set up under an OSHA-approved state safety and health plan. (For a list of states whose safety and health plans are OSHA-approved, see **Occupational Safety and Health Act,** earlier in this chapter.) Of course, if your employer is at all cautious, he will comply with both federal and state standards, or whichever one is stricter, just to be safe.

Federal Right-to-Know Law

Your employer's main concern has to be the federal right-to-know law, or state right-to-know laws that have the same or similar requirements. The following is an outline of the federal requirements.

Hazard Communication Plan: If your employer uses, produces, or distributes hazardous chemicals, he has to develop a *written* hazard communication (right-to-know) plan. The plan has to describe the chemicals in his workplace and how he will comply with OSHA's hazardous communication standard, which gives employees the right to know about the dangers of the chemicals they are exposed to. Among other things, the document has to cover compliance with labeling requirements, MSDS information requirements, and training requirements, and to contain a list of hazardous chemicals in the workplace.

Material Safety Data Sheets (MSDSs): Any company that manufactures, imports, or distributes hazardous chemicals has to provide something called a material safety data sheet (MSDS) to the companies they ship the chemicals to. The MSDS has to list the chemical's properties and dangers, the proper means of handling it, and appropriate medical treatment in case of exposure. If your employer receives hazardous chemicals, he has to make these MSDSs available to you.

Labeling: Manufacturers, distributors, and importers of chemicals have to label all hazardous chemical containers. Labels must identify the chemical (both trade and common names), warn of potential hazards, and give the name and address of the manufacturer, distributor, or importer. Companies that receive the chemicals have to be sure the labels remain intact.

Access to Records of Exposure: Your employer (or former employer) has to let you (or your attorney) see all records (including medical records) of your exposure to toxic substances and harmful agents within fifteen days of your request. OSHA representatives must be given immediate access to records of exposure. Employers must retain records of exposure for thirty years.

Notices to Employees: Your employer has to tell you about your rights under the hazard communication law, either by posting a notice or by informing you in person.

Training: Employers are required to provide employees with training on the handling of any hazardous chemical as soon as it is introduced into their work area or as soon as an employee is assigned to an area containing a hazardous chemical. Instructions have to include an explanation of the requirements of the hazardous communication standard and how to obtain copies, instructions on how to interpret MSDSs and labels on chemical containers, how to recognize when a hazardous chemical is being released into the work area, potential safety and health hazards of the chemical, and appropriate protective measures.

Community Right to Know: A law called the **Emergency Planning and Community Right-to-Know Act** requires employers who have hazardous chemicals in their workplaces to report them to various state and local emergency agencies and local fire departments. They also have to submit a list of hazardous chemicals they regularly release into the environment by March 1 of each year, and the quantity released; and notify emergency agencies of the release of any harmful chemical into the environment.

Other Right-to-Know Requirements

Under federal (and most state) right-to-know laws, employers must comply with other rather specific requirements regarding hazardous chemicals or toxic substances they use or produce. (A toxic substance includes any substance that has been identified as an air contaminant under federal OSHA.) The requirements generally include the following:

Notice to Employees, Hirees, and Transferees: Your employer has to provide you with information on all toxic substances he uses or produces:

☞ When you request it in writing. (Many requirements include a provision that if your employer does not give you the information within a reasonable time—say, four or five days—he can't make you keep working with the substance until he does give you the information.)
☞ Within a month of hiring you. Or,
☞ Within a month of transferring you to a new job that involves exposure to additional toxic substances.

The information has to include:

☞ The names of the substances, including generic and chemical names;
☞ The location of the substances you may be exposed to;
☞ The properties of the substances you may be exposed to;
☞ The symptoms and acute and chronic effects of hazardous levels of exposure to the substance, to the extent such infor-

mation is available from the manufacturer, supplier, and OSHA;

☞ Appropriate emergency treatment;

☞ Proper conditions for safe use of and exposure to the substances; and

☞ Procedures for cleanup of leaks and spills of the substances.

Note: Your employer has the right to require you to sign a statement acknowledging receipt of the information.

Posting Requirements: Your employer has to post a sign in plain view that informs employees of their right to receive information about all toxic substances he uses or produces.

Fetal Hazards: Employers must inform employees and prospective employees about any chemicals, toxic substances, and other substances in the workplace which they should have reasonable cause to believe will cause birth defects or constitute a hazard to an individual's reproductive system or fetus when the person is exposed to any of the substances on the job. However, the U.S. Supreme Court has held that so-called fetal protection rules that *ban* pregnant or child-bearing-age women from working on jobs that may cause birth defects are sexually biased and, therefore, illegal. See Chapter 5: Discrimination and Related Issues.

Note (trade secrets): If an employer or a supplier claims that revealing the identity of a toxic substance would force him to disclose a legally protected trade secret, he may register the information with the state labor commissioner as a trade secret. In most states, the commissioner will assign a registry number to the substance. Then, when providing required information, the employer or supplier may refer to the registry number of the substance and is not required to reveal its name. All other information must be provided as required. "Trade secret" refers to any unpatented secret commercially valuable plan, appliance, formula, or process used for making, preparing, or processing articles or materials, which is recognized by law as confidential.

Carcinogens: If your employer uses or produces carcinogens (cancer-causing agents) in the manufacture of any item, product, or material, or uses carcinogens in research, experimentation, or treatment, he generally has to comply with the same federal and state communication standards as relate to hazardous chemicals and toxic substances. That is, he has to post a list of carcinogens he uses or produces, provide a list to employees coming in contact with them, assure that substance containers are properly labeled, train employees in how to handle the substances safely, and familiarize employees with emergency procedures in case of exposure.

Discipline and Discharge: An employer may not discriminate against, discipline, or discharge you for exercising your rights under the right-to-know law. Also, any supposed waiver of your rights under the right-to-know law is considered null and void. In fact, if your employer even asks you to waive your rights under the right-to-know law as a condition of employment, that is considered to be discrimination. See Employee Complaints below.

EMPLOYEE COMPLAINTS

If you think your employer is violating safety and health laws, you can file a confidential complaint with OSHA. However, even if your employer finds out you filed a complaint, the law prohibits him from discriminating against you for exercising your rights under the act. That includes:

☞ Filing a complaint;
☞ Testifying; or
☞ Exercising any other rights under the law.

If your employer does retaliate against you for filing an OSHA complaint, you can sue to get your job back (if you still want it) plus twice the amount of your lost wages; and you may even be able to recover punitive damages.*

Note: You have to file your complaint within thirty days of your employer's alleged violation of the act.

"Whistleblower" Protection

Part of the **Occupational Safety and Health Act** protects you from retaliation—discipline or discharge—for reporting safety or

---

Reich v. Cambridgeport Air Systems, Inc., 26 Fed. 3rd 1187, 1st Cir., 1994.

health violations in your employer's workplace (i.e., "blowing the whistle" on your employer). In theory the protection is for the public good as well as your own, the idea being to encourage employers to obey safety and health laws and to encourage you to report them if they don't. However, in the real world it is you who may have to fight the stigma of being a "tattletale," and it is you who may have to face the long uphill fight to secure that protection. As was pointed out in Chapter 2: The Employment Relationship, whistleblowers can win big, but they can also lose big. And the fight always takes time—lots of time. Here are some examples of cases that went the other way—in the employer's favor:

☞ A low-level executive was fired after he reported what he believed to be a hazardous chemical spill. (Of course he had also received a couple of prior warnings about working excessive overtime and had had a number of poor performance ratings.) The court, noting that the employee's job description didn't call for him to give his opinion about business operations, upheld his firing. While the public interest is served by having employees report safety and health violations, said the court, the public interest is also served by allowing employers to maintain "peace, order and discipline in the workplace."*

☞ A tugboat captain was fired for refusing to set sail on a trip that was projected to take eighteen hours. He contended that to do so would have violated marine safety laws that limited the number of hours he could be made to work to twelve in any twenty-four-hour period. Oops, said the court. The captain should have taken the trip and *then* complained. But since he "never embarked on his journey . . . whether the law would have been violated is speculative."†

☞ An electrician who claimed he was fired for reporting safety concerns had actually merely pointed out "unpleasant working conditions about which little could be done," according to another court. The same court also noted that "some jobs are by their nature dangerous" and "every safety concern raised by an employee cannot always be resolved to the satisfaction of all."‡

*Smith v. Calgon Carbon Corp., U.S. Court of Appeals, 3rd Circuit, No. 89-3617, 1990.
†Feemster v. BJ-Titan Services Co./Titan Services, Inc., 873 Fed. 2d 91, 1989.
‡Walker v. Westinghouse Electric, 1 IER Cases 737, 1985.

☞ A mine worker who was fired after complaining about mine safety had no case for wrongful discharge because his union's collective bargaining agreement had grievance procedures that covered his situation, some of which the court said he had already pursued and lost and others of which he had failed to pursue at all.*

Note: The decisions in these four cases came an average of *four years* after the complaining employees were fired. We can only hope they weren't waiting around eagerly for the outcome.

Comment: Be resigned to one sure thing: Blowing the whistle on your employer is probably not going to make you the most popular person on your block. Before doing it, weigh your safety and health concerns against the very real risk of losing your job and make sure it's worth it. If you decide to go ahead, remember to make damn sure that you are right about your charges and that you have given your employer himself a chance to address the situation first. You will be on sturdier ground if you haven't been disciplined or been a "problem employee" prior to your complaint. If you already have one foot on a banana peel, blowing the whistle may grease the skids even more and your employer may still be able to prove he had just cause for letting you go despite your complaint. A final thought while you are standing at the edge of the pool: It may be a good idea to consult an attorney who specializes in this area of the law *before* you jump into the water. He or she may just be able to give you a good idea of how warm the water is. For help in selecting an attorney, see Chapter 11: I'm Getting Screwed; So What Can I Do about It?

For a more detailed discussion of federal and state whistleblower laws, see Chapter 2: The Employment Relationship and Chapter 8: Discipline and Discharge.

Refusal to Perform Unsafe Work

The **Occupational Safety and Health Act** also protects you from retaliation by your employer if you refuse to work on a job you legitimately feel is unsafe. But that doesn't mean you can just walk off the job. First of all, the unsafe condition must be one that presents a substantial risk of death, disease, or serious physical harm. And sec-

---

*Olguin v. Inspiration Consolidated Copper Co., 740 Fed. 2d 1468, 1984.

ond, it has to result from your employer's violation of safety and health standards. The risk you complain of can either be immediate or be caused by long-term exposure to the condition, but it must be something more than what would normally be expected on the job after all feasible safety and health precautions have been taken.

There are several other conditions placed on your protection against retaliation for refusing to work on a job you think is unsafe:

☞ The risk must be one that a reasonable person who is qualified to perform your job would recognize.
☞ The situation must be so urgent that there isn't enough time to eliminate the risk through normal enforcement procedures (i.e., an OSHA complaint). And,
☞ You must have asked your employer to correct the problem and he either couldn't or wouldn't do it.

If you refuse to work because of a good-faith belief that your job is unsafe, your employer should put you in another job with equivalent pay temporarily while he investigates your complaint. If, after a satisfactory investigation, your employer feels your complaint was valid, he obviously should correct the problem. If he feels it was unwarranted, he can require you to return to your usual job. (You don't have to do it if you still really think you are right. In that case, you would then file your complaint with OSHA.) In either case, the law protects you from retaliation if you acted "in good faith." But keep in mind the problems you can encounter as a whistleblower.

OSHA VIOLATIONS AND PENALTIES

OSHA issues citations to employers for varying degrees of violations and sets maximum penalties per violation according to severity. The following are the degrees of violations and the fines for each:

☞ *De minimis* violations: Minor violations not directly affecting employee safety or health. (No notice or penalty.)
☞ Nonserious violations: Conditions not likely to cause serious harm or death. (Maximum fine: $7,000.)
☞ Serious violations: Violations of the general standard or a specific standard resulting in a substantial probability of serious injury or death. (Maximum fine: also $7,000.)

☞ Willful violations: Deliberate or intentional violations. (Maximum fine: $70,000.)

☞ Repeated violations: Subsequent occurrence of a violation within three years. (Maximum fine: also $70,000.)

Employers have to make an immediate effort to correct any imminent threat of danger or hazard cited by OSHA.

Your employer, of course, has a right to contest any OSHA citations.

Criminal Penalties

An employer who is convicted of a willful violation of the **Occupational Safety and Health Act** that causes the death of an employee can be fined up to $10,000 and sent to jail for up to six months. A second conviction can bring a $20,000 fine and up to a year in jail.

STATE SMOKING LAWS

There is as yet no national smoking law. However, in reaction to nonsmokers' concerns about the health risks associated with "secondhand smoke" inhaled when working in close proximity to smokers, a number of states have enacted laws that require employers to restrict smoking in the workplace. Some of the laws affect employers directly, while others affect them indirectly by restricting smoking in certain public places. For an outline of state smoking laws that could affect your workplace, see **Table 13.**

Smoking Policies

Various studies conducted over the years have shown that smokers have higher rates of absenteeism, a greater number of health problems, higher mortality rates, and higher accident rates than nonsmokers. As a result, employers incur higher health insurance costs for smokers than for nonsmokers. Employers have also been successfully sued by nonsmoking employees who have been exposed to secondhand smoke on the job. These lawsuits have been based on an employer's general duty (under the **Occupational Safety and Health Act**) to provide a reasonably safe workplace, as well as on employees' claims that their sensitivity to cigarette smoke qualifies as a handicap that must be accommodated.

In one case, an employee was awarded almost $30,000 in workers' compensation benefits on his claim that he was permanently sensitized to secondhand smoke as a result of being forced to work in close proximity to heavy smokers.* In another, an employee who claimed to be unusually sensitive to tobacco smoke was ruled to be "handicapped" under the **Rehabilitation Act of 1973** because his sensitivity limited "at least one of his major life activities"—the definition of a handicap under the law. In this case, the major life activity that was limited was "his capacity to work in an environment which is not completely smoke free." His employer thus had to offer reasonable accommodation of his handicap, which involved separating him as much as possible from smokers.†

As a result of both changing laws and changing attitudes, more and more employers have developed smoking policies for their workplaces. Generally, these workplace smoking policies involve designating separate rooms or areas where smoking is allowed; using existing barriers and ventilation systems to minimize the effect of smoking on adjacent nonsmoking areas; putting smokers in work groups separate from nonsmokers; prohibiting smoking in "common" areas, such as hallways, meeting rooms, and cafeterias; providing education on the dangers of smoking; sponsoring efforts to get smokers to quit smoking, including providing incentives for quitting; or prohibiting smoking entirely inside the workplace.

Changing the Rules

Your employer has every right to have a smoking policy for his workplace. However, in order to enforce it without prejudice, he should make sure that everyone has been notified of the new rules and is given an adequate chance to adjust to them.

Smokers' Rights Laws

A growing number of states, perhaps in reaction to restrictions on smokers' rights in the workplace and generally, have passed laws prohibiting discrimination in hiring, firing, compensation, or other terms and conditions of employment based on whether or not an individual smokes *away from the job.*

Kufahl v. Wisconsin Bell Co., Wisconsin Labor and Industrial Review Committee, No. 88-000676, 1990.
†*Vickers v. Veterans' Administration,* U.S. District Court, Western Washington, 549 Fed. Supp., 1982.

TABLE 13

WORKPLACE SMOKING LAWS (STATE)*

Alaska *Covers:* All employers. *Requires:* No smoking except in areas designated by employer by posted signs; reasonable accommodation to protect nonsmokers from secondhand smoke, including separation, partitions, and ventilation.

Arizona *Covers:* Public employers. *Requires:* No smoking in most public buildings.

California *Covers:* Employers of more than 10 employees. *Requires:* Employers who permit smoking must clearly post the following warning: "Warning: This facility permits smoking, and tobacco smoke is known to the state of California to cause cancer."

Connecticut *Covers:* Employers of 20 or more employees in a structurally enclosed facility. *Requires:* Non-smoking areas (posted as such) sufficient to accommodate those who request them; use of existing barriers and ventilation to minimize effect of smoking in no-smoking areas. *Note:* Employers can designate entire workplace nonsmoking.

Dist. of Columbia *Covers:* All employers. *Requires:* Written smoking policy designating smoking areas; posting of smoking policy; posting of signs; use of barriers to minimize effect of smoking in no-smoking areas. *Note:* Employers are free to designate entire workplace as nonsmoking.

Florida *Covers:* All employers. *Requires:* Posting smoking policy designating smoking and no-smoking areas that reflect the ratio of smokers to nonsmokers; use of existing barriers and ventilation to minimize effect of smoking in no-smoking areas.

Hawaii *Covers:* Public employers; private employers receiving state funds. *Requires:* Written smoking policy; reasonable accommodation of nonsmokers by using existing barriers and ventilation to minimize effect of smoking in no-smoking areas. *Note:* If no accommodation can be reached, employer must make workplace entirely smoking or nonsmoking according to majority wishes.

Illinois *Covers:* All employers. *Requires:* No smoking except in areas designated by employer by posted signs; use of existing barriers and ventilation to minimize effect of smoking in no-smoking areas.

Iowa *Covers:* Employers with 250 square feet or more of floor space. *Requires:* No smoking except in areas designated by employer by posted signs; use of existing barriers and ventilation to minimize effect of smoking in no-smoking areas.

---

*This is an outline of the basic requirements of individual state smoking laws. Most state laws have exceptions, such as bars, factories, or warehouses not commonly used by the public, an employer's home used as a place of business, etc. For more details, contact your state department of labor or your state's occupational safety and health agency. See Appendix.

TABLE 13   *(Continued)*

Maine *Covers:* All employers. *Requires:* Written policy prohibiting smoking except in areas designated by posted signs.

Minnesota *Covers:* All employers. *Requires:* No smoking except in designated areas; smoking areas to be separate rooms where possible and, if not, non-smoking area must be at least 200 square feet; posting of smoking and no-smoking areas; use of existing barriers and ventilation to minimize effect of smoking in no-smoking areas.

Montana *Covers:* All employers. *Requires:* Designating no-smoking areas by posted signs.

Nebraska *Covers:* All employers. *Requires:* Designating no-smoking areas by posted signs; use of existing barriers and ventilation to minimize effect of smoking in no-smoking areas; limit or prohibit smoking if proximity of workers or inadequate ventilation adversely affects nonsmokers.

New Hampshire *Covers:* All employers. *Requires:* Written smoking policy available to employees designating smoking and no-smoking areas. *Note:* Employers may request policy suggestions from the department of health and human services.

New Jersey *Covers:* Employers of 50 or more employees in a structurally enclosed facility. *Requires:* Written smoking policy available to employees designating smoking and no-smoking areas and providing procedures to protect employees from the effects of smoke. *Note:* Where disputes arise, nonsmokers' rights have precedence over smokers' rights.

New York *Covers:* All employers. *Requires:* Written smoking policy available to employees designating no-smoking areas sufficient to accommodate those who request them (70% of seating capacity is considered sufficient accommodation); no smoking in common rooms (conference rooms) unless all occupants agree smoking is allowed; no smoking in common areas (elevators, hallways, etc.). *Note:* If employer is unable to accommodate nonsmokers, it must designate entire work area as no-smoking. Employers are free to designate entire workplace as nonsmoking.

Pennsylvania *Covers:* All employers. *Requires:* Posting any policy that restricts smoking in the workplace; no smoking in designated areas.

Rhode Island *Covers:* All employers. *Requires:* Written policy accommodating smokers and nonsmokers; reasonable accommodation of nonsmokers who object to smoking; use of existing barriers and ventilation to minimize effect of smoking in no-smoking areas.

Utah *Covers:* All employers. *Requires:* Voluntary designation of smoking areas in proportion to smokers and nonsmokers; use of existing barriers and ventilation to minimize effect of smoking in no-smoking areas. *Note:* Where disputes arise, nonsmokers' rights have precedence over smokers' rights. Employers are free to designate entire workplace as nonsmoking.

TABLE 13 *(Continued)*

Vermont *Covers:* All employers. *Requires:* Posting written policy prohibiting smoking or limiting it to specified enclosed areas (or unenclosed areas if at least 75% of employees in the area agree to allow smoking and it will not adversely affect nonsmokers); no smoking in common areas (halls, elevators, meeting rooms, etc.). *Note:* Employers may designate up to 30% of employee cafeterias and lounges as smoking areas.

Virginia *Covers:* Educational and health institutions and retail stores with 15,000 or more square feet. *Requires:* Designate and post reasonable no-smoking areas; use of existing barriers and ventilation to minimize effect of smoking in no-smoking areas. *Note:* Municipalities may require employers to designate and post smoking and no-smoking areas by agreement with employees, including prohibiting smoking entirely by majority vote (unless existing collective bargaining agreement does not allow the prohibition). Prior employer smoking policies supersede municipal requirements.

Washington *Covers:* All employers. *Requires:* Designating and posting smoking and no-smoking areas; prohibition of smoking in common areas; use of existing barriers and ventilation to minimize effect of smoking in no-smoking areas.

Wisconsin *Covers:* All employers. *Requires:* Designating and posting smoking areas; use of existing barriers and ventilation to minimize effect of smoking in no-smoking areas. *Note:* Employers cannot designate entire workplace smoking; cannot designate an entire room as smoking unless a majority smoke.

Note (preemployment questions): An employer shouldn't ask you whether you smoke when you aren't at work. In fact, he shouldn't ask you if you smoke at all. But he can tell you what his workplace smoking rules are (which may be no smoking at all while at work) and the consequences of violating them (which can include firing).

SUMMARY

Because OSHA is so incredibly understaffed, resulting in what can be described as only spotty enforcement, some employers are willing to take their chances on being investigated—or on having an accident—and will try to get by with unsafe conditions as long as they can. Often the cost of a resulting fine will be less than the cost of fixing the problem, so it becomes a "business decision" to them in the nature of a calculated risk. This may be true even with the 1991 increase in maximum penalties for serious violations (from $1,000 to $7,000) and for willful violations (from $10,000 to $70,000). Take, for example, the case of the shipyard where an overloaded crane collapsed, killing two workers. The company was cited for a violation of the general duty clause of the **Occupational Safety and Health Act** for "plain indifference" to the safety of its employees. Even though there was evidence that the company had operated the cranes unsafely for over five years—the proverbial "accident waiting to happen" situation—they were fined a whopping $8,000.*

The obligation may thus fall upon you to report unsafe conditions in your workplace if they are going to have any chance at all of being discovered before someone (like you) is seriously injured or even killed. However, understand that there is an inherent risk in taking that action. Unfortunately, as we have seen, whistleblowers are not often accorded much sympathy, even by the law that supposedly protects them. In fact, in 1992 a bill was introduced in Congress that addresses that deficiency. The **Comprehensive Occupational Safety and Health Reform Act** would put more teeth into OSHA's protection of whistleblowers and would give employees a more active role in the complaint process. At the congressional hearings to introduce the bill, much attention was given to how long it takes OSHA to investigate retaliation complaints, if they investigate them at all. One man testified that he was laid off three days after telling coworkers he was going to file a complaint about the persistent presence of unsafe levels of vinyl chloride fumes in the plant. After the South Carolina Occupational Safety and Health Administration dismissed his complaint outright, he appealed it to the federal agency, where it has been "under review" for over a year.

A woman who worked in a nuclear power plant testified that she was subjected to intimidation and then fired after raising her safety and health concerns to upper management during the plant's construction. She filed a retaliation complaint with OSHA, which she maintains OSHA failed to investigate properly and which, after four years, has still not been settled.

So there are those occasional big whistleblower verdicts, but remember, just as your employer may be taking a calculated risk that his safety violations won't be discovered or lead to an accident, you

Secretary of Labor v. Tampa Shipyards, Inc., OSHRC, No. 86-360, 1992.

are taking your own calculated risk if you "blow the whistle." You just might be better served by making a confidential report to OSHA or seeking the advice of an attorney. That way you may have a greater chance of protecting your safety and health while not jeopardizing your job at the same time. See Chapter 11: I'm Getting Screwed; So What Can I Do about It?

Finally, if your company has an *effective* internal procedure for investigating safety and health procedures, use it. To gauge its effectiveness, check out the results of previous complaints. Has the company really investigated them thoroughly? Have any of the complaints led to improved safety measures? Where are the "complainers" now? In the executive suite? Cleaning the executive washroom? Into the Great Beyond? Or did they emerge from the experience relatively unscathed? These are all very important questions. Before you take action, know the answers.

8

Discipline and Discharge

These days a lot of employers are afraid to discipline or fire an employee without having their lawyer with them. And for good reason. As we saw in Chapter 2: The Employment Relationship, there are a lot of situations where an employer *can't* discipline or discharge you even if you are an at-will employee (i.e., not under an express employment contract), including:

☞ When you are protected by a specific state or federal law;

☞ When you are protected by "public policy";

☞ When your actions are safeguarded by "whistleblower" laws;

☞ When your employment relationship is covered by an "implied contract"; and

☞ When the history of your relationship with your employer creates a duty on his part to treat you fairly and in good faith.

But on the other hand, there are a lot more reasons why your employer *can* discipline or discharge you, including:

☛ For insubordination;

☛ For violating company rules;

☛ For lying or making misrepresentations on your job application;

☛ For excessive absence or lateness;

☛ For low productivity;

- For incompetence;
- For negligence;
- For sleeping on the job;
- For violating safety rules;
- For harassing (i.e., sexual, racial, ethnic) coworkers;
- For stealing or misappropriating company property;
- For damaging company property;
- For fighting;
- For gambling;
- For drinking or possession of alcohol on the job;
- For use or possession of drugs on the job;
- For conviction of a crime;
- Because your job is obsolete;
- Because of a downturn in business; and
- Because you are physically or mentally unable to perform the essential duties of the job and there is no reasonable accommodation that would make it possible for you to do so.

The point is, even though the law stands behind you in certain situations—and stands behind some groups even more steadfastly than others—that doesn't mean you don't still have to show up for work, do your job, and stay out of trouble to keep drawing your paycheck. To paraphrase what the late John Houseman used to say in a popular television commercial about some investment company or other, "You have to make money the hard way. . . . You have to *earn* it."

WRONGFUL DISCHARGE (AND DISCIPLINE)

In Chapter 2: The Employment Relationship, you learned that unless you have entered into a written employment contract with your employer, the law refers to you as an "at-will" employee. In theory, that means your employer can fire you for any reason or for no reason at all, and you can quit for any reason or for no reason at all, and neither of you has any contractual (or other) liability to the other. However, you also learned that your at-will status has been modified over the years by both statutes and court decisions, making your employer a bit more responsible for the way he treats you. To recap briefly, your employer can't fire you (well, he can fire you but faces potential legal problems if he does) or "otherwise discriminate against you" under the following circumstances:

☞ In violation of a specific state or federal law, such as:
- Civil rights laws that prohibit your employer from discriminating against you on the basis of your age, race, sex, religion, ethnic background, or handicap (see Chapter 5: Discrimination and Related Issues);
- The **First Amendment to the U.S. Constitution**, granting you freedom of speech, freedom of religion, freedom of the press, and freedom of assembly (though your **First Amendment** rights are subject to the condition that the activity does not substantially interfere with your job performance or your working relationship with your employer);
- Laws that protect your right to engage in concerted activity or to belong to a union (see the Epilogue: Unions and Other Final Thoughts);
- Wage and hour laws (see Chapter 3: Wages and Hours);
- Laws designed to protect your safety and health (see Chapter 7: Health and Safety);
- Equal pay laws (see Chapter 5: Discrimination and Related Issues);
- Laws that protect your personal privacy (see Chapter 6: Right to Privacy/Access to Records);
- Laws that prohibit discipline or discharge because your wages have been attached. **Note:** Federal law allows your employer to discipline or fire you if your wages are attached for more than one debt, but most state laws make it illegal for your employer to discipline or discharge you even if your wages are attached for numerous debts. (See Chapter 3: Wages and Hours); and
- Workers' compensation laws (see Chapter 9: Workers' Compensation).

Remember, most of us are protected by at least one of the above laws, which is why employers (smart ones, at least) have gotten so paranoid about having documented justification for disciplining or discharging an employee.

☞ In violation of so-called public policy; that is, anything a court would consider to run counter to the interests of the general public. That includes when you are forced to miss work when you are summoned to serve on a jury, when you report your employer for breaking the law, when you report your employer for violating safety and health standards—so-called whistleblower laws—or when you assert your legal rights under any state or federal law (see Chapter 2: The Employment Relationship).

☞ When your employer has entered into an implied contract with you by virtue of promises he has made to you, usually either orally or in an employee handbook or manual, or possibly even in some more "informal" document—like in the margins of a memo patting you on the back for a job well done (see Chapter 2: The Employment Relationship). And,

☞ When your employer has implicitly undertaken a duty, because of the history of your relationship, to deal with you fairly and "in good faith"; for example, if you have a record of long and faithful service (see Chapter 2: The Employment Relationship).

"Otherwise Discriminate Against You"

As noted, your employer can get himself into hot water in the above situations not only if he fires you but also if he "otherwise discriminates against you." And what does it mean to "otherwise discriminate against you"? Simply stated, it means he can't refuse to hire you, demote you, deny you a promotion, deny you benefits, cut your pay, give you all your department's dirty work to do, or negatively affect any other terms and conditions of your employment. In fact, he's not supposed to reprimand or discipline you in any way at all.

"Constructive Discharge" (When Quitting Isn't Quitting)

In order to make a case for wrongful discharge, you must be able to prove that you, in fact, were discharged. In most cases that's pretty easy. Your employer says, "You're fired. Here's your pink slip. Have a nice life." End of story. But sometimes it isn't so clear cut. There are situations where a court will decide that you were fired even when you quit. It's called "constructive discharge," and it happens when your employer does something that makes it virtually impossible for you to continue on the job. Convincing a court that when you quit your job you were actually constructively discharged by your employer usually requires you to prove that:

☞ Your employer changed some working condition that led to your quitting. In other words, it won't do simply to point out some working condition that has always bothered you since the day you started the job. It has to be something he *changed* on you.

☞ The change in working conditions must have been recent enough that a cause-and-effect relationship can be established between the change and your quitting. That is, it has to have been recent enough that it could have been the factor that led *directly* to your quitting. And,

☞ The change in working conditions must have been so demeaning or upsetting or otherwise unfair or onerous that it would have caused any reasonable person in the same situation to quit, too. That means if your employer had to do what he did because of business reasons, you probably don't have much of a case. Likewise if you are particularly thin-skinned and most people would have accepted the change in working conditions with little more than a whimper, you'll probably fall short of proving constructive discharge; also, if it was merely a lousy new working condition but wouldn't be *intolerable* to a reasonable person. In short, your quitting has to have been *reasonable* under the circumstances. Or, as succinctly stated by one court, constructive discharge is when your employer makes working conditions so intolerable that you reasonably feel compelled to resign your position.*

Some courts tend to interpret constructive discharge fairly strictly, however. For example, an employee was found not to have been constructively discharged even though he alleged that the reason he refused to return to work was because his employer didn't adequately protect him from retaliation by coworkers whose criminal activities he had reported.† And another employee who quit rather than accept either a position that required him to double his production or an alternative one that required him to do the job of two or three insurance adjusters was unsuccessful in his claim for constructive discharge based on impossible job demands.‡

So before you resign thinking a court will treat you as having

Shawgo v. Spradlin, 1 IER Cases 164, 1983.
†*Beye v. Bureau of National Affairs, Inc.,* 477 Atl. 2d 1197, 1984.
‡*Duerksen v. Transamerica Title Insurance Co.,* 1 IER Cases 1492, 1987.

been constructively discharged, be darn sure a "reasonable person" would have considered the situation intolerable and that your employer doesn't have justifiable business reasons for having imposed the new working conditions. And remember, if you are an at-will employee, it may be immaterial that you were constructively discharged if your employer has followed all of the other rules against wrongfully discharging you.

Note (unemployment compensation): Being able to prove you were constructively discharged may or may not be important in establishing a wrongful discharge claim. However, it can be critical in making a claim for unemployment compensation benefits. That's because *voluntarily* quitting your job is one of several reasons you can be disqualified from receiving unemployment benefits. However, if you can show that you didn't quit voluntarily, but were forced to quit (i.e., were constructively discharged), you will not be disqualified from receiving benefits—at least not for that reason. For details see Chapter 10: Unemployment Compensation.

"RIGHTFUL" DISCHARGE AND DISCIPLINE (JUST CAUSE)

Though the law and the courts protect you against wrongful discharge or discipline, your employer has a generally recognized right to maintain an orderly, productive workplace. That means he is perfectly within his rights to discipline or discharge you, particularly when he has "just cause." As was pointed out at the beginning of the chapter, "just cause" can be any number of things, depending on the circumstances, including not only violations of work rules or standards of behavior or poor production, but a downturn in the economy. But there are things an employer must keep in mind in order to justify disciplining or discharging an employee, if he is called upon to do so. It's one thing to say an employer has a right to fire you for such and such behavior. But there is often more to the story than meets the eye. Let's take a look at a few situations by way of illustration.

Insubordination

Refusing to follow the directive of a superior is generally acknowledged as one of the most easily justifiable reasons for disciplining or discharging an employee. But not if the order was to do something illegal. So a fast-food store manager was wrongfully discharged by a district manager when he refused to sign a false and potentially defamatory statement about a former employee.* And a deckhand was wrongfully discharged for refusing to pump the boat's bilgewater into the harbor.†

Note: But remember the case of the tugboat captain who quit rather than break the law regarding the length of a trip he was ordered to make. The court found against him in his wrongful discharge case, reasoning that he only *anticipated* that he would be required to break the law, and that since he quit before making the trip, he in effect never actually found out if he had to break the law. Go figure!

Absence and Lateness

Of course, you can be disciplined or discharged for chronic absence or lateness, but you can't be disciplined or discharged for being absent or late because of compliance with a summons to serve on jury duty. Your employer may also get himself into problems if he has condoned your absence or lateness, or that of others, in the past.

Theft or Damage of Your Employer's Property

To further illustrate the more-than-meets-the-eye theme, consider a situation in which you are disciplined or fired for allegedly damaging or misappropriating your employer's property. Sounds pretty open and shut, doesn't it? Either you did it (and your employer can prove it) or you didn't (and he can't). But then there was the airline employee who transferred to another base and was subsequently fired for claiming moving expenses for a car he didn't move. Wrongful discharge, said the court. Why? The employee handbook clause regarding relocation expenses didn't specify that you couldn't submit expense claims before they were incurred.‡

Dress and Grooming Codes

Employers can impose dress and grooming codes in the workplace. However, the rules should bear some relationship to the job. And

---

Delaney v. Taco Time International, Inc., 681 P.2d 114, 1984.
†*Sabine Pilot Service v. Hauck,* Texas Supreme Court, No. C-3312, 1985.
‡*Aiello v. United Airlines, Inc.,* 818 Fed. 2d 1196, 1987.

even when they do relate to the job, they may be discriminatory if they affect members of a protected group more than they do other employees. Remember from Chapter 5 the case of the black pizza restaurant employee who successfully challenged his employer's requirement that employees be clean shaven? Even though the employer had a legitimate health reason for the shaving requirement, the court decided it was outweighed by the adverse impact the rule had on black males, many of whom are affected by a skin condition that makes it painful to shave.*

In the Course of Employment

In general, "just cause" relates to discipline or discharge for activity that occurs during the course of your employment. That is, while you are on the job. For example, you could be disciplined or discharged for smoking at work if your employer has a rule against it. But you can't be fired for smoking away from work. And you can be disciplined or discharged for drinking on the job. But, again, not for drinking at home. An exception, however, is when your off-duty conduct affects your job. For example, an employee of a local equal opportunities commission was fired because of his conviction for three felonies committed during off-hours. He challenged the discharge based on his union contract that specified he could be fired only for "just cause." The court upheld his firing because of the effect his convictions would have on the "credibility of all concerned in any future dealing as a public official."† Similarly, you might not be able to be disciplined or discharged for getting a traffic ticket in your personal car. But if you drive a truck for a living and your license is revoked, you wouldn't be able to perform your job.

These are only a few examples. Every situation is unique. These situations merely serve to point out that things are not always as they appear. Most of the time, maybe. But not always. Also, in assessing whether or not your employer had, or even needed, just cause to discipline or discharge you, it is always important to analyze how other employees with similar employment records have been treated in similar situations.

Bradley v. Pizzaco of Nebraska, Inc., dba Domino's Pizza.
†*In the Matter of: City of New Haven and AFSCME, Council 4, Local 3144,* Case No. 8889-A-416, 1991.

AFTER-ACQUIRED EVIDENCE

What happens if, after your employer fires you for what you think is a discriminatory reason, he finds out something that would have given him a legitimate reason to fire you anyway (e.g., you lied on your application form in violation of a written clause on the form stating that was grounds for termination; you stole from your employer; you made copies of confidential company records in violation of an express company rule, etc.)? Up until recently, it depended on where you lived and what courtroom you ended up in whether you could still recover damages. Now the U.S. Supreme Court has made a ruling that answers the question once and for all.* The answer? You can still recover damages if discrimination is proven, but not all the damages you could have recovered if you had, as lawyers say, come to court with totally "clean hands."

If a court determines that you were fired illegally but would have been fired eventually for a legitimate reason, you can still recover back pay, but only from the date you were fired until the time your employer discovers your wrongdoing, less whatever damage your employer might have suffered as a result of your wrongdoing. You cannot be reinstated or get front pay (damages based on amounts you may have earned in the future).

The real question here, left unanswered, is: What effect will this decision have on future employee lawsuits for discriminatory discharge? Will employers routinely try to dig up "dirt" on fired employees as fast as they can to try to minimize potential damages in the event the employee sues and eventually proves discrimination? And, if so, will that deter employees who think they were discriminatorily fired from filing lawsuits? Only time will tell.

WHAT ATTORNEYS TELL THEIR EMPLOYER-CLIENTS

It might be helpful at this point to get a little bit of insight into what "defense attorneys" are telling your employer about proper discipline and discharge procedures.

---

*McKennon v. Nashville Banner Publishing Co., 9 Fed. Repts. 3rd 539, 1995.

Defense Attorneys

They're the men and women who try to keep your employer out of trouble with his employees by advising him ahead of time what and what not to do; and who defend him when he screws up.

We all know there are times when an employee deserves to be disciplined or even fired. And, believe it or not, most employers find either to be a distasteful chore. But if they have to do it, they want to be sure they can do it without getting sued. And that is a legitimate worry. Because if they are called to task by an employee, it's going to cost them money. (That's why those defense attorneys love employers—because most have "deep pockets." You, on the other hand, have some options that may be able to keep you from having to reach into your somewhat shallower pockets. See Chapter 11: I'm Getting Screwed; So What Can I Do about It?)

As a matter of fact, statistics indicate that once your employer ends up in court, it's a sure bet it's going to cost him *lots* of money. According to Equal Employment Opportunity Commission studies, if there is sufficient evidence for the agency to back a fired employee's charges, the employee has an almost 90 percent chance of recovering something from the employer, either through a settlement or as a result of a court award. The ultimate cost to an employer of defending a wrongful discharge suit can easily run into the tens of thousands of dollars, even if they win, what with attorneys' fees and the time and resources it takes to defend themselves.

With the proliferation of employee rights legislation, employers have to be careful any time they make a potentially unpopular employment decision. Even though they have the right to discharge an unproductive or uncooperative employee, these days any time they sharpen the axe, they risk having the tree fall on them. So here are some of the suggestions defense attorneys make to help them reduce that risk:

Protected Groups: The first thing your employer's attorney will warn him about is all those protected groups out there that require a bit of extra attention. Over 70 percent of the work force is now in a protected group by virtue of being:

☞ A member of a racial or ethnic minority;
☞ Female;
☞ Over forty; and/or
☞ Handicapped.

Certainly employers can discipline or fire members of protected groups in appropriate situations. However, the main difference in dealing with a racial, ethnic, or religious minority, or a woman or an older or handicapped worker, is that the presumption tends to favor the employee rather than the employer. That is, if, for example, the fired employee is a female who says, "My employer fired me because I am a woman," and she has anything at all to back up her allegation, her employer will have to produce evidence that disproves her contention. She has something to hang her hat on, as it were, whereas a male, a Caucasian, or a nonhandicapped individual may not. That is the kind of "extra attention" the attorneys are talking about—making extra sure they have supporting evidence that their discipline or discharge of a member of a protected group is justified.

So the employer's attorney will remind the employer about those protected groups—that he must be sure work rules or cutbacks do not have more of an impact on any protected group when compared to his work force as a whole. The attorney will tell the employer-client that, particularly if the termination is due to economic causes (i.e., poor business or other cutbacks), he should be prepared to document a legitimate business reason for the firing, and that he should be absolutely certain his economic axe doesn't fall too heavily on older workers, minorities, women, or other protected groups.

Work Rules: Lawyers will also tell employers that it is a good idea to have written work rules. That way all employees know what's expected of them and what will happen if they break the rules (and, incidentally, the employer will have a yardstick against which he can measure workplace behavior and thus be better able to prove that specific conduct violated those rules). However, work rules have no meaning unless all employees are given a copy. Some employers even insist that each employee sign a statement acknowledging that he or she has received a copy of the company's work rules and has read and understood them.

To be effective as a buffer against lawsuits, work rules should be clearly stated (including the consequences of one or more violations), reasonable, and uniformly applied.

Progressive Discipline: It is important to defense attorneys that the employers they represent have a system of progressive discipline that includes a number of steps along the way to discharge and has as its primary goal the improvement of the disciplined employee's performance. It is probably the best way an employer can insulate himself from a wrongful discharge claim. It can also cut down on an employer's turnover rate by putting employees on notice about problems and giving them an adequate opportunity to correct the behavior or problem in question. Finally, it can boost morale, since we all feel a little more comfortable about our job security when we know that, under all but the most extraordinary circumstances, we will, in effect, be given a second and even a third or fourth chance. In any case, the steps in a progressive disciplinary procedure usually include the following:

☞ *Step 1:* A verbal warning (with written verification in the employee's personnel file).

☞ *Step 2:* A written warning detailing the exact nature of the problem and the measures the employee is expected to take to resolve it (including the time frame within which improvement is expected).

☞ *Step 3:* A specific period of probation during which the employee is put on notice that any further problems will result in more drastic disciplinary measures being taken.

☞ *Step 4:* Possible suspension without pay.

☞ *Step 5:* Termination.

Most lawyers counsel employers that decisions about disciplining or discharging an employee should never be made in the heat of the moment. In keeping with that, they will further advise that firing an employee "on the spot" should be done only in the most extraordinary situations (for example, when an employee strikes a superior). In short, *all* disciplinary action, including firing, should be well thought out and made only on the basis of calm, cool, calculated reason.

Grievance Procedures: Of course, standard union collective bargaining agreements include procedures through which union members can grieve disciplinary action taken against them, including firing. But the nonunion employee has no such luxury unless his or her employer has voluntarily set up such a procedure on his own. Many employers do exactly that these days—again, not only to ensure fairness on their part, but to protect themselves against charges of being arbitrary—or worse, discriminatory—in their employment decisions. The common grievance process involves a hearing before an impartial arbitrator, who renders a decision based on the evidence presented, including testimony of witnesses.

If your employer has such a grievance procedure, he should be held to it in all cases, including yours. If he didn't follow it, why didn't he?

Just Cause for Termination: Assuming an employer has appropriate work rules and a system of progressive discipline that he applies fairly and consistently, repeated violation of those rules would generally be considered just cause for dismissing an employee. And just cause is not restricted to situations involving unacceptable behavior or insubordination. An employer may have just cause to terminate someone's employment simply as a matter of business circumstances, such as:

☛ A reduction in force caused by economic conditions, a drop-off in business, or a cutback in operations;
☛ Business reorganization or technological changes that make an employee's job obsolete; or
☛ Poor job performance, inefficiency, negligence, or just plain incompetence.

Just as in the case of poor conduct or violation of work rules, the need to dismiss an employee because of any one of the above situations can be anticipated to some degree. So, again, attorneys will counsel employers that it is both wise (and, by the way, considerate) to give the employee a reasonable amount of warning that his or her job is about to be eliminated or his or her performance is not up to acceptable standards.

In any event, somewhere in here the piece of advice that every attorney will give to his or her employer-client is this: *All employment decisions should be documented in intimate detail.*

Documenting Disciplinary Action and Negative Performance Reviews: After counseling an employer about having work rules and progressive disciplinary steps, the next thing an employer's attorney will warn your employer about is to document in detail each and every action taken. Even an oral warning, they will say, should be noted in the employee's personnel file. (We've already learned about keeping our own "personal personnel file," but even more on that in a moment.)

Exit Interviews: Most attorneys will advise their employer-clients to try to conduct a so-called exit interview whenever they terminate someone. If your employer follows this piece of advice, he will probably do it on the pretext of explaining why the decision has been made and getting your feedback so presumably something positive can come out of the whole messy business for both of you. He may also say he's using the time for practical matters such as giving you your final paycheck, explaining terms of any severance package and/or payment of your vested rights in an employee retirement fund, and providing a written **Consolidated Omnibus Budget Reconciliation Act** (COBRA) notice detailing your right to continued group health insurance coverage. See Chapter 4: Fringe Benefits.

Beware: In most cases, that's not what he's really after. What he really wants is to have you sign statements that you were treated fairly and were discharged for just cause. If he's really clever—or well informed—he'll probably try to do it all in one swift maneuver (i.e., hand you your final paycheck and the waivers at the same time). If he's been following his attorney's advice all along (a rarity among employers, most of whom do exactly what you've always done—stumble along in the dark and wait until something bad happens before they call an attorney), the exit interview will go kind of like this: He'll summon you into his office and give you the bad news. He may even try to soften the blow a bit with a few tired platitudes. Then he'll move in for the kill while you're most vulnerable, while you're still sitting there stunned and wondering what you're going to do next. That's probably when he'll try to get you to sign the waivers. You know, like waivers of your ADEA rights, or your right to sue him, or maybe even your right to unemployment compensation. He may even offer you a favorable recommendation in return. Have none of it. Don't sign anything without first showing it to your lawyer. But take a copy of everything with you. It may be just the little bit of rope that you need to hang your employer out to dry.

Exit interview? The hell with it—and him. You are out. That's the cold, hard truth of the matter. Take your final paycheck, severance check, COBRA notice, and whatever else you can get out of your employer and scram. There is no advantage to you to hang around and possibly be talked (or scammed) into agreeing to something that will help only *your employer.* And, take note, if he wants you to sign documents relating to your firing, he's worried. An experienced labor and employment attorney will no doubt be able to squeeze a lot more out of him than he's offering you "out of the goodness of his heart" or "to avoid any unpleasantness." Keep that in mind. See Chapter 11: I'm Getting Screwed; So What Can I Do about It?

Note: Most attorneys will suggest that an employer make terminations effective immediately. They feel that having a disgruntled lame duck soon-to-be-former employee on the job for the remainder of the pay period, month, etc., can only lead to problems . . . both morale problems and, potentially, production problems. (You never want to be called into the boss's office on a Friday.) If your employer makes your discharge effective immediately and he, on the other hand, requests that employees give adequate notice (two weeks) of the effective date of a resignation, you should demand an equivalent amount of severance in lieu of notice of termination. If he doesn't agree, promise that you will make a stink over it.

Damage Control: And remember, your employer's attorney will no doubt remind him that even if he fired you wrongfully, he may be able to limit his damages if he can come up with some evidence against you that would have given him just cause to fire you anyway. (See After-Acquired Evidence, earlier in this chapter.)

STATEMENTS IN EMPLOYEE HANDBOOKS

If your company has an employee handbook, check to see if your employer has included a section on undesirable conduct and disciplinary measures that will be taken as a result, including steps in a progressive discipline policy. This could very well have the effect of limiting your employer's authority to discipline or discharge you to the behaviors listed; and the means of disciplining you to those steps outlined. That could be a big point in your favor in making a claim for wrongful discharge and/or for unemployment benefits.

Did your employer use all of the progressive disciplinary steps that are listed in the employee handbook in your case? Or did he skip some of the usual ones? If so, was there a valid reason? (For example, was yours a particularly serious offense?)

If you were put on probation, were the probation "conditions" reasonable?

Likewise, did he include a grievance procedure in cases like yours? If so, did he allow you to use it? Was it fair and impartial?

Note: A well-informed employer will be careful when he lists rules and the resulting disciplinary action that will be taken when those rules are violated. Specifically, he will note that the purpose of the list is to give examples only, and that it is not intended to be all-inclusive. He may also expressly retain the right to alter or amend stated progressive discipline procedures and tailor them to the facts of specific situations at his discretion. However, if the basis of a disciplinary policy is incorporated in an employee handbook, most courts will expect the employer to follow it—as your employer expects you to follow it.

MAINTAINING DISCIPLINARY RECORDS

It is imperative that you keep records of all disciplinary action taken against you. Detailed records are your first (and often only) defense against an unfair employment decision and your most powerful weapon in a legal battle against your employer. Even if you are given an oral warning, note it on paper. (Many employers will routinely note an oral warning in your personnel file.) And if keeping such records is to achieve its main objective of keeping your employer "honest"—making sure your side of the story gets told in some form—you must record events diligently and in minute detail. Any time disciplinary action of any kind is taken against you, keep not only the form you were given but your own detailed notes of the incident and what led up to it, as well as notes of the meeting, if there was one, in which the disciplinary action was explained to you.

Your own disciplinary records should include:

☞ The name and job title of the supervisor who disciplined you.
☞ A detailed description of the behavior he or she complained of, including the date or dates.
☞ If there is more to the incident than meets the eye, a detailed description of what precipitated the incident.
☞ What your supervisor indicated would be required of you to improve, including the date by which he or she expects that to be accomplished.
☞ What your supervisor told you the company would do to help you improve, such as giving you further training, counseling, or periodic performance reviews.
☞ Names of any fellow employee-witnesses. And,
☞ Your disciplining supervisor's signature, if you can get it without making a bad situation even worse. (**Note:** Often

your supervisor will have been instructed to get your signature on a disciplinary form. The implication is that, by signing it, you agree with its contents. If you do not agree with a statement in it, make a note of your disagreement next to the objectionable section. If you disagree with the whole thing, note that fact alongside of your signature. It would probably inflame what could already be a tense situation to insist on detailing your version of the incident on the form. Defuse the situation by simply noting your disagreement and calmly informing your supervisor that you intend to request that your own detailed report of the incident be included in your permanent record. Many state laws require that you be allowed to do so. See Chapter 6: Right to Privacy/Access to Records.)

As soon as you leave your disciplinary meeting, write out your version while you still remember every detail. Make a copy. Ask the personnel department to add the original to your personnel file. Bring the copy home and add it to your "personal personnel file." See Chapter 11: I'm Getting Screwed; So What Can I Do about It? for details on record-keeping.

FINAL PAYCHECK AND CONTINUATION OF INSURANCE

Remember, when you are fired, your employer has to pay you your final wages promptly. Under some state statutes, fired employees must be given their final paycheck as soon as the next business day; in any event, most fired employees are required to be paid at least by the end of the current pay period. See Chapter 3: Wages and Hours. Also, if your employer has a policy, practice, or contract by which he agrees to pay (or has set a precedent of paying) departing employees for vacations, holidays, sick days, and/or any other benefits that are accrued and unused at the time of discharge, you have to be paid those accrued benefits immediately upon termination, too.

Also upon termination, if your employer has a group health insurance plan, you have to be notified of your right to continue your membership in that group health insurance plan under the **Consolidated Omnibus Budget Reconciliation Act** (COBRA). In most situations you have to be allowed to continue in an employer-sponsored group health insurance plan for at least a year and a half following your termination, at your option. The only catch is that you have to pay the full premium yourself. That is, your employer no longer has to contribute toward the payment of your premiums. It may be tough to pay the full premium when you are out of work, but the group premium is still a lot less than an individual rate. See Chapter 4: Fringe Benefits.

UNEMPLOYMENT COMPENSATION

Remember, too, that if you are fired and have earned sufficient wages to qualify, you are eligible for unemployment compensation benefits. In most states you are eligible for benefits unless you were fired for:

☞ Repeated willful misconduct (more than one intentional act in disregard of your employer's interests in one year). Or,

☞ A single act of willful misconduct that seriously endangers the life, safety, or property of your employer, a fellow employee, or the general public.

See Chapter 10: Unemployment Compensation.

BLACKLISTING

A number of states have laws that specifically prohibit employers from blacklisting employees. States with blacklisting laws include Alabama, Arizona, Arkansas, California, Colorado, Connecticut, Florida, Indiana, Iowa, Kansas, Louisiana, Maine, Minnesota, Montana, Nevada, New Hampshire, New Mexico, North Carolina, North Dakota, Oklahoma, Oregon, Texas, Virginia, Washington, and Wisconsin. (Several states expressly exempt reference letters that truthfully state the reason for the employee's discharge.)

Generally, laws against blacklisting prohibit employers from circulating or being responsible for circulating the name of any employee with the intent of preventing the employee from securing employment elsewhere. But that doesn't prevent an employer from providing a truthful statement of facts about your employment when asked either by you or by a prospective employer. Remember, however, that your employer is treading on potentially dangerous ground here regarding *what* he can say about you and, in fact, whether he says anything at all (i.e., gives a reference) without your express permission. See Chapter 1: The Hiring Process.

Whether or not your state has a specific blacklisting law, it is an extremely risky proposition for an employer to circulate any information that is intended to keep you from getting a job with another employer (whether you are a current or former employee). In fact, if your employer is smart, he won't give any unsolicited information about either current or former employees—and certainly not without their written permission. If he does, he risks violating not only blacklisting laws but also privacy and defamation laws, depending on the nature of the information released.

PLANT CLOSINGS AND LAYOFFS

If you lose your job as part of a plant closing or a mass layoff, you may also be protected by a federal law called the **Worker Adjustment and Retraining Notification Act** (WARN), which went into effect in 1989. The law requires employers of one hundred or more workers to give employees sixty days' advance notice of a plant closing or mass layoff. Under WARN a plant closing happens when fifty or more full-time workers at an employment site "reasonably may be expected to" experience an "employment loss" during any thirty-day period. An "employment loss" is a termination (other than a voluntary quit, retirement, or discharge for cause), a layoff of more than six months, or a cutback in an employee's hours of more than 50 percent. (It's not considered an employment loss if an employer relocates or consolidates his business and transfers employees to a job site within reasonable commuting distance and there isn't more than a six-month break in service between the closing and reopening in the new location.)

A mass layoff, on the other hand, is when fifty or more full-time employees (amounting to at least one-third of all full-time employees) experience an employment loss during any thirty-day period. Where more than five hundred employees are being laid off, it does not have to amount to one-third of the work force.

Note (more than one group layoff): If unconnected events cause separate group layoffs at a single site and none alone is large enough to reach the minimum requirement, notice still must be given to employees if the total number laid off within a ninety-day period reaches the minimum requirement. (Notice does not have to be given if the employer can prove the layoffs resulted from different causes and its actions were not an attempt to evade the law.)

Notice That Must Be Given

Notices must be in writing in "language understandable to the employees." Notices must include:

☞ The name and address of the affected site;
☞ Whether the closing or layoff is temporary or permanent;
☞ Whether the whole facility is to be closed;
☞ The expected date the closing or layoffs will begin;
☞ The exact date on which terminations or layoffs are expected to begin;
☞ The name and telephone number of the company official to contact for more information;
☞ Whether bumping rights (i.e., the right to displace junior people in the same job classification) exist.

Note: Employers also have to notify state employment or dislocated worker units and the highest local elected official of the town where the layoffs or plant closing is to take place.

Delivery of Notice

Notice can be delivered to employees by any "reasonable" method, as long as it is received on time. U.S. Department of Labor rules expressly state that employers may not satisfy the requirement by routinely including a notice with employees' paychecks to try to sneak around the law.

Note (additional notice): If the expected date of the initial layoffs is postponed, the employer is required to give an additional notice of the new expected date.

Exceptions

In situations like the following, employers either don't have to give any notice of a closing or mass layoff at all, or are not required to give the full sixty days.

No notice required:

☞ At temporary facilities, on specific projects or contracts, or for seasonal work, where employees were hired with the clear understanding that their employment would terminate when the facility closed, the project or contract was completed, or the season ended.

☞ Where employees are on strike or the employer is engaged in a lockout that is not intended to evade the law. (But non-strikers who will experience an employment loss because of the strike must still be given notice.)

Full sixty days not required:

☞ If at the time the sixty-day notice would have been required, the "faltering business" was actively seeking new business or capital through "commercially reasonable" methods in order to keep from having to close. (The company must have had a reasonable belief that giving the notice would have prevented it from getting the new financing or business.)

☞ Where the closing or layoffs are caused by sudden, dramatic, and unforeseeable business circumstances that were beyond the employer's control.

☞ Where the closing or layoffs are caused by a flood, earthquake, drought, or similar natural disaster.

Sale of a Business

When mass layoffs will be caused by the sale of a business, affected employees must be given a WARN notice either by the seller (up to and including the time of sale) or by the buyer (from then on).

Violations of WARN

Employers who fail to give the required notice can be sued by each affected employee for up to three years' back pay and benefits.

Filing a Claim

Only recently has it finally (sort of) been settled as to how long you have to file a WARN complaint. There had been more than a little confusion, since WARN itself didn't specify how long you had to bring your lawsuit. Now the U.S. Supreme Court has decided that the statute of limitations in WARN cases should be the same as the limitation period for filing suit under the "most closely analogous" state law.* Huh? And what law would that be?

So now there is more than a little confusion over what the "most closely analogous" law is. The best advice? If you're even remotely considering suing under WARN, do it within six months of when you believe your employer violated it.

State Laws

A number of states also have various notice requirements in cases of plant closings or layoffs. See **Table 14.**

SUMMARY

Being reprimanded (or fired) is no fun. But it's even less fun when it is unfair. Your employer has every right to discipline or discharge you. If you are an at-will employee, he technically doesn't even have to have a reason. However, even if you are an at-will employee, he's setting himself up for a potentially hard fall if his reason for disciplining or discharging you is discriminatory, or is in violation of some other state or federal law or "public policy," or is in retaliation for your asserting your legal rights, or even (sometimes) is a breach of that ever-elusive concept of "good faith and fair dealing."

So here are a few things you should keep in mind when your employer metes out a little discipline (or a *lot* of discipline).

Discipline

Whenever you are disciplined, ask yourself the following questions:

☛ Was I informed of the rule or standard of behavior that I am accused of violating?
☛ Was the rule or standard of behavior clear and unequivocal?
☛ Did I violate it?

North Star Steel Co. v. Thomas, USSC, No. 94-834, 1995.

TABLE **14**

PLANT CLOSING AND MASS LAYOFF LAWS (STATE)*

Connecticut *Covers* employers of 100 or more employees relocating or closing. *Requires* continuation of health insurance for up to 120 days or until worker is eligible for other group insurance.

Hawaii *Covers* employers of 50 or more downsizing, closing, or relocating. *Requires* 45 days' advance written notice to affected employees and payment for 4 weeks of the difference between unemployment compensation benefits and workers' average weekly wages.

Kansas *Covers* employers in designated industries, such as manufacturers and transporters of food and clothing, as well as mining and public utilities (check with department of labor) downsizing or closing. *Requires* application to state department of human resources.

Maine *Covers* employers of 100 or more employees closing or relocating outside the state. *Requires* 60 days' advance notice to affected employees, state bureau of labor, and local governments, plus 1 week of severance pay per year of work for employees who have worked for the employer for 3 or more years.

Maryland (voluntary) *Covers* employers of 50 or more employees relocating or laying off at least 25% of their work force, or at least 15 employees, within a 3-month period. *Suggests* 90 days' advance notice to affected employees. (State employees are required to be given at least 90 days' notice before being laid off.)

Massachusetts *Covers* employers of 50 or more employees closing or having mass layoffs. *Requires* covered employers to give "prompt" notice to the commissioner of the department of employment and training of a pending plant closing; and requires a "good-faith" effort to give the longest possible notice to affected employees, as well as a good-faith effort to continue income and health insurance benefits as long as possible. (**Note:** The state has set up reemployment assistance and health insurance funds for eligible employees who lose their jobs because of a plant closing.) *Relocation:* Employers of 12 or more employees relocating within Massachusetts *must* file a report of the planned move with the state.

Michigan (voluntary) *Covers* employers of 25 or more expecting a closing or a relocation affecting 25 or more employees. *Suggests* notifying affected employees, the state department of job training, and the local government as soon as possible.

Minnesota (voluntary) Encourages employers anticipating downsizing, closing, or relocating to give advance notice to employees, union representatives, town officials, and the state department of employment and training.

---

*State plant closing and layoff laws are in addition to WARN requirements. Also, note that municipalities in a number of states also have ordinances that require that notice be given in cases of closings or mass layoffs.

TABLE 14 *(Continued)*

Montana Requires state agencies with more than 25 employees to notify employees when anticipating any layoff of 250 or more employees within 2 years.

New Jersey Employers required to give advance notice under WARN, must also give a WARN notice to the state dislocated worker unit.

New York (voluntary) Employers are free to join a state cooperative requiring advance notice of layoffs and discharges. Members of the cooperative must give such notice in order to be eligible for state economic assistance.

Oregon Employers required to give advance notice under WARN, must also notify the state department of economic development.

South Carolina All employers that require employees to give advance notice of quitting must give at least 2 weeks' notice (or the same period of notice that employees are required to give before quitting) of a closing.

Tennessee *Covers* employers of 50 to 99 full-time employees expecting a closing or relocation that will affect 50 or more employees in a 3-month period. *Requires* notice to be given to affected employees and the state department of labor. (Notice not required for closings or layoffs caused by labor disputes, closings of temporary facilities, or normal closing of seasonal operations.)

Wisconsin *Covers* employers of 50 or more employees expecting a closing affecting 25 or more employees or layoffs affecting 25 or more employees or 25% or more or the work force. *Requires* 60 days' written notice to affected employees, their union representatives, the state department of labor, and local governments

☛ Is the rule or standard of behavior reasonable? That is, does it bear a reasonable relationship to my job performance? Safety? My employer's business interests?

☛ Was I trained sufficiently to fulfill it?

☛ Does the company have records (or do I have personal knowledge) of previous infractions of this and other rules or standards of behavior and the disciplinary measures taken?

☛ Is my punishment consistent with prior action taken in similar cases, given my prior work record?

In short, did you know or should you have known about the rule? Is it reasonable? And was it fairly applied to you?

Discharge

If you are unfortunate enough to be discharged, consider the following:

☞ Was the discharge discriminatory?

☞ Did it violate a specific state or federal law (regarding payment of wages, hours of work, right to join or refrain from joining a union, equal pay, privacy, workers' compensation, attachment of wages, etc.)?

☞ Was it in retaliation for asserting your legal rights?

☞ Did it violate the terms of an employment contract between you and your employer? The contract may be either express (in writing) or implied. Check that employee handbook. Rummage through your personal employment file and pull out all those notes you took whenever your employer made anything that sounded even remotely like an assurance of continued employment.

☞ Particularly if your employer maintains that your termination is due to "business necessity" (i.e., economic reasons such as a drop-off in business), he should be able to document a legitimate business reason for your firing. That is especially true if you are a member of a protected group. Are you a woman? A member of a racial, ethnic, or religious minority? Over forty? Handicapped? If so, do your employer's economically motivated firings fall with disproportionate weight on members of your protected group? Are your main functions truly obsolete? Have they really been "consolidated" with other employees' jobs? Or is your employer "reorganizing" *you* out by simply renaming positions or shuffling work around?

☞ Did your firing come in the heat of the moment? Employers who act hastily, even irrationally, are less likely to have covered their tracks than those who act coolly and professionally. If he makes this obvious a mistake, there is a good chance he has made more along the way. Do a little research and find out what they are.

☞ Does your employer's action jibe with your performance reviews? That is, does it fly in the face of consistently good or even above-average job appraisals? If so, is there an ulterior (illegal) motive behind it? A new boss who doesn't like you?

☞ Did your employer try to convince you to sign any waivers (i.e., of your legal rights)—which waiver, by the way, may be meaningless; or acknowledgments (i.e., that your discharge was fair or for just cause)? If so, maybe he has something to be afraid of.

Maybe you will never face disciplinary action at work—or, ultimately, discharge. But if you do, be prepared. The importance of keeping detailed records of all employment decisions (both positive and negative) your employer makes concerning you and your job cannot be overstated.

9

Workers' Compensation

Once upon a time, you got hurt at work and you got fired and were replaced by somebody else. You were then left to bring a private lawsuit against your employer to recover medical bills and lost wages. Of course, while the lawsuit went on, you went broke paying doctors' and lawyers' bills, got thrown out of your house, were divorced by your spouse, disowned by your kids, and maybe even abandoned by your dog. And then you probably lost anyway.

You see, employers had these three very interesting defenses called contributory negligence, assumption of the risk, and the fellow servant rule. Contributory negligence is more or less self-explanatory. Your employer said, "Sure you got hurt working on my assembly line, but you wouldn't have if you'd been doing it right. In fact, except for your negligence, the accident wouldn't even have happened."

Assumption of the risk was a real beaut—but effective for a long time. The theory there was that, yes, the assembly line is a dangerous place to work, but you knew that when you signed on for the job, so you assumed that risk. Like, you knew I was a snake when you took me in, so stop complaining that I bit you.

Finally, the fellow servant rule came into play when you were working alongside someone else: a fellow servant. (You know you're in trouble when the law calls you a servant.) Let's say you were stacking inventory on a fork lift when the driver accidently put the fork lift into reverse and the boxes toppled over on you. You sued your employer. And he countered, "Hey, it wasn't *my* fault. It was his coworker who screwed up. Let him sue *him.*" That was fine, but of course your "fellow servant" was just as broke as you were, so suing him not only was pointless but didn't exactly endear you to the rest of your colleagues. (Your "fellow servant" probably wasn't all that thrilled, either.)

On the other hand, when you *were* able to prevail in your lawsuit, oftentimes you could win the store, financially crippling or even bankrupting your employer. (Of course your family and your dog were long gone, but at least you had the money—or what was left of it after the doctors and lawyers got finished picking the carcass.) That was because, as juries became more and more sympathetic, you were able to recover not only for medical expenses and lost wages but also for the more esoteric "pain and suffering."

Anyway, that's the short history of liability lawsuits for on-the-job injuries (which actually had a long history). And thus evolved workers' compensation laws. The theory of workers' compensation laws goes like this: You get hurt on the job. The law says *you* don't sue and expose your employer to a potentially outrageous damage award, and *he* will provide you with medical care and continued income while you are unable to work. In fact, workers' compensation laws require your employer to carry insurance that will pay all of your medical expenses from Day One and will protect you against loss of income if you are hurt in an on-the-job accident or contract an illness that's related to your employment. It also prevents your employer from disciplining you or firing you because you filed a workers' compensation claim (or because you testified at a workers' compensation hearing or otherwise assisted in someone else's workers' compensation claim). In fact, your employer may still have to pay you benefits even if he subsequently fires you *for cause.* Take the case of the employee who injured his hand and arm on the job and was out of work for a year. After returning to light duty—and while still receiving partial benefits—he called in sick. Seems his hand and arm were too sore for him to work that day . . . but apparently not too sore for him to play in a local golf tournament. His employer found out, fired him, and cut off his benefits. Penalty stroke, said the Maine Supreme Court. An employee's right to benefits (in this case, partial benefits) doesn't end because he is fired, even for cause, as long as his original injury made him eligible for benefits in the first place.*

On the flip side, in most situations workers' compensation is your

*Cousins v. Georgia-Pacific Corp., Maine Supreme Judicial Court, No. 5988, 1991.

exclusive remedy for an on-the-job accident or illness. The law doesn't allow you to sue your employer (or a "fellow servant") for damages either in addition to or instead of making a claim for workers' compensation. And it's a no-fault system. It doesn't matter anymore that you contributed to the accident through your negligence, or that your employer did. (Of course, he may have some problems if **Occupational Safety and Health Act** violations contributed to your accident or illness. But that, as they say, is a whole 'nother story.)

So, as they drew it up on the blackboard, this is the way it's supposed to go:

☞ Your employer buys workers' compensation insurance (or if he can prove he has the necessary financial resources, insures himself, which essentially means he pays claims out of his own funds instead of buying insurance).

☞ You get hurt on the job (or contract a work-related illness).

☞ Your employer's insurance carrier immediately starts paying your medical, hospital, and surgical bills.

☞ You file a claim for workers' compensation and your employer's insurance carrier immediately begins paying you benefits based on a percentage of your average weekly income (66⅔ percent of gross up to a maximum cap in most states, but in any event less than your full income, since you don't have to pay income taxes on workers' compensation benefits).

☞ The state workers' compensation board (or industrial commission, or whatever the agency happens to call itself in your state) quickly approves your claim—assuming they find it to be work-related.

☞ Your employer's insurance carrier continues to pay your medical bills and income benefits for the duration of your disability.

☞ As your condition improves, you return to "light duty."

☞ Eventually you are back to full duty and off workers' compensation entirely; or if you can never return to full earning capacity, workers' compensation makes up most of the difference between what you were able to earn before the accident and what you are able to earn with your disability.

You don't sue, your employer doesn't dump you, and everyone lives happily ever after.

But of course there are less appealing possibilities:

☞ Your employer disagrees with your claim.
☞ The workers' compensation commission holds a hearing to arbitrate the dispute. (Your employer may have to pay you benefits during the dispute process, though you may be required to reimburse him if the commission finds in his favor.)
☞ Following the hearing, and maybe an appeal or two—even to court—you win.
☞ Months pass. Even if you receive benefits while you remain unable to work, you have to tap into your savings to make up the difference between your regular earnings and your weekly benefits.
☞ You are dying to return to work and so have your doctor approve you for a return to work in a "light duty" role.
☞ Your employer says he has no "light duty" work available and cans you and cuts off your benefits, claiming you are fit to work—somewhere else.
☞ You can't get another job.
☞ Maybe you reinjure yourself and file another claim for benefits.

And it starts all over again.

☞ Your (former) employer disputes your claim.
☞ The workers' compensation commission holds a hearing. (This time, of course, you are no longer being paid benefits, so the fact that the hearing may be rescheduled a couple of times and may take a month or more to convene matters more to you at this point in time.)
☞ There is another hearing, at which your now former employer says you are faking it . . .
☞ You are required to submit to a medical examination. (See below.)

And on . . . and on . . . and on . . .

The problem, of course, is that often your employer assumes you are malingering. (It happens.) That is especially true for things like back injuries, stress, carpal tunnel syndrome, heart and lung disease, and a myriad of other occupational injuries and illnesses he can't actually *see*. (Employers are very *visual*.) To put it succinctly, as one employer was overheard to say at a workers' compensation hearing, he thinks you're "a big fat faker."

It is always, as they say, the few who try to take advantage of the system that ruin it for the many who have legitimate claims—in this case for benefits for a real on-the-job injury or illness. And, as usual, it is not always easy to separate one from the other. This has given rise to some of the most interesting and inventive attempts at recovery in any branch of the law. Take the guy who suffered a severe hand injury at work that required an extended stay at a medical center. The man, who was married, developed a romantic relationship with a medical center chauffeur (who, it was rumored, later had his baby). Well, the usual soap opera developed, they had an argument, and she stabbed him to death. The man's long-suffering wife claimed workers' compensation death benefits, maintaining that, except for his work-related injury, he wouldn't have been in the medical center, wouldn't have met the chauffeur, and wouldn't have wound up dead. Well, she had to keep on suffering, because the court denied benefits, saying that his death resulted from a strictly personal event and its connection to his job was so remote as to be nonexistent.*

A lot is at stake here, both for you and your employer. If you have a legitimate claim for benefits, you should get them—quickly and without a lot of hassles and a long, drawn-out lawsuit. On the other hand, if you don't have a legitimate claim for benefits, you shouldn't get them, because just like your automobile or homeowners' or any other kind of insurance, every claim against an employer's workers' compensation insurance raises his rates.

Workers' compensation laws were enacted and are administered by the individual states, so some of the requirements vary from state to state—like how long you have to file a claim and what percentage of your income benefits are based on. But the theories, and thus the main thrust of the laws, are very similar. (**Table 15**, at the end of this chapter, synopsizes the critical state-to-state differences in notice and filing requirements.)

There's a lot of technical stuff about which employers have to have workers' compensation insurance, where they get it, what their premiums are based on, which employees they have to insure,

Littles v. Osceola Farms Co., Florida Dist. Court of Appeal, No. 90-985, 1991.

their obligations to you if you are injured (or contract an illness) on the job, what benefits you are due if you are qualified to get them, and who makes sure they do what they're supposed to. This chapter will explain that stuff because you should know about it to really understand how the system works. But it will also examine in detail the issues that you and your employer will most likely butt heads over, like:

☛ What qualifies as an on-the-job injury and what does not? For example, what if you fall on the sidewalk in front of your employer's building while on your way to work? Or are in an accident in your delivery truck while deviating just a bit from your normal route? Or break your leg playing softball on a company athletic team?

☛ When is your employer relieved of his obligation to pay benefits? For example, what if you are hurt in a fight? Or while sleeping on the job?

☛ How long does your employer have to keep your job open before he replaces you? A week? A month? A year? Indefinitely? Not at all?

☛ Does your employer have to put you to work when you are ready? Or can he let you go the minute you get off workers' compensation?

Finally, the chapter will take you step-by-step through a sample claim procedure, including notice requirements, hearings, appeals, agreements, and settlements.

So put on your hard hat and safety goggles. Here we go.

ADMINISTRATION

Workers' compensation laws are administered and enforced by your state's workers' compensation commission or board or a comparable agency. In some states it is called the industrial accident commission or board and may be a subdivision of the state department of labor. Often the agency is broken down into geographical regions, with a commissioner assigned to each. The agency establishes rules and regulations regarding how and when claims for benefits must be made, how and when claims must be contested, and how and when hearings and appeals are conducted. Most workers' compensation agencies also have the authority to approve lists of doctors, surgeons, dentists, and other medical professionals who may treat injured or ill employees.

You can get the address and telephone number of workers' compensation agencies by consulting the Blue Pages of your telephone directory under state listings. There is generally a separate listing under "Workers' Compensation Commission" or "Industrial Accident Commission." If there isn't, check under "Labor Department" or call Information.

EMPLOYERS' INSURANCE REQUIREMENTS

Most of us hope we never get involved with the workers' compensation system. That's because the prerequisite is rather distasteful: We have to get hurt badly enough or get sick enough that we are not able to work, often for an extended period of time. And usually that means doctors, hospitals, medication, or even surgery. But for most employers there are no prerequisites. When he opens his doors and hires someone to help him out, he is automatically involved with the system. He now must deal with questions like: Do I have to have insurance? Where do I get it? Do I have to insure everyone who works for me? How much will the insurance cost? And, what kinds of injuries are covered?

Although all you, the employee, are really interested in at the outset is "Am I covered?," a brief outline of employer insurance requirements will help you understand how the system works.

Mandatory Coverage

Having workers' compensation coverage for their employees is mandatory for most employers in most states, whether they have only one employee or thousands. New Jersey, South Carolina, and Texas are the only states where insurance coverage is "elective." However, the "election" is a qualified one. If an employer in one of those states elects not to be covered, an injured employee can sue him for damages, just like in the old days. With one big difference: The employer has to fight with one hand tied behind his back. That's because the law won't let him assert certain key defenses, the most important of which is contributory negligence. Seeing as how assumption of the risk hasn't held water in a workers' compensation case in years, and the fellow servant rule isn't much help these days, either, the uninsured employer is pretty much up the proverbial creek.

A handful of states let very small employers in nonhazardous businesses off the workers' compensation insurance hook. In the following states, coverage is generally required only for employers of:

☞ *3 or more employees:* Arkansas, Georgia, New Mexico, North Carolina, and Virginia;
☞ *4 or more employees:* Florida, Rhode Island, and South Carolina; and
☞ *5 or more employees:* Alabama, Mississippi, Missouri, and Tennessee.

Again, however, this small-employer exception doesn't usually apply to construction and other hazardous employment. Plus, employers who do not have insurance may be taking an additional risk, since they can be sued for liability and can't always assert certain defenses that might otherwise have been available to them.

Employees Not Covered

Most jobs in most states are covered by workers' compensation. That usually includes employees who are hurt while working in another state. Some states even cover employees who are injured while working in their state but who are actually employed in another state if their home state doesn't cover out-of-state injuries. However, under most state laws, some or all of the following do not have to be covered:

☞ Sole proprietors and partners.
☞ Corporate officers who choose not to be covered.
☞ Members of the employer's family who live with the employer (i.e., spouse, children).
☞ Certain maritime employees, railroad workers, and federal employees who are covered by federal law.
☞ Some agricultural laborers.
☞ So-called outworkers, to whom materials or articles are given to be worked on away from the employer's place of

business, like people who knit garments at home on piece-work.

☞ So-called casual employees whose occasional employment isn't directly involved with the employer's business, like someone hired to plow snow from the employer's parking lot.

☞ Part-time housekeepers in private homes.

Note: Some states allow an employer to opt to cover some of these workers voluntarily—such as a sole proprietor, business partner, or corporate officer.

Independent Contractors

One of the most controversial employment relationships having an impact on workers' compensation coverage is the "independent contractor." That's because if you are an independent contractor, you are not considered an "employee" and do not have to be covered under the workers' compensation insurance policy of the company that hires you. (Neither does your "employer" have to make matching Social Security contributions for you or deduct and withhold income taxes, but those are Internal Revenue Service matters.) That being the case, many a sneaky employer will try to classify you as an independent contractor, as opposed to an "employee," so he will not be responsible for those extra costs of doing business. It may also seem like a good idea to you at the time, since as an independent contractor you can deduct your "business" expenses. But what about when you are hurt on the job? Do you have private disability insurance?

Well, the company that hires you may be responsible for workers' compensation coverage even if they call you an independent contractor—if you're really not. Whether or not you qualify as an independent contractor depends on the facts of your specific situation. But control is the key. You are likely an independent contractor if you hire out to do work by your own methods without being subject to the employer's control except as to the final result. However, if the person who hires you controls both *what you do and how you do it,* you are probably an employee.

So how do you know whether you are an employee or an independent contractor? Most workers' compensation agencies apply the same test as the IRS, which uses what they call the "common law factors" to decide. The "common law" factors essentially boil down to the following eight questions you can ask yourself:

☞ Do I get training or instruction on how to do the job?
☞ Do I perform the task in person, on company property, and during set hours?
☞ Is there a continuing work relationship (or do I work by the job)?
☞ Do I work exclusively for one company?
☞ Am I paid by the hour, week, or month, rather than by the job?
☞ Am I reimbursed for business and travel expenses?
☞ Does the company provide my tools or equipment?
☞ Can I be fired or can I quit without any contractual liability?

The more "yes" answers, the more "common law" control the company has and thus the more likely you are an employee—and probably have to be covered under the employer's workers' compensation policy.

Remember, it doesn't matter what the person who hired you and pays you calls you (or even what your written contract says). What matters is what the law calls you. And the foremost factor the law looks at is control. To illustrate: An employee who suffered a compensable injury (an injury that qualified for workers' compensation benefits) at his day job at a grocery store did some moonlighting on the local police payroll as an informant for the department's drug task force. The police treated him as an independent contractor, so the grocery store (who would be stuck with the extra workers' compensation bill) said his informant's pay shouldn't be included in computing his workers' compensation benefits. No way, said the court. The cops had rigid control over how the man performed his job. Decision: He's an employee and his benefits should be based on his total earnings from both jobs.*

Part-time Employees

The fact that you work only part-time doesn't relieve your employer from providing workers' compensation coverage. That means if he

*Buncy v. Certified Grocers, Florida Dist. Court of Appeal, 1st Dist., No. 91-984, 1992.

has to cover full-time employees who do the same work you do, he has to cover you, too.

Minors

In many states injuries to minors are covered at up to twice the usual rate. That is, they may be awarded benefits based on up to twice their weekly pay.

Voluntary Work

Unpaid volunteers are not considered employees and do not have to be covered, except that some states have special rules for volunteer fire and police work.

Multiple Employers

If you work for more than one employer, you are considered covered by the employer for whom you were working at the time of your injury.

EMPLOYERS' OBLIGATIONS

Employers have a number of obligations to workers who suffer compensable injuries. These obligations generally include:

☞ Carrying workers' compensation insurance (or self-insuring) in the first place.
☞ Payment of all related medical bills.
☞ Payment of weekly benefits as a substitute for lost wages.
☞ Payment of a lump sum for any permanent incapacity.
☞ Payment of death benefits.

In addition, many states also require:

☛ Continuation of the injured worker's group health and life insurance. **(Note:** The U.S. Supreme Court has ruled that ERISA, the federal law that governs employee benefit plans, preempts any such state requirement, so employers would not have to continue health insurance benefits for employees who are on workers' comp.* However, those employees may still be eligible for continued health insurance under the FMLA or ADA—and certainly would be eligible under COBRA. See Chapter 4: Fringe Benefits, and Chapter 5: Discrimination and Related Issues for more information.)

☛ Providing suitable work, if available, when the injured worker is able to return to "light duty."

☛ Returning a sufficiently recovered worker to his or her former job or an equivalent job, if one is available.

☛ Refraining from any form of retaliation against the worker for filing a workers' compensation claim (or helping someone else by testifying in theirs).

Insurance Carriers

Most employers carry insurance with private insurance companies. However, many states allow larger employers to self-insure—once they have proven they are solvent and are able to pay claims, and often after they have posted a bond. A few states, like Nevada, North Dakota, Ohio, Washington, West Virginia, and Wyoming require employers to insure employees through a state workers' compensation insurance fund.

In the matter of workers' compensation laws, your employer and his insurance carrier are essentially one and the same. Since the responsibility of carrying insurance is your employer's, this chapter will refer to him exclusively—even though it may, for example, actually be the insurer who pays the claim, requires you to take a medical examination, etc.

Medical Bills

If you are injured in an on-the-job accident, your employer is responsible for paying for all resulting medical treatment. Your employer may have his staff doctor treat you first, if he has one, or have you transported to the nearest emergency facility. But after that you have the right to choose your own doctor.

By the way, you have to be paid your regular wages for any work time lost for medical treatment.

Greater Washington Board of Trade v. District of Columbia, 1992 LEXIS 78471, 1992.

Weekly Benefits

Your employer has to pay you a weekly amount based on a percentage of your income while you are completely incapacitated and unable to work because of an on-the-job injury or illness. The percentage varies from state to state, but generally is either 66⅔ percent of your gross income or 80 percent of your disposable income (what's left after taxes, Social Security, and other deductions). States also put an upper limit on benefits, which is related to the state's average weekly wage for all workers. So, even though workers' compensation benefits aren't taxed, nobody ever got rich on workers' compensation payments and, in fact, most find it difficult to get by.

In some states benefits are adjusted annually to offset cost-of-living increases.

Partial Incapacity: If you aren't totally incapacitated, but are limited in the type of work you can do because of your injury or illness, or if you are not able to return to your full duties after a period of total incapacity, your employer has to make up the difference between what you could have earned had you not been injured and what you are able to earn since the injury. Again, what your employer has to pay is based on a percentage of the resulting difference in pay, as with total incapacity.

If you have diminished earning capacity and your employer has no suitable work for you and you cannot find another job in your area, your employer has to pay you full benefits as long as you can show that you are actively seeking work. (Many states require you to provide proof of your efforts, such as statements from employers whom you contacted about a job.)

Permanent Incapacity: There is also the matter of a permanent injury or incapacity. Most states have rather ghoulish "schedules" listing a specific number of weeks of benefits due to a permanently injured or disfigured worker depending on how much each particular type of permanent injury is "worth." For example, an injured worker might be due so many weeks of benefits for loss of a body part, depending on its "value," or so much for a facial scar or other disfigurement, depending on how extensive or visible it is and whether it prevents the individual from ever working again or being able to earn full wages. Often the payments will be translated into a lump sum payment.

Death Benefits: If a worker dies as a result of an on-the-job injury, his or her spouse will be paid a specified amount for burial expenses (usually about enough to bury the deceased in a cardboard box) as well as the worker's full weekly benefits for life or until remarriage. Dependents are also eligible for benefits until age eighteen.

Waiting Period

Generally, you must be paid full wages for the day you are injured. Then there is a waiting period before workers' compensation benefits kick in. Waiting periods range from a few days to a week. But if your incapacity lasts for a certain period of time (generally a couple of weeks), benefits will be paid retroactively back to the first day. See **Table 15.** Here's how it works. Take Connecticut, for example. In Connecticut, there is a three-day waiting period. But benefits are paid back to the first day after your injury if you are unable to work for seven days or more. So you wouldn't receive any benefits if you missed three days or less of work. If you missed four to six days, you would get benefits for only days four, five, and six. But if you missed seven days or more, you would get benefits from the first day. (Connecticut uses "calendar days" in its calculations, which means weekends and holidays are included.)

Start of Payments

Most states require your employer to start paying your benefits to you within a specified time after he agrees to pay benefits or benefits are awarded following a hearing—typically a week or two.

Group Health Insurance

A number of state laws require your employer to continue your group health insurance while you are unable to work because of an on-the-job injury or illness. However, remember the U.S. Supreme Court ruling that says ERISA preempts any such state requirement. That means your employer would not have to continue your health insurance benefits while you are on workers' comp. But you may still be eligible for continued health insurance under the FMLA or ADA—and under COBRA. See Employers' Obligations, earlier in this chapter.

"Light Duty"

If your injury incapacitates you only partially so you are unable to perform your usual duties but can do "light" or restricted work, or if you were totally incapacitated initially and have not recovered sufficiently to return to your old job but can do some type of work, your employer may be obligated under the workers' compensation law to provide you with suitable work, *if he has such work available.* Of course, that's the catch: *if he has such work available.* **Warning:** There are certain psychological as well as physical burdens that go along with being injured on the job and unable to work. Some employers (few and far between, but they are out there) keep in touch with injured workers, aid them as much as they can in their rehabilitation, and try to get them back to work as soon as possible. Which makes sense to both of you, since then he'll be paying you for *working* and you'll be back earning full pay. But most employers tend to lose touch with injured employees (once again, that malingerer syndrome). That leaves you floating around out there, not only physically hurting but bored and cut off from your work cronies not to mention stripped of your identity, of what you do.

So most injured workers are eager to get back on the job. A word to the wise: Don't be *too* eager. Know where your employer stands. Is your job still unfilled? If not, is an equivalent job open or opening soon? Does your employer have suitable light-duty jobs available? Is your employer ready to welcome you back into the fold? Or is he just waiting for you to get clearance for light duty so he can tell you he has no light-duty jobs and reduce or cut off your benefits now that your doctor has said you are ready to return to work?

This is not to suggest that you turn into a "big fat faker." It's merely a warning that before you get too anxious and try to return to work before you are ready, be sure your employer will be waiting with the welcome mat and not a banana peel.

Reduction or Discontinuation of Benefits

Once you return to light duty, your employer will apply to the workers' compensation commission for a reduction in your weekly benefit payments according to how much you are presently able to earn as compared with how much you were earning at full working capacity. Likewise, once your disability has completely ended, he will apply to have your weekly benefits discontinued. Most commissions do not allow the employer to reduce or cut off benefits without their express approval.

If you disagree with your employer's contention that you are able to resume light-duty work or that you are no longer disabled at all, the commission may require a further hearing to make that determination.

Note: You may be required to submit to a medical examination if your employer thinks you are sufficiently recovered that you no longer qualify for full (or partial) benefits. See below for details.

Reinjury

If you have returned to work and reinjure yourself, you are eligible for benefits based on the higher of your earnings either at the time of the original injury or the reinjury.

Retaliation

Your employer shouldn't fire you or discriminate against you in any way because you filed for workers' compensation benefits. But that doesn't mean he has to be happy about it. As mentioned earlier, neither does it mean he has to hold your job open indefinitely; or supply you with light-duty work if he doesn't have any for you.

How soon can he replace you? That depends on what is reasonable in the specific situation. Is yours a one-of-a-kind job that is necessary to the day-to-day operation of the facility? Then he wouldn't have to wait all that long before getting someone else to fill the position.

Should he hire a "temp"? Again, not an easy question to answer. Does the job lend itself to temporary workers? Does your employer often hire temps to fill in on your kind of job?

The question of replacing you depends on many factors, not the least of which is how long you are expected to be unable to perform your usual job and what is a reasonable period under the circumstances. It also depends on whether or not it appears that, in replacing you, your employer is making a statement: "This is what you get for filing workers' compensation and making me pay you for not working."

In many states, if you can show that your employer fired you under circumstances that indicate it was because you had the gall to file a workers' compensation claim, then you can go after him for reinstatement to your job, back pay, restoration of employee benefits, and your attorneys' fees.

Note: Other factors may also come into play. Are you an older employee? A woman? Black? Handicapped? How has your employer treated employees in nonprotected groups under similar circumstances? How long were their jobs held open? Was his dire need to fill your job only a pretext for the real reason: your age, sex, race, or handicap? Then you may have a discrimination or wrongful discharge claim, too. See Chapter 5: Discrimination and Related Issues.

ELIGIBILITY FOR BENEFITS

Now for the really good stuff. Your employer has workers' compensation insurance. You're covered. You're injured or you get sick. You are unable to work because of your injury or illness.

The big question and the one most of the disputes are over is: *Did your injury or illness "arise out of and in the course of your employment"?* If it did, you qualify for benefits. If it didn't, you're on your own. It's as simple as that. Which is about like saying it's as simple as putting a human on Mars.

"Arising out of and in the Course of Employment"

For you to be eligible for workers' compensation benefits, your injury or illness has to "arise out of and in the course of employment." What that means is that you must have been injured:

☞ During work time.
☞ In a place where you were supposed to be, or at least could have reasonably been expected to have been.
☞ In the line of duty. (That is, while you were doing a task associated with your job or a task that is "incidental" to your job.) And,
☞ Under circumstances where there is a cause-and-effect relationship between your job and your injury. ("But for" the fact that you were on the job, you wouldn't have been injured.)

But, depending on the facts of the case, you don't necessarily have to have been injured during working hours, or while you were on the job, or even while you were at work. And the causal connection between the job and the injury can be pretty remote. In analyzing a specific fact pattern, courts weigh time, place, and circumstances.

Common Situations

Some types of injury (and illness) situations just have a way of happening over and over again. So what follows are some examples of some of the more common ones. Keep in mind, though, that your workers' compensation case is as unique as your fingerprint.

Commuting ("Going and Coming" Rule): Injuries incurred while en route to and from work are not generally considered to "arise out of and in the course of employment" and thus are not covered by workers' compensation. As one court put it, hazards faced by employees during their daily commutes are common to the public at large, while workers' compensation benefits are designed to provide compensation for work-related injuries.* In other words, working at your job exposes you to specific hazards not encountered by the rest of us; and it is those hazards workers' compensation is designed to protect you against. Once you are back out in the big, bad world, you are on your own.

On the other hand, an employee who was injured walking to his car after he had left work and after he had left his employer's premises sustained a work-related injury and was eligible for benefits because his employer required him to bring his car to work every day to make occasional deliveries or to call on customers.† However, since the court noted that the injury occurred only a "few feet" from the employer's premises, it could be inferred that once the employee made it to his car and started home he would no longer have been covered.

Special Hazards: The *Fairchild Space Co.* case referred to above pointed out the general consensus that it is the special hazards of work that workers' compensation laws are designed to protect us

---

*Fairchild Space Co. v. Baroffio, 551 Atl. 2d 135, 1989.
†*Jenkins v. Tandy Corp.,* Oregon Court of Appeals, No. CA A40502, 1987; 86 Ore. App. 133, 1987.

against. And some courts stretch the connection between the special hazard and the job pretty thin. An Ohio court awarded benefits to a worker whose car was hit from behind as he took a left turn into his employer's driveway while rushing back from a lunch break. The court said that "but for" his job, he wouldn't have been at the location of the accident and that making the left turn put him at a greater risk than John Q. Public, who was just driving along in a straight line.*

Dual Purpose Trips (Business and Pleasure): You would be covered if you were injured on a business trip, of course, because the trip is work-related. But what if the trip mixes business and pleasure? Whether or not an injury on such a trip is covered depends on which factor was controlling—the business or the pleasure. If it is your work that created the necessity for the trip or work is a contributing factor in your taking the trip, an injury would qualify for workers' compensation benefits.† Look at it like this: If you would have had to take the trip for the business purpose even if the pleasure part hadn't existed, the injury is covered. On the other hand, if you wouldn't have gone except for the pleasure part of it, then the injury wouldn't be covered.

"On Call" (Special Errands): If you are "on call" for emergencies and are hurt when called to work, your injury would generally be covered as work-related (another exception from the "going and coming" rule). However, the court in the *Fairchild Space Co.* case (which has provided a fertile area of discussion) ruled that simply being called to work a little early or having to work a little late does not qualify as a "special errand," because it lacks the urgency to present a particular hazard to the worker.

Parking Lots: Generally, parking lot injuries are covered by workers' compensation only if the employer owns or has direct control over the area. So, if you are injured in your employer's parking lot, you will likely be covered. The area of your employer's responsibility can be extended by circumstances, however. One woman was hit by a car while crossing to a remote area of a parking lot adjacent to her employer's place of business but neither owned nor directly su-

---

Littlefield v. Pillsbury Co., 453 NE 2d 570, 1983.
†*Jacobs v. Consolidated Telephone Co.,* Nebraska Supreme Court, No. 90-410, 1991.

pervised by her employer. The reason she had parked so far away was because of a strict company policy that required nearby spaces to be left open for the convenience of shoppers. The court said that the policy gave the employer sufficient control over the woman at the time of the accident to remove her from the going and coming rule and make her eligible for benefits.*

Deviation from Route: If you are injured while making deliveries in a company truck or while you are being driven from one job site to another in a company van, you would almost certainly be covered by workers' compensation. But what if you deviated from your usual route for nonbusiness purposes? Well, that depends on the extent of the deviation. An employee injured in an automobile accident while his foreman was taking a circuitous route from the job site to the company's office via the bookkeeper's house could collect workers' compensation because the purpose of the trip was work-related—to pick up their paychecks—and the deviation was slight.† But the deviation can be too great. For example, a woman could not receive benefits for injuries sustained in a car accident even though she was chauffeuring around a customer at the time. Reasoning: She had taken the customer to a dog racing track, a deviation from her duties that was so extreme and so lengthy as to be beyond the scope of her employment.‡

Horseplay/Violation of Rules: Being hurt while "fooling around" can remove you from workers' compensation coverage. But not if the behavior is condoned by your employer. Take the case of the rubber band snapper. Returning from a break, this employee picked a rubber band up off the floor and snapped it. Apparently he wasn't too coordinated because it snapped back and hit him in the eye, partially blinding him. But because boxes routinely arrived at the company wrapped in rubber bands, and employees often picked them up off the floor, the court said getting hurt snapping them was a risk inherent in the job.§ The court did imply, however, that if the company had enforced a policy against the practice, such an injury might not have been covered.

*Livingstone v. Abraham & Straus, 524 Atl. 2d 876, 1987.
†Farris v. Huston Barger Masonry, Inc., Kentucky Supreme Court, No. 88-SC-788-DG, 1989; 780 SW2d 611.
‡Luddie v. United Advertising Corp., 5 Conn. App. 193, 1986.
§Davison v. The Florsheim Shoe Co., Missouri Court of Appeals, Western Dist., No. WD39907, 1988.

How about this one: An employee is hurt playing Ping-Pong before work with game equipment he and his fellow workers bought themselves. Decision: A compensable injury. Reasoning: Since the games occurred regularly on the employer's premises and with his knowledge and tacit approval, the conduct was "incidental" to the injured worker's employment.*

Acts Done for a Third Party: In general, where an injury occurs while doing something for a third party, the act must have been done to appreciably benefit the employer.

A cocktail waitress leaving her job stops to aid a motorist she recognizes as a guest while she is still on resort grounds. She is kidnapped and raped. When she later jumps from the man's car to escape, she is dragged some distance and severely injured. Decision: A compensable injury. Reasoning: Part of the woman's job was to offer any assistance possible to resort guests, which was of benefit to the employer and thus made the injury work-related.†

Willful Misconduct: Your injury may not be covered if it is caused by your own "willful and serious" misconduct. A man who worked part-time for a logging company showed up on one of his days off to try to borrow money from his employer. While there he began to climb a trailer to help out—against the owner's direct orders not to. He fell and was injured. But the court did not award benefits because the man went to the job site for purely personal reasons and was injured as a result of his own willful misconduct.‡ However, an employee who is injured by the "willful and wanton" misconduct of a *fellow employee* is covered under most states' workers' compensation laws.

Alcohol and Drugs: An on-the-job accident caused by your intoxication or addiction to alcohol or drugs normally does not qualify for benefits.

Fights: If you are involved in a personal fight with another employee, a resulting injury may not be covered. However, your injury would be covered if you were hurt while protecting your

---

McNamara v. Town of Hamden, 176 Conn. 547, 1979.
†*Culpepper v. Fairfield Sapphire Valley,* 377 S.E. 2nd 777, 1989.
‡*Lee v. Middleton Logging Co.,* Georgia Court of Appeals, No. A90A2159, 1991.

employer or his property or his interests, or if the assault was connected to some job duty. An employee who had punched out (no pun intended) but was still hanging around across the street from work with several fellow employees a couple of hours later came to the aid of his supervisor, who was being attacked by a group of men on his employer's property. Unfortunately, the employee was stabbed to death. His family was awarded death benefits because he was killed while furthering his employer's interests—by protecting a member of the employer's work force.* In another interesting case, a fellow took some heat from coworkers when his department got a raise and theirs didn't. One woman called his wife a rather unflattering name and he told her where to go. When the employee left work that afternoon, he was met in the parking lot by the coworker's husband (who wasn't an employee of the company). Injuries resulted and benefits were awarded. There was, said the court, a causal connection between his job and the injury.†

Causal Connection: As we just saw in the *San Antonio Shoes* case, whether or not there is a causal relationship between your employment and your injury often will determine whether benefits will be awarded. We also saw cause and effect working in the *Littles* case. (Remember "The Case of the Jealous Chauffeur," where the cause of the man's death was his extracurricular activities and not his job?) Even though your job led to a series of events that ultimately resulted in an injury, at some point the cause-and-effect relationship simply becomes too blurred. That was the case when a woman was injured on her job driving an eighteen-wheeler. She of course received workers' compensation for that injury. However, she was not entitled to benefits for injuries sustained in a second accident when somebody smashed into her car while she was on her way to get treatment for the first. Her claim was based on the fact that she was at the site of the second accident only *because of* the first, job-related one. Too remote, said the court. The negligence of the third party broke the causal connection with work.‡

Brind Leasing Corp. v. Workers' Compensation Appeal Board, Pennsylvania Commonwealth Court, No. 566 C-D, 1990.
†*San Antonio Shoes v. Beaty,* Arkansas Court of Appeals, Div. II, No. 88-356, 1989; 28 Ark. App. 201, 1989.
‡*Gayler v. North American Van Lines,* Indiana Court of Appeals, 4th Dist., No. 93A02-9001-EX-38, 1991.

Asleep on the Job: Workers accidentally injured while asleep on the job generally have been ruled to qualify for benefits.

Athletic Teams: Generally, whether or not an injury that occurs during competition on a "company" athletic team is covered by workers' compensation depends on the degree to which your employer is involved in or sponsors the team, including such things as whether or not:

☞ The employer provides uniforms and equipment or makes other financial contributions to the team.

☞ Games take place on company property or during working hours.

☞ The employer derives benefits from the team, such as advertising or a boost in employee morale.

A case in point: A 1991 Alaska Supreme Court ruled that supplying a softball team with T-shirts, caps, bats, and balls, paying the $250 rental fee for the field, and encouraging nonparticipating employees to attend games was sufficient sponsorship to qualify an injured player for benefits.*

Office Parties and Company Picnics: What if you are injured at a company-sponsored office party or picnic? Well, the injury would probably qualify for coverage as long as:

☞ Your employer paid for the party or picnic and employees were required (or "expected") to go.

☞ The party or picnic was held on work premises. (This would no doubt include a function held at your employer's home.) Or,

☞ The party or picnic was held during paid work time.

Note: Alcohol could add another dynamic to the situation, as a host who serves alcohol to someone who is already intoxicated can be held liable for injuries resulting from the person's intoxication. So if alcohol is served at the company picnic and you become intoxicated and are involved in an automobile accident while driving

LeSeur-Johnson v. Rollins-Burdick Hunter of Alaska, Alaska Supreme Court, No. S-3493, 1991.

home, your employer may be held liable for injuries to you and anyone else injured as a result.

Weakened Resistance: Personal injuries (i.e., those that are not work-related) do not qualify for benefits unless the cause can be directly traced to work. Most courts will require you to demonstrate that it was more than just "weakened resistance" caused by working that led to your injury.

OCCUPATIONAL ILLNESS OR DISEASE

Occupational illnesses and diseases are somewhat different than on-the-job injuries, and thus require a different standard of proof that they "arise out of and in the course of employment." The basic difference between accidental injuries and occupational diseases is that accidents are unexpected and occupational diseases really aren't, because to be compensable they must result from continued exposure to a *recognized hazard* of a particular job. Also, the onset of an occupational disease is gradual rather than sudden.

For example, if you claim your carpal tunnel syndrome (repetitive motion disorder) is caused by your job, you must prove that it is *characteristic* of your job; that is, that your job involves the kind of repetitive motion that would result in the type of injury you have.* It also helps if you don't have lots of nonwork factors that could contribute to the problem. Take the man who claimed his heart attack was caused by on-the-job exposure to gases in the refrigerators he moved. Not only was he unable to show a connection between the gases and his heart attack, the court pointed out that the fact that he was overweight and had high blood pressure and high cholesterol levels might have had something to do with his heart disease. No causal connection; no workers' compensation.†

Psychiatric Disability

To maintain a case for psychiatric disability, you have to be able to show that your condition resulted from an *abnormal* working con-

---

**Wood v. Allison Apparel Marketing, Inc.,* Virginia Court of Appeals, No. 0978-89-3, 1990.
†*Schmalz v. No. Dak. Workers' Compensation Bureau,* North Dakota Supreme Court, Civ. No. 890269, 1989; 449 NW2d 817.

dition. The presence of a mouse (or any other common pest) in the workplace is just too common an occurrence, for example, for a resulting psychiatric trauma to be considered work-related—even if you have always been afraid of mice.*

PREEXISTING CONDITIONS
Waiver of Liability

It may be difficult to get an employer to hire you if he knows you had a prior on-the-job injury that may potentially expose him to workers' compensation liability if you are reinjured. To insulate himself, he may require you to sign a waiver absolving him from responsibility in case of reinjury. In most jurisdictions, such a waiver is valid only with respect to the specific prior injury described and only if it is approved by the workers' compensation commission. It would not be valid as to any new injury. Also, in most jurisdictions, by executing such a waiver you don't forfeit your right to workers' compensation benefits even if you do sustain the same injury as before on your new job. So you have nothing to lose. All that happens is that your benefits come from a state "second injury fund" rather than from your employer. States assess extra premiums against employers, depending on the number of claims made against them, to set up these second injury funds with the express purpose of taking care of these types of situations.

Aggravation of a Preexisting Condition

What if you sustain a similar injury, only it's worse the second time than it was the first? Well, the benefits may come partly from your employer and partly from a state second injury fund, but if your injury is otherwise compensable, you will get benefits from somewhere. And, after all, who really cares where the money comes from as long as it comes?

*Marisco v. Workmens' [sic] Compensation Appeal Board, Pennsylvania Commonwealth Court, No. 1092 C.D. 1989, 1991.

WORKPLACE VIOLENCE

Some of the more chilling headlines we are reading in the newspapers these days involve violence in the workplace. Though we hear the usual sick jokes about another postal worker going berserk, the sad truth is that no workplace is completely immune from violence. The U.S. Department of Labor's Bureau of Labor and Statistics's figures show that over one thousand people are murdered and over two million are assaulted at work every year. Though these figures have remained relatively steady over the past fifteen years, they are disturbing nonetheless.

The obvious question is, what is my (or my family's) recourse if I am the victim of an assault at work? The answer, for now, seems to be relatively cut and dried. As with other on-the-job injuries, recovery for an injury caused by an attack at work is generally limited to filing a workers' compensation claim against your employer. (See Civil Lawsuits, later in this chapter.) Though a number of workplace assault victims have tried to hold their employers liable under the general duty clause of the **Occupational Safety and Health Act,** so far they have had little success. (The general duty clause requires employers to provide a workplace that is free from "recognized hazards" that are likely to cause death or severe physical harm. "Recognized hazards" include conditions or situations that are obviously dangerous, or that your employer knows about, or that are generally considered hazardous in his industry. See Chapter 7: Health and Safety.) It is certainly not a stretch to imagine a courtroom some time in the very near future where a jury will be called upon to determine whether an employer knew or should have known that an employee was dangerous. Likewise, a jury could easily view an injury sustained by a health care worker while treating a belligerent patient, or an assault on a police officer or firefighter responding to a call, or even an injury to an employee during a robbery of his workplace, as a foreseeable result of an employer's actions (i.e.: his failure to take reasonable precautions to prevent these things from happening). Also see "negligent hiring" in Chapter 1: The Hiring Process.

FILING A CLAIM

As you might expect, there are fifty different procedures for filing workers' compensation claims in the fifty different states. But it's only the nuances that vary all that much, such as time limits for giving notice, filing a claim, and appealing. See **Table 15**. The meat and potatoes requirements are basically the same:

Notice to Your Employer

Most states require you to notify your employer within a certain time that you are filing a claim based on an occupational injury or illness. Some states just say notice has to be given as soon as practicable, whatever that means. But most specify a time period, though notice requirements vary from immediately (Arkansas) to two years (New Hampshire). See **Table 15**. In order to be eligible for weekly disability benefits, you must give timely notice following the date of your job-related accident or the first appearance of symptoms of an occupational disease. (Most states don't require formal notice if your employer has actual knowledge of your injury, such as if he or your supervisor witnessed the accident, called an ambulance or doctor, sent you to the hospital, etc. But it is still a good idea to give formal notice anyway.) To be eligible for death benefits, your beneficiary must also give timely notice following your death—though most states extend the notice requirement in cases of death from an occupational injury or illness. Most states excuse late notice for a certain period of time if the delay was for a good reason. An employee was excused for missing the statutory deadline for giving notice of his back injury to his employer because he at first thought it was minor. But after it worsened day by day and conservative treatment failed to help, his doctor told him it was much more serious than his original diagnosis. The employee then notified his employer. However, by then the statutory deadline had passed. Excusable, said the court, since the employee was unaware of the seriousness of the injury until the later date.*

The best idea, of course, is to notify your employer immediately following your injury or the first symptoms of disease (or as soon as you realize it may be related to your job). Proper notice should include:

☞ Your name, address, and occupation, and your employer's name and address;

Peters v. Armellini Express Lines, Florida Dist. Court of Appeal, 1st Dist., No. 87-838, 1988.

☞ The date and site of the accident that caused your injury or the date you first noticed symptoms of the occupational disease; and

☞ A description of the injury or disease.

Though not universally required, the safest bet is to give notice in writing by certified mail, return receipt requested. And, of course, keep a copy for your file.

Filing a Claim with the Workers' Compensation Commission

Besides notifying your employer, you also have to file your claim with the workers' compensation agency within a specified period of time. Again, time limits vary. But they are most often a year or two either from the date of the accident or the first symptoms of illness; or from the date you first realized the connection between the injury or illness and your job. (If you had already been receiving benefits and they were discontinued for any reason, the time limit on filing your claim for continued benefits is measured from the date your benefits were discontinued.) See **Table 15.** Of course, as a practical matter, as with notice to your employer, you should file your claim immediately. Not only will you avoid any potential timeliness problems, but the quicker you file, the quicker you will receive benefits.

Your claim for workers' compensation benefits should include the same particulars as the notice given to your employer, as well as the relationship between your injury or illness and your job. In fact, you can type up (or print legibly) your notice to your employer and make two copies. Sign the original and a copy (a signed copy makes it a duplicate original) and send one to your employer and the other to the agency. (Send both certified mail, return receipt requested.) Keep the third copy for your file. **CAUTION:** Take care not to say anything that might prejudice your claim or make you ineligible for benefits or give your employer fuel to contest your claim. If you have any doubts, contact an attorney. For details, see Chapter 11: I'm Getting Screwed; So, What Can I Do about It?

Contested Claims

Your employer may agree to pay benefits. But since any valid claim will drive up his insurance rates, you can bet he will contest at any opportunity. (In fact, some employers hire specialists to scrutinize each claim for a potential basis for contesting it.) If your employer does decide to contest your claim, he too has to do it within a specified time period. If he doesn't contest within the time limit, he loses the right to do so. Your claim will be presumed to be valid and he will have to pay it.

Medical Examinations

Your employer has the right to require you to submit to a medical examination at any reasonable time to determine the extent of your injuries or your degree of rehabilitation. But he has to pay you for any work time you miss as well as for the examination itself. Your employer may also select the physician. However, you have the right to be examined by a physician of your own choice, too. Many jurisdictions have a list of approved health care professionals who may be consulted for specific types of injuries, including physicians, chiropractors, psychiatrists, psychologists, podiatrists, osteopaths, etc.

If you refuse a reasonable request to undergo a physical examination, you risk being declared ineligible for benefits until you change your mind.

Medical reports must be available to both you and your employer (and your respective attorneys). Your doctor is responsible for reporting the progress of your treatment to your employer. That includes reports of hospitalization, surgery, maximum improvement of your condition, your refusal to be treated or failure to make or keep appointments, and opinions as to your ability to return to work either in a light-duty capacity, to your regular job, or to alternate employment if you are unable to return to your old job.

Hearings and Appeals

In the case of a contested claim, there is a hearing process that gives both you and your employer a chance to air your side of the story in front of a workers' compensation commissioner. There are also avenues of appeal if either of you disputes the commissioner's decision. Of course, it would be impossible to detail the hearing and appeal procedures for every state. Instead, we'll take a look at a fairly typical scenario.

Informal Hearings: First, a regional commissioner convenes an informal conference at which you and your employer each get to state your case. The commissioner will try to effect a settlement at that time.

Formal Hearings: If your claim is not resolved or settled at the informal hearing, the commissioner will schedule a formal hearing at which both you and your employer are allowed to be represented by an attorney. The commissioner can subpoena witnesses and hear testimony, but he or she is not required to follow courtroom rules of evidence or procedure. (So, to that extent at least, even the "formal" hearing is relatively informal.) The commissioner will render a decision within a specified time of the formal hearing (which can be up to several months). If the commissioner decides in your favor, weekly benefits will begin being made. If your employer continues to contest by way of an appeal, most states will pay you benefits out of the state fund. But your employer will have to reimburse the fund, with interest, if he is ultimately on the losing end of the appeal. Of course, if you are denied benefits at the formal hearing, *you* can appeal.

Appeals: Either party may appeal a commissioner's award to the workers' compensation review board. In most cases, the board will simply review the record. It generally will not accept new evidence unless there was a good reason that it wasn't presented at previous hearings. (So it's easy to see that you'd better give it your best shot at the first two hearings.)

Further appeal can then be made to the appellate court. But only questions of law can be appealed at this point and not questions of fact. In other words, your appeal to the courts is confined to saying, "Okay, I accept the workers' compensation commission's determination of what *happened*. But I disagree with how they applied the law to those facts."

The procedure in your state will probably not be exactly the same as the one described, but you get the idea. Once you "get into the system" by filing a claim, your state commission will outline the exact nature of the hearing and appeals process for you and notify you of an award or denial of benefits and time limits on filing appeals. (If they don't, call them; or better yet, get right down there if you can and find out *why* you haven't received prompt action.)

What does all this mean? It means: *Shoot first and ask questions later!* If you are hurt or get sick under circumstances that can even remotely be considered to be connected with or caused by your job and it causes you to be unable to work, notify your employer and file a workers' compensation claim immediately. In the case of an occupational disease, that means notifying the workers' compensation commission as soon as you first experience symptoms of a disease that may have been caused by your work environment, even if it appears years later.

CIVIL LAWSUITS

In most situations, if you are injured or contract a disease that is attributable to work and you are eligible for workers' compensation benefits, you cannot sue your employer or a coworker for damages (a "civil" suit)—even for negligence. On the other hand, if your injury is deemed not to "arise out of and in the course of your employment," you can sue anybody you want. Remember, that's the workers' compensation trade-off: *You* get quick action and income replacement for a work-related injury or illness; *your employer* gets immunity from damage suits.

Exceptions

There are a few exceptions to the rule that workers' compensation is your exclusive remedy for a work-related injury or illness.

Injuries Caused by a Third Party: If your injury was caused by the negligence of a third party (someone other than your employer or a coworker), you are free to sue that person for damages. For example, someone ran a red light and hit your delivery truck while you were making a delivery. You are eligible for workers' compensation benefits, but you can also sue the driver who ran the red light and caused your injury. Your employer can sue the driver, too—to recover workers' compensation benefits he is required to pay you as a result of the driver's negligence. Or he can join your suit and seek reimbursement of his benefit obligations out of your damage award, if you are successful in your lawsuit. Most states require you to notify your employer if you decide to sue a third party, so your employer can join your suit.

Intentional Injuries: In some situations you might be able to sue your employer or a fellow worker for an intentional injury. For example, most jurisdictions allow you to bring a private lawsuit for assault and battery against a fellow employee who injures you in a fight. In the case of a potential lawsuit against your employer for an intentional injury, the injury generally must have been caused by a high-ranking company official—someone higher up than a manager, supervisor, or foreman.

Motor Vehicle Cases: Some states allow you to sue a fellow employee for injuries you sustain as a result of his or her negligent operation of a motor vehicle. States that do allow such lawsuits often restrict them to vehicles other than heavy equipment like bulldozers and backhoes being operated on the job site.

Americans with Disabilities Act Violations: Though workers' compensation laws prohibit most civil lawsuits, they do not prevent you from filing a discrimination charge under the **Americans with Disabilities Act** (ADA) if, as a result of your injury, you are a "qualified disabled individual," or under comparable state laws prohibiting disability discrimination. See below.

Note: Courts are fairly strict in their enforcement of the "exclusivity" of the workers' compensation remedy. It is a good idea to get the advice of an attorney if you think you might have a legal action over and above your workers' compensation claim.

ON-THE-JOB INJURIES AND ADA

How about your on-the-job injury and the **Americans with Disabilities Act?** To be protected by the ADA, your injury must have caused an impairment that "substantially limits a major life activity," or resulted in your having a "record of" such an impairment, or in your being "regarded as" having such an impairment. Obviously, not every on-the-job injury will qualify for ADA protection. The EEOC has a *Technical Assistance Manual* that uses the example of a construction worker who falls from a ladder and breaks his leg. Of course he would be eligible for workers' compensation. However, he would qualify for ADA protection only if the injury took much longer than normal to heal and he couldn't walk during that time; or if he ended up with a permanent limp; or if he recovered but another employer refused to hire him because he had a "record of" having a significant impairment.

Remember, an employer may check into your workers' compensation history *after* offering you a job. But he cannot base an employment decision on speculation that you might cause his workers' compensation rates to go up. He can refuse to hire you, or can fire you, only if you are presently unable to perform the job without posing a significant risk to yourself or others; and then only if the risk can't be eliminated or reduced by a reasonable accommodation.

Light Duty: ADA doesn't require your employer to put you on "light duty" unless the more strenuous parts of the job you can't do since your injury are just marginal tasks. In that case, reasonable accommodation would probably require your employer to have other workers do those marginal tasks. However, most light-duty jobs are entirely different jobs from the one you had before your injury, and ADA doesn't require employers to create jobs to fit an injured worker's disability. See Chapter 5: Discrimination and Related Issues, for details on the **Americans with Disabilities Act.**

SUMMARY

Workers' compensation laws were designed for the dual purpose of helping employees cut through the hassles of collecting benefits for on-the-job injuries and illnesses and protecting employers from potentially being wiped out by huge damage awards. Simple in theory, but not always so simple in practice. Employees often have to fight hammer and tong to get their employers to agree to pay benefits; or have to face hearing after hearing once they are awarded benefits by the workers' compensation commission. Even when their injury or illness does qualify them for benefits, weekly payments are often not enough to maintain their former lifestyle. Employers, on the other hand, are finding the cure to be as devastating as the disease, as workers' compensation insurance premiums skyrocket year after year.

But your challenge is to deal with the system as it is. And since workers' compensation laws are enacted and enforced on a state-by-state basis, the system as it is involves fifty different sets of rules.

So, if you feel that your injury or illness has even the remotest connection with your job, file for workers' compensation benefits and let the chips fall where they may.

As a practical matter, the first thing you'll want to do when you are injured or become ill under circumstances that either definitely are or could possibly be related to your job is contact your state workers' compensation agency. They will inform you as to notice requirements and filing deadlines, as well as hearing and appeal procedures. If your employer does contest your claim, you may find it to your advantage to hire an attorney for advice regarding your specific set of circumstances. See Chapter 11: I'm Getting Screwed; So What Can I Do about It?

You may or may not feel you need an attorney at the initial stages of the process. And one of the main purposes of this book is to help you save money, not to cost you money by suggesting you hire an attorney every time someone blinks. However, a word to the wise: It is inadvisable to make a final settlement of a workers' compensation claim without first consulting an experienced professional in the field.

TABLE 15

STATE WORKERS' COMPENSATION LAWS*

State	Waiting Period	Notice to Employer	Filing a Claim
Alabama	3 days; none if at least 21 days	5 days	2 years
Alaska	3 days; none if more than 28 days	30 days	2 years; 1 year (death)
Arizona	7 days; none if more than 14 days	immediately	1 year
Arkansas	7 days; none if at least 14 days	immediately; 1 business day if emergency treatment required	2 years
California	3 days; none if more than 14 days or hospitalized	30 days	1 year
Colorado	3 days; none if more than 14 days	2 days	2 years
Connecticut	3 days; none if at least 7 days	immediately	1 year (accident); 3 years (occupational disease)
Delaware	3 days; none if at least 7 days or hospitalized	90 days	2 years (accident or death); 5 years (last payment)†
Dist. of Columbia	3 days; none if more than 14 days	30 days	1 year
Florida	7 days; none if more than 14 days	30 days	2 years
Georgia	7 days; none if at least 28 days	30 days	1 year (injury or death); 3 years (last payment)
Hawaii	3 days	as soon as possible	2 years (effects of injury become manifest); 5 years (date of injury)
Indiana	5 days; none if more than 14 days	60 days	1 year

*This chart is a digest of a few aspects of state workers' compensation benefit and claim requirements. Its purpose is merely to provide a comparison of state-to-state variations in workers' compensation laws. It should not be used as a substitute for obtaining the EXACT requirements from the agency in your state that oversees workers' compensation claims.
†"Last payment" refers to the last date on which workers' compensation benefits were paid to the claimant.

TABLE 15 *(Continued)*

State	Waiting Period	Notice to Employer	Filing a Claim
Illinois	3 days; none if more than 14 days	45 days (90 for radiation)	3 years (accident); 3 years (last payment)
Indiana	7 days; none if more than 21 days	30 days (if given later, compensation starts at date of notice)	2 years
Iowa	3 days; none if more than 14 days	90 days	2 years (injury); 3 years (last payment)
Kansas	7 days; none if at least 21 days	10 days	200 days (accident or last payment); 1 year (death)
Kentucky	7 days; none if more than 14 days	as soon as possible	2 years
Louisiana	7 days; none if at least 42 days	30 days	1 year (accident or death); 2 years (if injury doesn't immediately develop)
Maine	3 days; none if more than 14 days	30 days; 3 months (death)	2 years (accident or last payment); 1 year (death)
Maryland	3 days; none if more than 14 days	10 days; 30 days (hernia)	60 days (injury); 18 months (death); excusable within 2 years of accident or disability
Massachusetts	5 days; none if at least 21 days	as soon as possible	4 years
Michigan	7 days; none if at least 14 days (or death)	90 days	2 years
Minnesota	3 days; none if at least 10 days	14 days; excusable up to 180 days with benefits starting date of notice	3 years (employer's report); 6 years (accident); 3 years (aware of disease)
Mississippi	5 days; none if at least 14 days	30 days	2 years
Missouri	3 days; none if more than 14 days	30 days	2 years
Montana	7 days; none if more than 7 days	30 days	1 year

TABLE 15 *(Continued)*

State	Waiting Period	Notice to Employer	Filing a Claim
Nebraska	7 days; none if at least 42 days	as soon as possible	2 years
Nevada	5 days; none if more than 20 days	as soon as possible	90 days (accident); 1 year (death)
New Hampshire	3 days; none if at least 14 days	2 years	3 years
New Jersey	7 days; none if more than 7 days	14 days (excusable to 90)	2 years
New Mexico	7 days; none if more than 28 days or death	15 days (excusable to 60)	1 year
New York	7 days; none if more than 14 days	30 days	2 years
North Carolina	7 days; none if more than 21 days	30 days	2 years; 6 years (death)
North Dakota	5 days; none if more than 5 days	none required	1 year (injury); 2 years (death)
Ohio	7 days; none if more than 14 days	none required	2 years
Oklahoma	7 days; none if more than 21 days	60 days; none if treatment	1 year
Oregon	3 days; none if more than 14 days or hospitalized	30 days	1 year
Pennsylvania	7 days; none if at least 14 days	21 days; excusable to 180 days but no benefits until notice	3 years
Rhode Island	3 days; none if more than 14 days	30 days	3 years
South Carolina	7 days; none if more than 14 days	90 days	2 years
South Dakota	7 days; none if more than 7 days	30 days	2 years
Tennessee	7 days; none if at least 14 days	30 days	1 year
Texas	7 days; none if at least 28 days	30 days	1 year
Utah	3 days; none if more than 14 days	180 days	6 years (accident); 1 year (death)
Vermont	3 days; none if at least 7 days; 7 days (partial disability)	as soon as possible	6 months

TABLE 15 *(Continued)*

State	Waiting Period	Notice to Employer	Filing a Claim
Virginia	7 days; none if more than 21 days	30 days	2 years
Washington	3 days; none if at least 14 days	as soon as possible	1 year
West Virginia	3 days; none if more than 7 days	as soon as possible	2 years (injury or death); 3 years (disease)
Wisconsin	3 days (not counting Sunday, unless employee works Sundays); none if more than 7 days	30 days	2 years
Wyoming	3 days; none if more than 8 days	30 days to employer; 10 days to court clerk	1 year

10

Unemployment Compensation

There is a small (but growing) segment of the population that the government tends to refer to as the "chronically unemployed." They seem to spend as much time in the unemployment lines as they do on the job. They know the system and how it works—and how to work *it*. This chapter is mainly for those of you (unfortunately also growing in number) who are about to deal with the system for the first—and hopefully last—time.

You are laid off or fired. Take heart. Even if you don't have a case for wrongful discharge, it's likely you have a claim for unemployment insurance benefits—a sort of government-imposed severance pay policy. The unemployment compensation system was designed to provide partial income payments to help tide workers over through short periods of unemployment. Employers pay quarterly taxes to finance both state and federal unemployment compensation systems. State systems provide basic benefits to qualified unemployed workers for a limited period of time—in most cases twenty-six weeks. The federal system is geared mainly to finance extended benefits in times of heavy unemployment, something it has already been called on to do several times in the early 1990s.

If you have a basic understanding of the unemployment compensation system and how it works, you will be light-years ahead of most employers. According to the chairman of one state's unemployment compensation commission board of review (the body—or its equivalent in other states—that hears contested cases), "Employers have a very poor understanding of how the system is structured and what it's designed to do." What the system is designed to do is pay benefits to claimants who are unemployed and eligible. While referees who arbitrate employer opposition to claims are supposed to be neutral, there is, in fact, a *presumption of coverage and eligibility.* In that regard, the same chairman said, "Employers shouldn't expect a totally level playing field."

As an example of the remedial nature of the system, in some states as many as 90 percent of claimants who were discharged by their employers are awarded benefits at the first, predetermination, hearing (where most contested cases are decided). Maybe even more telling, fully one-third of claimants who voluntarily quit (normally considered a disqualifying circumstance) are also awarded benefits. That's because, though the claimant may technically have quit voluntarily, he or she may have done so because of a "work-related" cause. In addition, many employers don't bother to contest claims, or don't take the trouble to contest as vigorously as required, or don't have adequate documentation of the circumstances of the discharge. (Remember, in most cases you don't have to prove you're eligible for benefits, it's *your employer* who has to prove you are *ineligible.*)

Of course, the reason that employers contest unemployment compensation claims is because, like workers' compensation, every claim affects their insurance rates. That's another reason why employers are getting more and more choosy about who works for them. High turnover can result in high unemployment insurance rates. However, what employers don't seem to understand is that some unemployment claims simply can't be avoided—or successfully contested. Layoffs, for instance, are generally not contestable, even if there is an economic necessity for them. Neither is a discharge for incompetence. Many employers (and employees) assume if there was a good reason to fire you, you shouldn't be eligible for unemployment benefits. But the way the system looks at it, putting you in a job that you were not qualified to do was at least partly your employer's fault. In any event, incompetence is not the kind of "fault" that makes someone ineligible for benefits. So your employer might have been completely justified in firing you but still might have no realistic prospect of winning his case against your receipt of benefits.

Another break in your favor—at least for purposes of the unemployment compensation process—is that you've got time: time to get your records together and time to appear at the hearing. Many employers are simply unwilling to commit the necessary resources to fight your claim. Though in most states an employer can file a form that outlines the reason(s) he feels you shouldn't be awarded benefits instead of appearing in person at an initial predetermination hearing, he generally puts himself at a great disadvantage by not showing up. ("Showing up" usually means producing the witness who has firsthand knowledge of the circumstances of your discharge: probably your supervisor, foreman, department head, etc.) If your employer just mails in the form, you are free to contradict it . . . and your version is likely to be given greater credence because you are *there* to defend your position.

Finally, even if your employer might otherwise have had the grounds for successfully opposing an award of benefits, he often loses for other reasons. Primary among them are:

☞ A failure to have any work rules at all;
☞ Having work rules but applying them inconsistently; and
☞ Not documenting disciplinary steps previously taken against you.

This discussion is not meant to encourage spurious claims. It is meant to encourage valid claims (okay, and even marginal claims). And it will do that by explaining how this arcane system works, thereby tilting the field even more in your favor. But having the field tilted in your favor isn't enough if you never file a claim. Unbelievably, it is estimated that more than 10 percent of those eligible for unemployment benefits never file a claim. And the main reason? They didn't realize they had one.

In the unemployment compensation system, at least, you start out one step ahead of your employer because you are *presumed* to be eligible for benefits. That's pretty nice: The law *presumes* you've won before you even enter the ring. This chapter will do something more: It will let you take the first swing. Because after you've read it, most of you will know more than your employer (or former employer) does about the system and how it works—and how to work *it*.

ADMINISTRATION

In most states, the unemployment compensation system is administered and enforced by the unemployment compensation division or employment security division of your state department of labor. Generally, the agency is divided into several branches: the unemployment compensation division, the appeals division, and a state job service. The unemployment compensation branch handles claims for unemployment benefits, the appeals division handles unresolved contested matters, and the job service is a sort of public employment agency.

These agencies will have a pamphlet that further details how the unemployment system works in your state. Information about your state unemployment compensation or employment security office or equivalent agency can be obtained by consulting the state listings in the Blue Pages of your telephone directory. It should be listed separately as "Unemployment Compensation Division" or "Employment Security Division" under the state Labor Department heading.

UNEMPLOYMENT COMPENSATION COVERAGE

As was the case with workers' compensation, a real working knowledge of the unemployment compensation system starts with knowing what your employer's obligation is to you, if any, in terms of coverage. So this section will tell you who is covered and who isn't, as well as briefly how your employer's tax is determined.

Remember, exact requirements as to which employers and what kinds of employment must be covered varies from state to state. Be sure to check with your state unemployment compensation commission for exact coverage requirements in your state if you are unsure as to whether or not you are covered by your employer's unemployment insurance.

Employer Coverage

Most employers are liable for both federal and state unemployment taxes. Federal tax liability is under the **Federal Unemployment Tax Act** (FUTA), and state tax liability is under individual state law. There are two basic tests to determine whether an employer is covered by the law and must pay taxes. In most states the tests are pretty much the same for both federal and state law. So if your employer is covered by one he is likely also covered by the other. (In fact, in most states, if an employer is covered by the federal law, he is *automatically* covered by the state law, too.) In general, your employer is liable for unemployment taxes if, during either this calendar year or last, he:

☞ Paid a total of $1,500 or more in wages; *or*
☞ Employed at least one person for any part of a day in at least twenty different weeks. (To qualify, the one person employed doesn't have to have been the same person, and the twenty weeks can be any twenty weeks and not necessarily twenty in a row.)

So, as you can see, most employers have to pay unemployment taxes and most employees are covered.

Special Situations: Besides the basic qualifications for coverage, the unemployment law addresses a few special coverage situations:

☞ Employers of agricultural laborers are liable if they paid at least $20,000 in wages in any quarter of either the current or previous year, *or* employed ten or more people for some part of a day in twenty different weeks;
☞ Employers of household help are liable if they paid $1,000 or more in wages in any quarter of the current or previous year; and
☞ Coverage of nonprofit corporations is deferred to the states, all of which impose coverage on nonprofit employers at least to the same extent as the minimum federal standards of coverage.

So, all in all, approximately 97 percent of our employers contribute to an unemployment compensation insurance fund that will—make that "may"—pay us benefits if we are discharged or laid off from our jobs.

"Employees" under Unemployment Laws

Your employer has to contribute to the unemployment fund on your behalf whether you are a full-time, part-time, or temporary worker, and even if you are a paid corporate officer. Sole proprietors and partners are not considered employees and don't have to contribute unemployment taxes for themselves.

Exceptions—Workers Who Do Not Have to Be Covered

The person who employs you doesn't have to cover you for unemployment (and thus you are not eligible for benefits if you are discharged or laid off) if you are:

☞ An independent contractor. There are a number of tests to determine whether or not you are an independent contractor. Among them are the degree to which you are free to perform your job without direction or control from the person who hired you, your performance of a service that's different from what your "employer's" business does, and whether you carry on an independent trade or business. Remember, it doesn't matter what the person who hired you and pays you calls you. What matters is whether you fit the description of an "employee" or an "independent contractor" under the law. See Chapter 9: Workers' Compensation for details. **Note:** Your employer may want to categorize you as an independent contractor even though you are technically an employee just so he won't have to pay unemployment insurance to cover you—or workers' compensation premiums, or deduct for income taxes and Social Security, etc. But if he categorizes you incorrectly, you may still be eligible for benefits.

☞ Under eighteen and employed to deliver newspapers.

☞ An insurance agent who works solely on commission. (This exception doesn't include industrial life insurance agents and real estate agents.)

☞ A student working for the school or university you attend (or the spouse of a student, *if* your employer informs you that you are not covered); or a student in a qualified work/experience program (a "co-op" student).

☞ A student nurse or intern working at a hospital.

☞ A volunteer worker.

☞ Employed by your son, daughter, or spouse; or are a minor and work for either or both of your parents.

Note: Your employer may cover you voluntarily except in the case of employment by a family member. The theory behind the exception here apparently is that there is enough fraud going on without *inviting* it.

Work in More Than One State

There are complex rules covering employees who work in more than one state. They determine not only where your employer pays his taxes, but, of course, how your weekly benefits are calculated and where you file your claim—since those are state matters. What is generally considered, in order of importance, is where you do most of your work, where your base of operations is, where you receive your orders from, and finally, where you live.

How Much Your Employer Pays

Your employer pays both state and federal unemployment taxes. True to form, each is figured a different way.

State Unemployment Tax: How much state unemployment tax your employer pays for you and every other person in his employ depends on two factors: your state's taxable wage base and your employer's experience rate.

Every state calculates an employer's unemployment tax obligation by taking a certain base amount of each of his employees' pay (taxable wage base), and multiplying it by a percentage based on the amount of turnover the employer has (his experience rate). Though the taxable wage base varies from state to state, it is the same for every employer in a given state. Say, for example, the taxable wage base in State A is $7,000. That means each State A employer pays unemployment taxes on the first $7,000 of each employee's pay. In State B, on the other hand, the taxable wage base is $13,000. Now, if you earn less than $7,000 (State A) or $13,000 (State B), your employer pays taxes for you based on what you actually earned rather than the taxable wage base. On the other hand, if you earn more than the taxable wage base, your employer still pays taxes on only the base amount.

Now, the percentage of that wage base that your employer pays is his experience rate. An employer's experience rate is exactly what it sounds like: It's the amount of experience he's had with the system—how much turnover he has. The more people he fires or lays off who then file for unemployment benefits, the higher his experience rate, and thus his unemployment taxes, will be. Let's take our State B example again. In State B, experience rates vary from a low of 0.4 percent (for employers with little or no turnover) to a high of 5.4 percent (for employers with high turnover). So a State B employer can pay as little as $52 per year per employee (0.4 percent of $13,000)—less if the employee earns less than $13,000; and as much as $702 (5.4 percent of $13,000). That's for each employee, though. So you can see that the expense can really add up for employers who don't keep an eye on their turnover rates. (Another reason for rigorous screening of job applicants.)

In most states a final factor in the equation is an annual surcharge imposed on every employer. The amount of the surcharge depends on the solvency of the state's unemployment fund. In recessionary times the surcharge tends to be higher than in good times when fewer unemployed people are drawing on the fund.

Federal Unemployment Tax: The federal government always seems to get its hand in there somewhere, and unemployment taxes are no exception. In addition to his state tax obligation, your employer pays a flat 6.2 percent of the first $7,000 of every employee's income in federal unemployment taxes. That's $434 a year. However, he gets a credit of up to 5.4 percent for state unemployment taxes he has already paid. (Other credits are available for having a low state unemployment tax rating.) In other words, an employer who pays 5.0 percent state taxes will owe only 1.2 percent federal tax. That eases the burden somewhat, but remember once again: Your employer pays unemployment taxes on every employee in his work force. So contributions to the unemployment fund can be significant, especially for an employer with high turnover rates.

ELIGIBILITY FOR BENEFITS

It's important, for an overall understanding of unemployment compensation, to know the basics of how the system works and how your employer's tax rate is determined. However, from a practical standpoint, the most important things to *you* are: Am I eligible to receive unemployment benefits? What do I have to do to stay eligible? How much will my benefit check be? And how long will I be able to draw benefits? First, let's take a look at the question of eligibility.

Minimum Work and Earnings Requirements

In order to eliminate people who just work occasionally and for only short-term periods, the unemployment compensation system requires that you work a minimum period of time and make a minimum amount of money for basic eligibility. The minimum qualifying work time is called your "base period," and the minimum qualifying earnings is called your "base period wages." Though, again, this time varies from state to state, in most states you have to have worked for at least three months during the past year to qualify to receive benefits. (This can be for one employer or for a number of different employers.) Ultimately, the amount of your weekly benefit check will depend on how much money you earned during your base period. See below.

Ready, Willing, and Able to Work

Assuming you have been employed long enough and had sufficient earnings during that time to qualify for benefits, you must then:

☞ Go down to your nearest unemployment office, file a claim for benefits, and sign up with your state job service, which lists available state civil service job openings. (Usually signing up with the job service is done automatically as part of the claim filing process.) Particularly in times of high unemployment be prepared to wait . . . and wait . . . and wait.
☞ Be physically and mentally capable of working. And,
☞ Remain available for work and make reasonable efforts to get a job.

In most states you will have to trundle on back to the unemployment office every week during your continued eligibility for unemployment and wait . . . and wait . . . and wait to collect your weekly benefit check. **Note:** Contrary to the prevailing view held only by people who have never been forced into a position of having to file an unemployment claim, you will definitely *earn* your unemployment checks.

DISQUALIFICATIONS

Okay, so you've worked long enough and earned sufficient wages to be eligible for unemployment benefits. But hold on. There's more. You may be disqualified for other reasons. In most states you are disqualified from receiving benefits if you:

☞ Quit your job without a sufficient work-related cause.
☞ Are fired for *repeated* willful misconduct.
☞ Are fired for just cause. In the unemployment context, just cause is a *single* act of willful misconduct that seriously endangers the life, safety, or property of your employer, a fellow employee, or the general public. For what constitutes just cause for dismissal, see Chapter 8: Discipline and Discharge.
☞ Are fired for committing a felony in the course of your employment, or for larceny of property or some type of service (like the phone company employee who hooked herself into "free" phone service)—also in the course of your employment. (Most states place a minimum value on the property or service that is stolen for the theft to disqualify you from unemployment benefits.)
☞ Take part in an illegal strike.
☞ Are terminated because you are participating in a labor dispute (other than a lockout).
☞ Are serving a prison sentence. (Most states set a minimum sentence, such as thirty days, for you to be ineligible for benefits.)
☞ Are a teacher between terms or a professional athlete between seasons and have reasonable assurance of returning for the next term or season.
☞ Voluntarily retire.

Now let's analyze some of these reasons for disqualification that need a bit of explaining.

Quitting Without a Sufficient
Work-Related Cause

The reason most people who would otherwise be eligible are disqualified from receiving benefits is because they just up and quit their job. That's because, as was noted earlier, the system is designed to pay benefits to individuals who become unemployed through no (or maybe only a little) fault of their own. However, even if you quit your job, you can still qualify for benefits if you quit for a good reason. Usually that good reason has to be work-related, though many states allow you to collect benefits if you quit to care for a seriously ill member of your immediate family or because you no longer have transportation to work and can't find an alternate means of getting there. (In most states this means loss of public transportation and doesn't include loss of your personal car.)

What, then, is a work-related cause that's a good enough reason for quitting that you remain eligible for unemployment benefits? Generally, it is some change in the job or working conditions caused by your employer that would make a reasonable person quit under the same circumstances. To maintain that you were justified in quitting, you would normally have to show that you apprised your employer of the situation and gave him a chance to rectify it and that his refusal left you with no alternative but to quit. (This is referred to as "constructive discharge." In other words, you may have quit, but only because your employer gave you no other choice.) An example might be if you worked the same shift for a period of time and then your employer changed you to another shift against your wishes. You would probably remain eligible to receive unemployment benefits if you quit, but only if you were unable to work the alternate shift for some good reason, you informed your employer of your situation, and he still demanded that you work the new shift.

On the other hand, leaving your job because your spouse got transferred out of the area is not sufficient cause to quit that would allow you to collect benefits in most states. That is true even though the law affects women in almost 90 percent of the claims filed in that situation. A federal court has determined that because such laws can affect men, too, they are not discriminatory.*

Other good reasons for quitting might be that your employer starts to require you to work overtime or weekends and you are unable to do so for some valid reason; or that he is going to require

*Austin v. Berryman, U.S. Court of Appeals, 4th District, No. 91-1750, 1992.

you to travel frequently and you can't accommodate your schedule to allow you to do so. Remember, a justifiable reason for quitting for purposes of still being able to collect unemployment must usually involve a change in the job caused by your employer. If he refuses *your* request to change something about the job (e.g., move you to a new shift, let you work more overtime, etc.), that is not a reasonable justification for quitting that will allow you to collect unemployment.

Other situations in which employers contested the award of unemployment benefits, maintaining that the employee left voluntarily—but the unemployment agency (or court) awarded the claimant benefits anyway: a claimant who was replaced and "offered" another job that amounted to a demotion; a claimant who told her employer that if anyone was laid off, she hoped it was her, and who was later laid off; a claimant who told her supervisor either to stop threatening to fire her or to do it, which he then did; and a claimant who was told that anyone off the street could do a better job and so quit.

This Could Be the Start of Something Big: In 1999 the State of Connecticut (Public Act 99-123) extended benefits to an employee who "leaves suitable work to protect the individual or a child domiciled with the individual from becoming or remaining the victim of domestic violence." The State of Maine has enacted similar legislation. Whether or not this is the beginning of a trend remains to be seen, but it is certainly a liberal application of the law. Note that in such cases the employer's account is not charged and so it does not affect his rate.

Warning: If you quit and nonetheless file a claim for benefits which your (former) employer contests, you will bear the burden of proving that you quit for a sufficient work-related reason. For that reason—among others—you should never sign anything that indicates you quit or resigned voluntarily; not unless you get something in return. Many a sneaky employer will conduct an "exit interview" in which he might discuss what went wrong with your employment. It is also called a "CYA" interview (as in "cover your ass"), because though he may be genuinely interested in finding out what it was that caused you to quit, so he can try to keep down future turnover, the most important reason for him to hold the meeting is to cover his butt in whatever manner he can. That includes getting you to sign statements that you quit voluntarily, that he didn't do anything wrong, etc.

The "something" he offers you that might make it worth your while to sign such a statement might be severance pay or a glowing job recommendation or both. It depends on how badly he wants your statement. (If he wants it *really* badly, you might think about seeing an attorney to figure out why.)

Warning No. 2: Although things often get heated at the climactic moment, remember that words and actions at the moment of departure can often supply critical evidence of whether you quit or were constructively discharged.

Discharge for "Repeated Willful Misconduct"

Unemployment benefits were intended for employees who are fired or laid off. But you can be fired and *still* be disqualified from receiving benefits, depending on the *reason* you were fired. The most common cause for claimants being disqualified from receiving unemployment compensation benefits is when they are fired for "repeated willful misconduct." Examples of willful misconduct include:

☞ Chronic absence from work (particularly if you give no plausible reason).

☞ Excessive tardiness (again, without a decent reason).

☞ Violation of workplace rules (if the rules are reasonable, you knew about them and your violation was intentional).

☞ Fighting, which can also qualify as "just cause" if it seriously endangers someone's life or safety. (Unlike willful misconduct, just cause requires only one incident. See p. 303.)

☞ Profanity, depending on the type of workplace. (For example, being fired for profanity on a construction site probably wouldn't disqualify you from receiving unemployment benefits.)

☞ Sleeping on the job.

What is "repeated willful misconduct" that is sufficient to disqualify a claimant? "Repeated," of course, means you must have done it more than once. "Willful," implies that you did it intentionally—or at least recklessly enough that it was for all intents and purposes intentional. (Generally, negligence is not enough to cause disqualification unless it was so frequent as to amount to willful misconduct. Neither is carelessness, lack of ability, incompetence, inefficiency, or good-faith errors in judgment.)

In some states, in order for you to be disqualified on the basis of repeated willful misconduct, you must commit a "final act" of willful misconduct that precipitates the discharge. It doesn't have to be the *same* conduct as previous episodes, but it has to be the kind of willful misconduct that, if repeated, would be sufficient cause for disqualification. For example, if you are constantly warned about being late and you are then fired for being absent without reporting it or asleep on the job, you may be disqualified. However, if you are constantly warned about your lateness and then you are fired because of a decrease in your production (not a cause for disqualification), you wouldn't be disqualified from receiving benefits. In other words, the "final act" generally has to be one that, if repeated, would disqualify you from benefits and thus is part of a pattern of similar acts of willful misconduct. Minnesota, appropriately enough, calls this the "last-straw doctrine."

Finally, the behavior that constitutes this "repeated willful misconduct" must occur in the course of your employment. Generally, the fact that what you did had an *impact* on your job isn't going to do it. Take, for example, this situation: You are a truck driver who is discharged because you lost your license for a traffic offense while driving off the job. In the majority of states you would still be entitled to unemployment benefits even though you were fired because the loss of your license meant you couldn't perform the job anymore.

How about the woman who was fired for defrauding the phone company she worked for but was not disqualified from receiving unemployment benefits because her ripoffs didn't have a close enough connection to her job as a phone directory editor?* Or the man who was fired for leaving his post during an LSD trip but was not disqualified from receiving benefits?†

You see why you should never just assume you won't qualify for benefits?

But there are even more factors that work in your favor. Your employer may have fired you for repeated willful misconduct, but if you reported your absences and they were for good cause (e.g., you have a doctor's excuse), or your tardiness was condoned (i.e., you weren't warned of the consequences), or if you were provoked into fighting or weren't told that profanity was unacceptable (or broke

*London v. Board of Review, Pennsylvania Commonwealth Court, 3636 CD 1986, 1987.
†Hammermill Paper Co. v. LIRC and Hoffman, 142 Wis. 2d 942, 1987.

another work rule that was unreasonable or that you had no knowledge of), that may mitigate your behavior to the extent that you will still be entitled to receive unemployment benefits anyway. (Not only won't you be disqualified from receiving unemployment benefits, but you may have a potential lawsuit if your employer's reason for firing you was a pretext for some other reason—for example, your age, sex, race, etc.—and he has no documentation to support his claims.) Other mitigating factors can include illness or emotional strain of some kind during the time the behavior took place.

Unlike when you quit your job, when the burden of proof is on you, when you are fired your employer has to prove that there is sufficient reason to disqualify you from receiving unemployment benefits. And the standard of proof is a pretty tough one. So even when you have doubts about your eligibility for benefits, go ahead and file a claim. The worst thing that can happen is your claim will be denied. But you have *no* chance of winning if you don't play the game.

Alcoholism or Drug Addiction: Most states treat alcohol or drug addiction as an illness. Therefore, if your employer fires you for repeatedly using drugs or alcohol on the job, you may still be eligible for unemployment benefits. You may have to document your addiction with medical evidence supplied by the physician who is treating you. But you may not. When a claimant's family and his employer both told him he had a drinking problem and his employer subsequently fired him for drinking on the job, the man was not disqualified from receiving unemployment benefits.*

"Just Cause"

Most state laws take the position that an employer shouldn't have to tolerate behavior at work that endangers his property or the health or safety of others, nor should he have to pay unemployment benefits for someone who was fired for such a "just cause." So you may be disqualified from receiving unemployment benefits if your actions are flagrant enough to give your employer just cause to fire you even if you did it only once. Examples might be fighting on the job (if the fight is violent enough or actually causes injury) or intentionally destroying your employer's property. One claimant was disqualified from receiving unemployment benefits after she was fired

*_Tompkins v. Unemployment Insurance Commission,_ Maine Supreme Judicial Court, 3721 Dkt Aro-84-258, 1985.

for choking a nurse hired by her employer when the nurse told her she'd have to get more information from her doctor to receive medical benefits.* The court noted that the assault was violent enough to have left marks on the nurse's throat. (Maybe if she'd just punched her in the stomach . . .)

Committing a Felony or Larceny

It should be obvious that there is a distinction between conduct for which you can be arrested and convicted, and conduct for which you can be fired and disqualified from receiving unemployment benefits. An employer needs much less proof to fire you than the law needs to prosecute you. But to disqualify you from receiving unemployment benefits, he must be able to offer some proof that you engaged in the felonious or larcenous conduct, and in many states he also has to show that the conduct occurred in the course of your employment. For example, the Connecticut Unemployment Compensation Board of Review determined that a school bus driver who was fired after being charged for dealing drugs was nonetheless eligible for unemployment benefits because his illegal activities took place while he was off-duty.† However, a morals offense that affects the performance of your duties or jeopardizes the interests of your employer might be a different story. For example, a school janitor was disqualified from receiving unemployment benefits when his employer learned he had been convicted of a sexual offense that involved a nine-year-old girl, even though the offense had occurred before the school had employed him.‡ As one court put it, "The fundamental issue is whether the result of the misconduct adversely affects the employee's ability to perform his duties to an appreciable degree."§

As for larceny, in most cases to disqualify you from receiving benefits, you must have stolen something not just from anybody, but from your *employer.* Also, most states place a minimum value on the goods or services you must have "appropriated" in order to justify denial of unemployment benefits. And remember: Your employer

*Tatum v. Labor and Industrial Relations Commission, Wisconsin Circuit Court, 739-914, 1988.
†Edmonds v. Town of Sherman, Case No. 447086-BR, 1987.
‡Ritz v. Kenowa Hills Schools and the Michigan Employment Security Commission, Michigan Circuit Court, 87-54793-AE, 1987.
§Dean v. Department of Labor and Pennington County Auditor's Office, 367 NW2d 779, 1985.

may be justified in firing you for pilfering a can of orange juice to wash down your lunch, as one court ruled, and yet have no chance to get the unemployment compensation commission to deny your claim for benefits.

Labor Disputes

Another activity that will generally disqualify you from receiving unemployment benefits is participation in a labor dispute—other than a lockout. By most definitions, you are participating in a labor dispute if you are part of a concerted action by employees to affect your wages, hours, or working conditions. That usually includes refusing to cross a picket line, unless your refusal is based on a legitimate fear of getting your head busted.

Lockouts: A lockout is when your employer simply closes his doors because of a contract dispute, or won't allow you to work until the dispute is settled, or says you can work only if you agree to work for less money, more hours, or under worse conditions than you were working in before the dispute began. If you are out of work because of a lockout, you are eligible to receive unemployment benefits. **Note:** It is not a lockout when your employer is willing to keep operating while negotiating in good faith.

Serving Prison Time

Many states disqualify you from unemployment benefits if you lost your job because you had to start serving time in prison. Still, some require the sentence to be a minimum length (like thirty days) for disqualification. (Note that, unlike a larceny or felony, for prison time to be reason for disqualification for unemployment benefits, the conviction doesn't have to be for a crime committed on the job.)

Voluntary Retirement

Unemployment compensation laws also disqualify you from eligibility to receive benefits if you voluntarily retire from your job. However, if you are forced to retire because of your age, you may still be eligible to receive benefits. (You may also have an age discrimination case. See Chapter 5: Discrimination and Related Issues.) You may be eligible for benefits even if you agree to mandatory retirement—rather than go out kicking and screaming—but probably not if you receive the "golden handshake" or some other financial inducement that acts kind of like severance pay.

REMAINING ELIGIBLE

All right, you're eligible for benefits. Maybe your eligibility was indisputable; or maybe your employer had a notion to contest but figured it wasn't worth the time and effort (and thus money) to contest it; or maybe he contested it and you won anyway. Whatever—you are eligible for unemployment benefits. The next trick is to *stay* eligible.

How do you stay eligible to receive unemployment benefits for the full time you have them coming to you? You have to remain ready, willing, and able to work. Basically, that means you have to do two things:

☞ Actively seek employment. And,
☞ Accept a suitable job when one is offered to you.

Actively Seeking Employment

Many unemployment compensation commissions require you to prove that you are actively seeking employment in order to continue receiving benefits. For example, you might have to supply them with a specified number of employment contacts in order to receive your weekly benefit check. The length of time you are disqualified for failure to actively seek employment varies greatly. Some states disqualify you just for the week you didn't look for work. Others disqualify you until you actually find another job and earn a specified minimum amount of money to requalify. States also vary greatly in the kind of verification required to show you are looking for a job. (**Note:** Unfair as it may seem, many states don't require as much proof—or any proof at all—of a job search by a white-collar worker, the assumption being that a person who is receiving only a small fraction of his or her usual pay while on unemployment *has to be actively looking for another job*.)

Suitable Work

Most state laws don't require you to accept just any old job—at least not right off. You are required to accept only an offer of "suitable" employment. What is suitable depends on such things as health and safety concerns, physical fitness demands, experience, education, skill and training requirements, salary, and length of unemployment. (The longer you have been unemployed, the more you may have to lower your job expectations. Forget unemployment compensation benefits—at some point you may have to do this to survive.) In any event, a job may be considered to be unsuitable if:

☞ The opening is the result of a strike or lockout;

☞ The wages, hours, or working conditions are significantly worse than average for the area;

☞ You would have to join a union or quit your present union to take the job;

☞ You would have to punch in or out at odd hours (like after midnight or before five or six in the morning);

☞ You would have no reasonable means of transportation to and from the job; or

☞ In order to get the job you would have to agree not to quit if your former employer called you back from a layoff.

Other Reasons for Loss of Eligibility

You can also lose your eligibility for other reasons. The length of time you will be disqualified varies depending on state regulations, but you will probably lose your eligibility for unemployment benefits for at least some period of time if:

☞ You receive just about any kind of pay during a given week, (e.g., severance pay, pay instead of a two-week notice, federal unemployment benefits, workers' compensation benefits, etc.). Loss of benefits is usually just for the week for which you receive pay.

☞ You leave your job to become a full-time student. In this case you are likely to lose benefits indefinitely. Or,

☞ You make false statements in order to receive benefits. Again, loss of benefits will probably be indefinite.

FILING A CLAIM

As you might imagine, the procedure for filing a claim for unemployment benefits is entirely a function of where you file the claim. You should check with your state or regional unemployment office for the exact requirements in your state. However, the following is fairly representative of the basic procedure in most jurisdictions.

The Unemployment Notice ("Pink Slip")

Most states require your employer to give you an unemployment notice—commonly called a pink slip—when you are terminated for any reason; and the reason must be listed. If the reason listed is "lack of work," you will usually qualify for benefits automatically. If your employer doesn't give you a pink slip, he may jeopardize his chances to rebut your claim for benefits. But that's his problem.

Filing and Initial Determinations

You should file your claim for benefits as soon as you lose your job, even though in most states there is a one-week waiting period before eligibility. (See below.) Generally, an agency representative will review your claim along with any evidence submitted by you and your former employer, if he contests it, and will make an initial determination either awarding or denying benefits. Both parties will be notified of the representative's decision and either of you may contest it within a certain number of days specified in the notice. If no appeal is filed within the time limit, the representative's decision becomes final. (If you are awarded benefits in the initial screening process and your former employer appeals the award, you will be paid weekly benefits pending the outcome of the appeal.)

Appeals

Appeals are generally held before an aptly named referee or similar agency representative. If the appealing party does not appear in person, the appeal may well be dismissed. In any case, whether it is you or your employer who has filed the appeal, you should show up in person and on time with all available documentation and witnesses to support your case. Appeal hearings are fairly formal, though formal courtroom rules of evidence and procedure are not followed. However, the referee has the power to subpoena witnesses when necessary. (It is necessary only when a witness won't appear voluntarily.)

A referee may either confirm, modify, or reverse the initial award or denial of benefits. Both parties are given written notice of the decision and their right to appeal to a review panel within a specified number of days. The review panel usually sees only the record of the original appeal and does not consider additional evidence.

Further appeals may be made through the courts.

Note: If there is any chance at all that your former employer will contest your claim for unemployment benefits, you should supply as much documentation as possible of your eligibility in your original complaint because the initial determination is given great weight in any appeal. Nationwide, more than 90 percent of claimants are awarded benefits in the initial stage of the claims process. So the dice are weighted heavily in your favor. Make the most of it.

Retaliation for Filing or Assisting in an Unemployment Claim

No employer may discriminate against you for having previously filed a claim for unemployment benefits. Neither may an employer discriminate against you or fire you for helping someone else with his or her claim for benefits by testifying at an unemployment compensation hearing or supplying other evidence of someone's eligibility for benefits. If an employer does discriminate against you or fire you for having made previous unemployment claims or helping someone else with a claim, you can sue him for reinstatement, back wages and benefits, court costs, and your attorney's fees.

AMOUNT AND DURATION OF BENEFITS

The amount of benefits you are eligible for and how long you are eligible to receive them is strictly a matter for state regulation. Therefore, the following discussion of benefits is necessarily a summary only. To find out exactly how weekly benefits are calculated where you live, contact your state unemployment office.

Weekly Benefit Amount

There are almost as many ways of calculating weekly benefits as there are states. However, every state bases the amount of your weekly check on both *your* average weekly earnings and the average weekly wage of *all of the employees in the state*. Most states use a rather complex formula that starts with a fraction of your average wages—often calculated by taking your average weekly earnings in your highest-paid three-month period over the past year. In most states that fraction is roughly half to two-thirds of what you usually earn. All states then impose a maximum based on the average weekly wage for all workers in the state who are covered by unemployment insurance. The maximums vary greatly, too, but most are somewhere between half and two-thirds of the average weekly wage for workers in the state. Many states add anywhere from $5.00 to $25.00 per dependent for up to four or five dependents. (States set minimum weekly benefit amounts, too.)

Waiting Period

Most states (and the District of Columbia) impose a one-week waiting period before you are eligible to receive unemployment benefits. (New York's waiting period is imposed by paying only three days of benefits for the first two weeks of unemployment.) Several states pay you retroactively for the initial one-week waiting period if you collect unemployment for a minimum number of weeks, as follows: Missouri—nine weeks; New Jersey—three; Texas—three; and Minnesota—four.

The following states have no waiting period, so you are eligible for unemployment benefits immediately: Alabama, Connecticut, Delaware, Iowa, Kentucky, Maryland, Michigan, Nevada, New Hampshire, and Wisconsin.

Duration of Benefits

In every state but Massachusetts you can collect weekly unemployment benefits for up to twenty-six weeks in a twelve-month period. (If you live in Massachusetts, you can collect for up to thirty weeks.) So if you are unemployed off and on during any twelve-month period, you can collect benefits for only up to twenty-six weeks during that time. (The twelve-month period starts with your initial week of unemployment.) However, you may not be eligible for the maximum number of weeks of benefits if you haven't been fully employed during the previous year or so—and thus haven't earned sufficient wages to qualify for full benefits.

A few states will extend benefits for a number of weeks in periods of high unemployment. Also, the federal government will occasionally extend benefits beyond the state's maximum payment period when unemployment is particularly severe, as has happened a couple of times in recent years.

Requalification for Benefits

Once your unemployment benefits run out, you can requalify only by getting a job and working long enough to earn the minimum amount of wages necessary—which is normally the same amount as was required to qualify in the first place. Usually you can't requalify until at least a year has passed since you received your first unemployment check the last time you qualified for benefits. (For example, let's say you got your first unemployment check on March 17, 2000, and received benefits for twenty-six weeks. You can't requalify for benefits again until March 17, 2001, and then only if you have been employed and earned the minimum amount of wages to qualify. Got it?)

Part-time Jobs and "Moonlighting"

You may also qualify for unemployment benefits if you lose your part-time job *if* you have earned enough money in the preceding year or so to qualify. Since the maximum amount of weekly benefits is based on your earnings, though, obviously your check is going to be pretty small if it's based on part-time work.

If you work more than one job and lose one of them in a manner that qualifies you for unemployment benefits, or if you take a part-time job after you become unemployed, you may still be eligible for unemployment benefits, but your benefits will be offset by whatever earnings you have from that other job.

Taxability of Benefits

Unlike workers' compensation benefits, unemployment compensation benefits are taxable. However, since the total amount of unemployment benefits you are eligible to receive is going to be below the annual amount of earnings necessary for you to be subject to income taxes, a lot of states won't withhold taxes from your weekly checks. However, be aware that the state will report your unemployment "earnings" to the Internal Revenue Service and your state income tax department. So you might want to have your next employer (during the same tax year) withhold a little bit more in taxes from each paycheck so you won't have a big personal tax deficit to make up come April 15.

SUMMARY

The most important lesson of this chapter on unemployment compensation is this: *When in doubt file a claim for benefits.*

Remember, the unemployment compensation system is designed to pay benefits to qualified unemployed individuals. So when you lose your job, the law assumes you are eligible to receive benefits. What that means is that if your (former) employer wants to contest your claim for benefits, he has the rather onerous burden of proving that you are ineligible for some reason (e.g., you quit without sufficient cause, you were fired for repeated willful misconduct, etc.). What that also means is that to have even the proverbial snowball's chance of keeping you from collecting benefits, your (former) employer will have to carry through by gathering his evidence and appearing in person at one or more hearings (or sending your supervisor, foreman, or other person who has firsthand knowledge of the circumstances of your discharge). For many an employer it simply isn't worth the trouble.

Why wouldn't it be worth the trouble? Because, though it is true that the more turnover your employer has, the higher his unemployment insurance rates will be . . . the fact is, he does have insurance. He's not going to be paying your entire weekly benefit check out of his pocket, but only a small fraction of it in the form of insurance premiums—which he's been paying every year he's been in business anyway. Take an employer who, for example, pays 2.0 percent of the first $15,000 of each employee's annual wages in unemployment insurance. That's about $300 per employee per year. That employer may not be willing to have a management employee who earns $800 a week spend days and days of his or her time gathering evidence and attending hearings for what may well turn out to be a lost cause anyway.

And forget any idea you might have had that collecting unemployment benefits is demeaning or somehow beneath you. Facing that line for the first time may not be the most uplifting experience you'll ever have; and you're not going to enjoy many fancy dinners out on your weekly checks. But your employer fired you or laid you off, and remember: *He's paying* to fund the unemployment compensation system. And, besides, that's what it's there for—to give you a little helping hand for six months while you try to get back on your feet. So take advantage of it.

Well, this chapter should give you a pretty good overview of how the unemployment compensation system works in your state. But keep in mind that, as a matter of state regulation, eligibility requirements, the amount and duration of benefits, and claim filing procedures vary in subtle but important ways from state to state. Therefore, you should always consult your state unemployment compensation agency for the exact requirements where you live.

11

I'm Getting Screwed; So What Can I Do about It?

inally we get to the part that tells you where to pick up your $10 million damage award: Will that be cash or check? No, on second thought, make it a $5 million settlement. Five million is plenty and then we don't have to go through all that messy—and lengthy—court stuff.

Well, if you think it's going to be that easy, you haven't been paying attention. If you are having—or had—a problem at work and you plan on doing something about it, plan on the process being a royal pain in the ass . . . whatever you decide to do.

Going directly to your employer (or other person responsible for your predicament)? Then plan on not getting a whole lot of sympathy. If his action—or inaction—was simply an oversight, or produced an unintended or unanticipated result, he may be understanding and do something to rectify the situation—if it's not already too late. But chances are whatever he did or didn't do, he either did it for what he figured was a valid reason or he did it out of a total lack of consideration for your rights. Either way, the fact that you are bringing his management skills into question is not likely to further endear you to him. In fact, you will first have to give serious thought to your travel plans: Is your complaint likely to be your passport to a better relationship with your employer? Or is it more likely to be the final painful stamp on your exit visa? Think about it.

GOVERNMENT AGENCIES

How about a government agency? Now, make no mistake about it, federal (and state) agencies do some wonderful things. And they work cheap. (That can be important, especially if you have only a few months' lost wages on the line.) But always remember those prophetic words: "You get what you pay for." Take the Equal Employment Opportunity Commission, for example. There's this toll-free telephone number the agency proudly displays on much of its literature: 1-800-USA-EEOC. Call free from anywhere for any information on equal employment opportunity in the workplace. In English, Spanish, Creole . . . you name it. Well, go ahead and try it if you've got the time and the patience. Better yet, let's just save you the aggravation. Depending on where you're calling from, one of three things will happen. Here's a brief synopsis of each:

Option One: "Your call cannot be completed as dialed. Please check the number and dial again."

Option Two (*You've already called the number approximately one thousand times between 8:30 A.M. and 4:30 P.M. and gotten a busy signal every time. You pick up the phone and give it one more try. It is 4:31.*)

"This telephone is answered between the hours of 8:30 A.M. and 4:30 P.M. Eastern Standard Time. Please call back during those hours. This is a recording."

Option Three: "You have reached the Equal Employment Opportunity Commission.

"If you want to hear this menu in Spanish, press 1 . . . now.

"If you want to hear this menu in Creole, press 2 . . . now."

(Of course, if you speak Spanish or Creole, you probably don't understand the first instruction, but that's another story.)

Once you get the right language, you'll hear something like this:

"If you want EEOC informational pamphlets sent to you in the mail, press 1 . . . now.

"If you want information on how to order Form EEO-1, press 2 . . . now.

"If you want information on how to order Form EEO-100, press 3 . . . now.

"If you are calling from a rotary phone, stay on the line and the first available representative will take your call."

Of course, what they don't tell you is that the first available representative hasn't been born yet!

State agencies are only slightly better. Call your state department of labor and if you can persevere long enough through the busy signals (a telephone redial function is a definite plus when dealing with any government agency), you will eventually get a human being. Not necessarily a *nice* one. (One thing we know for sure: They are not called civil servants for their telephone manner.)

Then there's your aunt Millie's brother's nephew, the lawyer. He did your cousin's divorce real cheap. Of course, it took three years—and they were only married six months. But you don't know any other lawyers.

Here's a bit of advice: Select a lawyer the same way you would select a doctor. Because, believe me, if the one you choose screws up, you will bleed; and you will bleed for a long time.

Your last option—which is actually your first option—is to do nothing at all. The reason it's your first option is because right from the beginning you'll have to decide whether or not this is the kind of situation in which inaction will produce better results than action. Are you, in fact, being subjected to the kind of treatment that no employee should have to endure? Is it because of your age, race, sex, or handicap? Or is this something more on the order of what my father used to refer to as "one of the minor indignities of everyday life"? Was it racial discrimination or just a one-time, embarrassing slip of the tongue? Is it sexual harassment or just an inept attempt at flattery? Will a firm, unequivocal statement from you nip things in the bud? Or will you be more apt to exacerbate the situation by calling attention to it? Would it be more likely to "go away" if you just ignore it?

These are the kinds of questions you should ask yourself right from the start. Trying to defuse a situation is almost always preferable to going straight for the head-on collision. But, then, there are times when the course of events is set, you did your best to swerve out of harm's way, but a head-on collision is unavoidable.

PREPARING YOUR CASE

You've been putting up with sexual harassment at work ever since you got this job. Your supervisor is always rubbing up against you, even tries to fondle your breast whenever he gets even half a chance. And the mouth on him! Always making some lewd remark.

You know sexual harassment is against the law but, really, what are you supposed to do? Go to your boss? He's just as bad—grabs you every time you get within arm's length of him.

So you've done your best to avoid both of them, which isn't easy, particularly your supervisor. After all, you have to *report* to your supervisor regularly and he has to approve your work. You'd quit but you really like what you do. And anyway, where would you get another job in this economy?

Then your supervisor tells you in no uncertain terms that unless you "go out" with him, which you know means only one thing, he will see to it that you get fired. That's the last straw. You finally get up your nerve and go to your boss. You tell him about your supervisor's objectionable conduct. You don't mention your boss's own less-than-professional behavior, thinking that to do so would not exactly be "political." Anyway, you figure he'll probably get the hint. He gets the hint, all right. He tells you that the only reason he hired you in the first place instead of hiring a man for the job was because you have a "cute little butt," and if you aren't willing to shake it a little for their amusement, then you'll be out on it in a heartbeat.

Humiliated and embarrassed, you quit on the spot. Now, home alone with your final paycheck, you are getting angrier and angrier. They can't do this to you. By God, you're going to do something about it. But what? You're going to file a complaint with the EEOC, that's what. Or go to a lawyer and sue the bastards. Or maybe you'll do both. But, of course, your boss and your supervisor will plead ignorance. You were just a lousy worker, they'll say. And no way were you forced to quit. You quit on your own. Which is a pack of lies, but what else would they do? Admit it? (The moral of the story here is that before you quit in a huff, you might want to think about seeing a lawyer for some advice on "constructive discharge." Also, see Chapter 10: Unemployment Compensation, for a detailed discussion of "constructive discharge.")

Well, to make any case at all, you've got to have some evidence.

Where did it all start? Let's see. When you filled out the application form, didn't it ask if you were married? But they've changed the application form since then. Where could you get a copy of the old one? And wasn't it Dave Lincoln, a coworker, who was there when your boss pinched you? Or was it Harry Swenson? And was it when your boss pinched you or when your supervisor propositioned you?

Or maybe it was Lincoln who was a witness in April and Swenson in July. Well, what difference does it make? Lincoln quit last month and moved, and Swenson was promoted and is now the boss's right-hand man . . . If only . . . If only . . .

If only you had thought about this situation when the first signs appeared—or even before. Because the most effective way to deal with a situation is to anticipate it. *An integral part of every job, from how you heard about it to when you leave it, should include keeping a file on it.* You know the employer is keeping a file on *you.* Why? Because, when push comes to shove—and he's probably been in business long enough to know it will (maybe not with you but with someone)—he's going to be ready. His file on you is going to be his ammunition in any claim or lawsuit you file against him.

Well, fair is fair. He's keeping a file on you? So keep one on him.

Remember, stripped to its bare bones, the employment relationship is essentially an adversarial one. At its worst it's a street fight. Are you going to go into a street fight unarmed? Well, that's what the woman in our example is going to be doing. Because she has nothing concrete. All she has are vague memories of when the unwelcome behavior might have first started, what she did to discourage it, what was said or done by whom and on what dates, and who might have witnessed it. And you can bet your lawsuit her employer has a file three inches deep documenting any negative performance reviews, and maybe including her supervisor's reports that the woman is a complainer or is insubordinate and his own similar comments. Remember the old labor lawyers' adage about agency complaints and employee lawsuits against employers: *The one with the biggest stack of papers wins!*

Well, the adage may not be true 100 percent of the time, but it is a good starting point. The only way you stand a chance when you take any action against your employer (or former employer) is if you walk in with a detailed file documenting everything that has happened to you from your very first contact with this company to your very last.

ABC Company File

Start by purchasing a manila accordion file folder for a couple of bucks—you know, one of those kind of reddish-brown things that starts out flat and expands as you fill it and has a bunch of separate compartments in it. Label it with the name of your new employer and the date of first contact and you're on your way. If you are really with it, you will start with the classified ad in the paper, or the name of the person who told you about the opening, or a note detailing the way you first learned about the job. You will also file copies of the cover letter and résumé you sent in response to the ad or by way of indicating your interest in the position. (You can keep your responses to a number of companies in the separate compartments, since you will probably be applying to more than one job at a time.) If everything is on the up-and-up through the application process and you don't get a particular job because the company hired somebody else who was more qualified, okay. Transfer the papers you've gathered on that company to another file (maybe even the "circular" file) and continue with those who send you an application form and invite you in for an interview. And start a new section with the next new company you apply for a job with. Keep it up until you get a job. Then you can devote the whole folder to your new employer. If you are conscientious about this process, you'll need it. (And if you have any real hope of maintaining a balance of power with your employer, you will *have* to be conscientious about it.) So, by your first day on your new job, you already have a working file.

Note: Leave your file at home. As you saw in Chapter 6: Right to Privacy/Access to Records, you may not always be able to count on being totally secure in your possessions at work. It could be embarrassing if your employer or supervisor stumbles on your file in your desk or locker. Besides, the best way to maintain the integrity of the file—as well as to avoid the worry over its discovery—is simply to keep it in a safe but readily accessible place at home. (You want it to be readily accessible because you're going to be adding to it regularly.)

Employer-Issued Documents

Starting with the job ad in the classified section that you answered, you want to keep every scrap of paper issued by your employer. That means:

That Job Application Form: Make a copy of the completed form and stick it in your folder.

Aptitude Tests and Any Other Preemployment Examinations: If you can get a copy. This may not be easy. The employer probably keeps them confidential so future job applicants won't get hold of them. You may just have to make a mental note of any potentially biased or objectionable questions, commit your mental note to writing at the first available opportunity, and add your notes to your file when you get home. (Remember, an employer can't ask you to take a medical or physical examination until *after* he has offered you a job—although he can make the job offer conditional on the results of the medical or physical exam.)

The Company's Employee Handbook: More and more companies are issuing new employees a company handbook that outlines everything from work rules to pension plans. See Chapter 2: The Employment Relationship. Most employers are smart enough (or have been burned enough) to have had a lawyer check out the handbook before they print it. That means the handbook's opening paragraph is usually a disclaimer that basically says the company isn't really responsible for any promises it may make in it. But that doesn't always wash in court. Especially if the handbook language is poorly drafted. (Your employer may not have read the section of this chapter on how to find the right lawyer.) A promise is a promise is the position many courts take. So, that handbook could amount to an employment contract of sorts. And even if it doesn't create an implied (and binding) employment contract between you and your employer, if it contains company rules and grievance procedures in the event of disciplinary action taken against any employee, then your employer had better have applied those rules to you in the same way he applied them to others before you, and adhered to his grievance procedures as outlined in that handbook. Get a copy. Photocopy it for your file in case your company, as many do, requires you to turn it in when you leave their employ and you think you might not be able to abscond with it easily. Read it. And know what it says. That's the only way you're going to know exactly what is going to be expected of you *and* what you can fairly expect from your employer.

Performance Appraisals: Most companies give regular (annual or semiannual) performance reviews. Many put them in writing. You've seen them. They tell you how you're doing and areas where you might need improvement. Don't just flip to the part that tells you if you got a raise. Check out the other stuff. Is it unbiased? Is it fair? Is it true? If not, maybe you should consider asking your employer to insert an explanatory comment in your personnel file. In many states you have that right. (See Chapter 6: Right to Privacy/Access to Records.) Keep those appraisal forms. Particularly if they are consistently good, your employer may have a difficult time proving later that he fired you for poor job performance.

Memos and Other Written Statements from Superiors: Anything your employer (or his agents) puts in writing should become part of your file. That includes everything from "formal" memos to comments penciled on the back of a napkin. If He (or one of His disciples) wrote it, it's worth saving.

Written Warnings or Notices of Disciplinary Action: You may want to cross-reference these with work rules listed in your employee handbook. You may also want to note your own version of the story and clip it to the company's version before inserting it in your folder. Do it while it's fresh in your mind.

The Termination Notice: Well, this is what all the preliminary stuff was building up to, of course. Most states require employers to give you a pink slip that indicates the reason you were discharged, for purposes of eligibility for unemployment compensation benefits. But it could be useful for other purposes if it doesn't jibe with previous documentation (for example, good performance reviews).

Other: There may be other employer-generated documents not listed here. Your employer may, for example, give the occasional written "pep talk" or issue a new company policy on something or other. You know, when he panicked along with every other employer in the aftermath of the Clarence Thomas confirmation hearings, back in the early 1990s, he may have issued a hastily drafted sexual harassment policy. Whatever. If it's in writing, you keep it.

Personal Notes

Besides written documents from your employer or his agents, your file should include any personal comments or notations you feel are appropriate under the circumstances. For example, explaining your version of what led to disciplinary action being taken against you: Was it fair? Did they treat other violators the same way? Or recording verbatim a racist or sexist remark or a comment that indicated age or handicap bias. Or documenting complaints you made to your supervisor or directly to your employer about unwelcome words or actions directed toward you, and your supervisor's or employer's response to your complaint, if any.

The thing about personal comments and notes is you have to record them *immediately,* before you forget what was said or done, who witnessed the exchange, and what you were feeling at the time.

Don't wait until you get home after work. As soon as you are alone and have a chance to write them down, do it. Go to the rest room if you have to. Remember to bring a pencil. Paper will help, too, or your comments are destined to be bathroom graffiti like so many other anti-employer sentiments.

Such notes should include date, time of day, place, those present, and details of what happened. The more detail, the more likely your version is to be believed. Who's going to believe a string of vague comments like, "I think it was the first week I started work," and, "Harry Swenson might have been there, too," and, "He said something like, if you don't wear tight clothes, I'm going to fire you."

On the other hand, if you can say, "It started during my first week on the job. It was May 15, 1994, when my supervisor, Leonard Harrison, said to me—and I quote, 'Look, honey, the only reason the boss hired you in the first place is because you've got a nice body. You don't cooperate and you're gone.' He winked at me really suggestively when he said 'cooperate.' It was at lunchtime in the cafeteria—12:45, to be exact—so a couple of people overheard him. There was . . ."

Got the idea? Details. Accuracy. Times, places, dates, names. The more the better.

Key Situations

There are some key job situations that you should really prepare for. Don't just walk blithely into these situations with the idea that you'll let the chips fall where they may. Think about what is about to happen—and what shouldn't happen—and clear your mental scratch pad for action.

The Job Interview: Making effective mental notes requires that you really pay attention during the interview (which is always a good idea, anyway). Of course, you will be nervous and you may be thinking, "How can I be expected to be worrying about objectionable questions or prejudicial conduct by an interviewer when all I'm trying to do is get this job?" Well, the answer is, You should have enough foresight to realize that you should be interviewing them, too. Do you want to work with people like these? In a place like this? Besides, remembering the interviewers' names (and dropping them from time to time in your responses to questions) will not only reinforce their names in your mind, it will impress the hell out of them; and paying strict attention to the questions they ask is the only way you're going to answer them intelligently anyway. So it's not really something extra you have to think about at all.

Performance Reviews: As previously mentioned, any written performance appraisals should be filed away in your folder. But pay attention to what is said in the meeting, too—things that may *not* be written down. For example, maybe your supervisor said something like, "As you can see from my memo, you are doing a fine job. Keep up the good work and you'll always have a job here." Or, "You still do a good job. It's too bad you're getting a little long in the tooth because I think the company is going to start looking to hire some young blood soon." Write it down immediately when you get out of that meeting. And, as they say in the vendetta business: "Take names."

Exit Interviews: As noted earlier, the "exit interview" is a relatively new concept, no doubt hatched by labor lawyers who represent management. In the "interview," your boss will probably give you your termination notice (the "pink slip"), then ask you what you think went wrong, what in your opinion management could have done or should do in the future to enjoy a more symbiotic relationship with employees such as yourself, and what changes in the work environment or working conditions could have made your experience a better, more productive one—none of which he cared enough to ask you while you were employed.

Get real. What he really wants to do is cover his butt. After he softens you up with kind words and understanding and mostly feigned interest in your opinions—and depending on how afraid he is of some kind of legal or agency backlash from your termination—he will invariably whip out the waivers for you to sign. You know, like I am voluntarily quitting or retiring, or I was fired for just cause or some other phrase of absolution. He may at the same time hold in his other hand your final paycheck, maybe another check for two weeks' severance pay in lieu of two weeks' notice, and a statement of your COBRA rights to continuation of your group health insurance as a sort of implied inducement.

To hell with him. *Don't sign anything before you show it to a lawyer.* Take your final paycheck and your continuation of insurance notice, both of which he legally has to give you within a specified period of time anyway. See Chapter 3: Wages and Hours and Chapter 4: Fringe Benefits. You also might try to "palm" the waivers he tried to get you to sign, if you can manage it without too much of a fuss.

Then there's the matter of keeping your ears open. What was said that is not in writing? Probably a lot more than was written. Because your employer isn't stupid. Even if, like most, he doesn't know the intricacies of labor law as well as you now do, he knows enough not to put really incriminating things in writing (and to tell his supervisors not to, either). So listen keenly to what is said. And again, take names.

Note: Obviously, proving someone said something is a lot easier when you've got it in writing. That's why it is so important to have details: dates, times, names, witnesses, and precisely what was said. You may still not be able to prove it in court if it comes down to your employer's (or supervisor's) word against yours, but at least this way you have a chance. Hearing his own statement repeated to him word for word, with details of time, place, and witnesses, might induce your employer to part with a little green by way of a settlement, or severance pay in exchange for forgoing a lawsuit. (For this kind of negotiation the services of a skilled attorney are highly recommended for most people. It will cost money, of course, but part of something is better than all of nothing.)

Now you have some ammunition (if you need it)—a complete life history of your relationship with your employer, from conception to last rites. Fortunately, in the world of work, there is an afterlife. So get on with it. Start a new file.

Now, as for the work life you just left: If it was a satisfying, productive one, then just let it go. Even if it was unsatisfying and unproductive but you were treated fairly, let it go. Learn from it, but let it go. On the other hand, if you were screwed, your file is your chance to get even.

FILING CHARGES WITH A GOVERNMENT AGENCY; PRIVATE LAWSUITS

As you already know, most of the alphabet is out there, in the form of federal agencies, to help you with many of your complaints against your employer. That includes the EEOC, DOL, OSHA, and INS. There are also state equivalents of the first three, as well as state unemployment compensation and workers' compensation commissions. Of course, which agency you go to depends a lot on what kind of case you think you might have and a little on protocol.

The Equal Employment Opportunity Commission (EEOC)

The EEOC is the agency you will go to if you have a discrimination complaint against your employer who denied you a job. You have to file an EEOC discrimination complaint before you can bring legal action on your own. (The same is not true of **Equal Pay Act** violations, which involve payment of wages issues. An EEOC complaint may still be appropriate, though, if your **Equal Pay Act** claim also involves other sex discrimination issues.)

Filing a Charge: You should file a discrimination charge either by mail (certified, return receipt requested) or in person. Charges must be in writing, signed and sworn to before a person authorized to take oaths (e.g., a notary), and give enough information for the EEOC to determine the nature of the charges (and for the employer to answer them). The statement should include the names of the parties and details of the act complained of—which you have in your file.

   Note: You don't have to identify yourself in the charges you file, and the EEOC will keep your identity confidential insofar as that is possible. Realistically, however, in most situations your employer is probably going to be able to figure out it was you who filed the complaint just by the nature of the charges. (If you've already been fired, of course, you'll probably *want* your former employer to know you're bringing charges. However, things could be a bit stickier at work if you're bringing charges while you still work for him.)

Time Limit for Filing Charges: Charges must be filed with the EEOC within 180 days of the act you are complaining about. Be careful here. It is reasonable to consider all of the possible ramifications of filing charges before doing so, but don't take too much time. You can be shut out if you do. It's important to know that the time period is considered to begin running as soon as you are notified of the action that will be taken against you. For example, if your employer gives you a two-week notice of your termination (which you feel is based on discriminatory reasons), the 180 days starts to run from the date of your receipt of the two-week notice, *not* from the date your termination actually becomes effective.

   If you live in a place where there is a state or local agency that handles discrimination complaints, the EEOC will defer any action on your complaint for a period of 60 days to give the state or local agency a chance to act on it. The EEOC will take over only if the state agency does not take action on the complaint within that 60-day period. **Note:** The 180-day time limit can be extended to as much as 300 days in this case. Check with the EEOC to be sure of your time limit for filing. Call your state or local agency, too. However, when in doubt, use the 180-day limit as your deadline.

Withdrawing Your Charges: You are the only person who can withdraw your complaint once you have filed it. Your lawyer can't do it without your signature. And you can't even do it without the approval of the EEOC.

Notice to the Employer: The EEOC has to notify the employer within ten days that you have filed a charge.

EEOC Powers: The EEOC has the authority to investigate your complaint, including inspecting employer records, interviewing other employees, summoning witnesses, requiring the production of relevant documents, and bringing legal action.

Settlement Efforts: If, after its initial investigation, the EEOC feels that the employer is guilty of age, race, sex, ethnic, religious, or handicap discrimination, it is legally bound to try to reach a reasonable settlement of the case between you and the employer before it does anything else. The agency has 180 days to try to negotiate a settlement between the parties. In making settlement attempts, the agency conducts hearings at which you and the employer may produce documents, witnesses, and other evidence to support your positions. You have the right to be represented by an attorney at all stages of the EEOC proceedings.

EEOC Streamlining Procedures: In 1995 the EEOC instituted a number of drastic (for a government agency) changes in the way it handles complaints:

The first change was to institute a system of "charge prioritization," by which the agency categorizes and handles charges according to the likelihood on first look that some kind of discrimination occurred.

The second change was to allow employers to offer "appropriate" (rather than "full") relief in the early stages of an investigation and "substantial" relief when the agency first discovers evidence of discrimination.

The third change was to give the EEOC's general counsel more latitude to delegate matters to EEOC regional attorneys and to decrease the amount of paperwork required.

And finally, starting in 1996 the agency instituted a voluntary alternative dispute resolution program that offers confidential hearings before a disinterested third party.

The streamlining was a necessary response to the realization that there was, according to the chairman of the EEOC, "more work than people to do it." The goal is to speed up the handling and resolution of cases and decrease the current case backlog. Whether or not it works, only time will tell. But at least it is a step in the right direction.

Lawsuits: If the EEOC can't get you and your employer to reach a settlement within the allotted 180 days, the agency will either bring legal action on your behalf, if it has reasonable cause to believe you have a valid discrimination case, or will issue you a right-to-sue notice. (In the case of federal government employees, the lawsuit is actually brought under the name of the Attorney General.)

Once you receive the right-to-sue notice, you have 90 days to file a lawsuit on your own. **Exceptions:** You can bring an age discrimination or **Equal Pay Act** lawsuit without receiving a right-to-sue notice from the EEOC.

Class Actions: In a situation where a number of people in a protected group (e.g., women, minorities, older workers, handicapped workers, etc.) were similarly discriminated against, those people may join in bringing a "class action" against the employer. In that case, one or more members of the protected group may bring the action on behalf of the entire affected class of employees (or job applicants). Or the EEOC may sue for the group.

Note: Remember, in order to have the right to bring a lawsuit for violation of **Title VII of the Civil Rights Act of 1964,** the **Age Discrimination in Employment Act,** or the **Americans with Disabilities Act,** you must first file charges with the EEOC. (That is not true, however, for violations of the **Equal Pay Act,** or the **Civil Rights Acts** sections guaranteeing equal protection of the law and the right to enter an employment contract.) You have every right to bring a lawsuit even if the EEOC decides it doesn't have enough evidence to proceed with its investigation.

Equal Pay Act Suits: As previously mentioned, unlike other discrimination cases, you don't have to file charges with the EEOC prior to bringing a lawsuit alleging an **Equal Pay Act** violation by your employer. You do have to bring your lawsuit within two years of the latest violation, though (three years if the violation is "willful").

Age Discrimination Suits: Prior to passage of the **Civil Rights Act of 1991,** you had to file an EEOC charge of age discrimination at least sixty days before bringing your own lawsuit; and there was also a two-year time limit within which you had to bring your lawsuit (three years for "willful" violations). Now the enforcement procedure is the same as for other discrimination claims under **Title VII**: You have to bring your lawsuit within ninety days after you receive your right-to-sue notice from the EEOC.

Bringing a Lawsuit: After the EEOC declines to bring suit (if they do), you may bring your own legal action. You probably will have hired a lawyer by this time, and if you hire the right one, he or she will certainly know which court a discrimination lawsuit should be brought in. But in the interest of being thorough—and because you *can* legally represent yourself if you choose to—I'll tell you anyway. Generally, there is joint state and federal jurisdiction over discrimination cases. State suits are brought in the judicial district (usually county) where you allege the discriminatory act your employer engaged in took place. Federal suits are brought in the federal district where the act you complain of took place. Recall that:

☛ **Title VII** (federal) complaints can be brought only against employers with fifteen or more employees;
☛ **Americans with Disabilities Act** complaints can be brought only against employers of fifteen or more employees; and
☛ **Age Discrimination in Employment Act** complaints can be brought only against employers of twenty or more employees.

Remember too that many states have similar laws that protect employees who work for smaller employers. See **Table 11**. If your employer is smaller than required under one of the above federal laws, you may be limited to filing your lawsuit under state law.

Note: If you bring a discrimination suit under either **Title VII of**

the **Civil Rights Act** or the **Americans with Disabilities Act** and can't afford to hire an attorney yourself, the court may appoint one to represent you. (But don't count on it.)

Burden of Proof: As the one filing the discrimination charge, you start out having to offer enough evidence to prove that you have a case against the employer (the burden of proof). That is, you have to show that you are in a protected group, are qualified for the job, and were adversely affected by the employer's action or practice. Once you have accomplished that, the burden shifts to the employer to show that the action or practice was not discriminatory or that there was a legitimate business reason for it. If he is able to do that, the burden shifts back to you to prove that the reasons the employer gave to justify the practice are simply a pretext or a subterfuge to mask the real, discriminatory reason for it. (Or you have to offer direct evidence that clearly discriminatory remarks were made.)

Jury Trials: Under the **Civil Rights Act of 1991,** the option of a jury trial is available to anyone seeking damages for employment discrimination of any kind. (Prior to that, you could opt for a jury trial only if you alleged age, racial, or ethnic discrimination. Those alleging sex, religious, or handicap discrimination could not.) The addition of the jury option is a great advantage to plaintiffs, since juries are known to be more sympathetic toward employees than they are toward employers—while judges, of course, are trained to be dispassionate toward both.

Court Awards

The purpose of laws against employment discrimination is, first, to prevent employers from discriminating against job applicants and employees in the first place. Next, to stop employers from engaging in ongoing discriminatory conduct or practices. And finally, insofar as possible, to make the victim "whole," financially.

Preliminary Injunctions: Where it looks as though you are likely to be able to prove that an employer engages in the discriminatory act you have complained of and irreparable harm may be done if it is allowed to continue, a court may issue a preliminary injunction demanding that the employer stop the practice pending the outcome of the case. (**Note:** This is something a court will rarely do.)

Permanent Injunctions: Of course, if you do win the case, the court can issue an injunction demanding that the employer stop the practice permanently.

Hiring: If you were qualified for a job you applied for but were turned down for a discriminatory reason, the employer can be required to hire you.

Reinstatement: If you were wrongfully discharged, a court can order that you be reinstated to your old job. A court can also order other "appropriate equitable relief." For example, if you were wrongfully denied a job or a promotion, the employer can be ordered to hire or promote you.

Back Pay: Generally, when a court orders you to be reinstated to your former job, it will award you back pay. It can also order back pay even if you are not reinstated. In either case, the amount of back pay is based on what you would have earned had you been allowed to continue in your job without interruption. In calculating back-pay awards, courts take into account not only your regular pay, but overtime, shift differentials, bonuses, vacation pay, holiday pay, loss of use of a company car, and any other "add-ons" you may have normally earned. They will also add interest from the time you were terminated to the time of the court award. (Back-pay awards for **Equal Pay Act** violations are limited to two years; three years if the violation was "willful." There could be further limitations under other laws, as well.) **Note:** You are usually required to try to "mitigate" the possible damages involved. That means, you have to try to cut down on your potential losses (by trying to get another job in the interim). Your back-pay award would then be offset by the amount of your interim earnings. However, you normally aren't required to take any old job—for instance, one you would be overqualified and/or underpaid for—just to mitigate the potential damages in the case. And you certainly wouldn't have to relocate to take even a comparable job.

Front Pay: Front pay is a rather interesting concept that works like this: If a court orders you to be reinstated, but your employer has already hired someone else to fill your old job or promoted someone else to the job you should have gotten—which would normally be the case—the court will order you to be put in an alternate job, but be paid what you would have been earning if you were still in your old job or had received your promotion. You would then have to be returned to your old job or promoted, as the case may be, as soon as the position became available. (The idea is to give you your due without compounding the inequity by ousting another innocent person from his or her job.)

Also, if the court feels it would be counterproductive to reinstate you (say, because of hostility arising out of the lawsuit), it might award you front pay for a certain period of time instead. It might be for only a couple of years, but the court's reasoning is that some pay in place of reinstatement will serve to make you "whole." (That is, put you in as good financial shape as you would have been if you hadn't been wrongfully fired in the first place.)

Benefits: When you are reinstated, you will be reinstated with full benefits restored. (Or you will be awarded the dollar value of the benefits you lost.)

Seniority: With reinstatement also comes a return to the seniority you would have had if you had continued on the job without interruption.

Damages: Potential damage awards are of two different types, "compensatory" and "punitive," and there's no mystery behind the adjectives: They are designed for exactly what they sound like they are designed for. Compensatory damages are awarded to compensate the victim of discrimination for damages suffered, including emotional distress caused by the employer's conduct. Under the **Civil Rights Act of 1991,** compensatory damages are available to anyone suing for intentional discrimination. (Prior to the enactment of that law, compensatory damages were available only to some victims of racial and ethnic discrimination, *not* to victims of sex, religious, or handicap discrimination. And even now, a victim of handicap discrimination won't be awarded such damages if the employer attempted a "reasonable accommodation" of his or her handicap.)

Punitive damages, on the other hand, are awarded to punish the employer for incidents of *intentional* discrimination. That means the employer must have "engaged in a discriminatory practice . . . with malice or with reckless indifference" to the victim's rights. Just as with compensatory damages, since the enactment of the **Civil Rights Act of 1991,** punitive damages are available to all victims of discrimination (whereas before that, punitive damages were available only to victims of racial or ethnic discrimination).

Limits on compensatory and punitive damage awards: The **Civil Rights Act of 1991** stirred up somewhat of a controversy by limiting the amount of damages that can be awarded to victims of intentional sex, religious, and handicap discrimination. Damage awards are limited by the size of the work force of the victim's employer, as follows:

☞ 15 to 100 employees: $50,000;
☞ 101 to 200 employees: $100,000;
☞ 201 to 500 employees: $200,000; and
☞ More than 500 employees: $300,000.

The theory behind these limits is apparently to prevent small employers from being forced out of business by huge damage awards. However, pointing out the inequity of limiting damages for victims of sex, religious, and handicap discrimination, while allowing victims of racial and ethnic discrimination to "shoot the moon," at least two U.S. senators immediately introduced legislation that would either eliminate or drastically modify these limits. (Since these damage limits were part of the overall compromise that allowed the **Civil Rights Act of 1991** to be passed at all, few in Congress see them being eliminated or modified in the near future.)

Attorney's Fees and Costs: A court can award you reasonable attorney's fees if you win your case. They may also award court costs, which include filing fees that can really add up. As far as what are "reasonable" attorney's fees, that is open to the interpretation of the court in which you brought your suit. By the way, you may have watched enough episodes of *L.A. Law, Law and Order,* etc., to know that attorneys routinely "judge-shop" (file a case in a particular court to get a judge who is known to be sympathetic to plaintiffs with their client's type of case). But did you know that some attorneys even "fee-shop" (pick a jurisdiction based on the court's reputation for awarding generous attorney's fees)? Again, for purely informational purposes, federal courts tend to be the favorites of "fee shoppers." (Remember, state and federal courts have concurrent jurisdiction in most discrimination cases. That means discrimination cases can be brought in either court.)

However, awards of attorney's fees are usually based on the number of hours your attorney would necessarily have spent on the case multiplied by a low estimate of the hourly rates for attorneys of comparable skill and experience in the community. (The fees of expert witnesses can also be awarded as part of your attorney's fee.)

Note: Your employer cannot recover his attorney's fees against you if he wins (unless your case is determined to have been completely frivolous). The rationale here is that to allow attorney's fees to a victorious employer would discourage employees from filing legitimate discrimination claims.

The Department of Labor

The department of labor is the agency to go to for wage and hour complaints. Usually if you call the U.S. Department of Labor, they will refer you to your state department of labor.

Filing a Claim for Unpaid (or Underpaid) Wages: If your employer owes you wages—for example, for unpaid overtime or for any other work performed by you but not paid for by him—you can file a "claim for unpaid wages" form with the department of labor. However, some state labor departments, overworked and understaffed as they are, take the "up-front" approach of replying that they are swamped and you might be better served hiring a private attorney to help you pursue your case than waiting around for them to get to your case. (And they might well be right.)

Time Limit for Filing: There is a two-year statute of limitations on filing a claim for wages under the **Fair Labor Standards Act.** That means you have two years from the time you knew or should have known of the violation within which to bring your action. Most courts have held that a new violation occurs every time you are illegally underpaid. So essentially you may be able to get away with filing years after you became aware of the violation and still win your lawsuit if you file your action within two years of the *last time* your employer either failed to give you a paycheck or underpaid you. However, it is best to file as soon as possible because you are also limited in the amount of back pay you can be awarded in a FLSA claim. See below. (**Note:** The time limit for filing is extended to three years if your employer's violation was "willful," which means he did it either on purpose or with reckless disregard for the law.)

Back Pay: Back-pay awards are limited to two years' worth of unpaid (or underpaid) wages. (Three in the case of willful violations.)

So, again, you can see the importance of filing your claim for unpaid or underpaid wages as soon as you realize what's going on.

Damages: Damages are also available when you make a claim for unpaid or underpaid wages. You can recover damages in an amount equal to your unpaid or underpaid wages. Like your recovery of the unpaid wages themselves, the damage award will also be limited to two or three years' back pay, depending on whether or not your employer's violation is ruled to have been willful. So, in effect, you can actually recover twice the amount of wages you are owed over a two- or three-year period (i.e., the wages themselves and damages in an equal amount).

Attorney's Fees and Costs: As with discrimination suits, reasonable attorney's fees and costs of suit are recoverable, too, if you win your case.

The Occupational Safety and Health Administration (OSHA)

Workplace safety standards are overseen by the federal Occupational Safety and Health Administration. About half the states have their own federally approved versions of OSHA. These states include: Alaska, Arizona, California, Connecticut (covers government employees only), Hawaii, Indiana, Iowa, Kentucky, Maryland, Michigan, Minnesota, Nevada, New Mexico, New York (covers government employees only), North Carolina, Oregon, South Carolina, Tennessee, Utah, Vermont, Virginia, Washington, and Wyoming.

The following is a brief synopsis of the inspection and complaint procedure. See Chapter 7: Health and Safety, for details.

Inspections: OSHA inspectors have the right to inspect an employer's workplace to ensure compliance with government-imposed safety and health standards. Inspections can be conducted without prior notice and can be undertaken on the agency's own initiative or in response to a complaint by an employee or a member of the general public. The usual inspection includes a check of the employer's records, a review of his compliance with right-to-know laws, interviews with employees, inspections of personal protective gear for employees, and an examination of fire prevention and evacuation procedures.

Complaints: You have the right to file a complaint against your employer for having unsafe working conditions. Your identity may be able to be kept confidential when filing such a complaint. In any event, the law protects you from being disciplined or discharged for reporting such a violation. And, in fact, as a practical matter, filing a legitimate complaint against your employer for a safety violation could even make your job a bit more secure, since any subsequent action taken against you would necessarily come under close scrutiny as a potential violation of these anti-retaliation or "whistleblower-type" laws.

Refusal to Work: You have the right to refuse to work if you have a reasonable belief that your employer's safety violation creates a substantial risk of death, disease, or serious injury. However, you must first notify your employer of the situation and give him a chance to correct it. It must also be enough of an emergency that normal enforcement procedures wouldn't take care of the problem quickly enough.

The Immigration and Naturalization Service (INS)

Under the **Immigration Reform and Control Act** (IRCA), it is illegal for an employer to recruit, hire, or continue to employ illegal immigrants who are ineligible to work in the United States. IRCA is administered and enforced by the INS. (For details see Chapter 1: The Hiring Process.)

I-9 Forms: Every employer is supposed to have every new employee fill out the appropriate section of the I-9, "Employment Verification Form." As a practical matter, many don't bother if they "know" you are a U.S. citizen—which could be a dangerous supposition, but that's their problem.

Filing a Complaint: You can file a complaint with the INS if you are required to supply more or different documents than other newly hired employees to verify your employment eligibility, perhaps because you "look" or "sound" foreign. You can also file a complaint if you know an employer hired an illegal alien instead of you (or instead of anyone, for that matter). A complaint has to be signed and in writing, giving dates, times, and places, identifying the employer, and giving details of the act complained of. The INS will then investigate if it feels your complaint has any validity. If the INS determines there has been a violation, it will bring a complaint by issuing a citation or a notice of its intention to level a fine. The employer can contest by answering the complaint within thirty days.

Private Lawsuit: If the INS notifies you that they will not be bringing a complaint against the employer, you will be given ninety days to bring your own discrimination lawsuit, if you choose to. The services of an attorney might be advisable at this point.

The State Workers' Compensation (or Industrial Relations) Commission

Your state workers' compensation commission—it may be called the industrial relations commission or something else in your state—administers and enforces workers' compensation laws. The following is a brief outline of the claims process. For details, see Chapter 9: Workers' Compensation.

Notice to Your Employer: The first thing you have to do when you file a claim for workers' compensation benefits is notify your employer that you intend to do so. Different states have different time limits on this requirement, but that is really irrelevant. You should do it immediately. Generally, it is sufficient to state your claim in enough detail to give your employer a chance to contest it if he wishes. Notices should be in writing and sent certified mail, return receipt requested. (Your workers' compensation commission will inform you of this obligation, as well.)

Filing a Claim: To be eligible for workers' compensation benefits, you must have an injury or illness that "arises out of and in the course of your employment" and causes you to be unable to work. So if you are hurt or become ill as a result of your job—even if the two might be only remotely connected—you should file a claim with the workers' compensation commission. Initially that simply involves filling out a claim form listing the details of the accident or illness and its relationship to your job. If your employer doesn't oppose your claim, you will normally begin receiving benefit checks within a couple of weeks.

If you break your leg falling off a scaffold at work, or are injured under similarly obvious work-connected circumstances, then there may be no doubt as to your eligibility for benefits and it is probably safe to file for benefits on your own. However, if the severity of your injury or its connection with work are not quite so obvious, and there is a chance your employer will contest the initial award of benefits, you might consider consulting an attorney from the outset. Someone who has "played the game" before and knows the ground rules may have the experience to phrase the details of an "iffy" claim and field hearing questions in terms that will give you the best chance to receive benefits and to win a contested claim. This option is not presented as a way to "beat the system." But, hell, you're *in* the system as a result of your injury or illness, so you might as well do your best to *win*. You know your employer will. If he thinks there is even the remotest chance of denying you benefits, you can bet your bottom dollar (and that may be exactly what you end up doing) he will oppose your claim as vigorously as he knows how.

Medical Expenses: Your employer is required (through his insurance company) to pay all of your medical bills resulting from an on-the-job injury or illness.

Medical Examinations: The workers' compensation commission can require you to see a doctor chosen by your employer or by the commission itself to confirm or refute the diagnosis given by your own doctor. Refusal to submit to such an examination is cause for suspension of benefits.

Informal Hearing: If your employer opposes your claim, you will each be given an opportunity to state your case, including presenting witnesses, medical documentation, and other evidence at an initial informal hearing. Failure to attend may be cause for discontinuing your benefits. You do not need to have an attorney present at this conference. If you have the evidence to back up your position, flying solo might get the job done. But keep this in mind: If your employer has come this far, he is obviously taking this contested business seriously.

Formal Hearing: If a settlement isn't reached at the informal hearing, the commission will call a formal hearing at which you and your employer are both "invited" to bring out the heavy artillery. It is inadvisable to go it alone at this stage and beyond.

Appeals: Either party has the right to pursue an appeal all the way through the workers' compensation commission and into the courts. But the chances of reversal on appeal are fairly remote, since the decision on appeal is generally based on the existing record. That is, no new evidence is allowed to be presented. For this reason, it is important to give it your best shot at the informal and formal hearings.

Benefits: You generally remain eligible for total benefits as long as you are incapacitated to the point that you are totally unable to work. Once you have recuperated enough to return to some type of work, you will be eligible for partial benefits, based on the difference between what you earned before the injury or illness and what you are able to earn after it. You will no longer be eligible for benefits once you are able to return to work. (You may, however, be eligible for a "permanency" award if you suffered some permanent impairment, such as scarring, partial or total loss of a limb, etc.)

Reviews: Once you are receiving benefits, you will be required to update your condition periodically so the workers' compensation commission can determine your continued eligibility for benefits. Additional hearings may be held if your employer contends you are, in fact, able to return to work.

The State Unemployment Compensation (or Employment Security) Commission

A division of your state's labor department, called the unemployment compensation commission, or the employment security department, administers and enforces the unemployment compensation system in your state. The following is a brief outline of the filing procedure. For details, see Chapter 10: Unemployment Compensation.

Filing a Claim: When you are laid off or fired for just about any reason, you may be eligible to receive unemployment benefits. The first thing you have to do is get on down to your local unemployment office and fill out a claim form stating the circumstances of your discharge. Generally, unless you quit voluntarily (without just cause) or were fired for repeated willful misconduct or for committing felonious or larcenous conduct, you will be eligible for benefits.

There are other requirements, such as having earned a minimum amount of wages over the past year, but if you even think you *might* qualify, file a claim.

Predetermination Hearing: If your employer contests your claim, the commission will hold an initial, predetermination hearing at which you will each be allowed to present evidence supporting your position. If you have solid evidence of your eligibility, you may not need an attorney, but you have the right to have one present. (**Note:** Because the presumption is in your favor in unemployment cases—that is, you will be awarded benefits unless your employer shows convincing evidence that you aren't entitled to them—there is probably less need for an attorney in the initial stages of the process than, say, in the case of a workers' compensation claim. However, this may not be the case if, in fact, your claim is based on shaky grounds.)

Hearing: If your case isn't resolved in the predetermination hearing, the commission will hold a formal hearing to resolve the case. (You may nonetheless be awarded benefits pending the outcome of this hearing.) As is the case with workers' compensation claims, the further along you go in the process, the more likely it will be that you will benefit by the services of an attorney.

Appeals: An award or denial of benefits may be appealed by either party through the unemployment compensation commission and on into the courts. As with workers' compensation cases, though, the outcome of the appeal is generally based on the existing record, so the chances of being awarded benefits at this point are pretty negligible.

ALTERNATIVE DISPUTE RESOLUTION

Alternative dispute resolution (ADR) has been in use for a long time, particularly in union collective-bargaining contracts. But it is being used more and more by nonunion employers as a potentially cheaper, quicker means of addressing employer-employee disputes. (The EEOC has expanded its use of ADR, too, and will soon be using it in various forms in many of its enforcement procedures.) Versions of ADR include fact finding by a neutral third party, negotiation, mediation, arbitration, open door policies that encourage employees to go to management with complaints, and even peer review. However, success of any ADR method depends on fairness, which can be ensured only by giving employees a voice in choosing the arbitrator, as well as access to relevant documents, the right to independent representation, the ability to recover the same awards (e.g., reinstatement, back pay, and punitive damages) as in a court of law, and judicial review of final rulings. If your employer uses ADR, do some research to determine if it is fair. Your first question should be: How has it worked for employees in the past? In any event, you may have to go through the process if your employer offers it, even if it seems to be an exercise in futility, simply to "exhaust your other remedies" prior to bringing a lawsuit.

HIRING LEGAL COUNSEL

Attorney at law, lawyer, counselor, "mouthpiece" . . . you all know one. In fact, you probably know more than one. Could be you've had to hire one before—to handle your divorce or to draft your will or to administer your aunt Mabel's estate. Maybe there's even one in the family. The best advice? Don't hire him (or her). Not unless he is an expert in that very specialized field of labor and employment law. And here's a bulletin: If he did your divorce or drafted your will or took care of your aunt Mabel's estate, he isn't a labor and employment law specialist. So how *do* you find the right lawyer?

Step 1: Do I Need a Lawyer?

The first thing to decide is whether or not you even need a lawyer. Not all situations merit one. Just because you got fired or laid off or passed over for that promotion doesn't necessarily mean you have a legal case . . . even if you're a woman or a member of a minority or over forty or handicapped—though, frankly, that helps. You have to assess your circumstances realistically before embarking on what may prove to be a long, arduous journey. Is it going to be worth the trouble—and the investment of time, energy, and money? That is something that, in the end, only you can decide. That decision will be based on a number of factors.

First, what do you have to gain? Is it money you're after? Your old job back? That promotion? Or is it principle? Or just old-fashioned revenge? And what do you have to lose—besides time, money, and wear and tear on your psyche?

Some situations may be fairly cut and dried. For example, you make a claim for unemployment or workers' compensation benefits which is uncontested. However, what happens to your workers' compensation benefit checks when your ability to work is called into question down the line? Can you handle the hearing process on your own against your employer and/or his insurance representative? If you have clear-cut medical evidence, perhaps. But if it was that clear-cut, your employer probably wouldn't be claiming you are capable of returning to work, would he?

On the other hand, if you are black and were fired for a first-time violation of a company rule that white employees regularly violate with impunity, the answer may be just as cut and dried.

But most will be in that gray area.

You've read this book. If you have been paying attention, you know what your rights are. But remember: Your case is a snowflake. It's different from every other snowflake that came before it and every one that will come after it. It may be big and wet like some; or light and fluffy like others; but it has its own unique characteristics that will determine whether it will melt or whether it will "stick." Sometimes the general weather conditions will give you a pretty good idea. But most times you just have to wait until it falls.

The irony here is that it may take the advice of an attorney to determine if you need one or not.

Step 2: How Do I Find the Right Attorney?

Finding the right attorney is almost like finding the right spouse. It's *exactly* like finding the right doctor. Only it's much more difficult. It's more difficult because for a doctor to hold him- or herself out as a specialist, he or she *has to be a specialist.* That means, for example, if her advertisement in the Yellow Pages says, "Dr. Mary Finch, Cardiovascular Surgery," she has to be a cardiovascular surgeon. She has to have done her residency in cardiovascular surgery, been board certified in cardiovascular surgery, and regularly retrained and recertified in new techniques in cardiovascular surgery. And you can bet it's all she does. She doesn't do noses. She does hearts.

Well, with lawyers, it's much different. If his advertisement in the Yellow Pages says, "Attorney Robert Johnson, Labor and Employment Law," he may have taken several labor and employment law courses in law school (if his law school had that many); he may have taken a two-year post-law-school course specializing in labor and employment law and earned his L.L.D. degree (Doctor of Laws); he may then have "interned" at a law firm that practices labor and employment law; and he may regularly pursue Continuing Legal Education (CLE) courses. On the other hand, he may never have taken a labor law course. He may have gravitated to the field because he handled a case or two and enjoyed it. Or he may have started out with a law firm that, because of the economy, found it had a lot of potential labor and employment clients and needed to start a labor and employment "department," and he was low man on the totem pole. Because believe it or not, most lawyers find their "specialty," if they even profess to have one, not by the process of *education,* but by the process of *elimination.* This is not to malign lawyers. That's just the way it is.

The fact of the matter is this: Any lawyer can practice any "specialty" he or she wants to practice without having demonstrated any proficiency in the field whatsoever—to the American Bar Association, to the state bar association, or to anyone else. Which certainly makes the selection process more difficult—and probably even more important—than that of finding a doctor.

So do some research. Suggestions, if you're starting from ground zero:

☞ If you know someone who sued his or her employer successfully, ask them for the name and telephone number of their attorney.

☞ Call your divorce lawyer or the lawyer who did your will or your aunt Mabel's estate (in light of the above discussion, I realize this is probably all the same person) and ask him or her to refer you to a labor and employment specialist. If he or she handled all of your other matters, he or she might suggest that he or she could handle this, as well. Proceed cautiously. If you were pleased with his or her work on the others, ask how many other cases like yours he or she has handled. What was the outcome? If you still prefer a specialist, consider a polite prepared statement such as "I appreciate all the fine work you've done for me and my family in the past and I certainly will call on you again in the future, but I really feel I need a labor and employment specialist in this case." If you can, get several names ranked in the order your attorney would call them if he or she had your problem.

☞ Call your state bar association. Ask for the president or other executive in the association and ask him or her for a referral or two. Also, most bar associations offer membership by specialty. Ask for the name and telephone number of the head of the labor and employment section. If the person is in your area, you might call for an appointment. (You would pay a regular fee for this.) If not, ask for a couple of referrals in your area.

☞ Ask the agency you are dealing with for a referral: EEOC, workers' compensation, unemployment compensation, etc. They may not want to give you *one,* but they may be more than willing to give you several. That way they won't feel like they are playing "favorites." It doesn't hurt to try.

☞ Check out a publication called *Martindale-Hubbell.* You can find it in most libraries. If your local library doesn't have it, the law school library does. Most law offices do, too. (Again, you could always call your divorce lawyer's secretary and ask if you could stop by and check it out.) *Martindale-Hubbell* contains a virtual résumé listing of most attorneys in the country by geographic area, including education and training, major achievements, notable clients, etc. It's probably not as good as a "live" referral, but it's definitely better than the Yellow Pages.

☞ Probably the best of all (but maybe the hardest to come by) is a book called *Best Attorneys in America.* Most attorneys don't even have a copy. But if you live in or near a large city, you may be able to find it at the state or university law library. (It's a good idea to call ahead to see if they have it.) State law libraries are open to the public. University law libraries usually are, too, though often on a limited basis. For example, you may be given a day pass. In any event, if you can get hold of a copy of *Best Attorneys,* you will find that it lists outstanding attorneys by specialty and locality as selected by their *peers.* For instance, "Labor and Employment" attorneys were picked for the book by asking numerous labor and employment lawyers in a locale which attorneys *they* would refer a case to if they couldn't handle it themselves. So what you end up with is a kind of all-star team; and the most reliable kind, at that—one picked by the other players.

Look at your list. Do any names appear more than once? Hey, that's a good place to start.

Step 3: When Should I See an Attorney?

The answer is sooner rather than later. The lament of most labor lawyers is "If only the client had come to see me sooner." The time to see a lawyer is when you first begin to read the handwriting on the wall, not after the story has already been written and has an ending. That way you have a chance to write the ending yourself—or at least have an effect on it. What you've learned in these pages should enable you to read that handwriting on the wall a little more clearly—and sooner—than before. And remember, just because you go to an attorney for advice doesn't necessarily mean you have thrown down the gauntlet and the war has begun. The lawyer's advice may be to sit tight and do nothing. It may be to approach your employer in the spirit of conciliation; to try to negotiate some kind of agreement that will be beneficial to both of you. It may be to try to get some degree of job protection by filing an agency (EEOC, etc.) complaint. Or it may just be to start looking for another job.

You have a "situation" on your hands involving one of your most important relationships—your employment. Your new attorney may be able to help you defuse it. Don't wait until the bomb has exploded.

Step 4: What about the Initial Consultation?

The interview with your prospective legal advocate goes both ways. You are both trying to figure out if you have a case that's worth pursuing and if he or she is the best one to do it.

When you call for an appointment, ask about the consultation fee. Some lawyers in this competitive market offer a free (albeit brief) initial consultation. Others charge a flat fee. Still others charge their regular hourly rate. Unless the consultation fee is totally out of line, it probably shouldn't override the careful selection process you went through to find this person.

Prepare for the Interview: Go through your file folder and familiarize yourself with it. Take notes. Bring your file folder with you. Don't listen to the radio on your way to the law office, think about what you will say and do when you get there. Time is money and you want to make the best of both.

Check Things Out: Is the office well organized? Or are things in a shambles? Does the office look successful? Or is it run down? These

(Continued on p. 348)

TABLE 16

ATTORNEY INTERVIEW WORKSHEET

The following worksheet will help you and your attorney through the initial interview. If a retainer is required to be paid prior to the initial interview, you may want to mail this worksheet in with the payment so that your attorney will be able to review it prior to your visit. Supplying your attorney with this information (if at all possible, ahead of time) could very well save you time—*and money.*

PERSONAL INFORMATION:

Name_____   Social Security #_____

Address_____   Date of Birth_____

Telephone_____   e-mail_____

EMPLOYER INFORMATION:

Name_____

Address_____

Telephone_____

Number of employees_____

Date hired_____

Salary or hourly wage_____

Bonuses_____

Awards_____

REASON FOR VISIT (check any and all that apply):

_____I was terminated from my employment

      date of termination_____

      date notified I would be terminated_____

_____I have been offered a severance agreement

      deadline to sign_____

_____I was denied a promotion

      date I learned I would not be promoted_____

_____I have been the victim of harassment

      _____racial

      _____sexual

_____I was denied benefits (i.e., wages, health insurance, etc.)

      date denial of benefits took place_____

TABLE 16 *(Continued)*

_____I was not hired for a job

      date_____

_____My employer violated terms of his own policies or handbook, or of my employment contract

      date violation occurred_____

_____I have been the victim of discrimination because of my (check any that apply)

      _____race; _____sex; _____; _____age; _____disability; _____national origin or ancestry; _____sexual orientation; _____marital status; _____religion; _____pregnancy; _____workers' compensation claim; _____illness or injury; _____other (specify)

_____I was retaliated against because I complained about (or reported) my employer's illegal conduct

      date of complaint or report_____

      date of retaliation_____

TERMS AND CONDITIONS OF EMPLOYMENT (check any and all that apply):

_____I am a member of a union

      the name of the union is_____

_____I received a letter when I was hired stating the terms of my employment, a copy of which is attached hereto

_____I believe the company violated the terms of this letter as follows:

      _____

      _____

      _____

_____I received an employee handbook (or personnel manual) when I was hired, a copy of which is attached hereto

_____I believe the company violated the terms of this handbook (or personnel manual) as follows:

      _____

      _____

      _____

_____The company has specific policies it goes by in making employment decisions, but employees do not get a copy of them

_____I believe the company violated the terms of these policies as follows:

      _____

      _____

      _____

_____I have received periodic evaluations of my performance, copies of which are attached hereto

TABLE 16 *(Continued)*

BASIS OF CLAIM(S):

_____I believe that I was treated unfairly

The following is a brief description of how I was treated unfairly:

_____
_____
_____

The following is my employer's explanation of why I was treated this way:

_____
_____
_____

The following is what I think was the REAL reason I was treated this way:

_____
_____
_____

_____I believe that I was the victim of discrimination

The following is the evidence I have that I was the victim of discrimination:

_____
_____
_____

_____I brought this discrimination to my employer's attention

I reported the discrimination on the following dates_____

I reported the discrimination to the following person(s)_____

The following action was taken as a result of my complaint(s):

_____
_____
_____

_____When I was terminated, I signed a resignation letter (waiver or release), a copy of which is attached hereto

Here are the circumstances under which I signed the letter (waiver or release):

_____
_____
_____

INJURY(IES) OR DAMAGES (if applicable):

I suffered the following physical and/or emotional damage as a result of my employer's actions:

_____
_____
_____

TABLE 16   *(Continued)*

_____I sought medical and/or psychiatric attention as a result

doctor's name_____; address_____;
telephone_____; diagnosis_____

_____I have lost wages as a result of my employer's actions

amount of wages lost to date_____

_____I have suffered other financial losses as a direct result of my employer's actions

amount of financial loss_____

description of loss_____

_____I have not received all of the direct payments I have earned and that are due to me from my employer:

salary due_____

bonuses due_____

vacation pay_____

commissions_____

other (specify)_____

PREVIOUS LAWSUITS:

_____I have filed complaints or sued an employer before (present or past employer)

date(s) of complaint or lawsuit_____

reason(s) for complaint(s) or lawsuit(s):_____
_____
_____

(Continued from p. 344)

first impressions are not always determining. There are a lot of messy, disorganized offices than run much more smoothly than some neat, fancy ones. But it *may* be indicative of general sloppiness. It's something to store in your memory bank for future reference.

The Conference: Make every minute count. You are paying for them. As you shake hands and introduce yourself, notice your surroundings, his or her manner. Is the attorney self-assured? Businesslike? Professional? Then get right down to cases.

Outline the basics of your situation. Provide specifics as necessary. Whether you are paying an hourly rate or a flat rate or the consultation is free, it should not take more than an hour for your attorney to tell you if he or she can help you and, if so, how.

You know the score by now. You know what you should be listening for. Note things like:

☞ Does he or she ask the right questions?
☞ Does he or she explain things clearly?
☞ Does he or she outline options and both the possible benefits and the potential consequences of each?

Note: Beware of attorneys who promise you will win lots of money. None can promise you that—especially at your first conference! (Even if they could, they would be fools to do it.) Cautious but realistic optimism is what you are looking for.

At the same time he or she is considering whether your case is worth his or her (and your) while, you should be asking:

☞ What are the fee arrangements? See below.
☞ Who will handle the case, the partner you are speaking to right now or an associate? (In legal parlance, a partner is one of the owners of the firm—a bigwig; an associate is a junior attorney who does research and handles the less significant matters to gain experience—a gofer.) Is your case "significant" enough to them that a partner will handle it? This may be one of the first clues you'll get about the attorney's feeling as to the merits—and potential payoff—of your case.
☞ Will the firm keep in close contact with you? Some send "FYI" (for your information) copies of every document they file and every letter they write to anyone, along with regular case updates and itemized statements of hours spent. Some send nothing but the bill. Obviously, you want the former.
☞ How soon does he or she return phone calls? Attorneys are notorious ignorers of phone calls and messages. Granted, often they really are "in court" or "on the other line" or "in a client conference." But will they return your call within a reasonable period of time? Ask. It's a valid question. There is *nothing* more frustrating than a lawyer who won't return your phone calls.

You might also ask when is the best time to call. For many

it's the afternoon. (Court calendars are generally called in the morning.) Some reserve an hour at the end of the day to take or return calls.

☞ How long will the proposed action take? See below.

After the Interview: Back in your car on the way home think about what just happened. Do I have confidence in this person? Did he or she answer my questions to my satisfaction? Is this the person I want to handle my case? Should I get a second opinion? (If you don't feel comfortable that you have a case or that this is the person to handle it, you might go back to your list and pick the name that appeared the second-most number of times or that had the next best or next most reliable reference. You may have just spent $200 or more, but that doesn't commit you. If you stick with a lawyer you aren't comfortable with, you could be throwing good money after bad.) When in doubt, follow your gut.

Step 5: How Much Will This Cost?

Consultation fee arrangements—how much it is and how and when it is to be paid—should, of course, be among your first questions to your prospective barrister. Further fee discussion is then probably best left to the end of the initial consultation. Is the fee:

Hourly: The rate depends on where you live (and often on what the traffic will bear). Okay, you want an estimate? Here's an estimate. High-cost-of-living areas: $125-an-hour is probably low-end; $300 is high-end; $150–$200 is about average. Low-cost-of-living areas: $75–$200, with $125 about average. Firms charge higher-end rates for a partner's time, lower-end rates for associates. For advice on strategy, early negotiations with your employer (or former employer), and review of severance proposals, expect to pay an hourly rate. (Lawyers are fond of quoting Abe Lincoln—an old lawyer—who said that time is a lawyer's "stock in trade.")

Out-of-pocket Expenses: Your attorney will charge you for his or her out-of-pocket expenses in addition to the legal fee. Make sure you find out what these expenses will be up front. Out-of-pocket expenses can include:

☛ The sheriff's fee for serving the defendant (your employer and maybe your supervisor) with the complaint: This includes travel expenses as well as his or her services. Charges depend on the number of defendants and how difficult they are to find, but generally fall in the neighborhood of $35 to $75 for a single defendant.

☞ The filing fee: This is what the court charges for bringing a complaint. It varies according to the court and the type of action, but can be anywhere from a few dollars to well over a hundred dollars.

☞ Your attorney's travel expenses, where required.

☞ Depositions: Depositions are pretrial examinations of witnesses. They can include depositions your attorney takes of your employer's witnesses, including your supervisor, and depositions your employer takes of your witnesses, including you. They can be few or many, depending on the case. Where your attorney "deposes" someone on your behalf, you will pay for your attorney's time and expenses, if any, as well as for the services of the court reporter or stenographer who will record the proceedings, and for sheriff's fees to summon any reluctant witnesses. If you are deposed, you will have to pay for your attorney's time and expenses. Obviously, the cost of a single deposition can easily run well into the hundreds of dollars, plus fees.

Contingency: A contingency fee is based on winning a lawsuit. An attorney will charge a percentage—usually 33⅓ percent; sometimes more—of the gross amount of your award. But you will bear any out-of-pocket expenses, win or lose. Some firms will charge you in advance for filing fees, sheriff's fees, and other expenses. Others will pay the expenses themselves and deduct them from any monetary award over and above their fee.

Note: Whether or not an attorney will accept your case on a contingency fee basis may be a good barometer of its merit. If you have a good chance of winning some big bucks, he or she is not going to want to let you get away. If you have a *really* good case, they will be more than willing to eat the out-of-pocket expenses up front, too, and take them back off the top after the matter is settled or tried. Absent big bucks potential, however, few lawyers will take a time-consuming (and they often are) employment law case on a complete contingency basis. Expect to make some financial investment, but think about approaches you can afford, such as installment payments, and the ultimate dollar limit you are willing to go to.

Flat Fee: Some lawyers in some situations charge a flat fee for a specific service. This is usually done only where the time he or she will spend on the case can be calculated fairly accurately. Most labor and employment cases do not lend themselves easily to that kind of estimate.

Combination Fees: Some lawyers will combine, for example, hourly and contingency fee rates. For example, they may quote the fee as $150 an hour or one-third of your award, whichever is less. Or they may charge you an hourly fee for a certain period of time and then, if there ends up being a lawsuit, switch to a contingency fee or some kind of "tailored" fee based on a comparison of risk and potential reward. Most attorneys won't start out with a straight contingency fee arrangement simply because there are too many variables. They aren't going to want to risk spending a lot of time on your case only to have you drop it to take a higher-paying job. You, on the other hand, wouldn't be too happy having to pay one-third of a settlement negotiated in only a few hours. So most attorneys will at least start with some type of hourly fee arrangement.

Note: Know the fee arrangements in advance. Most attorneys will have you sign a retainer agreement in which you agree that they will represent you in this particular case and that the fee will be such and such. Don't sign it unless you understand it and agree with it.

Step 6: What about Tactics?

This is another case-by-case thing. Most workers' compensation and unemployment compensation cases and the procedure for pursuing them, for example, are fairly straightforward. On the other hand, there are more options for potential discrimination or wrongful discharge cases. To be sure, many—perhaps most—cases are not lawsuit material. If you get to the right attorney early, he or she may be able to rattle your employer's (or his attorney's) cage enough to negotiate some kind of "severance pay" package for you in lieu of stirring up the waters. Or your attorney may instruct *you* on how to get a better severance deal. If you have a really good case, your employer may want to settle early rather than dragging it into a costly, and maybe an ugly, fight with attendant bad press. But then he may try to drag things out as long as possible, figuring he has more resources for a war of attrition than you do.

If you get to an attorney early enough, he or she can sometimes not only defuse a situation by contacting your employer about it, but by going on the record with your complaint, you may actually be able to improve your job security. Your employer, for example, had better be pretty sure of his ground before firing you (or continuing the unwelcome behavior) after your attorney has contacted him about sexual harassment or other illegal behavior. At the very least, you may be able to gain a period of job protection while you look for another job.

Your prospective attorney should discuss potential tactics with you and what, in his or her opinion, is the most likely direction your case will take.

Step 7: How Long Will All This Take?

The only answer is: It depends. It depends on a lot of things but primarily on how strong a case you have against your employer. Most attorneys will want to try to settle a case rather than go to the mat. The stronger your case (and the uglier any attendant publicity), the more likely a quick settlement can be reached. The weaker your case, the more likely your employer (through his attorney) will drag his feet. He may figure that you don't have the stomach—or the resources—for a protracted legal battle. He may consider going the legal distance as simply another cost of doing business. Unless you are able to reach a quick settlement, chances are this is going to take a while. Getting to trial court can take a year or more—as many as four or five in some cities or states with really congested dockets. Appeals can add another year or more. So, though a settlement is possible anywhere along the line, meandering your way through the legal system can take several years. In short, you'd better not be counting on your court award to survive in the short term. (If you are, you may have to settle sooner and for less.)

It's Your Call

So, do you go for it? Or don't you? It's rarely an easy call, but it's one you'll have to make. Do you have the time? Do you have the money? Do you already have another job? Does your spouse work? Do you have the perseverance needed to follow through? And is your case worth it? What are the potential rewards? What are the costs? What are the chances of success? In the end, only you can decide what to do.

SUMMARY

Your employment situation is as unique as your fingerprint. What you do to resolve it will depend a lot on your instincts . . . and your knowledge of the law . . . and the advice you get. No matter what you do or don't do about it, it will be on your mind for a long time. To you, your case is the most important one in world. Unfortunately, it will not be so important to the agency that handles it. Be prepared to face the frustration that goes along with that dose of reality. You are just another file number to them. If it's an uncontested workers' compensation or unemployment compensation claim, a minimum amount of "bugging" them should get your benefit checks coming within a fairly reasonable time. If it's more than that, it may take making a total nuisance out of yourself to get any action. Or it may take a skilled professional who is versed in the ways of the system.

If you choose to hire an attorney, do it carefully. Any old lawyer definitely will not do. Take the time to do it right. The right person should make you feel as though your case is just as important to him or her as it is to you—as it should be.

Epilogue: Unions and Other Final Thoughts

Well, there you have it: Everything you always wanted to know about your employment rights but didn't know where to look for the answers. In these pages you have learned how the law protects you, from the hiring process right on through to the firing process—and even beyond. You have learned what your rights are in virtually every employment situation and what to do to protect them. In fact, the only situation that hasn't been covered in detail is union membership and how that affects your job.

There is a good reason why I have left unions for last; and it's not because fewer of us belong to unions than ever before (only about one in six as of 1995—and that figure is decreasing every year). It's because, if you do belong to a union, your employment relationship is pretty well covered by your collective bargaining contract. You have problems with your employer (passed over for a promotion, disciplined, demoted, fired), you visit your union steward and the union decides if you have a grievable beef or not. But that doesn't mean you should be ignorant of your rights; or that the rest of us don't need to know how unions work; or that we have a right to join one—or not to join one; and how unions go about trying to get recognized as the certified representative of a company's employees.

Note: If your union refuses to back you up, you become just like every other (nonunion) employee. That is, you still have the right to seek redress of your complaint on your own through any of the means described in this book. You simply must exhaust your grievance procedures through the union first. If the union doesn't back you, or the grievance process doesn't end to your satisfaction, you in effect become a free agent, able to take up your cause on your own.

UNIONS

The **Labor-Management Relations Act** (also called the **Taft-Hartley Act**) regulates the activities and outlines the rights of unions, employers, and employees and prohibits certain unfair labor practices. It was enacted in 1947 after it became apparent that its forerunner, the **National Labor Relations Act** (also called the **Wagner Act**), which had been enacted in 1935, had given too much leverage to unions, to the detriment of the rights of both employers and employees. Thus, the basic purpose of the **Labor-Management Relations Act** (LMRA) was to effect a balance of bargaining power between employers and employees by allowing employees to organize and bargain collectively and also to impose certain restrictions on how far unions can go in organizing a company's employees. The law is administered and enforced by the National Labor Relations Board (NLRB).

If you are among the roughly 16 percent of employees who currently belong to a union, your employment relationship is governed by your union's collective bargaining agreement. That means most, if not all, of the terms and conditions of your employment, such as wages and hours, work schedules, bonuses, seniority, vacations, insurance plans, physical examinations, retirement and pension plans, work rules, safety rules, lunch and coffee breaks, discipline and discharge, and grievance procedures, are regulated by that contract. If you have a problem, you discuss it with your union representative and he or she will take it up with union brass to determine if you have a reasonable gripe. If you do, the union will file a grievance on your behalf; and the grievance will be decided by a procedure that is also detailed in the collective bargaining contract. (But remember, if they don't file that grievance for you, or if you aren't pleased with the results, you can still proceed on your own.)

Who Is Covered By the Law?

The LMRA applies to most employers, though it does specifically except certain workers from coverage, like agricultural laborers, domestics (housekeepers), people who work for their spouses or parents, independent contractors, and supervisors and managerial personnel, as well as workers who are covered by the **Railway Labor Act** (which applies to disputes between air carriers and railroads and their employees).

Protected Activities

Whether or not you belong to a union, the LMRA protects your right to:

☞ Join a union;
☞ Bargain collectively through representatives of your own choosing;
☞ Participate in concerted activities, such as strikes and picketing; or
☞ Refrain from doing any of these things. (**Note:** You may not have the right to refuse to join a union if the collective bargaining agreement between the union and your employer has a clause that requires all employees to be members of the union. (See Closed Shops and Union Shops, p. 360.)

Employer Unfair Labor Practices

Your employer is expressly prohibited by the act from interfering with the exercise of your protected rights of organization, and from trying to restrain or coerce you in the exercise of those rights. For example, he can't refuse to bargain in good faith with a union that is the recognized or elected representative of his employees; and he can't discriminate against you because of your union activities. In fact, he can't even discriminate against you if you are a paid union organizer and one of the reasons you want to go to work for a particular company is so you can try to organize the other workers.[*]

Note: The protections of the LMRA apply to all concerted activity, even if employees are not represented by a union. Thus, even the actions of a single employee are protected if he or she is acting on behalf of coworkers.

Here are some more protected activities:

Distributing Union Literature: Your employer generally can't prohibit the distribution of union literature by an employee in non-

[*]*NLRB v. Town & Country Electric, Inc.,* U.S. Supreme Court, No. 94-947, 1995 LEXIS 8311, 1995.

working areas during nonworking hours. However, your rights are subject to your employer's right to maintain discipline and keep his business running smoothly. For example, retailers can prohibit distribution of union literature in selling areas even on nonworking time and hospitals can prohibit distribution of literature in hallways and other places near patient-care areas.

An employer can prohibit off-duty employees from entering the building to solicit on behalf of a union, but only if he prohibits off-duty employees from entering the workplace for any purpose. He may also prohibit nonemployees from distributing union materials on his private property as long as the union has other reasonable means of reaching employees.

Unilateral Wage Increases: It is also generally considered an unfair labor practice for an employer to increase or promise to increase wages or improve working conditions on his own while a union is trying to organize workers. (You know, to make it look like his employees don't need the union to improve their lot.) It's also illegal to decrease or threaten to decrease wages or withdraw privileges when faced with a union organization campaign.

Asking Employees' Views on Unions: Your employer isn't supposed to ask your opinion of a union unless he's expressly trying to determine that the union actually has the majority support it claims to have. Even then he has to do it by secret ballot and promise not to retaliate against employees based on their responses to his poll.

Predictions by Employers: Your employer can't coerce you into joining or not joining a union, but he can give his opinion or prediction about what will happen if employees do join or form a union. But the opinion or prediction can't be threatening and is supposed to be based on legitimate economic projections.

Surveillance: Employers are prohibited from spying on or eavesdropping on employees' union activities.

Discipline or Discharge: It is illegal for your employer to discipline or discharge you for filing charges under the LMRA or for testifying in a proceeding conducted under the act. *If you are a union member, you have the right to have a union representative present at any meeting with management that may result in disciplinary action being taken against you for any reason.*

You are also supposed to have the right to be told ahead of time what will be discussed at the meeting and be allowed to talk to your union representative about it beforehand.

Blacklisting: Employers can't blacklist employees because of union activity. ("Blacklisting" is the act of trying to prevent a worker from securing employment with another employer.) Many states also have specific statutes that prohibit blacklisting. See Chapter 8: Discipline and Discharge.

Dominating a Union: Employers can't support a union, either financially or otherwise, so as to dominate or control its activities. Such a union is referred to as a "company union."

Past Union Membership: An employer may not ask you about your past union membership.

Grievances: An employer can't refuse to discuss an employee's grievances with the employee's authorized union representative.

Union Unfair Labor Practices

There are certain things unions cannot do under the LMRA, too. Most of them relate to their dealing with employers during organizing campaigns and their right to strike and/or picket. (See below.) However, one in particular has a direct effect on employees. That's the clause that says it is an unfair labor practice for a union to cause an employer to discipline, discharge, demote, or otherwise discriminate against an employee because he or she does not support the union.

Unions and Civil Rights

Unions, like employers, are subject to **Title VII of the Civil Rights Act of 1964.** Thus, it is illegal for a union to discriminate against an individual on the basis of race, sex, age, handicap, national origin, or religion.

Can Membership in a Union
Be Required?

There are various clauses in collective bargaining agreements between unions and employers regarding membership in the union, all of which are addressed by the LMRA.

Closed Shops and Union Shops: There is a slight but subtle difference between a closed shop, which is illegal under the LMRA, and a union shop, which is legal. In a closed shop an employer agrees to *hire* only members of the union. In a union shop, he can hire nonunion members, but the individual hired must join the union within a specified time of hiring (usually thirty days). In a union shop, current employees must join the union, too. (**Note:** Often a modification of a union shop agreement lets current nonunion employees remain nonunion if they wish.)

Agency Shop: In an agency shop, an employee doesn't have to join the union, but has to pay union dues. The theory here is that the nonunion employees shouldn't get the advantages of the union—since under the LMRA the union must represent all employees in the unit whether they are members or not—without paying their fair share toward its financial support.

State Right-to-Work Laws

Many states have so-called right-to-work laws which make union security agreements, such as union shops and agency shops, illegal. These right-to-work laws have been given precedence over LMRA union security provisions in federal court decisions.

Strikes and Replacement of Strikers

Employees have the right to strike (i.e., refuse to work) either because they want to gain better wages, benefits, or working conditions or because their employer is engaged in an unfair labor practice. Under the LMRA employers are within their rights to hire permanent replacements for employees who are engaged in an economic strike. However, they can replace employees striking over an unfair labor practice only until the strike is over.

Picketing and Boycotts

Picketing and boycotting are a means not only of trying to get an employer to settle a labor dispute in the union's favor, but also of bringing the labor dispute to the attention of the general public. Peaceful picketing generally is lawful, as are primary boycotts, in which the union prohibits its members from working for the targeted employer and tries to get people to stop patronizing the employer's business. However, secondary boycotts, which are boycotts of other employers who do business with the targeted employer, are considered to be unfair labor practices.

Lockouts

An employer, on the other hand, has the right to close his place of business and not allow employees to work as a means of trying to settle a labor dispute in his favor.

Choosing a Union

Union organizers can petition for an election to be recognized as the exclusive bargaining representative of a group of employees. However, to call for an election the union must be able to prove that they have the support of at least 30 percent of the employees in the bargaining unit. (In disputed cases, the NLRB will determine which employees make up a specific bargaining unit, according to the similarity of their interests.) Elections must be by secret ballot and generally may be called for only once a year.

The Labor-Management Reporting and Disclosure Act

The **Labor-Management Reporting and Disclosure Act,** also called the **Landrum-Griffin Act,** was enacted in 1959 to require unions to file their constitutions and bylaws with the government, detailing their day-to-day management policies, including rules for participation, election of representatives, holding of meetings, and the like; and to file annual financial statements. Financial statements have to include such things as income and its sources, salaries of officers, loans to officers or union members, and an accounting of all significant payments made by the union.

Claims of Violations and Remedies

Claims of violations of the LMRA are filed with the NLRB. Upon investigation and a finding that your employer or a union has committed an unfair labor practice, the NLRB will order it to cease the practice and take whatever remedial action is necessary or possible to fix the situation. The NLRB can take the offender that refuses to obey to federal court, which may issue an order to comply with the NLRB's directive. Failure to comply with the court order can result in a fine and/or imprisonment.

Summary

The LMRA is a complex law that regulates a complex relationship—the delicate one that exists between unions and employers. It also governs the fallout from that relationship that directly affects you as an employee, *whether you are a union member or not*. The foregoing has been a necessarily abbreviated outline of some of the major provisions of the act, particularly as they affect you, the employee. As a practical matter, if you are a member of a union, any complaints you have against your employer, as well as disciplinary measures he proposes to take against you, up to and including discharge, are subject to a grievance procedure as outlined in your union's collective bargaining agreement. If you are unsure of what your grievance rights are, contact your union representative.

A LOOK BACK
Know Your Rights

The whole idea of this book is to arm you for combat that, hopefully, will never come. You know, to be forewarned is to be forearmed. And maybe knowing your rights in the workplace—especially if your employer *knows* you know your rights—will help you ward off some or all of that unfair, discriminatory, or illegal behavior before it even starts.

Remember, not all unpopular employment decisions made by an employer are morally—or legally—wrong. Sometimes employers simply have to make them for economic reasons; or because an employee just isn't working out no matter how many chances the employer gave him or her to try to improve his or her conduct or work product. But sometimes those unpopular employment decisions are also against the law, or a breach of an employer's express or implied promise, or a violation of public policy or good faith and fair dealing. Still, there isn't *always* anything you can do about it—at least anything that will improve or rectify the situation. But often there is. Many times it comes down to making a difficult decision whether to accept the status quo or take a risk and try to do something about it. And, unless you've already been fired and have nothing to lose, there's always a risk. But there are ways you can reduce that risk. Knowing your rights is one of them. Keeping your own personnel file is another.

Documentation

Throughout the pages of this book I have harped on documentation as your greatest weapon against arbitrary, unfair, and even illegal action by your employer. But to be worth the effort—and it will take some effort—your recordkeeping must be detailed, accurate, and an automatic part of your workday. It must begin when you first hear of a job opening and make your first move to investigate it. Adding to your file must become almost a reflex action. If your employer (or supervisor or other "agent" of your employer) reprimands you, disciplines you, makes a sexually or racially motivated comment, or does or says anything with negative implications, write down exactly what happened, what was said, who was present, dates, times, and anything else that may be relevant. Do the same thing if your employer or his agent says or does something positive, particularly if it contains express or implied assurances of continued employment. And file every document you get from your employer (performance reviews, commendations, memos, warnings—*everything*). And, remember, many states allow you to submit your own explanation of negative entries your employer makes in your personnel file. (See Chapter 6: Right to Privacy/Access to Records.) But even if your state doesn't, write down your explanation anyway—immediately, while it is still fresh in your mind—and put it in your *own* personnel file. If push comes to shove, it may be your word against your employer's, but a judge or jury may believe your word if it's backed up by detailed records. And maybe it won't be just your word against his if some of your records contain names of witnesses who are willing to support your side of the story.

Documentation: It's essential.

What to Do

Another thing you can do to reduce the risk of retaliation when you decide to fight your employer's actions, or increase the chance of prevailing in an all-out war, is to get help before it's too late. That requires that you have a little foresight: Read the handwriting on the wall. Don't just sit there and hope a bad situation will go away by itself. Usually it will get worse. If an employer sees he can get away with something (discrimination, sexual harassment, underpayment of wages or overtime, or some other violation of the law), he will likely continue to do it. That's just human nature. Call the EEOC; call OSHA; call the Department of Labor; or call an experienced labor and employment lawyer. A call to the appropriate agency for advice is free. And a call to that attorney, though it may not be free, may be worth the expense. It may cost you a couple hundred bucks, but the advice could solve your problem, or even save your job.

Law Is Not an Exact Science

I have done my best to explain state and federal labor and employment laws and the effect they have on you and your job in such a way that you don't have to be a lawyer to understand them. (A lot of lawyers don't even understand them.) I have presented you with the options available to you when your rights are being violated. But remember, the law is not an exact science. Yours is a unique situation with a unique set of facts, and the specific course of action that is best for you will depend not only on the facts of your case but also on what state you live in, changes in the law since the publication of this book, and even the unique tendencies of the particular court that will have jurisdiction over your case, if the courtroom is its ultimate destination.

THE LAST WORD

Our jobs are extremely important to us. Not only do they allow us to keep a roof over our heads and food on the table and otherwise provide for our families, but in a very real sense they define who we are. What's the first question your spouse asks—or you ask your spouse—when you get home? "How was work today?" Meet up with a good friend and how long does it take for him or her to ask, "How's work going?" And how deep into a conversation with a new acquaintance will you get before he or she asks the inevitable question "What do you do for a living?" The fact is that even though most of us probably wouldn't even work if we didn't have to—well, at least we wouldn't work as hard or as long—we spend more time working than we spend doing just about anything else.

At its best, your job can be a satisfying and rewarding experience. You enjoy what you do, you're good at it, it pays a fair wage, you like the people you work with and they like you, and the environment is safe and healthy. But at its worst, it can screw up your whole life (and even your family's). So what is it that determines which one *your* job will be? Is it the pay? The hours? The benefits? What?

My grandfather worked in a Boston shipyard for most of his life. When I was a young boy the family would drive up from Connecticut to visit him and my grandmother, and I'd see him come home on the train with his lunch pail swinging in his hand, tired and dirty but always with a smile on his face. He and my grandmother lived in a modest neighborhood and didn't have much in the way of luxuries. I remember one time asking him why he liked his job so much when it couldn't have paid that well and was obviously such hard physical labor.

"The bosses are good," he said.

"The bosses are good." A simple answer, but one that said it all. Well, that was many years ago and work, like much of life, is a far more complex place than it was in my grandfather's day. But that universal truth still holds today. When the bosses are good, then you can bet that the job is pretty good, too. But, of course, the bosses can't always be counted on to hold up their end of the deal. And when that happens, your job can end up more like a street fight than the rewarding life's "calling" you had hoped for. And if that happens, you'd better be armed for combat. I hope this book has given you all the ammunition you need: number one, to improve your chances of getting the most job security and best working conditions you can get. Number two, to create a balance of power that will neutralize the potential for all-out war between you and your employer. And, number three, to give you a better chance of winning if the day ever comes when that dreaded war does arrive.

Good luck. And have a great day at work.

Appendixes

Glossary of Employment Law Terms

ADA: The **Americans with Disabilities Act,** which protects disabled individuals from employment discrimination and requires employers to offer reasonable accommodation of their disability.

ADEA: Age Discrimination in Employment Act, which protects people forty and over from discharge or discipline based on their age.

Administrative remedy: A claim made through a governmental agency, such as the EEOC or DOL; as opposed to a claim pursued through the courts.

ADR: Alternative dispute resolution, which employs various methods, including fact-finding, negotiation, mediation, arbitration, open door policies, and peer review to encourage settlement of employer–employee disputes without litigation.

Adverse impact: A negative effect; as in work rules that have an adverse impact on a protected group.

Affirmative action: A policy of giving an advantage in hiring or promotion opportunities to members of a protected group to atone for past discrimination.

After-acquired evidence: Evidence an employer discovers after an employee is fired (usually wrongfully) which, if it would have provided "just cause" to fire the person, can be used to limit the employer's damages.

Agency shop: A clause in a collective bargaining agreement that requires nonunion members to pay the union an amount equal to the amount of members' dues. (I.e., in an agency shop employees do not have to belong to the union, but in effect have to pay union dues.)

Assumption of the risk: A legal theory which states that an individual who is aware of the hazards of an activity but engages in that activity nevertheless cannot recover damages if he or she is injured by that hazard.

Back pay: A damage award in a lawsuit allowing recovery of wages an employee would have earned if he or she had not been illegally fired or denied a promotion.

Base period: The minimum period of working time required to qualify for unemployment compensation benefits.

Base period wages: The minimum amount of base period earnings required to qualify for unemployment compensation benefits.

Blacklisting: Circulating or publishing a person's name with the intention of interfering with his or her chances for employment.

Bona fide occupational qualification (BFOQ): A normally discriminatory job requirement which is legitimate under specific circumstances (e.g., seeking only female candidates for a job playing a female acting role).

Bottom-line test: A comparison of actual hiring rates rather than selection methods, to determine whether or not hiring practices have an adverse impact on members of a protected group.

Boycott: A refusal to work for or patronize an employer with whom a union is involved in a labor dispute.

Burden of proof: The obligation placed by the court on a specific party to establish a case.

Business necessity/justification: A valid economic reason for an employer to make an employment decision. (E.g., a loss of customers may cause a business necessity or be a sufficient business justification for layoffs.)

COBRA: The **Consolidated Omnibus Budget Reconciliation Act,** which gives terminated employees the right to continuation of health insurance coverage at group rates (usually for up to a year and a half).

Carcinogen: A cancer-causing substance.

Casual employee: A worker who performs a job that is not within the scope of the employer's usual business, such as a person who cleans carpets in a doctor's office.

Causal connection: A link between events that is close enough to establish a cause-and-effect relationship.

Chain of custody: The course taken by a blood or urine sample between its donor and its analysis, which must be guarded to ensure the integrity of the sample.

Civil lawsuit: A lawsuit brought by one individual (or entity) against another, as opposed to a criminal lawsuit, which is brought by the government against an individual or entity.

Class action: A lawsuit undertaken by one or more members of an aggrieved group on behalf of all its members.

Closed shop: An agreement between a union and an employer whereby the employer agrees to hire only union members. Closed shops are illegal under the **Taft-Hartley Act.**

Company union: A union supported by and effectively controlled by an employer, either financially or otherwise.

Comparable worth: A theory that people doing *different* jobs that are of roughly equal worth to their employer should be paid the same wage, regardless of sex (an extension of the **Equal Pay Act,** requiring equal pay for people doing the *same* job).

Compensatory damages: Damages awarded by a court to repay an individual for losses suffered (i.e., lost wages and benefits, pain and suffering, emotional distress).

Compensatory ("comp.") time: Time off given in lieu of overtime. Generally not allowed for private employers under the FLSA.

Conflict of laws: Laws (usually one state and one federal) that impose different requirements in similar circumstances. In the case of a conflict of employment laws, employers must follow the law that gives employees the most rights or protections.

Constructive discharge: "Voluntary" resignation caused by intolerable changes in working conditions imposed by an employer.

Contingency fee: An attorney's fee based on a percentage or fraction (usually one-third) of the amount recovered, rather than an hourly or flat rate.

Continuation: The right of employees, under COBRA, to remain on their employer's group health insurance policy after termination, usually for up to a year and a half.

Contributory negligence: A legal theory that reduces a damage award if the plaintiff's negligence contributed to his or her own injury.

Conversion: The right of an employee, following the expiration of his or her right of continuation of group health insurance under COBRA, to convert to an individual policy.

Court costs: The fees required to bring a lawsuit, including the fee for filing the action in a specific court. Often awarded to the victorious party in addition to other relief.

DOD: The Department of Defense.

DOJ: The Department of Justice.

DOL: The Department of Labor.

DOT: The Department of Transportation.

De minimis: Minor, as a *de minimis* violation of the **Occupational Safety and Health Act.**

Defamation: An oral or written statement impugning a person's character. See "libel" and "slander."

Defendant: The person (or entity) being sued by another (the plaintiff).

Defined benefit plan: A pension plan in which a specified payout is guaranteed on retirement. The employer's contribution may vary depending on market conditions.

Defined contribution plan: A pension plan in which the employer's contribution is fixed, but the payout may vary depending on market conditions.

Deposition: A statement taken under oath prior to trial.

Disparate impact: A negative effect (as of a work rule) that falls more heavily on one group than on another.

Disposable earnings: The net amount of wages remaining after lawful deductions, such as for taxes, Social Security, health insurance, and pension contributions.

Docking: The practice (prohibited by the FLSA) of paying employees for fewer hours than they actually worked as a form of punishment (e.g., for being late for work).

Dual-purpose rule: A theory that makes an employee who is injured on a trip with both business and personal purposes eligible for workers' compensation benefits if business was the dominant purpose of the trip.

EEOC: The Equal Employment Opportunity Commission, which administers and enforces civil rights laws.

ERISA: The **Employee Retirement Income Security Act,** which outlines legal requirements for employer-sponsored retirement plans, pension plans, and other plans established for the benefit of employees.

Employment at will: A noncontractual employment relationship in which the employer is free to fire the employee for any reason or no reason and the employee is free to quit with no contractual obligation.

Employment eligibility: Legal qualification to work (in the United States).

Essential function of the job: The primary duties of a job, as opposed to its incidental duties.

Et seq. (et sequens): And the following; a citation reference (e.g., Title 29, U.S. Code, Section 1001, *et seq.*), meaning the cited material begins at Section 1001 and continues for an unspecified number of sections following it.

Exempt employees: Employees who are not subject to the minimum wage and overtime provisions of the FLSA, such as white-collar employees.

Experience rate: An unemployment insurance premium based on an employer's turnover rate.

FLSA: The **Fair Labor Standards Act,** which governs federal wage and hour laws.

FMLA: The Family and Medical Leave Act, which requires employers of 50 or more employees to allow eligible employees to take up to 12 weeks of unpaid leave in any 12-month period for family or medical emergencies without risking loss of their jobs.

FUTA: The **Federal Unemployment Tax Act,** under which employers are obligated to pay federal unemployment taxes.

Fellow-servant rule: An antiquated rule of law that required an employee who was injured by the actions of a coworker to sue the coworker for damages, rather than their employer.

Fetal protection policy: A company rule prohibiting women of child-bearing age from working in certain hazardous jobs. Ruled unconstitutional by the U.S. Supreme Court in *United Auto Workers v. Johnson Controls, Inc.,* 1991.

Four-fifths rule: An EEOC guideline that says a preemployment test has an adverse impact if the selection rate for any group is less than four-fifths (or 80 percent) of the group with the highest selection rate.

Front pay: A damage award that pays a discharged or "unpromoted" employee (instead of reinstating him or her) the additional pay he or she would have earned if reinstated. (Awarded in situations where someone else has already been hired for the higher-paying job.)

Garnishment: The attachment of wages (or other moneys due to an individual) to pay a debt.

Gas chromatography: A method used to test for the presence of drugs in the blood system.

Going and coming rule: The rule of law that says an employee who is injured during his or her normal commute to and from work is not eligible for workers' compensation benefits.

Grandfather clause: A provision in a law or rule that exempts from coverage anyone who has engaged in a practice since prior to passage of the law or rule that prohibits the conduct.

Gross misconduct: A breach of work rules or behavioral standards that is so substantial as to warrant immediate discharge.

Handicap: A limitation in the capacity to perform one or more of life's major functions (e.g., breathing, walking, seeing, hearing, working, etc.).

Hostile working environment: An environment created by a pattern or practice of unwelcome behavior (usually sexually or racially motivated) that unreasonably interferes with an individual's job performance.

Hours worked: All hours that an employee is either required or allowed to work and for which he or she must be paid under the FLSA.

I-9 Form: "Employment Eligibility Verification" Form; must be filled out by all employees and employers in order to establish an individual's eligibility to work in the United States.

INS: The Immigration and Naturalization Service, which administers and enforces the **Immigration Reform and Control Act.**

IRA (Individual Retirement Account): A tax-deferred account into which the Internal Revenue Service allows an individual to contribute up to $2,000 per year ($2,250 if the individual has a nonworking spouse).

IRCA: The **Immigration Reform and Control Act,** which outlines eligibility and verification requirements for legal employment in the United States.

Illegal alien: A foreign national not legally eligible to work in the United States.

Implied contract: A contract that is suggested by the conductor actions of the parties rather than by any specific written instrument or oral agreement.

Just cause: A legitimate reason, as opposed to an illegal or discriminatory reason (e.g., for firing someone).

LMRA: The **Labor-Management Relations Act,** also called the **Taft-Hartley Act,** which governs the relationship between unions and employers.

Last-straw doctrine: The principle that for an employee to be ineligible for unemployment compensation benefits based on discharge for repeated willful misconduct, the final act, or "last straw," must also have been willful misconduct.

Legal holidays: Paid days off traditionally given to employees for major holidays. Not required of private employers in the absence of an employment or union contract.

Libel: Defamation that is in writing.

Lie detector: Any electronic device used to determine the truth or falsity of the statements of the individual being examined; a polygraph.

Light duty: A nonphysical or less physical alternate work assignment offered to a workers' compensation claimant to get him or her back to work prior to full recovery.

Liquidated damages: An amount of damages that is preset or calculated exactly, rather than using an estimate. (Used in cases where damages would otherwise be speculative or difficult to determine. For example, in cases of willful ADEA violations, damages may be preset to equal back-pay damages, in effect doubling them.)

Lockout: A labor dispute in which the employer prevents employees from entering the workplace until the dispute is resolved.

Mass spectrometry: A method used to test for the presence of drugs in the blood system.

Mitigation of damages: The obligation to minimize the amount of damages insofar as reasonable, such as by a fired worker using reasonable efforts to find a new job (thus reducing any potential back-pay and/or front-pay award).

Modified union shop: An agreement that newly hired employees must join the union, but that existing nonunion employees may remain nonunion.

NLRB: The National Labor Relations Board, which administers and enforces the **National Labor Relations Act,** the law that defines the relationship between employers and unions.

NRC: The Nuclear Regulatory Commission, which oversees the operation of nuclear energy plants.

National origin: Ethnic background.

Negligent hiring: Employing someone for a job that would give him or her the opportunity to commit a crime against a customer or client, where an adequate background check would have revealed prior offenses (and where the employee then uses his or her position to commit the type of crime he or she had a history of committing).

Noncompetition clause: A clause in an employment contract which seeks to limit the employee's right to work for a competitor of the employer or open a competing business.

OFCCP: The Office of Federal Contract Compliance Programs, which oversees federal contractors' compliance with equal employment opportunity laws.

OSHA: The Occupational Safety and Health Administration, which administers and enforces the **Occupational Safety and Health Act,** regulating safety and health in the workplace.

On-call time: Time during which an employee must remain available to report to work on short notice, and for which the employee must be paid if he or she has to wait in a place designated by his or her employer.

Permanency award: A payment made for permanent incapacity caused by an on-the-job injury or illness; often based on a statutory "schedule" of injuries.

Permanent injunction: A court order to refrain from doing something that may cause irreparable harm if allowed to continue.

Picketing: An action informing the general public of the existence of a labor dispute; usually involving strikers walking outside the employer's premises carrying signs and passing out leaflets stating the union's position.

Plaintiff: The person (or entity) bringing a legal action against another (the defendant).

Polygraph: Any electronic device used to determine the truth or falsity of the statements of the individual being examined; a lie detector.

Predetermination hearing: An initial, informal workers' compensation hearing conducted to determine the merits of a contested claim for benefits.

Preexisting condition: An injury or condition an individual already had prior to his or her employment or prior to the current injury or condition.

Preliminary injunction: A court order to refrain from doing something that may cause irreparable harm if allowed to continue pending the final outcome of litigation.

Pretext: An excuse or rationale that masks the real (illegal) reason for an employment decision.

***Prima facie* case:** The basic evidence which "on its face" establishes grounds for a lawsuit. For example, a prima facie case of race discrimination would require evidence that the alleged victim was a member of a racial minority and negative employment action was taken under circumstances that tend to show it was for that reason.

Private employer: A nongovernmental employer.

Profit-sharing: A retirement plan in which employer contributions are tied to company profits.

Protected group/class: People who, because of historic class discrimination, are given extra protections by the law (racial, ethnic, and religious minorities, women, older workers, and the handicapped).

Public employer: A federal, state, or municipal governmental unit or any subdivision or agency thereof.

Public policy: A policy designed to promote the general good.

Punitive damages: Damages awarded to a victim by a court as a means of penalizing the wrongdoer (awarded over and above compensatory damages).

Qualified disabled person: An individual whose disability substantially limits his or her ability to work but who is still able to perform the essential duties of the job.

Quotas: Employment practices that aim to hire in strict conformity with the statistical makeup of the local work force (racially, sexually, etc.).

Reasonable person standard: The yardstick by which courts often judge a person's actions. (I.e., would a reasonable person have acted or been affected in the same way?)

Reasonable woman standard: The yardstick by which some courts judge sexual harassment claims. (I.e., would a reasonable *woman* have been affected in the same way?)

Recognized hazard: A dangerous condition of a particular job or industry that is generally acknowledged to exist despite reasonable safety precautions.

Reverse discrimination: Employment practices which unfairly and illegally disadvantage traditionally unprotected groups (i.e., whites and/or males).

Rule of thumb: *See* four-fifths rule.

Scope of employment: The range of an employee's job duties. (I.e., something occurs within the scope of someone's employment if it happens while he or she is doing something reasonably connected with his or her job.)

Secondary boycott: A refusal to work for or patronize a company that continues to do business with an employer with whom a union is involved in a labor dispute. (Considered an unfair labor practice.)

Sexual harassment: Unwelcome sexual advances, the acceptance of which is either expressly or implicitly made a condition of employment; or sexually oriented behavior that creates a hostile working environment.

Slander: Oral defamation.

Speak-English-only rule: A workplace rule that requires employees to speak only English on the job (usually unlawful unless restricted to specific situations, such as face-to-face contact with customers).

Special errand: The act of reporting to work while on emergency "on-call" status; injury while on such a "special errand" generally qualifies for workers' compensation coverage.

Special hazard: The risk associated with work, which risk workers' compensation insurance is designed to cover; as opposed to everyday risks faced by the general public.

Statute of Frauds: The law providing that a contract for a term of longer than a year must be in writing to be enforceable.

Statute of Limitations: The legal time limit for bringing a lawsuit or filing a lawful claim.

Stock options: A retirement plan in which employees are either given stock in the company or an option to purchase stock in the company.

Strike: A work stoppage designed to force an employer to submit to workers' demands.

Subpoena: A legal summons requiring an individual to appear in court.

Suitable work: Employment that reasonably matches an individual's qualifications, education, and experience, an offer of which generally cuts off the person's eligibility for unemployment compensation benefits.

Taft-Hartley Act: The law that governs the relationship between unions and employers; also called the **Labor-Management Relations Act.**

Taxable wage base: That part of each worker's wages used to determine his or her employer's unemployment compensation tax liability.

Temporary partial disability: A physical impairment that causes an individual to be incapable of full employment for a limited period of time.

Temporary permanent disability: A physical impairment that causes an individual to be totally incapable of working for a lim-

ited period of time; usually followed by a period of temporary partial disability.

Timeliness: The bringing of a legal action or filing of a legal claim within the time limit set by law.

Title VII: The section of the **Civil Rights Act of 1964** that prohibits employers from discriminating on the basis of age, race, sex, color, religion, or national origin.

Undue hardship: A unreasonable (usually economic) burden that relieves an employer from being required to accommodate an individual's handicap.

Union shop: A clause in a collective bargaining agreement which states that an employer may hire nonunion members, but employees must join the union within a specified period of time, most often thirty days.

USERRA: The Uniformed Services Employment and Reemployment Rights Act, which protects the jobs of employee/military reservists who are required to attend periodic meetings or training sessions, or are called to active duty.

Validation: A means of verifying the alleged nondiscriminatory effect of preemployment tests or other selection procedures.

Vesting: The establishment of an absolute right of ownership (i.e., in the proceeds of a retirement fund).

Vietnam-era veteran: A veteran who served during the Vietnam War (August 5, 1964, to May 7, 1975) and who must be given employment preference in work on federal government contracts under the **Vietnam Era Readjustment Assistance Act.**

Waiting time: Time an employee is required to remain at the workplace waiting to work (for example, because of a machinery breakdown) and for which he or she must be paid.

Waiver: An agreement to forgo a right conferred upon a person by law.

Weakened resistance: A theory that bases eligibility for workers' compensation benefits for a nonwork injury or illness on lowered resistance caused by work.

Whistleblower: An employee who reports his or her employer's violation of the law.

White-collar exemption: The exemption of executive, administrative, and professional employees from the minimum wage and overtime provisions of the FLSA.

Willful misconduct: Unsuitable behavior that is engaged in either intentionally or with reckless disregard for the consequences.

Discharge for repeated willful misconduct can be cause for denial of unemployment compensation benefits.

Wrongful discharge: The termination or firing of an employee in violation of the law or public policy or in breach of an employment contract, either expressed or implied.

Summary of Federal Labor Laws

AGE DISCRIMINATION IN EMPLOYMENT ACT (ADEA)

Coverage: The ADEA applies to employers of twenty or more workers.

Requirements: The ADEA prohibits employers from discriminating against workers who are between the ages of forty and seventy years old on the basis of age. (**Note:** Some state antidiscrimination laws apply to workers who are under forty and over seventy years old.) This includes discrimination in hiring, compensation, and other terms and conditions of employment.

Exceptions: The law does not apply in cases where age is a bona fide occupational qualification of the job.

Enforcement: The law is administered and enforced by the EEOC.

Claims: Claims must be filed with the EEOC within 180 days of the violation complained of.

Lawsuits: You may bring a private lawsuit if the EEOC doesn't sue on your behalf. But the lawsuit must be filed within 90 days of receiving a right-to-sue notice from the EEOC, or within 60 days of receiving a notice that the EEOC will not be pursuing the matter.

If You Win: If you win, you can be reinstated to your job with back pay and full benefits; you can get liquidated damages of double your back pay; you can be awarded attorney's fees and court costs; and the court can order your employer to stop the practice.

Library Reference: 29 U.S. Code, Section 621.

AMERICANS WITH DISABILITIES ACT (ADA)

Coverage: The ADA applies to employers of fifteen or more workers.

Requirements: The ADA prohibits employers from discriminating against qualified disabled workers. This includes discrimination in hiring, compensation, and other terms and conditions of employment. The law also requires employers to make reasonable efforts to accommodate the disability of an individual who is otherwise qualified to perform the essential functions of the job, as long as the accommodation wouldn't be an undue hardship on the employer. The law specifically applies to victims of AIDS.

Exceptions: The law does not protect individuals who currently use illegal drugs, and allows employers to hold alcoholics to the same standards as other employees. In addition, employees with certain communicable diseases that can be spread through contact with food may be transferred from food handling jobs to other jobs, where available.

Enforcement: The law is administered and enforced by the EEOC.

Claims: Claims must be filed with the EEOC within 180 days of the violation complained of.

Lawsuits: You may bring a private lawsuit within 90 days of receiving a right-to-sue letter from the EEOC.

If You Win: If you win, you can be reinstated to your job with back pay and full benefits; you can be reimbursed for your attorney's fees and court costs; you can get compensatory and punitive damages, within certain limits; and the court can order your employer to stop the practice.

Library Reference: Title 42, U.S. Code, Section 12101 *et seq.*

"Guide" Reference: Chapter 5: Discrimination and Related Issues; Chapter 11: I'm Getting Screwed; So What Can I Do about It?

CIVIL RIGHTS ACT OF 1991

Coverage: The Civil Rights Act of 1991 applies to employers of fifteen or more workers.

Requirements: The Civil Rights Act of 1991 is really an amendment to Title VII of the Civil Rights Act of 1964. Its major effects are:

☞ Reversing the effect of a number of U.S. Supreme Court decisions, making employment discrimination laws applicable to all facets of the employment relationship, not just hiring and certain promotion decisions;

☞ Allowing women, handicapped individuals, and members of religious minorities to sue for damages for intentional discrimination. (Racial and ethnic minorities were already allowed to do so under Section 1981 of the Civil Rights Act of 1870.) **Note:** Damage awards for women, handicapped individuals, and members of religious minorities are limited by size of employer, however, while damage awards for members of racial and ethnic minorities are not.

☞ Allowing women, handicapped individuals, and members of religious minorities to choose trial by jury. (Racial and ethnic minorities were already allowed to do so under Section 1981, but not under Title VII.)

Enforcement: The law is administered and enforced by the EEOC.
Claims: Claims must be filed with the EEOC within 180 days of the violation complained of.
Lawsuits: You may bring a private lawsuit 90 days after receiving a right-to-sue letter from the EEOC.
If You Win: If you win, you can be reinstated to your job with back pay and full benefits; if the discrimination was intentional, you can be awarded damages within certain limits; you can be reimbursed for your attorney's fees and court costs; and the court can order your employer to stop the practice.
"Guide" Reference: Chapter 5: Discrimination and Related Issues; Chapter 11: I'm Getting Screwed; So What Can I Do about It?

CONSOLIDATED OMNIBUS BUDGET RECONCILIATION ACT (COBRA)

Coverage: COBRA applies to employers of twenty or more workers.
Requirements: COBRA requires employers to offer to continue employees (and their covered dependents) in their company's group health insurance plan when their employment terminates for just about any reason except gross misconduct. In most cases continua-

tion is for eighteen months, but it can be for up to thirty-six months. Employers are required to notify employees of their COBRA rights both when they join the group health insurance plan and when their employment terminates. The (former) employee (and/or his or her covered dependents) must pay the entire premium. The employer is no longer responsible for making contributions.

Exceptions: COBRA continuation rights may end prematurely either when the covered individual fails to pay the premiums or when he or she becomes eligible for membership in another group health insurance plan.

Enforcement: The law is administered and enforced by the IRS.

If You Aren't Offered Continuation of Coverage: If your employer doesn't notify you and your covered dependents of your right to COBRA continuation benefits, he can be held liable for any medical expenses you incur as a result of your lack of insurance or under-insurance.

"Guide" Reference: Chapter 4: Fringe Benefits.

CONSUMER CREDIT PROTECTION ACT

Coverage: The Consumer Credit Protection Act applies to all employers.

Requirements: The act limits the amount of an employee's wages that can be attached by court order and withheld by his or her employer for payment of a judgment. For court orders other than for support of a spouse or dependent child, the limit is 25 percent of weekly disposable earnings or the amount of disposable earnings over thirty times the federal minimum wage, whichever is less. For support orders, up to 60 percent of the employee's disposable earnings can be attached (only 50 percent if the individual is already supporting another spouse or dependent child). **Note:** Some states allow less of an employee's wages to be attached than does federal law, which means only the lesser amount can be withheld from the employee's wages. In addition, under the act an employer cannot discipline or discharge an employee if his or her wages have been attached for a single indebtedness. **Note:** Some states prohibit an employer from disciplining or discharging an employee even if his or her wages have been attached for numerous debts.

Exceptions: Amounts payable for federal and state taxes are not subject to the above limits.

Enforcement: The law is administered and enforced by the U.S. Department of Labor, Wage and Hour Division.

Lawsuits: An employee whose wages were attached in an amount greater than that allowed by law may sue his employer (or the attaching creditor) for the excess amount attached. An employee who was discharged in violation of the law can sue for reinstatement and back pay.

Library Reference: Title 15, U.S. Code, Section 1671.

"Guide" Reference: Chapter 3: Wages and Hours.

EMPLOYEE POLYGRAPH PROTECTION ACT

Coverage: The **Employee Polygraph Protection Act** applies to most employers except those in the security business with respect to employees directly involved in security matters, and employers in the prescription drug business with respect to employees who directly handle those drugs. It specifically doesn't apply to public employers or to private employers with subcontracts with the Department of Defense, the Department of Energy, and government agencies guarding the national security.

Requirements: The act prohibits most employers from requiring or even requesting that a job applicant or employee submit to a polygraph, or lie detector test, as a condition of employment.

Exceptions: The law does not apply in cases where an employee is reasonably suspected of workplace theft or otherwise intentionally causing a monetary loss to his or her employer, if the employee actually had access to the property in question. In that case, strict testing requirements must be followed, including giving advance notice to the employee of his or her legal rights, including questions that may not be asked and the right to discontinue the test at any time.

Enforcement: The law is administered and enforced by the U.S. Department of Labor, Wage and Hour Division.

Complaints: Complaints of violation of the act may be filed with the U.S. DOL, Wage and Hour Division.

If You Are Illegally Required to Take a Lie Detector Test: If you are fired or denied a promotion on the basis of a lie detector test, you are entitled to reinstatement to your job, or the promotion you were denied, with back pay and full benefits. Your employer is also subject to a fine of up to $10,000 for illegally requiring you to take a lie detector test.

Library Reference: Title 29, U.S. Code, Section 2001.
"Guide" Reference: Chapter 6: Right to Privacy/Access to Records.

EMPLOYEE RETIREMENT INCOME SECURITY ACT (ERISA)

Coverage: ERISA applies to all employers who sponsor pension or retirement plans for their employees.

Requirements: ERISA has specific requirements regarding plan participation, vesting of employer contributions, and funding of plans. In addition, it has numerous reporting and disclosure requirements that depend on the kind of pension or retirement plan in question. Annual reports to employee-plan members must include a statement of total benefits and the percentage of benefits that are fully vested. Employers must also provide regular reports to the U.S. Treasury Department, the IRS, and the Pension Benefit Guaranty Corporation.

Enforcement: The law is administered and enforced by the U.S. Department of Labor, the U.S. Treasury Department, the IRS, and the Pension Benefit Guaranty Corporation.

Lawsuits: You may bring a private lawsuit if your ERISA rights are violated.

If You Win: If you win, you are entitled to restoration of full benefits, and attorney's fees. Your employer can also lose his tax exemption for the plan. Intentional violations of reporting and disclosure requirements can result in a fine of between $5,000 and $100,000 and imprisonment for up to a year.

Library Reference: Title 29, U.S. Code, Section 1001 *et seq.*
"Guide" Reference: Chapter 4: Fringe Benefits.

EQUAL PAY ACT

Coverage: The Equal Pay Act applies to all employers with two or more employees.

Requirements: The Equal Pay Act requires equal pay for equal work, regardless of sex. Work is considered equal if the jobs require substantially equivalent skill, effort, and responsibility and are done under similar conditions.

Exceptions: The act does not apply where different wages are paid according to a bona fide merit or seniority system, or a system based on quality or quantity of production, or any other system that is not based on sex.

Enforcement: The law is administered and enforced by the EEOC.

Claims: An employee may file a claim with the EEOC, which must bring a lawsuit within two years of the violation (three years if the violation was willful).

Lawsuits: You may bring a private lawsuit rather than filing a claim with the EEOC. However, once you file a complaint with the EEOC, you may bring a private lawsuit only if the EEOC doesn't sue on your behalf.

If You Win: If you win, you can be reinstated or promoted; you can get double your back pay; you can be awarded attorney's fees and court costs; and the court can order your employer to stop the practice. Your employer can also be fined up to $10,000. Fines can be greater, and prison sentences imposed for subsequent willful offenses.

Library Reference: 29 U.S. Code, Section 206(d).

"Guide" Reference: Chapter 5: Discrimination and Related Issues; Chapter 11: I'm Getting Screwed; So What Can I Do about It?

FAIR LABOR STANDARDS ACT (FLSA)

Coverage: The FLSA applies to virtually all employers.

Requirements: The FLSA contains a series of wage and hour laws that require employers to pay employees at least the minimum wage and pay overtime for hours worked in excess of forty in a week. **Note:** Many states require employers to pay a higher minimum wage than does the federal law. Some also require the payment of overtime for hours worked in excess of eight in a day. In those cases, employees must be paid according to the law that requires employers to pay the higher amount. The FLSA also sets limits on the number of hours employees may work in a day or week. In addition, the FLSA regulates hours of work for minors and restricts minors from working in hazardous jobs. **Note:** Many states have stricter limits on hours of work for minors and jobs they may be hired to do than does the federal law.

Exceptions: The FLSA excepts executive, administrative, and professional employees, outside salespeople, and certain computer professionals from coverage of the minimum wage and overtime provisions of the act. Certain other jobs are also specifically excepted from minimum wage and overtime coverage. In addition, certain learners, apprentices, and trainees may be paid less than the minimum wage with permission from the commissioner of labor. Tipped employees may have up to 50 percent of their tips credited toward payment of the minimum wage.

Enforcement: The law is administered and enforced by the U.S. Department of Labor, Wage and Hour Division.

Claims: Employees can file a claim for unpaid wages with the DOL within two years of a violation (three years if the violation was willful).

Lawsuits: If the DOL doesn't sue on your behalf, or if you do not file a claim with the DOL, you may bring your own lawsuit.

If You Win: If you win, you can recover twice the amount of your unpaid wages and be reinstated to your job with back pay and full benefits if you were fired in retaliation for seeking your FLSA rights. Employers can also be fined up to $10,000 for a child labor law violation.

Library Reference: Title 29, U.S. Code, Section 201 *et seq.*

"Guide" Reference: Chapter 3: Wages and Hours.

FAMILY AND MEDICAL LEAVE ACT (FMLA)

Coverage: FMLA applies to all employers with fifty or more workers within a 75-mile radius.

Requirements: Eligible employees (those who have worked for the employer for at least a year, including at least 1,250 hours in the last year) may take up to twelve weeks of unpaid leave in any one-year period for the birth or adoption of a child, or the serious illness of the employee or the employee's spouse, child, or parent. The employee must be returned to the same or equivalent job with equivalent pay and benefits.

Enforcement: FMLA is administered and enforced by the U.S. DOL.

Claims: Claims must be made with the DOL within two years of the alleged violation.

Lawsuits: An aggrieved employee may bring legal action for the appropriate redress, including promotion, reinstatement, and monetary damages.

Library Reference: Public Law 103-3.

"Guide" Reference: Chapter 4: Fringe Benefits

EXECUTIVE ORDER 11246 (E.O. 11246)

Coverage: E.O. 11246 applies to all employers with contracts with the federal government worth more than $10,000.

Requirements: E.O. 11246 prohibits discrimination by federal contractors and subcontractors and requires them to have written plans that outline the affirmative action they will take to hire and promote minorities and women.

Enforcement: E.O. 11246 is administered and enforced by the Office of Federal Contract Compliance Programs (OFCCP), a division of the DOL.

Claims: Claims of violations of the law may be made with the OFCCP. Discrimination claims may be made with the EEOC.

Violations of the Law: Employers who are found to be in violation of either the discrimination or the affirmative action sections of the law may have their federal contracts canceled and may be denied future contracts with the federal government.

IMMIGRATION REFORM AND CONTROL ACT (IRCA)

Coverage: IRCA applies to all employers.

Requirements: IRCA prohibits employers from employing illegal aliens. IRCA requires employers to verify that job applicants are eligible to work in the United States. In so doing, employers must check specific documentation presented by applicants to verify both their identity and their eligibility to work in the United States. Both the employer and the employee must fill out the applicable sections of the Immigration and Naturalization Service's I-9 Employment Eligibility Verification Form. Applicants can be asked for proof of their identity and verification of employment eligibility only after they have been offered a job. Employers may not require more or different identity or employment eligibility verification from anyone because they may "look" foreign or speak with a foreign accent. **Note:** It is not considered discriminatory for an employer to hire a U.S. citizen over an equally qualified alien.

Exceptions: The law does not apply to employees hired prior to November 6, 1986, the effective date of the law. Also, the antidiscrimination provisions of IRCA don't apply to employers with under four employees.

Enforcement: IRCA is administered and enforced by the INS and the Department of Justice.

Complaints: Discrimination complaints under IRCA are investigated by the DOJ. If an employer who is engaging in discrimination employs fifteen or more workers, the victim may bring a complaint with the EEOC instead of with the DOJ.

Lawsuits: Victims of discrimination who file complaints with the EEOC may bring a private lawsuit if the EEOC doesn't sue on their behalf. As with other EEOC complaints, the lawsuit must be filed within ninety days of receiving a right-to-sue notice from the EEOC, or within sixty days of receiving a notice that the EEOC will not be pursuing the matter.

If You Win: If you win a discrimination action, you can be awarded back pay for up to two years. The employer can also be fined from $100 to $1,000 for failing to keep proper records; up to $1,000 for a first offense of knowingly hiring someone who is not authorized to work in the United States, up to $5,000 for a second offense, and up to $10,000 for a subsequent offense.

"Guide" Reference: Chapter 1: The Hiring Process.

LABOR-MANAGEMENT RELATIONS ACT (LMRA)

Coverage: The Labor-Management Relations Act, also called the Taft-Hartley Act, applies to virtually all employers.

Requirements: The LMRA gives employees the right to organize and bargain collectively. It prohibits employers from engaging in unfair labor practices, such as coercing employees to join or refrain from joining a union, refusing to bargain in good faith with a certified bargaining unit, retaliating against employees for union activity or otherwise interfering with employees' rights to engage in concerted activity.

Exceptions: The law does not apply to agricultural workers, housekeepers, people who work for their spouse or parents, independent contractors, supervisors and other managerial employees, or employees subject to the Railway Labor Act (i.e., employees of airlines and railroads).

Enforcement: The law is administered and enforced by the National Labor Relations Board (NLRB).

Claims: Claims of unfair labor practices must be filed with the NLRB within six months of the violation complained of.

Remedial Action: If the complaining party wins, the NLRB can order the violation to be stopped. If the employer or union in violation of the act doesn't comply, the NLRB can seek a court order. Violation of the court order can result in a fine and/or imprisonment.
Library Reference: Title 29, U.S. Code, Section 141 *et seq.*
"Guide" Reference: Epilogue: Unions and Other Final Thoughts.

OCCUPATIONAL SAFETY AND HEALTH ACT (OSHA)

Coverage: The Occupational Safety and Health Act applies to virtually all employers.
Requirements: The act requires employers to comply with safety and health standards set by the Occupational Safety and Health Administration (OSHA). A general standard requires employers to ensure that their workplaces are free from ordinary hazards that are likely to cause serious injury or death. Specific standards apply to particular industries. There are also requirements regarding employees' basic comfort and needs, such as general housekeeping requirements, provision of drinking water and sufficient toilet facilities, and maintenance of a temperature range that is not likely to cause illness. (**Note:** A number of states also have safety and health laws that are approved by OSHA.)
Enforcement: The law is administered and enforced by OSHA. OSHA has the authority to conduct inspections of workplaces on its own initiative or in response to specific complaints.
Complaints: When a complaint is made, OSHA can investigate. If a violation is discovered, the employer will be issued a citation and will be ordered to correct the violation. An employer can be fined up to $1,000 a day for failing to correct a violation. He may also be fined up to $7,000 for a serious violation and up to $70,000 for a willful violation.
If You Win: If you successfully sue your employer for firing you in retaliation for reporting OSHA violations, you may be awarded double the amount of your lost wages as well as punitive damages.
Library Reference: Title 29, U.S. Code, Section 651 *et seq.*
"Guide" Reference: Chapter 7: Health and Safety.

THE REHABILITATION ACT OF 1973
(REHAB ACT)

Coverage: The Rehab Act applies to most federal contractors and subcontractors.

Requirements: The Rehab Act prohibits employers from discriminating against handicapped people and requires them to take affirmative action to employ and promote the handicapped.

Exceptions: The Rehab Act does not apply to illegal drug users or alcoholics whose problem prevents them from performing their job.

Enforcement: The law is administered and enforced by the U.S. Department of Labor's Office of Federal Contract Compliance Programs (OFCCP).

Complaints: Complaints must be filed with the OFCCP within 180 days of the violation complained of. Employers who are found to have violated the law can be ordered to cease the discriminatory practice. They can also have their federal contracts revoked and be denied further federal contracts. Employees who are discriminated against based on their handicap can also bring a complaint with the EEOC.

Lawsuits: Handicapped individuals who are discriminated against may bring a private lawsuit if the EEOC doesn't sue on their behalf. The lawsuit must be filed within ninety days of receiving a right-to-sue notice from the EEOC, or within sixty days of receiving a notice that the EEOC will not be pursuing the matter.

If You Win: If you win, you can be reinstated to your job with back pay and full benefits; you can be awarded attorneys' fees and court costs; and the court can order your employer to stop the practice.

Library Reference: Title 29, U.S. Code, Section 701 *et seq.*

"Guide" Reference: Chapter 5: Discrimination and Related Issues.

SECTION 1981 OF THE CIVIL RIGHTS ACT
OF 1870 (SECTION 1981)

Coverage: Section 1981 of the Civil Rights Act of 1870 applies to all employers.

Requirements: The original intent of Section 1981, which was passed in the aftermath of the Civil War, was to give blacks "full and equal benefit of all laws . . . enjoyed by white people," specifically including the right "to make and enforce contracts." Courts thus construed the law to apply to the right to enter an employment contract, whether written or not. Several U.S. Supreme Court decisions narrowed the application of the law strictly to discrimination in hiring and some promotional decisions, and not other aspects of the job (i.e., harassment once the person was on the job). However, part of the Civil Rights Act of 1991 expanded Section 1981 to prohibit discrimination in all aspects of the employment relationship.

Lawsuits: Anyone who is denied equal protection of the law (and the right to contract) under Section 1981 may bring a private lawsuit.

If You Win: If you win, you can be reinstated to your job with back pay and full benefits; compensatory and punitive damages may be awarded in cases of intentional discrimination; you can be awarded attorney's fees and court costs; and the court can order your employer to stop the practice.

Library Reference: Title 42, U.S. Code.

"Guide" Reference: Chapter 5: Discrimination and Related Issues; Chapter 11: I'm Getting Screwed; So What Can I Do about It?

TITLE VII OF THE CIVIL RIGHTS ACT OF 1964 (TITLE VII)

Coverage: Title VII applies to employers of fifteen or more workers.

Requirements: Title VII prohibits employers, unions, and employment agencies from discriminating against job applicants and employees on the basis of race, sex, age, handicap, religion, and national origin. The law prohibits discrimination in hiring, firing, discipline, compensation, and other terms and conditions of employment.

Exceptions: The law does not apply in cases where an otherwise discriminatory requirement is a bona fide occupational qualification of the job (BFOQ). However, the BFOQ exception is very narrowly construed by courts. An example of an acceptable BFOQ would be to hire only women to fill a female acting role.

Enforcement: The law is administered and enforced by the EEOC.

Claims: Claims must be filed with the EEOC, which generally defers action for sixty days to give the equivalent state agency an opportunity to act on the charges. If the state agency does not take jurisdiction, the EEOC will take over the case. If the EEOC finds a violation, it will try to reach a settlement between the parties. If that fails, the EEOC may bring suit on your behalf.

Lawsuits: You may bring a private lawsuit ninety days after receiving a right-to-sue letter from the EEOC.

If You Win: If you win, you can be reinstated to your job with back pay for up to two years preceding the filing of your EEOC complaint, and full benefits; you can be awarded damages, within certain limits; you can be awarded attorney's fees and court costs; and the court can order your employer to stop the practice.

Library Reference: Title 42, U.S. Code, Section 2000e.

"Guide" Reference: Chapter 5: Discrimination and Related Issues; Chapter 11: I'm Getting Screwed; So What Can I Do about It?

UNIFORMED SERVICES EMPLOYMENT AND REEMPLOYMENT RIGHTS ACT OF 1994 (USERRA)

Coverage: The Uniformed Services Employment and Reemployment Rights Act of 1994 applies to virtually all public and private employers.

Requirements: USERRA requires employers to allow employees to take unpaid leave of absence for active military service, either voluntary or involuntary; and to attend required military reserve or national guard meetings, training sessions, and drills. Employers must reinstate returning service personnel to the same or equivalent job at the same level of seniority, status, and pay upon their honorable discharge and return from active duty of up to five years.

Notice: Employees called to active duty must give their employer advance notice, either oral or written, of the need to take a leave of absence, except where giving notice is impossible, or unreasonable, or is precluded by military necessity. A returning reservist must, except if it would be impossible or unreasonable, give his or her employer notice of the intention to return to work. The length of notice required varies according to the length of military service.

Enforcement: The law is administered and enforced by the U.S. Department of Labor.

Complaints: Complaints must be filed in writing with the DOL.

If You Win: If you win, the court can order your reinstatement, double the amount of your lost wages, and reimburse your attorney's fees and court costs.

Library Reference: Public Law 103-353.

"Guide" Reference: Chapter 4: Fringe Benefits.

VIETNAM ERA VETERANS' READJUSTMENT ASSISTANCE ACT

Coverage: The Vietnam Era Veterans' Readjustment Assistance Act applies to most federal contractors and subcontractors.

Requirements: The act requires employers to give preference in hiring and promotion to:

☞ Vietnam veterans who served at least 180 days and weren't dishonorably discharged; and

☞ "Special disabled" veterans who have at least a 30 percent military disability or were discharged because of a service-related disability.

The act also prohibits discipline or discharge of military reservists and members of the National Guard who must miss work for training drills, and gives those who enlist in the military or are called to active duty certain reemployment rights.

Employers with fifty or more employees and federal contracts worth $50,000 or more must develop affirmative action plans for the hiring of Vietnam veterans and special disabled veterans.

Enforcement: The law is administered and enforced by the Veterans Employment Service.

Complaints: Complaints must be filed with the local branch of the Veterans Employment Service. Employers who are found to have violated the law can be ordered to cease the discriminatory practice. They can also have their federal contracts revoked and be denied further federal contracts. Disabled veterans who are discriminated against based on their handicap can also bring a complaint with the EEOC.

If Your Complaint Is Valid: If your complaint succeeds, you can be awarded the job or promotion you were denied with back pay and full benefits; and the employer will be ordered to stop the practice. (As noted above, an employer can also lose his federal contract and be denied future federal contracts.)

Library Reference: Title 38, U.S. Code, Section 2011 *et seq.*

"Guide" Reference: Chapter 5: Discrimination and Related Issues.

WORKER ADJUSTMENT AND RETRAINING NOTIFICATION ACT (WARN)

Coverage: WARN applies to employers of 100 or more full-time workers, or 100 or more workers, full- and part-time, if they total more than 4,000 hours a week.

Requirements: WARN requires employers to give employees (and their union representatives and local government officials) at least sixty days' notice of a plant closing or mass layoff, including the expected date of the closing or layoffs. A plant closing or mass layoff happens when fifty or more workers will either lose their jobs or have their hours cut in half over a thirty-day period. (**Note:** In the case of layoffs, the fifty employees laid off must total at least one-third of the employer's work force, unless more than 500 workers are being laid off.)

Exceptions: Notice doesn't have to be given or may be shortened in circumstances such as: at temporary facilities, on specific projects, or for seasonal employment where workers knew of the temporary nature of their jobs when they were hired; when closings or layoffs are caused by a natural disaster; where the company was seeking financing to stay in business and notice would have kept it from being able to get the financing; when employees are striking or the employer is engaged in a lockout that isn't intended to evade the law; or where the situation is caused by sudden, unforeseeable business circumstances beyond the employer's control.

Enforcement: The law is administered by the U.S. Department of Labor. Enforcement is left to the affected employees and union or government officials.

Lawsuits: Affected employees, unions, and government officials in the town where the plant closing or layoffs occur can bring a lawsuit against the violating employer in federal district court. The statute of limitations for bringing suit under WARN is the same as that for the "most analogous state law."

If You Win: If you win, you can be awarded up to three years' back pay and benefits. The employer can also be fined up to $500 a day for failure to notify local government officials, up to a maximum of sixty days.

Library Reference: Public Law 100-379.

"Guide" Reference: Chapter 8: Discipline and Discharge.

Common Questions
(with Answers)

The following is a set of questions employees have often asked themselves (and labor attorneys) over the years. All of them have been covered in one place or another in this book. The answers aren't always easy—or strictly black and white. Loosen up: This isn't a pop quiz. It's just for fun. (Answers follow.)

1. I have gone through a personal bankruptcy recently. Can an employer deny me a job because of that?

2. Every job application form I get, of course, asks for the name of my last employer. But they also ask if they can contact him. I'm afraid to say no, because that looks suspicious. But, since I got fired from my last job, I'm afraid my former employer will bad-mouth me. Is there anything I can do?

3. I thought I was doing a good job at work and all of a sudden my supervisor calls me in and tells me I'm being let go. I asked him why, since I've always gotten good performance reviews, and he just said they're making cutbacks and I was the most expendable. I've got more seniority than other people they are keeping and I know I've had just as good performance reviews as others. Do I have any job rights?

4. If my company's employee handbook has a blanket disclaimer saying, in effect, that it's not meant to be binding or create any kind of duty on my employer's part or contract rights of any kind, is it pretty much worthless as far as reading through it to try to hang something on him, like that he didn't give me any warnings or do the other things the hand-

book says he'd do before firing anyone? Or that it says you can be fired for "just cause" only and I wasn't?

5. I never get time off to eat lunch. If I get to eat at all, it's while I'm working. And forget about coffee breaks. I thought I had to be given at least half an hour off to eat in peace; and a coffee break in the morning and in the afternoon.

6. I have to wear a beeper so my employer can call me in case of an emergency. I can be called out of a restaurant or off the golf course or anything and he expects me to rush right in. Shouldn't I have to be paid for the time I have to wear the beeper and be on call?

7. Not only did I have to work Christmas Day, but I didn't even get time and a half for it. Christmas is a legal holiday. Isn't that against the law?

8. My former employer never told me I had a right to continue in the company's group health insurance plan. I didn't know until I became ill and required hospitalization that I could have continued my group insurance with my former employer even after I was let go. What can I do now?

9. I decided not to continue in my former employer's group health insurance plan because, without a job, I couldn't afford it. I have since been hospitalized. Can I get coverage now or is it too late?

10. Do I have an age discrimination case if my boss holds me to higher performance standards than younger, less experienced workers?

11. I hurt my back at work. Am I protected by the **Americans with Disabilities Act**? Does my employer have to accommodate my injury?

12. Can my boss bug my office telephone?

13. My employer asked me to take a lie detector test because he thought I stole some money from the till. I said okay because I didn't steal the money and I wanted to clear my name. Then the tester starts asking me questions about my religious beliefs, my ethnic background, my sexual practices, and other really personal stuff. When I objected, he said it was necessary background information to check the machine's readings on basic questions. I walked out and my employer fired me for refusing to take the test. Can he do that?

14. They've been doing some work outside my office and I have to breathe in all these dust particles. I'm worried it may cause me health problems. It particularly worries me because the

workers are wearing dust masks. What can I do about this situation? I don't want to make waves, but I don't want to get sick either.

15. We're supposed to punch in at 8:00 A.M. every day. But if we're even one minute late, our supervisor won't let us punch in until 8:15. If you come in at 8:16, he won't let you punch in until 8:30, and so on. Can he do that?

16. My employer accused me of stealing company property in front of other workers and then fired me. He had no real proof and, in fact, I didn't do it. What can I do?

17. I got a little tipsy at the company picnic, which was held at my employer's home out by the swimming pool. I was fooling around with some other guys and slipped and broke my leg. Am I eligible for workers' compensation benefits?

18. I was on a business trip to Florida and a bunch of us sneaked off to play a round of golf one day when we finished our meetings early. I was hit in the head with an errant tee shot, which caused dizziness that made it impossible for me to work. Am I eligible for workers' compensation benefits?

19. I'm a company driver and I got fired because I lost my license while driving my own car when I wasn't at work. Am I still eligible for unemployment compensation benefits? My employer says he's going to contest my claim because losing my license meant I *couldn't* work.

20. I'm on workers' compensation and I'm afraid my employer will fire me as soon as I recover enough to return to work. Can he do that? I thought I couldn't be fired for going on workers' compensation.

ANSWERS

1. Your credit history is not supposed to be a factor in determining your qualifications for a job. Also, under the **Fair Credit Reporting Act,** an employer is required to notify you in writing within three days of asking a credit reporting agency to check on you and can use the results only to verify the fact that you were employed. (Requiring good credit has been shown to have an adverse impact on women and minorities.) However, since bankruptcy filings are a matter of public record, even though he is not supposed to figure credit into the employment equation, an employer could

check on bankruptcy filings without a great deal of difficulty. Also, credit history could possibly be considered a legitimate job criterion where the job involves the handling of cash or some other fiduciary relationship with customers or clients.

2. A person who leaves a job under less than desirable circumstances is in a rather delicate position regarding his or her résumé and job applications. Leaving a gap in an employment history is not a good idea, since a prospective employer will wonder what you were doing during that time. But giving permission to contact that employer may amount to a death sentence for your job prospects, depending on how bad parting feelings were. There is no way you can ensure that your former employer won't bad-mouth you. But if you are really afraid he might, try contacting him and telling him you have been asked to get a reference from your most recent employer and that you would appreciate it if he would mail it directly to you. (There's less chance he'd say something negative about you if he knows you'll see it.) It might be easier to get this kind of hand-delivered reference as soon as you are given your pink slip. (Of course, it probably wouldn't occur to many people who have just been fired to ask.) In any case, he may refuse. So you may just have to take your chances. These days employers are so paranoid about being sued, most will avoid putting anything really negative about an employee or former employee in writing. The biggest risk may be that dreaded "old-boy network." Your prospective employer has lunch at The Club with your former employer and asks about you "off the record." **Note:** If your former employer tells lies about you, he could be liable for defamation. He could also be liable for defamation if he promises not to give you a bad recommendation and then does anyway (*Holton v. Lockheed Corp.,* California Superior Court, No. 642082, 1991). And if he circulates information about you that is designed to keep you from being employed anywhere else, he could be guilty of blacklisting. Of course, you would have to have proof. (If you "negotiate" your severance with your employer—either on your own or with the help of an attorney—you should include an agreed-upon letter of recommendation, or a statement to be added to your personnel file as to exactly what your employer will say about you in response to a reference request.)

3. Whether or not you have any job rights when you are let go for "no reason" depends on the specific facts of your case. Having more seniority and better performance evaluations than others who are kept on certainly provides food for thought. Why were you let go when they were kept on? Do they do different work than you? Are you sure your job evaluations were better than theirs? Do they have other skills your employer needs or may reasonably need in the near future that you don't have (i.e., because of growing technological needs in the industry, etc.)? Or is there some other legitimate reason for your discharge (e.g., disciplinary actions against you, lateness, absence)? If your employer is unable to point to a specific reason for picking on you as opposed to less senior and no more qualified or experienced coworkers, you may have an argument for wrongful discharge, particularly if you have something else to hang your hat on, like that you are over forty, female, a minority, or handicapped.

4. A blanket disclaimer in an employee handbook can certainly limit an employer's exposure to lawsuits based on what's in there. However, that doesn't mean he can just make all sorts of promises in the handbook and go merrily along breaking them at his whim. Courts vary greatly in their interpretations of the binding nature of clauses in employee handbooks. However, many courts hold employers to their promises, even when the handbook also contains a disclaimer, as long as the employee's expectation (e.g., of continued employment, progressive discipline, right to a hearing on any disciplinary action, or discharge only for "cause," etc.) was reasonable in light of the wording in the handbook, as well as his or her employment history and how the company has interpreted the applicable handbook section in the past (*Badgett v. Visiting Nurses Association,* Iowa Court of Appeals, No. 0-651/90-443, 1991).

5. Federal law has no requirement that you be given time off to eat (though some state laws do). But if you are given at least thirty minutes off to eat, you don't have to be paid for the time. If you are required to keep working while you eat, or even if your employer *lets* you keep working while you eat, you have to be paid for the time. (The states that require time off for meals generally let you work straight through by arrangement with your employer—as long as you are paid, of course.) There is no law that requires employers to give

employees coffee breaks. But any break of less than twenty minutes has to be paid time.

6. An employer has to pay employees for time they are on call, but generally only if they have to stay in a specific place designated by the employer while they are waiting. If they are allowed to go anywhere they want and only have to keep their employer informed of their whereabouts, or if they are required to wear a beeper so their employer can track them down easily, the employer generally doesn't have to pay for that time. However, if you are called to work for an emergency while on on-call status, you are supposed to be paid from the time you respond to the call to the time you finish your assignment.

7. A private employer doesn't have to give employees paid holidays off, even so-called legal holidays; and he doesn't have to pay time and a half to employees who have to work on holidays, unless that brings their hours to over forty for the week (and/or eight for the day in a few states). However, an employer could be involved in a discriminatory practice if he requires one employee to work on holidays and not other similarly situated employees (i.e., employees who do roughly the same job, have roughly the same seniority, etc.). This may be especially so if you are a member of a protected group and he is singling you out for that reason.

8. Your employer and his insurance carrier can be held liable for any medical expenses you incur as a result of their not telling you about your right to continue on your employer's group health insurance plan. (This can also be true if the new insurance you get on your own offers less extensive coverage than your former employer's plan.) To escape liability, your employer would have to prove that he (or the insurance company) actually did give you the required notice, and that the required time period has elapsed without your election of continuation or payment of the premium.

9. You may still be able to get health insurance coverage through your former employer's group health insurance plan even if you didn't elect to continue coverage before your injury or illness and haven't paid any premiums, if fewer than 105 days have gone by since your termination. That's because, under COBRA, you have sixty days to elect continued coverage and another forty-five days to pay the first premium.

10. According to one court, it's okay for an employer to hold older, more experienced workers to higher standards than their younger, less experienced coworkers. An inference of age discrimination is raised only, said the court, if younger workers of the *same* level of experience weren't held to the same standards; or if there was no real basis of distinction between the older worker's job and that of the younger workers, and thus no real reason to judge them differently (*Fallis v. Kerr-McGee Corp.*, U.S. Court of Appeals, 10th Circuit, 1991).

11. Whether or not you are protected by the ADA with regard to an on-the-job injury (meaning your employer would have to offer you a reasonable accommodation) depends on whether your injury caused an impairment that "substantially limits a major life activity." You would, of course, be eligible for workers' compensation. But you would be protected by the ADA only if the injury was severe enough or developed complications that, say, prevented you from being able to walk during a prolonged period of rehabilitation, or if it required surgery that left you with a permanent limp or chronic pain when you walked or sat. Then, if you weren't able to return to your former job, your employer would probably be required to accommodate your incapacity by considering your qualifications for any job openings in the company.

12. To date, the law generally lets your employer tap into telephone conversations at work, as long as he does it for a legitimate business reason, like improving production or customer relations. In fact, the **Omnibus Crime Control and Safe Streets Act of 1968** says it's okay for him to intercept communications "in the ordinary course of business." But he's supposed to butt out as soon as he determines the communication is personal. And he isn't supposed to do it to try to get information he isn't supposed to have. For example, a company can be liable for damages for invasion of privacy when they intercept telephone conversations in an attempt to identify union sympathizers (*Parrish v. Northern Telecom, Inc.*, District Court, Middle Tennessee, 1992).

13. If an employer has a legitimate basis for requesting you to take a lie detector test (which, in most cases—except if you are a police officer or a firefighter, or are employed by a security or pharmaceutical company—is limited to reasonable

suspicion of theft of property you had access to), there are specific rules for the conduct of the test. One of those is that you cannot be asked to answer questions that would give your employer information he has no right to have. That includes things like your age, religion, sexual practices, etc. You can also refuse to take the test or ask to discontinue the test at any time. And you can't be fired based on the results of the lie detector test alone. In fact, given the rigid requirements for asking an employee to take a lie detector test at all, the notice that must be given to test subjects, and then what is required of the tester, any employer who asks an employee to take one is taking a pretty big chance of having it come back to haunt him.

14. Under the **Occupational Safety and Health Act,** you have a right to a workplace that is "reasonably safe from recognized hazards that are likely to cause death or serious physical harm." You should bring any condition that you feel might be unsafe to the attention of your employer. If he does nothing about it, you can file a complaint with OSHA. Disciplining or discharging you for reporting an OSHA violation is against the law. However, if you are afraid your employer would fire you and take his chances, you might want to make your complaint confidential (assuming you aren't the only person affected by the situation, which would make it pretty easy for your employer to figure out who filed the complaint). If the situation is serious enough that you have a legitimate and reasonable fear that it is unsafe and that there isn't enough time to go through the normal OSHA enforcement process, you can refuse to work under the unsafe conditions. However, you first have to point out the situation to your employer and give him an adequate chance to correct it. And he must have refused or failed to do so.

15. "Docking" someone's pay—for being late, for example—is acceptable only if you are not allowed to work and if you are free to use the time as you wish. For example, if you report in at 8:02 and your supervisor says you can't punch in until 8:15, you must not be allowed to work and you must be free to go to the cafeteria for a cup of coffee, or to go outside and enjoy the sunshine or read the paper, or to do whatever else you want to do in the few minutes you have before being allowed to punch in. You can't be required or

even allowed to work from 8:02 on and not be paid for actual time worked.

16. An employer can be held liable for defaming an employee: making negative false statements about the person, either orally or in writing. Such statements must be published—that is, heard or read by others—and generally must be made maliciously or with blatant disregard for their consequences. Disregard for the consequences of a statement can be shown where the employer didn't undertake a reasonable investigation of the charges before making the statement. An employer can also be held liable for wrongful discharge for firing an employee based on erroneous charges.

17. You will normally be eligible for workers' compensation benefits if you are hurt at a company-sponsored party. That is especially true if your employer paid for the party and it was held at work (or at his house) and during working hours, and if employees were required or "expected" to attend. The important things that the workers' compensation commission will consider are the employer's contributions, financial or otherwise, whether attendance was required or essentially so, and what he gets out of it, like a boost in employee morale.

18. Employees who are injured "in the course of employment" are eligible for workers' compensation benefits. Most courts consider an injury sustained while on a business trip as having occurred in the course of employment. Usually the test of whether or not an injury is covered is whether the main purpose of the trip was business, with any personal activities being merely incidental.

19. Even if you were fired for "just cause," you will generally be eligible for unemployment benefits. That includes a situation where you lost your job because you no longer had the license required to perform the job.

20. You can't be fired *because* you were hurt on the job and were out of work and receiving benefits. However, your employer can replace you if yours is a one-of-a-kind job and he needs someone immediately, or if you are out for long enough that he has to replace you. If that's the case, he doesn't *have* to re-hire you if your job or a similar one is not available when you are ready to come back to work.

Acknowledgments

I am extremely grateful to labor and employment attorneys Paul W. Orth and Henry J. Zaccardi of the Hartford, Connecticut, law firm of Shipman and Goodwin for contributing their time and expertise to a review of my manuscript.

Index

notice to employer of claim of, 277–78, 285–88, 336

occupational illnesses and, 274–75, 281

on-the-job injuries and, 252, 253, 256, 267–74

OSHA and, 207, 253

partial incapacity and, 263

permanent incapacity and, 261, 263

preexisting conditions and, 275

psychological injuries and, 274–75

records on, 176

reduction of benefits, 265–66

references and, 36

reinjury and, 266

reviews of, 338

second injury funds for, 275

by state, 256–59, 261–62, 275, 276–77, 285–88

third-party injuries and, 271, 281–82

wages and, 261

waiting period for, 264, 285–88

workplace
conditions of, 203–6, 229, 365; *see also* Occupational Safety and Health Act; Occupational Safety and Health Administration

privacy in, *see* privacy

rules in, 235, 246–48, 270

safety violations in, *see* safety violations

surveillance in, 184–87

violence in, 39, 276

About the Author

Lewin G. Joel III has been a member of the Connecticut and Massachusetts bars for more than twenty years. He currently practices law in Connecticut, where he lives with his wife, Carolyn, and daughter, Sophie.